MAY IT PLEASE
THE COURT

From the Gray's Inn Portrait of Harringdon Mann.

JAMES M. BECK

MAY IT PLEASE THE COURT

By

JAMES M. BECK, LL.D., D.Lit.,

Formerly Solicitor General of the United States

Edited by
O. R. McGUIRE, A.M., S.J.D.

"Those who design to be partakers in the government should be sure to remember those two precepts of Plato; first, to make the safety and interest of their citizens the great aim and design of all their thoughts and endeavors, without ever considering their own personal advantages; and, secondly, so as to take care of the whole collective body of the Republic, as not to serve the interest of any one party, to the prejudice or neglect of all the rest." Cicero, "The Offices," No. XXV.

Essay Index Reprint Series

BOOKS FOR LIBRARIES PRESS
FREEPORT, NEW YORK

First Published 1930
Reprinted 1970

STANDARD BOOK NUMBER:
8369-1694-8

LIBRARY OF CONGRESS CATALOG CARD NUMBER:
75-121447

PRINTED IN THE UNITED STATES OF AMERICA

TABLE OF CONTENTS

PART I
ADDRESSES

Early Philadelphia Bar—Illustrious members—Compares
Academy to Inns of Court—The Philadelphia Bar and the
Supreme Court of the United States—That court and the
Constitution—Superstructure erected by that court—Early
days of the court—Public interest in hearings before the
court—Some great cases—Extended arguments in early
days—Weariness of court with such arguments—Rule of
court limiting time of argument—Time allowed in recent
years insufficient for extended presentation of cases—Some
greater modern cases—Comparison of old and new forensic
arguments—Necessity for skilled advocacy—Decline of public interest in proceedings of the court—Questions wisdom
of expedition in arguments—Necessity for limitation on
number of cases coming to that court.

Beaumarchais entitled to interest and affection of Americans
for aid in the Revolutionary War—Meagre supplies of muni-
tions of war in the Colonies—Beaumarchais aided in supply-
ing the deficiencies—His origin and rise to influence at the
French court—His varied interests and accomplishments—
Beaumarchais as a litigant and his own lawyer—Difficulties in
litigation in France in that period—Author of two famous
plays—Meeting of Beaumarchais and American agents in
London at home of John Wilkes—His scheme to aid the
Colonies without involving the French government—Establishment of private commercial house on funds partly borrowed from the French king—Failure of Continental Congress to pay for the supplies sent by Beaumarchais—
Beaumarchais and the French Revolution—His declining
years—Continued refusal of America to pay Beaumarchais—
Fraction of debt paid years later to heirs of Beaumarchais
through deduction from the French Spoliation Claims—His
memory entitled to gratitude of America.

Eulogy of Washington superfluous—The Master Spirit of the
early political life of America—His self-education made him

iii

PART II
ARGUMENTS

ILLUSTRATIONS

INTRODUCTION

James Montgomery Beck—A Biographical Note

*"I have observed that a reader seldom
peruses a book with pleasure 'till he knows
whether the writer of it be black or a fair
man, of a mild or choleric disposition, married or a bachelor, with other particulars of
the like nature that conduce very much to
the right understanding of an author."*
        —*Sir Roger de Coverley.*

Few American lawyers of this generation have less need
of an introduction to the members of the American Bar
than the author of the arguments and addresses in this
volume, for few have been the recipient of so many honors as James Montgomery Beck.

While he has never restricted his activities exclusively
to the legal profession, for both in his native city of Philadelphia and in his country he has for half a century been
active in the civic life of the nation, yet his achievements
and reputation are largely those of a lawyer. He never
held any public office outside of his profession until elected
to Congress in 1927. Admitted to the bar of Philadelphia
in 1884, he has held the offices of Assistant District Attorney (1888-92); United States District Attorney for Pennsylvania (1896-1900); Assistant Attorney-General of the
United States (1900-1903), and Solicitor-General of the
United States (1921-1925).

Few lawyers have had a more varied experience at the
bar, for after practicing law for seventeen years in his
native city, Mr. Beck spent three years as Assistant Attorney-General in Washington, under the administrations of
Presidents McKinley and Roosevelt, and speedily won such
general recognition that he was, in 1900, admitted to one
of the oldest law firms in New York and successfully practiced in that city for seventeen years.

Notwithstanding the tempting opportunities in New York, from a material standpoint, he preferred, after a successful career at the bar of that city, to return to the public service and was appointed by President Harding as Solicitor-General of the United States in 1920, and it is safe to say that for four years he bore as onerous a burden of professional obligations as ever fell upon the shoulders of any American lawyer. The greatest war in history had ended and, in the liquidation of that war and in the application of three new amendments to the Constitution, the legal work of the United States Government had reached a peak never reached before and not likely to be reached again for many years.

In his four years' service as Solicitor-General, Mr. Beck had charge of over eight hundred cases in the Supreme Court. This meant that he was the active counsel for the Government in at least one-fourth of all the cases on the calendar of the Court. While many of these cases were only applications for a certiorari, which the Government either presented or opposed, yet at least two hundred cases were orally argued cases and many of them of great importance. Of these Mr. Beck personally argued at least one hundred.

Great as was this service, Mr. Beck rendered even greater service to his country and civilization during the World War. In October, 1914, he wrote, at the request of the New York Times, in the form of a juridical judgment, an analysis of the diplomatic papers of the various nations, in order to determine the moral responsibility for the war. This article made an immediate and profound impression all over the world. It was translated into almost every language and millions of copies were circulated. Subsequently, he expanded this notable article into a book, called "The Evidence in the Case," which was also translated into two other languages and enjoyed a world-wide reputation. In 1916 he went to England and France and, in the course of a number of addresses in both countries, sought to interpret the sympathy of the American people with the cause of the Allies. At that time the feeling towards America in England and France was none too

kindly and Mr. Beck's mission was similar to that of Henry
Ward Beecher, when he went to England during the Civil
War to bring about a better feeling between the two nations that were soon destined to be allies in a common
cause. Mr. Beck spoke in Paris, London, Manchester, Edin-
burgh and Glasgow and over two hundred thousand copies
of his first speech, as to the true attitude of America, were
circulated in England alone.

It is not unnatural that great honors came to him by
reason of his services to the cause of the Allies. When,
after the close of the war, he returned to England, he
was paid the unprecedented compliment of being called
to the Bar of England without the obligation of being
"screened" or observing the time-honored formality of
eating the requisite number of dinners in one of the Inns
of Court. He had previously been made a Master of the
Bench of Gray's Inn, one of the historic Inns of Court.
Under the joint auspices of the Universities of Manchester, Oxford and London, he was invited to deliver a series
of lectures, but as he was unable to reach England in
time to deliver the lectures at Manchester and Oxford,
he delivered five lectures on the American Constitution
in 1922 and 1923 under the auspices of the University
of London in Gray's Inn. Later, when he visited Paris,
he was given a series of receptions, in which the Minister
of Justice, University of Paris, Chancellery of the Legion
of Honor, and other civic institutions participated and
was paid the honor—said to be unprecedented—of being
formally received by the Cour de Cassation, the highest
court of France. After his reception in open court, he
later delivered in the court room a lecture on the Supreme
Court of the United States to the Bench and Bar of France.

The fruit of these lectures and studies was Mr. Beck's
now classic work on the Constitution of the United
States.* Few law books have been better introduced, for
President Coolidge wrote the introduction to the American
edition, the Earl of Balfour that to the Oxford University

---

* The Constitution of the United States published by Doran Doubleday & Co.,
of New York, and by the Oxford University Press in England.

Press edition; Dr. Larnaude, Dean of the Faculty of Law of the University of Paris, for the French edition, and the Chief Justice of Germany the introduction to the German edition.

It is safe to say that no book on the Constitution has been more widely read since Bryce's "American Commonwealth." The subject is treated in an altogether different way than in previous works on the Constitution.

Among the many tributes that have been paid to Mr. Beck's professional and public achievements, possibly none is more noteworthy than that of President Coolidge, who, in accepting Mr. Beck's resignation as Solicitor-General, said:

> "In accepting your resignation I wish to make particular acknowledgment of the faithfulness and distinguished ability with which you have discharged the duties of your high position. Your record, as Solicitor-General, will stand as one of the most notable proofs that the Government is so many times fortunate in being able to enlist the most eminent of talents and highest fidelity, not because of the compensation, but because of the fine sentiments of patriotism which animate those who thus do honor to the public service. At a great sacrifice to yourself in everything save only reputation, you have given your splendid energy and exceptional capacity to the furtherance of the national interests. Contemplating your record of achievement, I have to express the hope that it may be alike an inspiration and a model to many others."

Mr. Beck's first appearance at the Bar of the Supreme Court was in 1896, when he argued the case of *Durland* v. *United States*, 161 U. S. 308. Since then he has appeared in a long line of important cases, many of them involving questions of constitutional law and all of them referring to cases of more than ordinary importance. Thus, he argued *Neely* v. *Henkle*, 180 U. S. 109, in which the constitutional power of the Government to govern Cuba after the Treaty of Paris was involved. This was regarded as the forerunner of the famous *Insular Cases*, 182 U. S. 244, in which Mr. Beck was also engaged as Assistant Attorney-General and which involved the power of the United States to govern permanently colonial dependencies free from the limitation of the uniformity clause of the Constitution. In the famous *Danbury Hatters case*, 208 U. S. 274, Mr. Beck successfully argued the application of the Sherman Anti-Trust law to a nation-wide labor boycott on a manufacturer's products.

Among the greatest of his cases was the *Lottery Case*, 188 U. S. 321, which rounded out the doctrine of *Gibbons v. Ogden* by holding that the constitutional power to regulate commerce included the power to prohibit commerce for federal purposes. This case has always been regarded as one of the great landmarks of constitutional jurisprudence and has taken its place among the leading cases on constitutional law.

Mr. Beck successfully argued for a further expansion of the commerce power in the case of *International Textbook*, 217 U. S. 91, which involved the applicability of the interstate commerce power to the transmission of educational matter by correspondence schools. In *Lewis Publishing Co.* v. *Morgan, Postmaster of New York City*, 229 U. S. 288, he defended—although unsuccessfully—the freedom of the press from a form of censorship. In the *Boston Store* case, 246 U. S. 8, he argued the validity of resale contract prices and although his contention was unsuccessful in thus seeking to overrule the decision in the *Miles-Parke Medical case*, he had at least the satisfaction of convincing a minority of the court that the previous decision was incorrect.

Among other important constitutional questions was the *Alaska case*, 258 U. S. 101, which was unique in that it involved a question of constitutional law in which there had been no prior expression of opinion by the Supreme Court, that of the applicability to a Territory of the Constitutional requirement that no preference should be given to the ports of one State as against another.

In the case of *Stafford* v. *Wallace*, 259 U. S. 44, Mr. Beck successfully sustained the constitutionality of the Stockyards Act and in the case of *Fairchild* v. *Hughes, Secretary of State*, 258 U. S. 126, the validity of the Nineteenth Amendment.

Next to the Lottery case, the most important case which Mr. Beck argued was that of *Myers* v. *United States*, 272 U. S. 58, in which the century-old controversy as to the President's power of removal was at length finally settled. Mention must also be made of the Great Lakes controversy, possibly the greatest of all litigations between the States, in which the right of Illinois to divert the waters of Lake Michigan into the Mississippi watershed was involved. Mr. Beck first argued this case for the Government in *Sanitary District* v. *United States*, 266 U. S. 405, and sustained the power of the Federal Government to control such diversion. Later, when he had ceased to be Solicitor-General and the Sanitary District of Chicago was defending its right to make such diversion under the permit of the War Department, Mr. Beck, now representing the Sanitary District, again sustained the supremacy of the Federal Government.

To review his exceptional record in the Supreme Court, it would be necessary to consider many other cases of a widely varying character which he has argued, but enough has been cited to indicate that few lawyers of this generation have argued more cases which involved the Constitution and helped to determine the form of our government.

Mr. Beck has not been of that class of lawyers, who restrict their energies exclusively to the practice of their profession. He has taken a deep and continuous interest in the civic activities of his native city and in varied public affairs. During the last fifty years he has made many public addresses in Europe and in all parts of the United States and it has been difficult for the editor to select from nearly two hundred addresses and arguments those that will best illustrate the variety of his activities and the nature of his art of advocacy.

As this book is primarily intended for members of the

bar and those interested in jurisprudence, the editor reluctantly found it necessary to exclude from this compilation a great many addresses of an historical and literary character.

Mr. Beck has delivered many formal orations at college commencements and at the dedication of statues to eminent Americans and, if this compilation were not restricted to legal topics, it would have been a satisfaction to the editor to have included his formal orations on Washington, Franklin, Hamilton, Jefferson and other master builders of the Republic, and to have added some of the literary addresses, especially on Shakespearean topics. Mr. Beck has been a life-long student of Shakespeare and the editor feels safe in saying that nothing has given Mr. Beck greater intellectual satisfaction, or been a better relief to his arduous legal work than to turn from the dusty highways of the law to the flowery fields of Shakespeare's poetry.

The reader, who has never heard Mr. Beck, may be interested in his style of speech and the methods of his art. Upon this the editor can speak with authority, as he has very frequently heard Mr. Beck in the Supreme Court and on the floor of the House of Representatives. As a rule, he speaks extemporaneously, with the exception of formal lectures or academic orations, and rarely uses notes. He discusses nothing unless he has studied the subject, but when he has studied it, he generally speaks without first reducing his intended speech to literary form. His theory of public speaking is that the speaker should be wholly unconscious of himself and should concentrate his attention upon the thought that he is trying to convey, rather than upon the impression that he is making upon his audience. Indeed, the editor believes that Mr. Beck, when speaking, is largely unconscious of the existence of an audience. Possibly none of his auditors is more interested in the line of thought that he is following than the speaker himself. He becomes absorbed in his theme and in a natural and unaffected way expresses his thoughts in a nervous and terse phraseology. He makes few gestures and neither seeks nor stops for applause. When speaking, his face is animated and his eyes glow with intensity and throughout his speech there is a ring of sincerity without which no speech can ever be convincing.

As an omnivorous reader from early childhood and with a tenacious memory, Mr. Beck enriches his discourses with many literary and historical allusions, which come quite spontaneously to him.

It must not be understood that the speeches herein published represent the addresses in their extemporaneous form, for Mr. Beck carefully revises the stenographic transcript of his speeches when they are to be used for publication, but neither must the reader assume that the "purple passages" in the contents of this compilation were always after-thoughts. On the contrary, owing to the ardor of his speech and to the intensity of his emotions when speaking on a great subject, many of the finer passages came spontaneously to the speaker.

When the publishers honored the editor by an invitation to select and edit some of Mr. Beck's more important arguments and addresses, the editor was confronted with no easy task. He hopes, however, that the selections will find favor with members of the bar, law students, and those generally interested in public affairs. The editor has preceded each speech by a brief headnote, in order that the reader may understand the nature of the occasion and the subject-matter of the address.

O. R. McGuire.

Washington, D. C.
March 1, 1930.

Part I

ADDRESSES

I

THE OLD AND THE NEW SUPREME COURT OF THE UNITED STATES

This series of Mr. Beck's addresses on varied topics can profitably begin with his interesting and illuminating address on the Supreme Court, past and present. It was delivered before the Law Academy of Philadelphia, an association of law students and young lawyers, which was formed in Philadelphia more than a century ago in imitation of the English Inns of Courts. Once a year the Academy invites a distinguished lawyer to address them, and in 1923 Mr. Beck was the orator of the occasion. His picture of the old Court in its Golden Era and his description of the Court in this later period of steam and electricity, where even in judicial procedure speed is a vital factor, will interest members of the Bar and all classes.— EDITOR.

Gentlemen of the Academy and Fellow-Members of the Philadelphia Bar:

To me this is a homecoming, and as such most grateful to my feelings. As the shadows of life are now for me fast lengthening, the honor of the invitation to deliver this annual address before this venerable institution of the historic bar of Philadelphia is one that I greatly value.

Nearly forty-two years ago I registered as a student of law in this city, and next April it will be thirty-nine years since I appeared at the bar of the Court of Common Pleas to take the oath of office as one of its members. I have gone far afield in my professional career, for it has been my fate—may I say privilege?—to have practiced law in three cities, Philadelphia, Washington and New York, and to have had a delightful, though honorary, connection with the bar of England as a Bencher of Gray's Inn.

I only mention this as a matter of inducement to a tribute to the bar of Philadelphia.

Of that bar today I know too little to speak with

1

knowledge, but so far as my experience qualifies me to express an opinion, it is my deliberate conviction that the bar of Philadelphia in the "eighties" was excelled by none in this country.

Then it still retained something of its characteristics of the earlier days of the Republic, when the ancient fame of the Philadelphia lawyer had already become a proverb. The mellow glory of the simpler days had not altogether passed. The courts were still held in that most sacred building in America, Independence Hall, designed by a Philadelphia lawyer, who had studied law in Gray's Inn —the Inn of Gascoigne, Nicholas Bacon, Francis Bacon, Holt, Romilly and many other illustrious names in the annals of our profession. The lawyers' offices were still clustered about Independence and Washington Squares, and there were still some who, as in the earlier days of the Nineteenth Century, had their offices in their residences.

Some of the leaders of these earlier days were still living. As a young man I might well have met, though such was not my privilege, the greatest advocate that Philadelphia ever gave to the Nation—Horace Binney. He was a connecting link between the colonial bar and the bar of the Nineteenth Century, for in his early youth he had seen Washington and Franklin conversing in front of Independence Hall.

When I was called to the bar, the day of the skyscraper was but beginning, stenographers and typewriters were few, and the old-fashioned letter press duplicated the documents which students had laboriously transcribed in longhand. The personality of a lawyer was not then merged so generally as today in a partnership. Men still felt a pride in a sense of individual work in a great and noble calling. The old-fashioned loyalty to a leader in the profession led his associates and law students to the *court in banc* on Saturday mornings, if it were only to hear him argue a motion. The bar was then a somewhat exclusive profession and not a promiscuous trade. The age of specialization, which creates the effective machinery of a modern law office, but which prevents the rounded development of the true lawyer, was then only in its incipiency.

The Philadelphia Bar of 1884 was approximately twelve hundred members. The successful lawyer was bound to know his profession as an entirety, from the preparation of the *praecipe* to the bringing down of the mandate from the appellate court.

Let me recall by name a few of the lawyers of Philadelphia of that time, although I fear that many of them will be little more than names to the younger portion of my audience, for unhappily a lawyer's reputation is generally little more than footprints on the ocean strand: Arnold, the Biddles, Bispham (master of equity), the two Brewsters, Jeremiah S. Black (a modern Erskine), Cuyler, Richard C. Dale, Cassidy (a towering figure at the criminal bar), Dallas, Dickson, Dougherty (a finished orator of the old school), Earle, Flanders, Fraley, Gibbons, Hagert, Harrity, the two Gowens, the Junkins, McMurtrie (a master of the common law), Wayne MacVeagh, Coppee Mitchell, Outerbridge (the ideal reporter), Pettit, the elder Porter, Page, Price (master of real estate law), Pritchard, Rawle, the two Shapleys, Sellers, Furman Sheppard (a true master of his profession), White, Wilson, and many others, and last, but not least, the lawyer who was as indisputably the leader of the American bar in his generation, as Daniel Webster and Horace Binney were in theirs, John G. Johnson. To these could be added many others who, happily still living, now form the "Old Guard" of a remarkable generation of lawyers.

Such were the men, and they were worthy successors to the illustrious men who, at the beginning of the Nineteenth Century, gave such peculiar distinction to the bar of Philadelphia.

To return to this bar fills me with a feeling of pride that although the greater part of my professional life has been spent in other cities and in other courts, yet I am, as I began, a Philadelphia lawyer. Tonight, I come back to the Temple, where I began my novitiate, and hang my few and insignificant trophies on its walls, proud at least of the fact that as Solicitor-General of the United States

I represent for a little time the world's greatest client in the world's greatest court.

I fear that I have already dwelt too long upon my voluntary exile from this delightful city, and have thus exposed myself to the satirical reproach which once greeted a Roman lawyer when he, after an absence, returned to the bar of his native city. After an absence of some years as Pro-consul to one of the Roman provinces, Cicero was returning to Rome. He landed at Baiea, the seashore resort of the imperial city, and almost the first person whom he met on disembarkation was a Roman lawyer. When Cicero asked him, with plaintive curiosity, "What do they say in Rome of my return?" his friend quizzically replied: "Oh, Cicero, they have not yet commenced to talk of your departure."

In selecting a theme for my address tonight I have had an embarrassment of riches. At one time I thought of describing to you the Inns of Court, as Spenser says:

"those bricky towers
Where now the studious lawyers have their bowers.
There whylome wont the Temple Knights to byde
Till they decayed through pride."

They were the true fountain head of the legal profession in America, for of the small Colonial Bar, a relatively great number (115) had studied in the Inns of Court. While now largely superseded by schools of law, they still remain not only as proud monuments to the past but as effective methods to preserve the *esprit de corps* of the profession and to keep its older and younger members in constant contact.

This venerable Academy is in truth an Inn of Court, and it is to be regretted that, like its ancient prototypes, it was not able to build a noble Commons Hall where the younger members of the profession could dine from week to week with their seniors and thus have the inspiration of their personal influence. To this end the Inns of Court still remain, and as a continuing bond between successive generation of lawyers, they still are, as Ben Jonson called

them in his *Every Man in His Humor* "the noblest nurseries of humanity and liberty in the Kingdom." How
fine it would be if the Law Association and your Academy
could unite to erect such a Hall as Gray's Inn with an
annex Library building in lieu of the present unhappily
located library in the City Hall.

If I may address you on this interesting theme, it must
be on another occasion, for I have selected, as of greater
interest to my audience, a subject which also has its great
roots in the past, and which enables me to contrast for
a little while the old and the new. I shall therefore ask
your attention to a brief and inadequate discussion of the
argument of cases in the Supreme Court of the United
States, as they once were and as they now are.

No institution of our country is of greater interest to
the lawyers of other nations than the Supreme Court of
the United States. When I was invited last summer to
deliver an address to the French Bench and Bar in the
Cour de Cassation (the Supreme Court of France), and
asked them what subject they wished me to treat, they
replied: "The Supreme Court of the United States." The
admiration of jurists of every land for this unique tribunal
is well deserved.

No court ever occupied a larger space in the life of a
nation than the Supreme Court in the first half century
of our history. It was the greatest forum of intellectual
debate of which civilization has any knowledge. There
had been great courts before, but none had had its peculiar and extraordinary function of determining in like
measure the very form of the Government whose laws
it was interpreting. It was in truth a super-Senate, or,
more properly, it was in fact, if not in theory, a continuance of the Constitutional Convention of 1787. The
men of that Convention had, with unerring sagacity,
only indicated the ground plan of the future edifice of
our constitutional form of Government. The august duty
devolved on the Supreme Court to erect the superstructure. That superstructure, compared with the original
Constitution, is as the present Capitol building to the
original edifice, and is largely the work of the Bench and

Bar of the United States. The principles of Government were to be developed, not in the heated atmosphere and selfish conflicts of political strife, but in the serene air of the Temple of Justice, after full debate by the greatest lawyers of the time, and by a court which acted not as partisans but as the sworn interpreters of constitutional liberty.

There is no better evidence of the spirit of self-restraint, which is the very genius of American liberty, than the fact that after the storm of party strife and the earthquake of popular resentment, which at times marked the reaction of the people to the great pioneer decisions of the Supreme Court, its "still small voice" was more potent than either. This Nation, and indeed the civilized world, has given praise in ungrudging measure to Marshall and his great associates, but too little has been said of the great men of the bar who primarily fought out the mighty issues of constitutional liberty and from whom, in so many instances, the court received its inspiration. Marshall's greatest opinion, that of *Gibbons* v. *Ogden*, was but a re-statement of the powerful argument which Daniel Webster had made against the steamboat monopoly, as his great decision of *McCulloch* v. *Maryland* was the judicial synthesis of Pinkney's wonderful argument.

Possibly the greatest debates on the nature of government that ever took place within a short period of time were those of the Constitutional Convention of 1787, but, unhappily, only a fragment, a few bones of the great mastodon, remain to posterity in Madison's Journal. Only second in dignity and importance to these debates were the equally prolonged and masterly arguments that were addressed in the first half century to the Supreme Court by the leaders of the bar, and we of the Philadelphia bar can take proud satisfaction in the fact that so many of those leaders were of our own bar. Wilson, Tilghman, Ingersoll, John Sargent, Joseph Hopkinson and Horace Binney were among the foremost gladiators in that half-century struggle between conflicting governmental ideas which made us a powerfully unified Nation.

During the first half century no limitation whatever

was placed on the length of arguments by counsel, for happily the docket of the Supreme Court was not crowded with cases, and trivial private litigation did not prevent the Court from giving that deliberate and profound consideration to the essential nature of our Government which in the tremendous pressure of modern conditions is unfortunately impossible. No cases of any description came before the Court during its first three semi-annual terms. From 1793 to 1803 the Court decided only sixty-four cases. The first volume of Reports devoted exclusively to the Supreme Court was not published until thirteen years after its establishment. In the six years beginning with 1809 and ending in 1815 the Court sat on an average of thirty days in the year. Between 1822 and 1846 the Court only decided forty cases a year, and even between 1846 and 1850 the annual average was seventy-one cases. This may be compared with the annual average of the last five years, which is over one thousand cases. Thus the Court was then able to give a full and patient consideration to every case, quite impossible in these strenuous days, when counsel can only ask, as of right, an hour to present his contention.

With the judiciary, as with every institution of human society, the period of which I speak was the age of quality rather than, as at the present time, an age of quantity. The mechanical era, which has so profoundly affected human life by substituting a quantitative for a qualitative production, has not been without its effect even upon the administration of justice. Probably it is as admirable for our present-day judiciary to turn out so many useful and sound decisions as it was in former days to deliver so many great decisions. It was the age of the wheelbarrow as contrasted with the present age of the aeroplane. Men had still time to think with patience and deliberation of the supreme issues of life, a luxury which unfortunately is no longer afforded the present generation. The tendency towards bankruptcy of present-day civilization seems to me to be largely due to the fact that the complicated processes of modern life have placed an excessive strain upon the very limited ability of man. Our Government in all its branches is slowly breaking down under this inordinate pressure.

As late as 1818 the Justices had abundant time for dining out when they were at the Capital, and they were apt to begin the day's session, after robing and taking their places, by receiving from the marshal and then answering their cards of invitation. Their annual session in Washington was too short to make it their residence, and, as a result, the Justices boarded together in the early days of the Nineteenth Century in a common boarding house, sitting from eleven to five o'clock in Court, dining at five o'clock, and then consulting until midnight. As the cases were comparatively few, and as the Court was sincerely desirous to do its part in developing the principles of our Government, technical objections and jurisdictional difficulties played little part in their deliberations. In *Marbury* v. *Madison* the great Chief Justice first decided the two disputed questions, and then proceeded to hold that the Court was in that form of action without jurisdictional power to decide them. In the famous case of *Hylton* v. *United States,* argued by Alexander Hamilton, a fictitious statement of facts was made to create a justiciable controversy, and the Government stipulated to pay the counsel fees on both sides; but nevertheless the Court proceeded to a judgment which was to play a fateful part in the great discussion nearly a century later when the power of the Government to levy an income tax without apportionment was in controversy.

The fact is that the Court did not then regard itself as primarily a court to adjust private controversies. It regarded—and as the event proved properly—its function as the higher one of being the balance wheel of our constitutional system.

For many years the Court permitted counsel to consume an unlimited amount of time in the argument of their cases. On three occasions counsel consumed eleven days in each of the cases. *McCulloch* v. *Maryland* took nine days, the *Girard Will Case,* ten days. Leading counsel, like Pinkney, Wirt, Webster, John Quincy Adams and

Horace Binney, repeatedly consumed three or four days in a single argument.

To the modern practitioner this borders on the incredible, for it is difficult to understand how they could possibly have taken so much time to establish principles which were generally more important than complex.

Take, for example, the case of *McCulloch* v. *Maryland*. It involved two elementary principles of infinite moment to the efficacy of the Constitution.

Did the Federal Government have any powers except those that were expressly conferred, and if it had the implied power to create a fiscal agency, could the States interfere by taxation with its operations?

No one can question the importance of these two principles, for if they had been wrongly decided it is difficult to understand how the Constitution could have functioned; but, after all, they were reasonably simple questions, and it would have been difficult for a modern practitioner to have spent two hours in discussing principles which were so obvious. The great question in *Marbury v. Madison* was extraordinarily simple, and admitted of but one answer. That answer was not novel and had long been anticipated, even in the Constitutional Convention. No new planet swam into Marshall's ken on that occasion. He only stated an obvious truth, to which only a few, notably Jefferson, dissented. The extraordinary skill with which Chief Justice Marshall answered this question serves to blind us to its simplicity; and if it be asked why he should have rendered on this and other occasions extended opinions to discuss the obvious, the answer is that in both cases the opinions were far more than judicial decisions. They were in the highest and truest sense political documents, and, like the Federalist Papers, addressed to the people of the United States, and their real purpose was to reconcile to a consolidated Union a people, whose traditions and conventions were altogether opposed to such a unification. As political documents they deserve their high place in the annals of political government, but as judicial opinions it is difficult at this day to understand how counsel could have argued them for many days and why it should have taken so much judicial argument to announce the conclusion.

Gibbons v. *Ogden,* on the contrary, was something more than an obvious answer to a simple question. That decision required the experience of a statesman and the prescience of a prophet, and if Chief Justice Marshall had written nothing else than his great opinion in this case, he would have justified his place among the immortals.

The Justices themselves were not unconscious of the inordinate length of the arguments on questions which, while important as pioneer decisions, were not inherently difficult. Justice Story thus wrote at the very beginning of his judicial career in 1812:

"The mode of arguing cases in the Supreme Court is exceedingly prolix and tedious."

Again, in 1831, when the *Charles River Bridge Case* was before the Court, he wrote:

"We have been sadly obstructed of late in our business by very long and tedious arguments, as distressing to hear as to be nailed down to an old-fashioned homily."

And again, in 1835, after listening eight days to argument in *Mitchell* v. *United States,* and looking forward to five more days of speechmaking, he wrote:

"I firmly believe that it ought not to have occupied one-third of the time to have developed all the merits, * * * but this is the very region of words."

It was not until March, 1849, that the long-suffering Court adopted a rule which limited the length of each argument to two hours, and it took this course only after its indulgence towards counsel had been severely criticized in Congress. In the course of debate a Senator said:

"It is quite familiar to us all that in a case which attracted some attention one of the learned counsel occupied an entire day for the purpose of demonstrating this very difficult proposition in America, that the people are sovereign; and then pursued his argument on the second day by endeavoring to make out the extremely difficult conclusion from the first proposition that, being sovereign, they had a right to frame their own Constitution."

The stage-setting for this unrivaled display of oratory was not in itself picturesque. The Court met on the basement floor of the Capitol, underneath its present chamber, the room now occupied by the library of the Court. Here for forty years were argued nearly all of the great constitutional cases, from *McCulloch v. Maryland* to the *Dred Scott* case. The Justices, who for lack of private rooms robed themselves in Court, sat on a long seat at the east end of the room on a raised platform. On the floor was a long table with chairs for the lawyers and for the audience. The room was so often crowded with people that every inch of space was taken and the judges were on more than one occasion almost pushed off their platform by the society ladies of Washington, who sat behind and before them. At times Congress would be deserted, as its leading members crowded into this small room to see Webster and Clay cross swords, for it was then recognized that the forum for the foremost debaters of the Senate was not on its floor but in the Supreme Court.

Such was the arena of the great gladiators of the bar upon whom the Judges raised or turned down the thumb in their subsequent decisions.

"What a crowded hour of glorious life" it would be if we could avail ourselves of Wells' time machine and travel back nearly a century to the year 1824 and be present when the supremely great case of *Gibbons* v. *Ogden,* which did more to unify America than any other decision that was ever announced, was argued in the Supreme Court of the United States. Imagine ourselves as one of that generation, crowded into that little court room, to witness the long-expected duel between the Hector (Mr. Pinkney) and the Achilles (Mr. Webster) of the bar. For a year past the subject of the Federal power over the great waterways of the country, and in a larger sense over all the tremendous commerce of the Nation, which was then developing through the potent agencies of steam, had agitated the minds of men throughout the Nation; and now the great issue was to be determined, after an agitation of nearly a quarter of a century, in the arena of reason.

Death had taken the then leader of the bar, Mr. Pinkney, from the combat, but Daniel Webster and William Wirt remained to plead for the freedom of commerce in opposition to Emmet and Oakley, leaders of the New York Bar, for the State of New York. Many awaited the tourney of intellect with the same eager interest as that with which the foremost men of England thronged Westminster Hall to hear Burke and Sheridan in the Warren Hastings trial.

On the eve of the argument Wirt wrote to his brother-in-law:

"Tomorrow week will come on the great steamboat question from New York. Come on and hear it. Emmet's whole soul is in the case and he will stretch all his powers. Oakley is said to be one of the first logicians of the age, as much a Phocion as Emmet is a Themistocles, and Webster is as ambitious as Caesar. He will not be outdone by any man, if it is within the compass of his power to avoid it. It will be a combat worth witnessing."

Such a combat it indeed proved to be. Webster opened the case, and a contemporary writes:

"It was one of the most powerful arguments we ever remember to have heard. The court room was excessively crowded. He devoted almost his full time, two and one-half hours, to developing his broad thesis as to the plenary and exclusive power of Congress over the commerce in question."

Webster himself described his own justifiable elation of spirit as he slowly developed the great principle which was to be so fateful in the development of this Nation. He said:

> "I think I never experienced more intellectual pleasure than in arguing that novel question to the great man who could appreciate it and take it in; and he did take it in as a baby takes in its mother's milk."

Judge Story, referring to Webster's argument, thus described its characteristics:

> "His clearness and downright simplicity of statement, his vast comprehensiveness of topics, and his fertility in illustrations drawn from practical sources; his keen analysis and suggestion of difficulties; his power of disentangling a complicated proposition and resolving it in elements so plain as to reach the common minds; his vigor in generalizations, planting his whole argument behind the whole battery of his opponents; his wariness and caution not to betray himself by heat into untenable positions or to spread his forces over useless ground."

Oakley followed with a two-day speech, in which he sought to countermine the argument of his great opponent, and it was pronounced "one of the most ingenious and able arguments ever made in this court." The veteran Emmet then argued for two days, and the court room was so densely packed that the ladies of Washington found seats on the judicial dais and among the lawyers.

Wirt closed the argument in a speech of two days, and his peroration was declared by a contemporary to be—

> "the finest effort of human genius ever exhibited in a court of justice, a powerful and splendid effusion, grand, tender, picturesque, and pathetic. The manner was lofty and touching; the fall of his voice towards the conclusion was

truly thrilling and affecting, and I never witnessed such an effect from any burst of eloquence; every face was filled with the fine trans-
port and prophetic fury of the orator, and all
united in applauding the peroration as affording
in matter, diction, manner, happy application,
and striking effect the most powerful display of
real oratory that they had ever witnessed."

Allowing for the greater and more ingenuous enthusiasm of those days, it must have been an extraordinary
combat of wit, learning, and eloquence—such as could
never happen in these swifter but more prosaic days.
Today the Court will tolerate an occasional witticism,
but frowns upon any studied effort at eloquent expression, especially if it "smells of the lamp." I remember
when I argued the case of *Neely v. Henkle,* which
involved the right of our Government to govern Cuba as
temporarily acquired territory free from many limitations of the Constitution, I concluded a two-hour argument by quoting, in answer to an attack upon the manner of such occupation, the fine lines from the play of
Richelieu where the great Prime Minister defended his
country, and I remember the surprised expression of Chief
Justice Fuller at any attempt to enrich an argument with
an historical analogy or a quotation from the theatre.

Seventy-eight years after the argument in *Gibbons* v.
Ogden it was my privilege to argue the great question,
unanswered in the former case, as to whether the power
to regulate commerce included a power to prohibit. We
argued it on three different occasions before the Court
finally reached its conclusion, and my opponents were
William D. Guthrie, George F. Edmunds, and the then
leader of the American Bar, James C. Carter. (As Mr.
Carter retired from the case before the third argument,
his name does not appear in the Reports.) I do not recall
in either of those three arguments, each of which lasted
four hours, made in a case which was recognized as of
unusual importance in the development of Federal power,
that either I or my opponents ever lightened the argu-

ment with any of that old-time grace of expression or richness of allusion which must have made the arguments of the older days so illuminating and inspiring. Mr. Carter filed a two hundred page brief in support of the extraordinary proposition that the right to print a lottery ticket was safeguarded by the "liberty of the press" guarantee and he gave the Court all the learning on that subject from Milton down.

In the *Lottery Case* all that was attempted by counsel was to dig deep into the strata of successive decisions interpreting the commerce power in order to discover the textual foundation of the Constitution, to ascertain whether its framers included in the power to regulate the so tremendous and potentially subversive power as the power to prohibit.

One advantage of these interminable arguments of the earlier days was that they obviated the long delays in the decisions which are now so frequent. Following the custom of the English courts, the Supreme Court generally reached a decision very shortly after the conclusion of the argument. There were then no lengthy printed briefs to be examined and necessitating a postponement of such decision. Moreover, the possibilities of discussion had been exhausted in the patient and exhaustive analysis of the subject in the oral argument; and generally the Court, after listening to all that eminent counsel could say in many days of argument, had then reached a conclusion and it only remained to formulate it in a written opinion. Thus, *Chisholm* v. *Georgia* was decided fourteen days after the argument. *Penhallow* v. *Doane's Administrators,* which took eleven days to argue, a week after the conclusion of the argument. *McCulloch* v. *Maryland,* which was argued for nine days, three days after Mr. Pinkney had made the concluding argument. *Cohens* v. *Virginia,* two weeks after the argument. *Osborne* v. *Bank of the United States,* one week thereafter, and the *Girard Will Case,* which was argued for ten days, was decided two weeks later.

Another circumstance, which conspired to focus public interest on the Court, was the small number of the

Supreme Court bar and the greatness of many of its members. The public was attracted to these gladiatorial exhibitions of forensic skill apart from the interest in the questions that were discussed, and took the same interest in their champions as today it takes in the latest baseball phenomenon or moving picture favorite.

A bar that could include such men as Wilson, Hamilton, Luther Martin, the two Ingersolls, Lewis, Rawle, Dallas, Duponceau, Hopkinson, Sargent, Binney, Pinkney, Wirt, Oakley, Emmet, Rufus Choate, Benton, Quincy Adams, Webster and Clay was one of unequaled brilliancy, and even this small number could be reduced to an even smaller number who appeared on one side or the other of nearly all the great cases. Webster argued in the Court for nearly forty years, and in nearly every important case we are apt to find his name. In one volume of the Supreme Court Reports (8 Cranch) Pinkney's name appears in one-half of the forty-six cases that were argued.

Probably one of the greatest field days of the Court, and one of peculiar interest to Philadelphia, was the *Girard Will Case*, argued in 1844. Walter Jones and Daniel Webster were opposed to Horace Binney and John Sargent. They were all of them veterans.

We have the following contemporary pen picture, as given in The New York *Herald* of February 7th of that year:

"The highest judicial officers of the Nation, each robed in a black silk gown and sitting in a large armchair before his separate table. * * * In front, and some distance off, are four mahogany tables. Seated at one of these was a small, old gentleman. This is the celebrated General Walter Jones. Next is Daniel Webster, with beetled brow and dark eyes, poring over the papers, books, or printed statements of facts in the case; behind him sits John Cadwalader, of Philadelphia, and, in this case, the principal grubber after facts and documents. He is Horace Binney's son-in-law. At the table parallel to

Mr. Webster, and a little behind, sat Horace
Binney, white-haired, a large head and frame,
wearing spectacles and with strongly marked
features. Next to him is John Sargent."

One of the interesting features of this argument was
that, during its progress, President Tyler offered John
Sargent the position of Associate Justice, to fill a vacancy.
Mr. Sargent declined, and, believing that it would then
be offered to Mr. Binney, requested that the fact of the
offer should be kept secret during his life, and never disclosed to Mr. Binney. It was then tendered to Mr. Binney
and he declined and made the same request—that the fact
of such declination be not disclosed to Mr. Sargent. Was
not this the very flower of old-time courtesy?

Returning to the argument, the contemporary account
tells that the court room had been densely crowded from
a very early hour in the morning. Mr. Binney, in the
course of his argument, quoted from one of Mr. Webster's
arguments in a preceding case, and Webster laughingly
replied: "That was a bad case, and I had to make my
argument to suit my case."

Under the rule, Webster, having the closing argument,
was obliged to furnish his points and authorities to Mr.
Binney before the latter commenced his argument. This
he did, just as Binney was about to begin. In so doing
Webster apologized for his tardiness, and when he had
concluded Binney sarcastically said, with a slight wave
of his hand, that he "fully excused his brother for his
delay of citation, for he (Binney) would have no occasion to touch a single point or anything cited by him."

A contemporary account thus describes the scene:

"Throughout the court room there is a great
silence, save now and then when a bevy of ladies
come in. In fact, it looks more like a ball-
room sometimes; and if old Lord Eldon and the
defunct judges of Westminster would walk in
from their graves, each particular whalebone in
their wigs would stand on end at this mixture
of men and women, law and politeness, ogling

and flirtation, bowing and courtesying, going on in the highest tribunal in America."

Binney argued for two days, and, as he proceeded with his masterly exposition of a very difficult subject, to which he had given many months of research, Webster was literally stunned by the power of an argument to which he could make no adequate reply. As a contemporary said of that argument: "It was like a huge screw slowly turning around on its threads." If Binney today tried to read at length old chancery precedents, some Justice would discouragingly ask him whether they were not in his brief.

It was now Webster's turn. It is said that there were never so many persons in the court room. Hundreds were turned away. Senators, Members of the House, Foreign Ministers, Cabinet officers, social leaders of both sexes, were there to hear the Olympian Webster answer the first of Philadelphia's lawyers. His argument is thus, in part, described by a spectator:

> "The opening of the argument was remarkable for all the impressiveness of manner, clearness of expression and power of analysis for which Webster is so distinguished. The closing part of his address produced a thrilling effect upon those who heard him, and many at times were shedding tears from his eloquent defense of the power and influence of the Christian religion."

A Member of Congress wrote in his diary:

> "One day a Member came into the House and exclaimed that 'preaching was played out. There was no use for ministers now. Daniel Webster is down in the Supreme Court room eclipsing them all by a defense of the Christian religion.' As I entered the court room, here are his words: 'And these words which I command thee this day shall be in thy heart.' Then again: 'Suffer little children to come unto me,' accent-

ing the word 'children.' He repeated it, accent-
ing the word 'little.' Then rolling his eyes
heavenward and extending his arms, he repeated
it thus: 'Suffer little children to come unto
Me, unto *Me,* unto *Me,* suffer little children to
come.' So he went on for three days, and it was
the only three days' meeting that I ever attended
where one man did all the preaching and there
was neither praying nor singing."

If Webster were today to inflict such oratorical effects
upon the Court, its impatience would soon quench the
fire of his eloquence. The belief was that he had a two-
fold purpose in his emotional appeal, one to make a fee
of $50,000 (at that time unheard of), and the second,
by his appeal to the religious elements, to win a nomination for the presidency. In both he failed. As you know,
Webster, fortunately for Philadelphia and for the orphan
children, lost his case, and indeed it may be here noted
that Webster lost more than one-half of all the cases he
argued. It was with him, as later with John G. Johnson,
his very fame at times made him a coroner for the dead
rather than a physician for the living.

Pardon one final picture of the old Court, and then
from these specimen bricks we can judge the edifice. It
was the year 1848, and the case assigned for argument was
Houston v. *City of New Orleans.* The question was a
very simple one under the bankruptcy law. But Henry
Clay was to argue. I quote from a contemporary:

"At an early hour the avenues leading to the
Capitol were thronged with crowds of the aged
and the young, the beautiful and the gay, all
anxious to hear, perhaps for the last time, the
voice of the Sage of Ashland. On no former occasion was the Supreme Court so densely packed.
Every inch of space was occupied, even to the
lobbies leading to the Senate. Mr. Clay arose a
few minutes after eleven o'clock, the hour at
which the Court is organized. It has been often
said, and truly, that he never was and never

could be, reported successfully.   His magic manner, the captivating tones of his voice, and a
natural grace, singular in its influence, and peculiarly his own, can never be transferred to
paper."

Another spectator dwells upon the gallantry of his
bearing, the dignity of his gestures, the warmth of his
manners, his sonorous voice, and the many graces which, as
the writer said, made him "the proper favorite" of the
ladies who so thronged the bar and even the Judges' platform as almost to push them from their seats. The writer
adds the audacious pun that "the liberty of the press"
was never carried to a more dangerous extent; and all
this about a sordid question of the bankruptcy law.

Such was the Court of yesterday—a Court of leisure, deliberation and dignity, where men had the time and took
the pains to exhaust the possibilities of reasoning, and where
the clash of mind with mind attracted an attention, to
which today the latest prizefight or football match is the
only thing comparable in the intensity of interest.

Let me now speak of the Court today, as I have had
occasion to see it in the thirty years in which I have been
a member of its bar.

Today there is no distinctive bar of the Supreme Court.
No one knows exactly its living membership, but it is estimated that it is at least thirty thousand. Of these the
greater number never had a case in the Court, and only a
few have had many cases. This is undoubtedly due, in
part, to the facility of transportation, for in the old days a
lawyer at a distance could not come to Washington to
argue his case without discomfort and great expense of
time and money. Today, the remote lawyer, even if he
is of the Alaska or Philippine Bar, feels repaid for a
delightful journey by steamship and railroad, if only for
the fact that he has made his bow to the Court.

The thousands of cases that have been argued in the
last half century have been largely argued by men, who
made their first and only appearance in the Supreme
Court, and, for this reason, the close intimacy of the Court,

as it prevailed in the earlier days, when the same men
year after year crossed swords in intellectual combat, is
almost wholly gone.

In the second place, the growth of litigation in the
Supreme Court has been such as to make impossible the
careful and deliberate consideration of cases which was
possible in the old days.

Prior to 1825 the Court disposed of an average of
twenty-four cases a year. From 1826 to 1830 the average was fifty-eight. From 1846 to 1850 the average was
seventy-one cases. In October, 1891, term there were
1,582 cases on the docket, of which 496 were disposed
of, and at that time it took three years to reach a case
for argument. The Circuit Court of Appeals Act gave
temporary relief, but only temporary, for in the past
five years the Court has had on the average of 1,054 cases
pending each term, and of these it has disposed of an
annual average of 625 cases. At the present time, unless
a case is advanced, it requires about fifteen months after
it has been docketed before it is heard.

This condition of affairs has required the Court to
reduce the time of argument from two hours to the present one hour for each side, and while the time is occasionally extended the extension is a short one, generally not in
excess of a half-hour. I can only recall in recent years
three cases where, as in the old days of the Court, a full
court week (or five days) was allowed for the argument.
They were the *Income Tax cases*, the *Insular cases* and the
National Prohibition cases, and on these occasions something of the old glory of the Court was revived when many
of the greatest living lawyers, with sufficient time to discuss a great subject fully, crossed swords in a forensic
discussion of great dignity and power.

Generally, however, each argument must be concluded
in an hour, and as this is all too short to make an elaborate argument, any attempt to enrich it with the graces of
literature or the power of wit is not welcomed by the
Court. An argument, such as Jeremiah S. Black made in
the case of *Ex parte Milligan*—one of the greatest ever
made in a court of justice—would today be quite impos-

sible in the Supreme Court. One historical reference would be tolerated, but if any advocate today should imitate Black in a lengthy rhapsody on human liberty he would soon get such a reaction from the Court that he would stop in the full tide of his oratory. A great argument, in the sense that the arguments of Webster, Binney and Jeremiah S. Black were great, namely, in their exhaustion of the subject by every possible resort to literature, history, philosophy and law, would be quite impossible today, for, even if the advocate had the time to make such an argument, the Court would not have the patience to listen to it.

One reason and possible justification for this marked change is the fact that the brief has largely supplanted the oral argument, and yet it is too often a poor substitute for it. Chief Justice White once said to me that the lawyer who submits his client's case upon a printed brief betrays that client. This seems to me too sweeping,— the late Chief Justice was given, with his love of emphasis, to sweeping generalizations,—for exceptional cases may be advantageously submitted on a brief. Nevertheless, in substance, the Chief Justice's observation is true, for the brief is no more a true substitute for an oral argument, even in these days of prosaic argument, than a chromo is a substitute for an oil painting.

This is especially true in view of the great number of cases that the Court must dispose of in each term. The rapidity of business and the swift succession of cases gives little time to the Justices to examine briefs, much less records, and some of them rely upon the impressions of the oral argument far more than may be generally suspected.

The art of the advocate of today is not to charm and enthrall the judgment of the Justices by the graces of old-fashioned oratory, but rather to waken the interest of men, already overstrained, in the subject, to indicate its nature, and to stress the contention upon which the case can be won. I imagine that this was true even in the old days, for it was probably true of Webster, as it was said of Erskine, that his statement of facts was worth

another man's argument.   No barrister ever made so deep
and permanent impression as Judah P. Benjamin upon the
English bar, and I once asked Lord Halsbury, a former
Lord Chancellor, the secret of his power, and he replied
that it was in his convincing statement of fact.   He instanced a case that he had heard Benjamin argue, where the
Court was opposed to his contention as developed by his
junior. When Benjamin arose the Court was impatient of
further discussion. In an aggressive voice the great advocate said:

> "If your Lordships please, if you will listen to
> me for ten minutes I will convince you that my
> contention is correct."

Lord Halsbury added that Benjamin in ten minutes
completely changed the opinion of the Court.   In fact,
there may be more merit in a lawyer in this day and
generation in a speech of an hour driving home a great
contention, which in former days would have taken a
week to argue, than the elaborate discussions of the earlier
days of the Court. The great merit of John G. Johnson
was in his exceptional power to select out of the many
points the one which could be most plausibly argued and
then to drive that point home with the blow of a sledge-
hammer.   I doubt whether Mr. Johnson ever argued a
case in the sense that Pinkney, Wirt, Binney or Webster
presented their causes. Rarely did he enrich his argument
with any graces of expression or any of the riches of
literature or philosophy. Rarely did he exhaust the possibilities of his case by dwelling upon the many points
that favored his contention. Tersely and abruptly he
would state the main point, and his strength was in the
wisdom with which he selected the point and the power
with which he drove it home.

It would be interesting to compare Johnson, as the
leader of the Bar in our time, with Webster, the leader
of the Bar in his time. They were so different as to suggest a contrast, rather than a comparison.

Mr. Webster had an unusual combination of great gifts,
and his speeches, notably his great Reply to Hayne—in

my judgment, the greatest piece of forensic oratory in our literature—showed the impassioned oratory of Fox, the philosophic grasp of Burke, and the acute logical analysis of Marshall.

Johnson had, in some measure, the latter quality; but he was never the orator, and rarely the philosopher. On the other hand, as an all-around practitioner, combining the work of both solicitor and barrister, he has possibly never had his equal at the American bar. He probably disposed of more legal business in one year than Webster did in five. Indeed, this was his limitation, for in my judgment he to some extent wasted his giant energies in a mass of trivial litigation. Had he entered the Senate and become both a lawyer and a public man and devoted his splendid energies to the really great questions of the day, he might have ranked with Webster. One thing is clear—his prodigious industry and capacity for work has rarely, if ever, been equaled.

Another difference between the present and the past is the lack of public interest in the deliberations of the Court. It does not lack great questions. Measured by any standard, there are now argued each year greater questions than were argued in the first half century of its existence, if we except the few notable pioneer decisions of Marshall. Today, cases of enormous importance are argued without attracting any public interest whatever. Cases which involve millions, and in some cases hundreds of millions, are constantly arising. In jurisprudence, as in economics, this is now, as Speaker Reed once said, "a billion-dollar country." The Court is no longer impressed, when counsel suggest that the importance of the case is measured in millions. At the last term of Court I argued the case of *United States* v. *Southern Pacific Railroad,* which involved to an important extent the transportation destinies of the Trans-Mississippi region and affected securities valued at hundreds of millions of dollars. Even twenty years ago the case would have excited widespread interest and would have affected the great financial exchanges of the country because of the immensity of the interests involved; but in these times, when events of world-wide importance crowd upon each other's heels so that history, which was formerly made in centuries, is now made in decades, when the cinematographic mind of man hardly grasps some fact of world-wide interest in the morning paper before it is crowded out by a fact of equal importance in the evening paper, it is not unnatural that cases, which would formerly have awakened nation-wide interest, today hardly get a paragraph in the daily papers.

Constitutional questions of great importance to our form of Government continue to arise, and each term witnesses a clash of conflicting constitutional ideas which in former days would have been of very general concern and interest to the whole people, but today they are unnoticed outside of our profession.

I doubt whether even the average practitioner at the bar attempts to keep pace with the rapid progress of constitutional law. Few appreciate how many questions of constitutional interpretation are still arising. In the last thirty years, nearly eight hundred cases have arisen under the Fourteenth Amendment, and over two hundred cases under the commerce clause. It is probably a conservative estimate to say that, in the last thirty years, over fifteen hundred cases involving an interpretation of the Constitution have been argued, in which the question was one of substance. I do not include the innumerable cases in which constitutional questions are raised for purposes of delay, or are otherwise frivolous in character.

Today, the Supreme Court attracts little popular interest or attention. In the first half century of the Republic it was not undervalued either to the Executive or to Congress in the profound concern with which its deliberations and decisions were followed. One has only to read Warren's History of the Supreme Court (a very admirable book which every lawyer should read), to know that for a full century, and as late as reconstruction days, violent storms of public opinion raged about the Supreme Court. Probably no single cause did more than the *Dred Scott* decision to precipitate the Civil War, but in this respect that fateful decision differed only in degree and not in kind from the many prior decisions, from *Marbury* v. *Madison* down, about which the storms of public opinion raged so violently.

Today the Supreme Court is no longer an asset for the all-important city editor. Public interest in its deliberations is moribund. The only spectators in the Supreme Court room are groups of tourists who, under the ciceronage of a professional guide, file into the court room, remain five minutes, and then depart. As I once heard one of these guides say to his group of tourists: "Now, we are going into the Supreme Court. You won't want to stay long, for no one is interested in what they do." There is more truth than poetry in this remark. The interest of the public either in the bench or the bar is very slight. I know of no living lawyer whose appearance in the Supreme Court room, even if previously announced, would half fill the court room as Pinkney, Wirt, Webster, Clay and Binney once crowded it.

Happily, one dignified ceremonial of the old Court remains; and while it is, from a practical standpoint, unquestionably a loss of time, yet there are few of us, who are privileged to be in Court on Monday mornings, when the Court is in session, who would willingly forego this survival of the days of leisure. I refer to the custom of the Court to deliver orally the substance of their opinions. The room is then crowded with members of the bar to hear the latest utterances of the Court of last conjecture. Each Justice, in turn, commencing with the junior Justice, announces an opinion "by direction of the Court." When the Court is divided on some important question this oral delivery of opinions almost takes the form of a debate, and not infrequently, where acute differences have developed, the opinions are delivered with the oral graces of oratory.

Well do I remember when the opinions were delivered in the so-called *Insular cases* in 1901. The reading of the opinions on that occasion consumed nearly six hours, and the historic old chamber darkened with the fading light of day as the last of the Justices concluded. Both the place and the occasion were historic, for the court room is the old Senate Chamber of the United States, and if Webster, Clay, Calhoun and Benton could have on that occasion revisited the great arena, in which they had fought as gladiators for nearly a half century, they would again have felt the old thrill of combat as they listened to the vehement expressions of the different Justices.

The reading of these opinions on successive Mondays does involve a loss of valuable time, but it serves to preserve an intimate personal relation between the bench and the bar and to emphasize the deep interest which the bar should have in the continuous development of our constitutional jurisprudence by our highest Court.

Fortunately, the value of the Court does not depend upon its character as a spectacle. It is just as useful whether there is an audience and whether the tourists remain, or, as always, depart.

The more serious concern is how the Court, with its ever-growing calendar, can attend to its tremendously important work unless in some way there are fewer cases and therefore more time for extended discussion, both orally in court and in the consultation room. The Court today literally does ten times as much work as it did in Marshall's day, and it may be added that its problems are ten-fold more complex. It must content itself with hearing from the advocate a hurried and often superficial explanation of the nature of the controversy and the character of his contention.

The only compensatory advantage is the elaborate briefs, sometimes amounting to treatises, which the bar inflicts upon the Court, but the inordinate length of these bulky briefs defeats the good that they might otherwise do. I once heard Chief Justice White say, about the first of the year, that if he did not hear another argument he could not possibly before summer read all the records and briefs which had been filed from October to January, and yet the Court had four more months in which to hear arguments and receive briefs. It is a matter of simple calculation to show that the Court could not possibly consume in the five months of their annual session the ocean of printer's ink in which they are engulfed. Printed briefs alone cannot be less than 60,000 pages each year, and transcripts of records, often consisting in a single case of twenty volumes, cannot be less than another 60,000 printed pages. This makes 120,000 pages each term, and on the basis of 200 working days in each term, it means theoretically a reading *each day* of 600 pages. That is impossible, as the judges sit for four hours each court day to hear arguments.

Hence the enormous importance, despite the hour rule, of skillful advocacy in impressing upon the Court the nature of the case and the even greater necessity of making "briefs" brief in fact as well as in name. Today it takes more ability to write a brief "brief" than a long one, and it is twice as effective; and yet lawyers, especially my brethren of the New York Bar, with their great machine-like offices, turn out briefs which are encyclopædic in nature and generally defeat their own purposes by their inordinate prolixity.

All this increases my wonder as to the ability with which the Supreme Court of the present day disposes of the intolerable burden of litigation that each term is pressed upon its back. The present term began October 2, 1922, and the Court has already disposed of nearly 300 cases, and this may be compared with the twenty-four cases a year which the old Court disposed of prior to 1825, or the sixty-five cases which it disposed of each year in the next quarter of a century. Which is most admirable, the old Court of meticulous care or the new Court of unequaled industry? The greater credit for sustained intellectual exertion is due to the Court of today. I say this so that I may not be accused of being merely a *laudator acti temporis*.

To me this is a very serious situation, for if the past has made one thing clear in American history, it is that our form of Government cannot survive unless the Supreme Court functions, and the Supreme Court cannot function if an undue strain is put upon it. For this reason, a bill has been introduced in Congress, with the approval of the Court, and indeed on the initiative of the present hard-working Chief Justice, whose purpose, broadly speaking, is to make all appeals, with the exception of a few classes of cases, as of grace and not of right. This would enable the Court to select out of the mass of applications for appeals the cases to which it could justly give its time and consideration, and more than that, it seems to me, no one should wish. In my judgment, if a way could be found to eliminate the frivolous appeals and those merely intended for delay, and to select the cases which are of real concern to the development of law and to the public interests, then greater time could be allowed for oral argument, and in that event some of the vanished glories of the Court, as one of the greatest of forensic tribunals, might return.*

To me it is a matter of deep regret that the great constitutional cases that are always arising can now only be hastily and perfunctorily argued by counsel because of the limitations of the hour rule. Of the thirty-five cases that I argued the last term of Court, I am confident that at least ten presented constitutional questions. All of the great issues of the Constitution have not been decided. Indeed, cases even now arise of first impression. I argued one the last term of court (*Alaska* v. *Troy*), as to whether the clause of the Constitution which forbids preference to the port of one State over the port of another State included the port of a Territory. This clause had not been construed with respect to this point, and I was virtually treading the untrod paths of the Fathers, and yet I had to argue the case in an hour. My opponent came all the way from Alaska to argue this case and could only have an hour to present a contention which was undoubtedly of great importance to that Territory.

I gravely question the wisdom of such express-train methods in solving fundamental problems of Government; and if this be true of oral arguments, it is even more true of the time necessary for consultation by the Justices and the preparation of their opinions. They cannot give due care to these great expositions of the Constitution, which, when rendered, become a part of our jurisprudence for all

---

* This reform has been enacted into law since this address and the work of the Court thus greatly reduced.—EDITOR.

time, unless they have abundant opportunity to think out the question from every angle and all its phases, and it is sadly true that such is not the condition at the present time.

It is true that many great questions have been simplified by the successive strata of decisions; and yet, on the other hand, these decisions sometimes make the question more difficult than the original text of the Constitution, for those of us who argue constitutional questions in the Supreme Court know full well that it would be far easier, as in Marshall's day, to interpret the virgin text of the Constitution than to interpret and reconcile the successive strata of judicial decisions, which have covered the Constitution as the ashes of Vesuvius once covered Pompeii.

These innumerable decisions in over 270 volumes of reports justify the words of Tennyson:

> That codeless myriad of precedents,
> That wilderness of single instances,
> Through which a few, by wit or fortune led,
> May beat a pathway out to wealth and fame.

Young gentlemen of the Law Academy, and of the Bar, for each of you I express the wish that you may be of that happy "few" who will achieve great things in our noble profession and be privileged from time to time to argue cases in a tribunal which still remains the greatest court of the world. Whether, however, you are thus privileged or not—and such success is not merely a matter of deserving, but, too often unhappily of fortuitous circumstances—may I express for each of you at this period of the year so near to Christmas time the season's wish of Thackeray in one of his Christmas books:

> Come wealth or want, come good or ill,
>   Let young and old accept their part,
> And bow before the Awful Will,
>   And bear it with an honest heart.
> Who misses or who wins the prize,
>   Go, lose or conquer as you can;

But if you fail, or if you rise,
  Be each, pray God, a gentleman.

My song, save this, is little worth;
  I lay the weary pen aside,
And wish you health, and love and mirth,
  As fits the solemn Chritsmas tide,
As fits the holy Christmas birth,
  Be this, good friends, our carol still—
Be peace on earth, be peace on earth,
  To men of gentle will.

II

THE CASE OF THE LOST MILLION

Beaumarchais rose from obscurity and poverty to become the friend and confidant of Louis XVI of France. The career of this nimble-witted son of France is even more interesting than that of Cellini, the Italian. Beaumarchais was a friend of the Thirteen Colonies in their death grapple with the Mother Country and was able to assist the continental army under Washington with arms and ammunition when their need was acute. The story of his remarkable career as poet, dramatist, publicist and orator, his service to America, and the ingratitude of our country to its benefactor, are interestingly told by Mr. Beck in the following address in the form of a legal argument to an imaginary Court, which he delivered on May 1, 1914, at a joint meeting of the Bar Associations of the States of Mississippi and Louisiana. Unconsciously he delivered it on the eve of a great war, in which the United States was destined to come to the relief of France, as France had come to America in its hour of need.   EDITOR.

Mr. Chairman, Gentlemen of the Joint Associations, Ladies and Gentlemen:

Let me in the first place express my very deep appreciation of the great honor that has been done me by your two associations in inviting me to address you upon this occasion. I only hope that your experience will not be that of a small boy who, having valorously struggled with the alphabet for a space of forty-eight hours, remarked that he was doubtful whether it was worth while to go through so much to learn so little. I fear you will share the experience of an old farmer in New England, who went to Boston to hear the great philosopher, Ralph Waldo Emerson, and it so happened that Artemus Ward was to lecture in the adjoining hall, and, by some mistake, the farmer entered the wrong hall, where Artemus Ward was delivering a humorous lecture. As he emerged from the hall, someone said to him: "What did you think of Ralph Waldo Emerson?" "Well," he replied, "he was pretty good, but it was not quite what I expected."

My address will be something of an innovation at a bar meeting. Its theme, although it has some distant relation to both the bench and the bar, is not, I may frankly warn you, strictly a legal subject. I chose it for two reasons. In the first place, if I had selected such a legal subject as those with which my own professional career has been most connected, I might inadvertently wander into the sphere of controversial public questions, and that, for obvious reasons, I was anxious to avoid. But there was another and, perhaps, better reason. I have often been impressed at bar meetings at the pained distress of the fairer portion of humanity, trying, with their most polite, and at the same time, praiseworthy attention, to follow a discussion on some technical subject—as the nature of a contingent remainder, or the rule in Shelly's case—somewhat in doubt as to whether the rule related to poetry or law. It occurred to me, therefore, that if I could select a subject which, while having some distant relation to the law, would also be of some general interest to the ladies, who honor us with their presence, perhaps you would, even if my effort resulted unfavorably, give me the credit of a praiseworthy intention.

My subject ought to appeal—unless the narrator shall hopelessly fail in his effort to present it to this audience— to your patient attention, because it relates to one of the most dramatic episodes in the history of our nation. A comparatively unknown episode, which has a most intimate connection with two epoch-making revolutions— the one, the American war for independence, and the other, its swift-following sequel, the French Revolution. Upon the other hand, it will, I trust, be of some interest to an audience of lawyers, because it concerns the remarkable and picturesque career of one who was not only one of the most extraordinary personalities of the eighteenth century, but also one of the most persistent litigants, of whom I have any knowledge. From his twenty-first year until his death, he was almost incessantly embroiled in law suits, and I am sure I cannot commend him better to the good favor of this audience of lawyers, because the persistent litigant is one in whom the Bar especially delights. But he was remarkable in this, as you will presently see, that he gave the most successful refutation to a maxim almost universally accepted by the Bar, that a layman who is his own lawyer has a fool for a client. He was often his own lawyer, but he was neither a fool as an advocate, nor as a client. Finally, it ought to interest a group of American citizens, because it is my thesis to suggest to this audience that, but for his indispensable contribution to the cause of American liberty, it is probable that our nation would never have come into existence, at least at the time it did.

My address shall take the form of a legal argument, because that will make it a little more pertinent to the occasion. I shall constitute you all members of an extraordinary court. This may not be disagreeable to any judicial aspirants here assembled, for I suppose there are some young lawyers here, as in my own state, who say, with Absalom, "Oh, that I were made judge in the land, that every man which hath any suit or cause might come unto me, and I would do him justice." These I shall not offend by making them *pro tempore* judges. To the judges who are judges, *de facto et de jure,* let me only say that if I am inflicting a double burden upon them of hearing another argument in vacation time, they may resort to that most ancient and honorable prerogative of the bench—they may take a nap.

Richard Brinsley Sheridan, when he produced his tragedy of *Pizarro,* learned that Lord Eldon was to be among his auditors, and when it was over, and his friends were congratulating him, said: "What did Lord Eldon think of my tragedy?" One of his quizzical friends replied: "To tell you the truth, Sherry, at the most pathetic part of your tragedy, I looked at his lordship, and he was fast asleep." Sheridan calmly replied: "Ah! his lordship thought he was on the Bench."

May it please your Honors, this is an imaginary action brought by the estate of Pierre Augustin Caron, of Paris, France, against the United States of America, for the recovery of two million, eight hundred thousand francs, of which one million is "the lost million," referred to in the title of this address.

In order to defeat any defense based upon lapse of time, let me say that, if the statute of limitation, which is an altogether popular plea these days, is interposed as a barrier to my client's claim, now preferred again after more than one hundred and thirty-seven years, that this suit is but a continuation and revivor of a suit pending at the Bar of Humanity for considerably more than a century to recover not merely money, but a long over-due debt of appreciation and gratitude. For I venture to say that I could take a poll in any part of the United States of ten educated men, and only one of the ten would be familiar with the facts which I am about to outline, and which, although I am stating them as an advocate, I give you my assurance that they are based upon authenticated historical records.

The gravamen of my action is that Pierre Augustin Caron rendered services to the United States, at a time of acute need, without which Washington's army would have perished before the end of 1777.

Let us consider the situation at the beginning of the Revolution. That Revolution was an act of sublime audacity. It is very hard for us today, in this hour of our acknowledged power and almost invincible strength, to appreciate that no reasoning man could, at the beginning of the Revolution, regard the triumph of our cause, as more than a remote possibility. So much was this the fact, that, if we were to take the utterances of the great leaders of the Revolution at the beginning of the struggle, we would find that there was hardly one who did not disclaim any purpose of separation from the mother country.

The desperation of our cause was not due to the lack of fighting men. We had in this country, it is computed, about two million, one hundred thousand white inhabitants, and, assuming that half of these were men, it left a homogeneous population, descendants of path-finders and pioneers, who were accustomed to fighting man and the elements. If equipment had been available, the Colonies could have placed in the field at least fifty thousand men, and even with the meagre facilities of transportation, we would have been, if other things were equal, invincible to any force that England could have placed in the field against us in the days of the sailing vessel.

But apart from the fact, which we in our patriotic pride are now apt to ignore, that the people of the Colonies were by no means agreed as to the policy of the Revolution, there were then many other obstacles which we must take into consideration. There were few, if any, manufactories of ordnance and powder in this country. It had been the policy of the Lords of Trade, to strangle American manufactures, and when the American farmers fired the first shot on the village green at Lexington, there was not a powder mill in the United States. There were, so far as can be accurately determined, only two manufacturers of muskets, and those painfully inadequate to supply arms to carry on any campaign of even short duration. The result was that while at the first shot which "went around the world," sixteen thousand men gathered at the gates of Boston and besieged Gates' army, yet they were without tents or uniforms. They did not have powder enough to last more than a few months. Each man carried his own rifle and powder horn.

The Massachusetts Committee of Safety made an accurate estimate of the existing supplies for the hastily improvised army.

On April 19, 1775, this committee could only count twelve field pieces, 21,000 firearms, 17,000 pounds of powder, 22,000 pounds of ball; and, for food, 17,000 pounds of salt fish and 35,000 pounds of rice.

There was thus barely a pound of powder for each soldier, in a war that might last, as it did last, for years! So destitute were they in the wherewithal to fight, that Washington, when he assumed control at Cambridge, had kegs of sand labeled "powder" rolled into the camp in order to delude his soldiers into the apparent security that there was plenty of ammunition. This was the main reason why Washington's rapidly mobilized army of sixteen thousand minute men shrank to approximately three thousand after the siege of Boston, why he was later defeated in New York, and fled in orderly retreat across New Jersey. Franklin—the wisest man in the eighteenth century—actually advocated the use of bows and arrows in order to fight the invader! While the idea was absurd in the extreme, it showed the desperation of the cause, that so great a man could gravely advocate the arming of men with bows and arrows, scythes and farming implements, to face the trained and equipped grenadiers of the British army. And Washington—the great-hearted, leonine, magnanimous Washington—one of the greatest in soul of all men since the tide of time began—so clearly recognized the desperation of the cause—that he said if worst came to worst, "we must then retire to Augusta County in Virginia. Numbers will repair to us for safety, and we will try a predatory war. If overborne, we must cross the Allegheny Mountains."

All this noble leader, whose courage seemingly never failed him, could see in the immediate prospect, was that there might be, as was later the case of the Boers in South Africa, a great trek across the mountains into the unbroken wilderness. In order to prevent this, men went about the streets of Philadelphia and begged the pendulums off the clocks in order to turn them into lead bullets, and the settlers upon the remotest outskirts of the wilderness gave up their powder horns in order that the few ounces of the indispensable commodity could be placed in the general store!

Where could these brave men look for any relief? What probability was there that any nation would aid them? Remember that England was then the first power of the world, and that no nation would, without the greatest hesitation, challenge such a power by openly helping us. There was also this very substantial reason that France—as every other European country with the exception of Switzerland—was an absolute monarchy, and why should their governments encourage in the smallest degree a democratic revolt against monarchical auhority?

How then, did it come that France came to help English colonial yeomen—who had climbed with Wolfe and his English grenadiers the Heights of Abraham and wrested the Canadian empire from France?

My client, may it please the Court, Pierre Augustin Caron, was the first and most potent factor in reversing the policy of France and in bringing us her assistance. Long before Franklin reached Paris, late in 1776, and before there was a suggestion of an open alliance—France was secretly helping us; but this was due to my client, for whose claim to gratitude I am pleading at the bar of this Court.

Caron was the son of a watchmaker in the City of Paris, and himself a watchmaker. He was not without education. His father was a man of intellectual force and varied accomplishments, and Caron's four sisters were accomplished musicians. When the day was over, the evenings in the Caron household were spent in literary work and musical pleasures, in which all the family were proficient.

When young Caron, who received a very limited school education, was twenty-one years of age, he invented an improved escapement to a watch, which made it possible for watches to be made far smaller than had been theretofore possible. In an imprudent moment he showed his invention to a rival watchmaker, and was surprised to find a few weeks later in the Journal of the Academy of Sciences of Paris, an announcement of the invention, claimed by the disloyal friend as his own.

At a time when justice was administered with slight regard for human rights, and frequently bought and sold, an unknown watchmaker of twenty-one would not have much opportunity for redress against his rival for stealing his invention. This young Caron was, however, a man of unusual attainments, and he wrote a memorial to the Academy of Science, so cleverly worded that he not only persuaded them to look into the case, but, like Byron, after writing Childe Harold, he awoke one morning to find himself famous. A committee of inquiry was appointed, which reported in favor of young Caron, and he thus won, in his first contest, a signal victory.

This suggested to his mind that possibly there might be a larger career for him than at the watchmaker's bench, and for this there was abundant reason. He was a man of more than ordinary personal beauty; of engaging presence, brilliant and witty in conversation, with a mind that even in his last days and during all his troubles, never failed in effervescent gaiety. He was also gifted with the pen to a degree so remarkable that his writings are to this day among the classics of French literature.

The day of the commoner was then dawning in France

and penetrating even the Court at Versailles. Caron determined to try to climb the slippery ladder of court preferment. He went to Versailles, Louis XV being King, and opened his career by presenting the King with a watch, and followed this as a discerning young man, by presenting the King's reigning favorite, the Marquise de Pompadour, with a watch so tiny that she could wear it as a ring upon her finger. She and the King were so delighted that they gave the young watchmaker an audience and, presuming on this familiarity with the Court, he assumed the title of "Watchmaker to the King."

With this first start he awaited an opportunity for a larger field of usefulness. Louis XV had four daughters, who were fond of music, and young Caron could play, with a great deal of proficiency, the flute, violin and also, an instrument which was then comparatively new in France, the harp. The young princesses sent for Caron and asked him whether he would not teach them to play the harp and thereby he became for the princesses a kind of *arbiter elegantiarum*.

He fell in love with the wife of an officer of the Court, who was known as the "Clerk of the King's Kitchen." As you may remember, Louis XV, like his father, the so-called "Sun King," often dined in public. The result was that the serving of the table was a pompous ceremony and the officials of his kitchen were men of considerable importance. On the death of this "Clerk of the Kitchen," Caron married his widow and gained the husband's position.

At that time he was a comparatively poor man, and to live in a court as luxurious and profligate as that of Versailles required considerable money. A rich contractor named Duverney, had made a great fortune, and in the manner of many financiers of the present day, determined to build a philanthropic institution to attest his public spirit. He erected on the Champ de Mars, where you may see it today, a military school. He was very anxious to have Louis XV give it the prestige of a royal visit, but the indolent and luxurious King refused to do so. Duverney heard of the resourceful Caron who was making such marked headway in court, and enlisted his good offices to arrange the royal visit. Caron induced the princesses to visit the school and then influenced them to ask their royal father to do so and, finally, Louis, accompanied by the more intimate members of his family, made a visit of state to the Duverney school.

Duverney was so pleased with Caron's resourcefulness that he took him into partnership, and young Caron rapidly became rich, in the manner of those days, when army contracts were swollen with inordinate profits. Such profits have not altogether passed away.

In the court, where almost every man had noble blood in his veins, Caron was naturally subject to all manner of insults, and was not liked by many because he was a commoner. It was still regarded as the height of presumption for a commoner to penetrate within the sacred precincts of royalty. On one occasion a courtier took out his watch and said: "Will you be good enough to repair my watch? It is out of order." Caron, knowing that the man intended to insult him, said: "Be it so, but I have not practiced my art as a watchmaker for several years; I fear I have grown somewhat awkward. But I will try." He then deliberately let it drop. It broke into a thousand pieces, whereupon, bowing sardonically to the courtier, he walked away.

Another courtier, who was an expert swordsman, deliberately picking a quarrel with Caron, challenged him to a duel which, because of the strictness of the laws against duelling that then existed in France, was fought in a lonely part of the royal forest without seconds or witnesses. It illustrates the fine chivalry that existed even in that most profligate period that, after Caron had fatally wounded his challenger, the stricken man begged him to fly, as a fatal duel meant almost certain punishment in the Bastile, but Caron refused to escape without first trying to save his enemy. He went to the nearest town, aroused the surgeon in the middle of the night, and told him where he would find the wounded man and then betook himself to Paris, in order to determine what his next step should be. The man lingered for nine days and, although he was pressed by all his family and friends to reveal the man who had given him the fatal wound, he died without disclosing the secret. The fine chivalry of the dying man thus protected Caron from punishment. Caron, not knowing this, finally determined to go back to court and face the music. He went to the princesses, whose closest friend he was, told them of his danger and they spoke to Louis XV, who, in his indolent way, said: "Oh, well, arrange it any way you please, only do not let me know anything about it." Thus Caron escaped punishment.

Caron, having bought a fictitious title, assumed the name by which he is best known in history. Thenceforth he was known as Pierre Augustin Caron de Beaumarchais which has been shortened in the history of the stage and literature to Beaumarchais.

Duverney died, leaving his estate to a nephew, Count de la Blache, who was a very influential man at the French Court. Upon his uncle's death, de la Blache alleged that Caron was indebted to his uncle's estate. Caron produced a receipt, which showed that, far from owing Duverney's estate anything, there had been a mutual cancellation of debits and credits.

La Blache charged that the instrument was a forgery and instituted a suit against Beaumarchais to cancel the document as fraudulent. Beaumarchais defended the claim and in the court of first instance secured a judgment in his favor. An appeal was taken to the highest court in Paris, known as the Parliament of Paris (*Parlement de Paris*). The old Parliament of Paris was one of twelve provincial parliaments, having both legislative and judicial duties, and it was the only organ through which the voice of the people could reach the court. But under Louis XIV, the parliaments were rarely called into session, except for judicial purposes, and when Louis XV ascended the throne he became so annoyed and embarrased by the continual complaints welling up from the submerged people through the Parlement de Paris, that, shortly before the Duverney suit, he had abolished the Parisian Court and substituted for it a new parliament, whose judges were his own royal minions. This was called the Meaupeau Parlement. It was the custom of that time for the Parlement to delegate one judge, called a reporter, with whom the litigants had personal hearings. In addition to these personal interviews and investigations, such controversies were conducted by a kind of trial by pamphlets, in the form of so-called memorials, which passed from litigant to litigant and which sometimes attracted public attention, especially when they were well written.

Beaumarchais thus found himself face to face with a corrupt court upon this appeal, pitted against an antagonist of noble blood who stood very high in the French court and had behind him the prestige of the Duverney millions. Beaumarchais was already involved at that time in another personal controversy with an even more powerful antagonist concerning a lady of the opera. A certain Duke de Chaulnes had been attentive to a Mademoiselle Menard and had become very jealous of Beaumarchais. Mademoiselle Menard having made an imprudent remark, which was favorable to Beaumarchais' personal attractiveness, the Duke, a man of violent and almost maniacal temperament, said he would before night search all Paris for Beaumarchais and kill him on sight. With the insanity of a jealous man he went, sword in hand, through the city trying to find Beaumarchais. Among Beaumarchais' many court duties was that of presiding over a little court which tried cases of poaching upon the King's hunting preserves. While the Duke was looking for him, Beaumarchais was administering justice on the bench of this little court. The Duke rushed into court and, after making a very unseemly disturbance, Beaumarchais adjourned the court in order to invite the Duke into the Judge's chamber and ask what his pleasure was. The Duke replied: "I am going to kill you, tear your heart out and drink your blood." "Well," Beaumarchais calmly said, "in that case it must be business before pleasure. I will resume my place on the bench."

When Beaumarchais had leisurely prolonged the proceedings as far as possible, he adjourned court, and came out in his bland and inimitable style, and said he was now at his royal highness' pleasure. The Duke then told him that he wanted to fight an immediate duel, and suggested that they repair at once to a certain nobleman who would second him, and from whom they could get the necessary swords. This nobleman, thinking that a few hours might possibly have a cooling effect on the irate Duke, said he had an engagement at the palace, and could not see them until four o'clock, but would endeavor to accommodate them at that hour. Beaumarchais turned to the disappointed Duke and coolly said: "Can I have the pleasure of having you dine with me?" The Duke, strange to say, accepted, and when at the table in the bosom of the Caron family the Duke became so exceedingly offensive that Beaumarchais said: "Let's go into my room, and we can talk it out there." Then they went into the room, and the Duke, bent on murder, saw on the bureau a short sword, and suddenly seized it with the idea of murder. Beaumarchais, who was himself a very powerful man, threw his arms around him, and two or three of his servants flung themselves upon the would-be murderer with the result that the Duke was held until a commissary of police arrived. A trial was had before a magistrate, the Duke was imprisoned and Beaumarchais was acquitted.

That did not suit the Versailles Court. The result was that under a royal warrant—*a lettre de cachet*—Beaumarchais was sent to prison. Thus he found himself in prison at the very time when he was obliged to try his case against the Duverney estate. After considerable trouble, he received through influential friends, of whom he always had an abundance, permission to go out by day, provided he would return by night, and always be accompanied by a guard. Leaving his prison for these short periods of time, he was then told that it would be impossible to have his personal interview with the judge, whom the court had delegated as reporter and whose name was Goezman, unless he would first pay to the judge's wife two hundred louis, and give an extra fifteen louis for the judge's secretary. Bribery was then a common occurrence in France and it being the only way to get the interview, Beaumarchais gave to Madama Goezman the two hundred louis and the extra fifteen for the secretary. Then he had his interview with Goezman, and two days later Goezman decided the case against him, holding that the receipt was a forgery.

The frail wife of the judge, possibly scenting danger,

returned to him the two hundred louis, but failed to return the fifteen louis, on the ground that she had not received it. Beaumarchais then went to the judge's secretary and asked him whether he had received fifteen louis. The secretary replied that he had not. Thereupon, the resourceful Beaumarchais sent a letter to the judge and his wife, demanding the immediate return of the fifteen louis. The judge, knowing that he was now in danger, felt that the safest way was to openly face the charge. He went before his brother judges of the Meaupeau Parlement, upon whose fidelity he felt he could count, and charged Beaumarchais, not only with being the forger of the Duverney receipt, but also guilty of bribery.

There was not a lawyer in Paris who would defend him because the aristocracy and the Parlement de Paris were behind the corrupt regime; but Beaumarchais placed his reliance in that which was becoming a new force in French society; he invoked public opinion against the Meaupeau Parlement, and without stopping to count the cost, launched against the whole Meaupeau Parlement a series of charges, as Zola impeached, in our time, the military tribunals, and, as we will see, with the same result. He wrote philippic after philippic against the French judicial system, and showed its unquestionable corruption.   As a result of his efforts, all Europe became tremendously interested in his mighty struggle.   Each memorial was succeeded by another with more biting wit and sarcasm in which this man, with his back to the wall, and no advocate to defend him, branded his accusers and judges with judicial infamy. Finally, as I have said, all Europe was stirred with the excitement caused by the Beaumarchais trial and after seven months of these attacks and counter attacks, it was announced that the Meaupeau Parlement would render its decision. All Paris was on tiptoe to learn what the Meaupeau Parlement would do with the problem. It was no longer Beaumarchais who was on trial. It was the highest court in France.

A great crowd gathered around the courtroom. Finally the judges tried to solve the difficulty by one of those judicial compromises which have rarely been effective in the history of litigation. Upon the whole their decision was not unreasonable. They condemned Goezman, their colleague, *au blame*—that is, to be dismissed from the bench. They condemned him and his wife to civic degradation. This carried with it absolute incapacity to hold any public office, and, ordinarily, it would have meant social ruin. They also condemned Beaumarchais for bribery.

When Beaumarchais came out of the courtroom the great crowd cheered him with enthusiasm, and as the judges came out they were hooted and hunted to their very doors.

Thus Beaumarchais became, for the time being, the most talked of man of his day, supplanting in popularity men like Voltaire and Rousseau, who were then sowing the seeds of revolution against a rotten regime.

After his release, Beaumarchais reached the conclusion that another effective way to destroy a rotten institution was through the stage and for that purpose he wrote a comedy, of which all of us have heard and to which some of us have listened in the form of an opera. It was *Le Barbier de Seville*. Having lived for a short time in Spain, he had acquired some knowledge of the Spanish character. The character of *Figaro* became his mask. Beaumarchais was the witty, resourceful, irrepressible barber and he presented his own struggle for justice so directly and plainly in his comedy that the censor at first refused to allow it to be produced.

One witticism of the *Barbier de Seville* will appeal to us as lawyers. We often say, and it has almost passed into proverb, that every litigant who loses his case has the constitutional right to swear at the court. In the *Barbier de Seville*, he says in substance: "I know it is the custom of the Palais de Justice that a man has only twenty-four hours to curse the court, but I have twenty-four years on the stage." (I quote from memory). After several years of adverse action by the censor, this witty comedy was finally produced in 1775 amidst universal *eclat*. It pilloried the judiciary of France, and the court itself, so that he became the rising genius of the French democracy.

Louis XV soon realized that this resourceful courtier was too valuable to languish in the Bastille and he determined to employ him in the secret service. There having appeared in London a brochure entitled *"Memoires secrets d'une femme publique,"* a scandalous account of the then reigning favorite, the Comtesse Du Barry, Louis XV, having vainly insisted on the extradition from England of Charles Theveneau de Morance, the author, determined to utilize Beaumarchais. Louis sent for him and told him that if he were able to accomplish this task, the sentence of civic degradation would be cancelled. Beaumarchais crossed to England, found his quarry and in a short time secured every copy of the offending pamphlet and burned them in a lime kiln near London. He returned to Paris with the joyful news, only to find that Louis XV had died during his absence.

After Louis XVI had ascended the throne, a printer in Amsterdam published a political document of grave import against Marie Antoinette, which incidentally accused her of not being able to give France an heir. Louis XVI, remembering the success of Beaumarchais in the preceding episode, sent him to Holland to suppress this book. Beaumarchais went to Amsterdam and made a contract with the publisher to purchase the entire edition. He paid the money and destroyed the copies and was returning to France when he learned that the rascally bookseller had kept one copy and was on his way to Germany, apparently to republish it. Beaumarchais hastily pursued this man and at last caught up with him near Nuremberg. He threw him from his horse and rescued from his satchel the last copy and then, fearing that perhaps there might be some other copy in the printing shops of Nuremberg, which were then so justly famous, he determined to go to Vienna and see Marie Antoinette's mother, Maria Theresa, and have her take immediate and summary steps to stop the republication. His passports were in an assumed name and Maria Theresa could not believe that he was the famous Beaumarchais, the author of *Le Barbier de Seville.* As a result, he was thrown into prison and remained there until a month later, when the word came from Louis XVI that this was indeed the famous Beaumarchais; whereupon the Austrian government released him, with apologies, to return in disgust to Paris where a third secret mission was given to him.

There happened to be at that time a curious character by the name of Chevalier d'Eon. For forty-five years he had been known as a man, but he suddenly assumed the attire of a woman and played the part so well that all Europe became interested in the question of his real sex. Chevalier d'Eon, whether man or woman, had secured a number of confidential state documents when he represented France in the diplomatic service, which the government was very anxious to secure.

Beaumarchais, the ever resourceful, was sent again to England to secure them. He arrived in London in September, 1775, about five months after Lexington, and among the men he met in his confidential mission was John Wilkes, the radical Lord Mayor of London and the leader of the radical party in England. At Wilkes' house congregated the radical spirits of the time. Among them was Arthur Lee of Virginia. Lee had been a law student in the Temple and when Benjamin Franklin had given up his position in England as agent for the Colonies, he asked Lee, although only a law student, to represent the cause of the Colonies. Arthur Lee, as such representative, met Beaumarchais and they frequently discussed the opportunity which the revolt in America offered to France to embarrass England. Beaumarchais afterwards claimed that Lee assured him that if France could openly or secretly send powder, shot and guns to Washington's army, the Colonies, if they were ever established as a free nation, would give to France a monopoly of commerce for a period of years, such as England then enjoyed. Beaumarchais quickly appreciated this unique opportunity for France to humiliate her ancient foe and gain for herself substantial material advantages. Abandoning the mission, which had brought him to London, he crossed the Channel and returned to Versailles and, in his capacity as secret diplomatic agent of the King, obtained access to the King's royal Cabinet and submitted substantially this proposition:

He admitted that France could not then openly champion the cause of the Colonies. "But," he said, "let us give aid to them secretly and if your Majesty will give me the necessary money I will be responsible for the necessary purchases of arms and ammunitions and my purchases and sales can take the form of an individual commercial undertaking, payable by the Colonies in tobacco, indigo and rice."

Thus, as early as September, 1775, long before Franklin reached Paris and before the men of the Revolution had any idea that France would help us, Beaumarchais had laid his plans and anticipated their pleas to give us aid, secret but substantial.

As a result, on June 10, 1776, Beaumarchais received from the French government a receipt, upon which the Case of the Lost Million, as it subsequently developed in our diplomatic history, turns.   I want to read the receipt, because if my subject has any legal aspect at all, it will have it in the wording of the receipt.

Let us resume the fiction that I am addressing a Court. May it please your Honors, in this document, which I now produce, dated Paris, June 10, 1776, Pierre Augustin Caron de Beaumarchais signs this receipt:

> "Received from M. Duvergier, in conformity with the orders of M. de Vergennes, dated the 5th instant, which I have handed to him, the sum of one million, *of which I am to render an account to the said Sieur Count de Vergennes.*
>
>   Caron de Beaumarchais
>
> Good for a million of livres tournois.
> Paris, June 10, 1776."

Beaumarchais also obtained an equal loan under similar terms from Spain, then an ally of France, which was first paid into the French treasury to conceal its source, and then paid to Beaumarchais. He gave a similar receipt and with these two million livres, he opened a commercial house under the fictitious name of Rodrigue Hortalez & Cie.

Before 1777 he had purchased arms, ammunition, clothing, tents and guns for an army of twenty-five thousand men; had not only transported them across the Atlantic in his own chartered vessels and, in the face of the English cruisers which swarmed the seas, but before the campaign of 1777 began, he had sent to Washington's army two hundred cannons and two hundred and fifty thousand rounds of ammunition. Moreover, DeKalb, Pulaski, Steuben and others were employed by Beaumarchais to come to our country to serve as officers in the Colonial armies.

Vergennes, in substance, said to Beaumarchais: "We will give you secretly these two million francs, but no one must ever know it. We are not prepared to quarrel with England. If you ever allow the secret to be discovered, we will disavow you. If it becomes necessary, we will stop the ships from leaving France. We will repudiate any possible agreement with you. Therefore, it must take the form of a commercial venture, at your risk and subject to our repudiating you if it becomes necessary."

Silas Deane was sent over by the Colonies as the first representative in France. He reached Paris in August, 1776, and in paying his respects to the Comte de Vergennes, Deane asked him whether there was any way in which our armies, in dire need of powder and shot, could obtain a loan of war materials from the French arsenals. The great foreign minister replied: "France cannot help you. We will not in any way countenance any violation of our neutrality obligation." As Deane was about to leave the count's office, Vergennes significantly said: "There is a Spanish merchant who trades under the name of Rodrigue Hortalez & Cie. Possibly it might pay you, Mr. Deane, to go to him." Deane took the hint and went to the Hotel de Hollande, found Beaumarchais there, and asked him if he was the head of the house. He said: "Yes, I am the head of Rodrigue Hortalez & Cie., and I shall be most happy, indeed, to send over to the Colonies whatever war supplies you need, with officers to man the guns, provided that you ship back to our firm tobacco, indigo and rice in payment." The colonists had no currency with which to pay.

Thus, an agreement was made between Hortalez & Cie. and Silas Deane on the faith of which Beaumarchais continued his shipments, having obtained the war material from the arsenals of France and then awaited the promised payments.

Unfortunately, Arthur Lee, who was a congenital marplot, sent word to the Continental Congress that Beaumarchais' claim that these cargoes of ammunition were sent as an ordinary commercial speculation was merely a blind, and that these shipments were an absolute gift on the part of France, and that nothing whatever should be shipped back to Beaumarchais against these shipments.

Meanwhile, Beaumarchais, in addition to these two millions, had enlisted a great deal of private capital in his commercial house, and it was essential, as he had to account not merely to his creditors but to the government for his expenditures, that he should get payment from the Continental Congress. Two years and six months passed, and as no payment came, he found himself facing financial ruin. To bring matters to an issue Beaumarchais sent an agent, by the name of De Francy, to Philadelphia, who warned the Continental Congress that no more cargoes would be shipped unless Congress made some payment on account. The committee of Congress replied that they understood the shipments were a free gift from the King of France. De Francy speedily undeceived them. Congress then instructed Franklin, who by that time had arrived in Paris, to ask Vergennes whether or not the shipments were gifts and the minister told Franklin to advise the Continental Congress that the French king had nothing whatever to do with the shipments. This in a technical sense was true. He had given nothing. He had simply loaned the money to Beaumarchais to be accounted for to Vergennes, his Foreign Minister.

The Continental Congress then paid a small sum on account, and was about to liquidate the balance, when in 1783, the Treaty of Peace with England was signed and, there being no further need for subterfuge, the French government drew up a contract, in which, for purposes of accuracy, they stipulated what the United States had theretofore received by way of loans or gifts. They recited that, before 1778, the king of France, had given to the Colonies as a free gift three million of livres, and later an additional six millions and had loaned them quite independent of these gifts several millions more.

When Congress read that treaty they remembered that they had received two millions, which Franklin had in 1778 received from Vergennes, independently of Beaumarchais' two millions, in order that Franklin could support his embassy at Passy. When the treaty recited a gift of three million before 1778 Congress not unnaturally asked: "Where is the third million?" It is now beyond dispute that the missing million was in fact the one given to Beaumarchais on June 10, 1776. Our forefathers suspected this, and not knowing the form of the receipt which Beaumarchais had given to Vergennes, or the nature of this secret transaction, they naturally believed that Deane's contract to pay for the supplies in tobacco, indigo and rice was merely to deceive England, and that Beaumarchais was attempting to collect from the Congress a free gift.

They asked him the question whether or not that million had not been given to him directly for their benefit. He said, "No, not at all." He had to equivocate somewhat, because he had accepted this as a secret service fund from the king, and the king's honor was pledged in a certain sense to England that his government had not, prior to the open alliance in 1778, given help to the Colonies. Therefore the mission having been an exceptionally confidential one, Beaumarchais could not, without the permission of the French king, reveal the fact that this million was, in point of fact, a secret subsidy. His royal master, and his immediate superior, the French foreign minister, repudiated the suggestion that the third million was the million given on June 10, 1776, to Beaumarchais.

He had by this time assisted the American government to the extent of over five millions of livres in arms and ammunition, and of this he received until his death only a small fraction. Despairing of his debt ever being paid by our country, he resumed his varied work as a financier and dramatic author, poet, speculator, diplomat, and secret service spy, because he was one of those extraordinarily versatile men, of which the eighteenth century, as the sixteenth, was so productive.

He determined to write a successor to "The Barber of Seville," and called it "The Marriage of Figaro (*Mariage de Figaro*)." As Shakespeare, to please Elizabeth, wrote "The Merry Wives of Windsor," to depict Sir John Falstaff in love, so Beaumarchais determined to show *Figaro* in love. But his real purpose was deeper and very radical. His target was this time much higher than the corrupt judiciary of France; it was the royal court itself, and the whole system of hereditary privilege. When the play was first submitted to the censor he forbade its production on this account.

Great pressure was brought upon Louis XVI to have the play produced, and finally the king agreed to hear it read, and you will find in the *Memoirs* of Madame de Campan that she read it to the king, and when they reached *Figaro's* monologue in the third act, where he attacks the very foundation of the ancient *regime,* the king sprang up with the angry protest: "You might as well tear down the Bastile as to permit such a play to be produced."

Beaumarchais was a good deal of a Barnum, and he knew perfectly well, as he made *Figaro* say, that the surest way to make a thing popular is to try and suppress it. So he read it in manuscript in the aristocratic salons. It was read in many salons in Versailles to the representatives of that chivalry of France which he was laughingly hunting to its death. Beaumarchais, far more than any of the liberty-loving philosophers who preceded him, literally smiled away the French Monarchy, and I have the highest authority for the statement, for Napoleon later said that the Memorials and Comedies of Beaumarchais were the French Revolution in action.

Beaumarchais wrote the "Barber of Seville" in 1781, and for three years the king would not withdraw his royal interdict, Beaumarchais simply kept it in his desk, giving occasional readings of it in private houses. Finally, the pressure became so great upon the king, that, to please Marie Antoinette, he agreed that it should be produced in a small and insignificant theatre of Paris.

When that became known the crowd was so great that it was an historical event of the French stage. The auditorium was crowded to suffocation with the aristocracy of France to hear a play about which everybody had been hearing for three or four years.   Just as the curtain was going up, a royal guard came upon the stage, held up his sword and said: "By order of his majesty, the king, this play is not to be produced here or anywhere, now or at any time."   The audience sprang to its feet, crying "Tyranny! oppression!" and insulted the messenger of the king.

Beaumarchais merely said: "Very well, my play goes back to its portfolio," and he continued to read it in many private homes. Finally, Louis XVI, always a vacillating monarch, again agreed to let it be produced.   The great night came when it was to have its *premiere*. The crowd—almost a mob—gathered in the dawn of the preceding morning and waited patiently the whole day for the night to come.   Titled ladies of the most exclusive circles slept in the actresses' rooms in order to be sure of a seat.   A great crowd gathered about the iron grating which stood outside the theatre, and finally, in its impatience, surged forward, broke down the iron barrier and sprang toward the doors of the theatre, suffocating three people in the melee.   In the twinkling of an eye, the theatre was filled, and the *Mariage de Figaro* was thus, in 1784, given for the first time.

It ran for three hundred nights, a thing unprecedented at that time, and Beaumarchais gave his share of the royalties to a hospital for nursing mothers, which, of course, added to his fame and popularity.

The Comte de Provence had been one of the most insistent that the play should not be produced, and shortly after the *premiere* of the *Mariage de Figaro*, the count made a bitter attack on the triumphant dramatist. Beaumarchais, who could never repress a witty saying, even if the subject was of royal blood, replied to the attack by saying in substance: "What?   Shall I, who have fought with lions now waste my time on a louse?" The Comte de Provence indignantly went to the king and said: "This infamous man is calling your majesty a lion." Louis XVI was playing cards, and, taking up the three of spades, according to an authenticated memoir, he wrote on the spur of the moment: "Send Beaumarchais to St. Lazare."

That was not the Bastile where the political prisoners were imprisoned. It was the most loathsome jail in Paris, where degenerates were imprisoned. This man of fifty-two years of age, then the most splendid figure in the literature of his country, and who had rendered signal service to Louis XVI, was thus taken from his family and home and consigned to this loathsome jail.

The first day Paris woke up and characteristically laughed. "Figaro in prison?" A great joke! The second day they said: "Whose liberty is safe in France today?" The third day it became a rising, sullen murmur. Finally, word reached the king that there was danger of revolution in France, if this distinguished poet and dramatist was not released. Louis XVI, who was at heart one of the kindest of men—and what irony that this kind-hearted and generally just king should have expiated with his head the mistakes of his predecessors—sent an order to release him. Beaumarchais, when the message of the king was delivered, said: "I will not stir from here until I know the charge that was made against me," because he was in ignorance of the cause of his detention. They came back to him and said: "You are charged with having insulted his Majesty by likening him to a lion." Beaumarchais replied: "Is it an insult for the king's most loyal subject to liken him to such a king of the forest?"

Beaumarchais was then released, and Louis XVI, in partial expiation commanded a special performance of *Figaro*, and ordered the leading members of his Court to attend it. He even permitted a little later a performance at the Trianon of the *Mariage de Figaro*, in which Marie Antoinette played the part of Rosina, and the Comte d'Artois the part of *Count Almaviva*. He invited Beaumarchais to be the special guest of the court to see the Queen of France, and daughter of Maria Theresa, tread the boards of the theatre and play the part of the vivacious Spanish flirt. Could royal self-abasement go further?

Napoleon boasted that he had given Talma an audience of kings and emperors, but Beaumarchais could claim that he staged his play with royal actors and actresses and was himself the audience!

The rest of Beaumarchais' stormy life can be very quickly sketched. Having spent his life in controversy, and having a sharp tongue, he was almost continually in some heated controversy. He never lost his good humor, never attacked a man unless he was attacked, and was always generous to a fallen foe. His papers after his death contained promissory notes aggregating 900,000 francs— of actors, authors, politicians, nobles and commoners, to whom he had loaned money from time to time, many of whom had been his personal enemies. He was most generous in his disposition, whatever his other personal faults.

However, in the latter part of his life he became involved in two controversies, from which he did not emerge with credit. He had organized a company to bring water to Paris from the outskirts. A firm of Paris bankers were short of the market, as we now express it, and were anxious to drive the shares down. Beaumarchais, who was the chief financial backer of the water company, proceeded to put the shares up, as he was as much an adept in finance as in poetry. The bankers employed a young advocate, whose name afterwards became famous, Mirabeau, and the latter launched an oratorical thunderbolt against Beaumarchais, in which he accused Beaumarchais of poisoning two of his three wives, of forging the Duverney receipt, of bribing the Meaupeau Parliament, and various other offenses, winding up with an attack upon the morality of both *Le Barbier de Seville* and *Le Mariage de Figaro*. While neither is a play calculated to be read in Sunday School, yet Mirabeau was not the one to cast a stone in this respect. Mirabeau's attack was terrible in its intensity, and, for the first time in his career, and for some reason hard to understand, Beaumarchais made no reply, and with that his popularity commenced to wane.

Then followed the so-called Kornmann litigation. He was an Alsatian nobleman, who had imprisoned his wife under a *lettre de cachet* in order to confiscate her fortune, and some friends appealed to Beaumarchais. He did not even know Madame Kornmann, but the case appealed to his sympathy. The idea of a young, beautiful woman languishing in jail, under an arbitrary warrant, while her husband was squandering her fortune, spurred him into action. Accordingly, he used his influence to obtain the release of the lady and thereupon Kornmann commenced a divorce action against his wife, and among other co-respondents named Beaumarchais. A young advocate, who thereafter made himsef famous, as Beaumarchais had done in the case of the Duverney receipt, whose name was Bergasse, came to the front. He had no humor like Beaumarchais, but he had, like Mirabeau, a tremendous power of invective, and he followed the tactics of Beaumarchais in not attacking the latter's action in the immediate controversy, as to which Beaumarchais was really innocent, but launching a tremendous attack upon the existing order, against which Beaumarchais, with somewhat lessened intellectual activity, and now himself rich and powerful, found it difficult to reply. He was no longer the poor young commoner with his back against the wall, but the rich and powerful banker and financier who was fighting a comparatively unknown young lawyer. At all events, the Bergasse affair greatly lessened Beaumarchais' waning popularity.

In the meantime, the Revolution broke with volcanic violence. Members of the convention, headed by Danton, Marat and Robespierre, knew that there were 75,000 muskets in Holland and wanted to get them. They sent Beaumarchais on this mission. They gave him five hundred thousand francs in *assignats,* but made him put up, as collateral for the success of his attempt, seven hundred fifty thousand francs of money that was current. Beaumarchais went to Holland, and had to work very secretly, because England was attempting to confiscate these arms, if they became the property of the French nation.

While in Holland in 1798, the Committee of Public Safety concluded that Beaumarchais was a secret royalist, proscribed him and confiscated his beautiful home near the site of the Bastile. What a situation! An exile, minus his seven hundred and fifty thousand francs, his wife and daughter thrown into prison, and daily awaiting, probably, that sad procession to the *Place de la Concorde,* where heads were falling by hundreds into the basket. He, however, returned to Paris, attended a meeting of the Committee of Public Safety, and defended himself in a spirited speech, in which, ridiculing the personal appearance of Marat, he defiantly asked who Marat was, to assail him, citizen Beaumarchais, who had done so much for French liberty. The Committee of Safety, concluded that France needed Beaumarchais' services more than his head, and sent him back to Holland to recover the arms. He returned to Holland, and had arranged by devious ways to get those arms for the French Government, when the Committee of Safety again proscribed him and confiscated his fortune. He remained an exile in Holland until Napoleon planted his guns upon the steps of St. Roch, ended mob rule in France and restored law and order.

It only remains for me to tell you what became of "The Lost Million." I have sketched briefly and very inadequately Beaumarchais' career. Certainly Dumas never wrote anything more romantic than the sober facts I have had the pleasure of relating to you in the most cursory way.

Beaumarchais had assured the Continental Congress that his demand for five million francs—call it one million dollars—spent for ammunition and guns was not a gift, and his failure to receive the promised and long overdue payment was ruining him. Although Congress had previously assured him that it would pay, nevertheless, after its usual custom, it failed to do so. While an exile at Hamburg, and practically ruined, he wrote a pathetic letter to our Congress, which gives an idea of his style, as well as points the pathos of this story.

"Americans, I served you with untiring zeal! I have thus far received no return for this but vexations and disappointment, and I die your creditor. On leaving this world, I have to ask you to give what you owe me to my daughter as a dowry. When I am gone, she will, perhaps, have nothing, on account of other wrongs against which I can no longer contend. Through your delay in discharging my claims Providence may have intended to provide her with a resource against other destitution. Adopt her after my death as a worthy child of the country! Her

mother and my widow, equally unfortunate,
will conduct her to you. Regard her as the
daughter of a citizen* * * Be charitable to your
friend, to one whose accumulated services have
been recompensed in no other way! *Date obo-
lum Belesario.*"

He died without the slightest recognition of his claim.

In 1778, after Louis XVI had given him assurance that
the million of June 10, 1776, the receipt for which I read
to you, had not been given by the king to Beaumarchais,
which was a diplomatic falsehood, the American Congress
persisted in thinking that it was a gift. In 1794, when
there came a lull in the political storm, Congress instructed our minister in Paris to request information as to when
the missing million had been given to our country, credit
for which the French government had claimed. The
French foreign minister then advised our representative
that the million in question had been given on June 10,
1776, to Beaumarchais. This naturally confirmed the suspicion of Congress that Beaumarchais was attempting to
defraud this country. Congress claimed that the million
was given to Beaumarchais for our benefit, and therefore
deducted it from the balance of his account of 3,600,000
livres.

You would have thought that our country, having had
such signal benefits from this man, who, mark you, had
hazarded every one of the forty ships he chartered, would
have paid it without "looking a gift horse in the mouth;"
but Congress refused either to adjust the question of the
lost million or to pay him the remainder of his claim. Taking the disputed item as a pretext, it refused to make any
adjustment. In 1785, it did instruct our consul general
in Paris, Mr. Barclay, to make another examination of the
account, against which Beaumarchais for nearly a year
protested, and as a result of such examination, while the
claim was somewhat reduced by our consular representative, it still left, independent of the missing million, a
large balance in Beaumarchais' favor.

Although he was then in sore need of the money, Congress turned a deaf ear to all his entreaties. In 1787 he
addressed the following letter to the President of Congress:

"What do you suppose is the general opinion here of the vicious circle in which you have involved me? 'We will not reimburse M. Beaumarchais until his accounts are adjusted by us, and we will not adjust his accounts, so as not to pay them!' With a nation that has become a powerful sovereign, gratitude may be a simple virtue unworthy of its policy; but no government can be relieved from doing justice and of discharging its debts. I venture to hope, sir, that, impressed by the importance of this matter and the soundness of my reasoning, you will oblige me with an official reply, stating what decision the honorable Congress will come to, either to promptly adjust my accounts and settle them, like any other equitable sovereign, or submit the points in dispute to arbiters in Europe with regard to insurance and commissions, as M. Barclay had the honor of proposing to you in 1785, or, finally, to let me know without further shift that American sovereigns, unmindful of past services, deny me justice. I shall then adopt such measures as seem best for my despised interests and my wounded honor, without lacking in the profound respect with which I am, sir, the very humble servant of the general Congress and yourself, Monsieur le President,
CARON DE BEAUMARCHAIS."

In this letter, which I have only quoted in part, he agreed to submit the disputed question to any arbitrator with the single exception of his inveterate enemy, Arthur Lee and our Congress actually had the indecency to appoint Arthur Lee to make a further investigation. That envious, suspicious and vindictive marplot revised the figures with such obvious want of fairness that he actually brought Beaumarchais into debt to the United States to the amount of 1,800,000 francs.

The report was such a shocking travesty on justice that Alexander Hamilton, then Secretary of the Treasury, ordered another investigation, which resulted in finding that the United States did owe to Beaumarchais the sum of $2,-

800,000, provided that he was entitled to the lost million, and $1,800,000, if the disputed million properly belonged to our government as a gift from France.

Still our country refused to pay, and Beaumarchais died in 1799 without having received even so much of his claim as our country did not dispute.

In 1816 in a spasm of virtue our government, through Mr. Gallatin, advised the French foreign minister, that if he would give Congress his personal assurance that the disputed million was not given to Beaumarchais as a gift to us, and was not used by him in the purchase of military supplies for which his estate was then charging the United States Government, Congress would accept the million as a debt, and settle the rest of the account.

Thereupon the French foreign minister replied that, while it was true the million in question had been given to Beaumarchais, yet it was not given for arms and ammunition, but as a *"mystere de cabinet,"* for secret political purposes, for which his estate was accountable to the French government.

Our government refused to accept that explanation as satisfactory, and insisted in a strong diplomatic communication of Mr. Gallatin, that, as this million dollars had been paid to Beaumarchais for our use, and the French government had included it in the three millions as gifts, it must be so treated. Mr. Gallatin contended that the bailee had a duty not only to the bailor, but to the beneficiary for whom the bailee had given the sum of money.

On the other hand, the French government said that Beaumarchais' accounts in the seven years with the French government, showed he had received twenty-one million livres, and that there had been a cancellation of accounts between the French government and Beaumarchais. They suggested, rather than stated, that Beaumarchais, in settling the account with the French government, had been charged with this lost million.

The dispute was not settled until Andrew Jackson became president of the United States and he cut the gordian knot in a characteristic way which almost brought on war between France and the United States. You will remember that after Napoleon became First Consul and the French fleets had almost swept our commerce from the seas, we preferred against the French government the so-called "French spoliation claims."

Andrew Jackson determined to force a settlement of these claims and instructed our minister, Mr. Livingstone, to negotiate a treaty to that effect, and without any diplomatic delay.

Livingstone finally secured a treaty, under which it was agreed that the French would pay five million dollars for the relief of our citizens, provided France could deduct, for the heirs of Rochambeau and the estate of Beaumarchais, certain sums, in the latter case, eight hundred thousand francs. Beaumarchais' claim was three million, eight hundred thousand francs, and as found by Alexander Hamilton, two million eight hundred thousand francs, even if the disputed million was a gift. And yet all that the heirs of Beaumarchais ever received under this settlement, and they did not get that until 1835, was eight hundred thousand francs, and they only received that through the settlement of the French Spoliation Claims.

The treaty was made in 1831, and the French Parliament, possibly taking a leaf from our note book, would not appropriate any money to carry out its provisions. Finally, in 1834, Andrew Jackson's patience was exhausted and his wrath was great. He sent a message to Congress in which he intimated rather brusquely that France had no intention of respecting its obligations, and he advocated a seizure of the property of French subjects in our own country, until we had received the five millions due us.

You can imagine the effect of such an undiplomatic threat to a great and proud nation. There was an uproar in France. The French government handed our minister his passports, recalled its own representative, demanded an apology, and served notice upon Andrew Jackson that, unless our country apologized for his offensive language,, it would neither pay the Spoliation Claims nor resume friendly intercourse with us. Andrew Jackson was not the man to apologize on demand. Like Falstaff, he would never give reasons "on compulsion." Thereupon, the French government, which was very much in earnest, determined to send a fleet to our harbors to make a hostile demonstration, and "Old Hickory" in turn asked Congress to appropriate money for the national defense. In the meantime, our dismissed minister was hurrying back to Washington, and Jackson had sent word that as soon as he arrived, he was to come at once to the White House. As soon as Livingstone reached Washington, he was put in a carriage and hurried to the White House, where Jackson and his cabinet awaited him.

Livingston's story was to the effect that France was very much in earnest and would make war unless our government apologized. Jackson replied: "That's like the French; they never pay unless they have to."

Let it be gratefully remembered that it was England that intervened and tendered her good offices to both France and the United States. As a result, Jackson disclaimed an intentional affront, the French government withdrew its demand for an apology, and the French Parliament promptly passed the appropriation to pay the French Spoliation Claims, less the specified deductions. France in turn paid to the daughter, as the sole heir of Beaumarchais, the platry sum of 800,000 francs.

I need not remind this audience, composed in part of New Orleans lawyers, that it was only about ten years ago that Congress, having received in 1835 the five millions from France for our citizens, appropriated two million dollars to pay the first French Spoliation Claims.

Ladies and gentlemen, who have constituted my Court, this is my Case of the Lost Million. I hope I have proved to this Honorable Court a just claim for judgment on behalf of my client.

When you attend the French Opera and hear Rossini's florid music of the *Barbier de Seville*, or Mozart's far nobler music of the *Mariage de Figaro*, think of the man who wrote so pathetically to our country in his dying hours, "Give an obolus to Belisarius." and to whom no monument has been erected by this country.

Let us hope that the time will come when our country will not only honor DeKalb, Lafayette, Rochambeau, Steuben and Pulaski, but will also remember that great foreign minister of France, the Comte de Vergennes, who rendered as the inestimable service, which finally culminated in the great alliance. Without the aid of France, the war of independence would probably have been lost. Louis XVI, who, for helping our cause out of his own private purse, also deserves our gratitude; and last, but not least, we should honor in our grateful memories that *Figaro* in life, Pierre Augustin Caron de Beaumarchais, whose cause I have pleaded and for whom I ask a judgment, payable in the only way now possible, viz., the enduring gratitude of the great Republic, to whose foundation he made so signal a contribution.

III

WASHINGTON AND THE CONSTITUTION

It is the custom of both Houses of Congress on Washington's Birthday to have the Farewell Address read by one of the members in each House. In 1929 the House of Representatives departed from this custom and extended an invitation to Mr. Beck to deliver an address on Washington. He chose for his subject "Washington and the Constitution." The address made a deep impression upon the House of Representatives and on its conclusion, the entire House rose in honor of the speaker.

As Washington was not a lawyer or a jurist, he is not especially associated in the public mind with the Constitution and Mr. Beck's address is interesting in that it brings out how clearly Washington realized that a nation could not be created merely by a written agreement, but must rest upon the foundations of sentiment and economic solidarity.—EDITOR.

Mr. Speaker, Ladies and Gentlemen:

We do well, my fellow members of the House of Representatives, to pause in our deliberations to recall the immortal memory of the noble founder of the Republic, and I am greatly honored in being the interpreter on this occasion of the grateful sentiments which this sacred anniversary inspires.

Nothing is further from my purpose than to attempt either an eulogium or an apologia—certainly not the latter, for of recent petty aspersions upon Washington's fair fame one need only say, as Franklin in Poor Richard: "Dirt may cling to a mud wall, but not to polished marble."

Eulogy seems equally superfluous. His great fame has long since outstripped the power of praise. Even Lincoln, master of felicitous phrase, confessed his inability to pay any adequate tribute to Washington, and simply said:

"In solemn awe pronounce his name, and in its naked, deathless splendor leave it shining on."

Indisputably "first in the hearts of his countrymen," yet a larger and more splendid fame has been Washington's—and he shares it with no character in profane history—he is also first in the affection of the world. If the wise and the good of every civilized nation could be polled as to the three noblest characters in history, Washington alone would be on almost every list. The greatest of the Victorian novelists, Thackeray, has thus voiced the verdict of posterity:

> What a constancy, what a magnanimity, what a surprising persistence against fortune. * * * The chief of a nation in arms, doing battle with distracted parties; calm in the midst of conspiracy; serene against the open foe before him and the darker enemies at his back; Washington, inspiring order and spirit into troops hungry and in rags; stung by ingratitude, but betraying no anger, and ever ready to forgive; in defeat invincible, magnanimous in conquest, and never so sublime as on that day when he laid down his victorious sword and sought his noble retirement —here indeed is a character to admire and revere, a life without a stain, a fame without a flaw.

It is true that a few hypercritics—not worthy to untie the latchets of his shoe—have questioned his intellectual powers.

A sapient college professor, speaking a few years ago at an English university, patronizingly said that Washington was "a man of few natural gifts, self-educated, and somewhat slow-witted."

Again, in a recent biography of Aaron Burr, the authors refer to Washington's "failure to rise above the mediocrity of a small Virginia planter."

My good friend, Claude G. Bowers, in his otherwise admirable book, *Jefferson and Hamilton*, gives these two the center of the stage, and relegates the august figure of Washington to the wings.

Such was not the judgment of those who best knew him. Jefferson—not wholly a friendly critic—spoke of his intellect as "great and powerful"—no mean praise— and Patrick Henry said that, of all the members of the

First Continental Congress, Washington was foremost for "solid information and sound judgment."

The indisputable fact is that, from the beginning of the struggle for independence until the end of his half century of useful service, George Washington was the master spirit in the political life of America. He was the one man who commanded the confidence of all, and this fact alone would refute the theory of his intellectual inferiority, for the Fathers were not fools. Always he was the "tower of strength, that stood foursquare to every wind that blew." Of what act in his whole career is America today ashamed? What doctrine of his would it now disavow? What writing of his would it delete? None. Name one of his contemporaries, indeed, name any statesman of any era of the world, of whom this could be said in equal measure.

He *was* largely "self-educated." Farmer, hunter, frontiersman, pioneer, and pathfinder, realities and not verbal abstractions interested him. The formative years of his life were spent on the plantation and in the forest. Doubtless he often thought, as did Shakespeare's banished duke in the Forest of Arden:

"Are not these woods
More free from peril than the envious court?
Here feel we but the penalty of Adam,
The seasons' difference, as the icy fang
And churlish chiding of the winter's wind,
Which, when it bites and blows upon my body,
Even till I shrink with cold, I smile and say,
'This is no flattery. These are counsellors
That feelingly persuade me what I am.' "

Yes, he was "self-educated" in the arduous school of nature, and his keen mind, even as the banished duke, found—

"Tongues in trees, books in the running brooks,
Sermons in stones and good in everything."

This life-long communion with nature gave him little patience with the more artificial institutions of man. He listened with ill-concealed impatience to the lengthy speeches of the lawyers in the Constitutional Convention, in whose deliberations of four months he spoke only once.

The quarrels of two lawyers in his Cabinet, Jefferson and Hamilton, embittered him.

On August 23, 1792, he addressed a letter to Jefferson, Hamilton, and Randolph, in which, after deprecating the fact that internal dissension should "be harrowing and tearing out our vitals," he added:

> "That unless there could be more charity for the opinion and acts of one and another in governmental matters * * * it would be difficult to manage the reins of government, or keep the parts of it together, * * * and thus the fairest prospect of happiness and prosperity that ever was presented to man, will be lost perhaps forever."

He therefore asked that—

> "instead of wounding suspicions and irritating charges there may be liberal allowances, mutual forbearance, and a temporary yielding on all sides."

As I read the history of those eventful days, my sympathies are not with Jefferson or Hamilton. They are with Washington, who stood alone, and who could have said in truth: "A plague o' both your houses."

For editors, with their "I am Sir Oracle" snap judgments upon matters, of which they knew little, he had a profound contempt. Charged by one with being a "Nero," he said he "would rather be in the grave than emperor of the world."

There is little evidence that he placed any great dependence upon doctors, and this is not surprising in that age of Sangrados, for two doctors, after torturing him with blisters, finally bled the grand old man to death for a swollen windpipe.

Washington, as all the supremely great men of history, was a realist. For legal abstractions he had little patience. With him "things were in the saddle" and only facts counted. He was not an empiricist. He distrusted phrase making. He doubted panaceas by law. He knew that no constitution could be devised that would be fool-proof. Far better than the lawyers and jurists of his time, he knew the futility of leagues or confederations patterned on the Greek models, whose authority was only moral. He summed up all the folly of the old Articles of Confederation in the one terse phrase: "Influence is not government."

No one saw more clearly and advocated more earnestly the necessity of creating a nation and not a mere league of states, but he did not believe that this could be done alone by paper constitutions, but only by an antecedent spiritual union, based upon sympathies and economic solidarity. He saw more clearly than the learned legal theorists that, in the last analysis, no government can be essentially different from the spirit of the people which created it.

Give me your indulgent attention while I seek to show these facts from the text of the "Farewell Address," for it contained the statement of his political philosophy.

On an autumn day of the year 1796 President Washington, weary of official life, worn out by his public service of half a century, and desiring to seek the retirement which he had so richly earned, sent for the editor of a Philadelphia newspaper, and handed him a manuscript, with a request that he publish it. It was his farewell testament to the people whom he loved so well and whom he had led to high achievement. The political literature of the world contains nothing nobler.

It was not written upon a hasty impulse or with scant preparation. Gray required seven years to write his famous "Elegy." Washington had made the first draft of the Farewell Address five years before he sought its publication. A diffident and modest man, he had sought the advice of Madison, Jefferson, and Hamilton, but the final form was his own and he twice corrected it in the proofs before it was published in the Philadelphia *National Advertiser*.

I am first impressed with the fact that it is dated September 17, 1796. He could have selected any date and it is possible that he chose that date because it was the ninth anniversary of the final formulation of the Constitution. In the nine years that had intervened, he had brought that sickly infant—as it then seemed—to a vigorous youth and, as the message was largely devoted to a vindication of the Union and its organic instrument, the Constitution, it is possible that the date was deliberately selected. There was, in any event, great propriety in the date, for if the Constitution is "the most wonderful work ever struck off at a given time by the brain and purpose of man," then the great fame of Washington could be safely rested upon that achievement alone.

He may not have written a line of the text, but it is incontrovertible that, without his great influence, it would never have been formulated by the convention or ratified by the states, and it is probable that the new government would have had short life had not the practical statesmanship of Washington in its first eight years put it on a firm foundation and gained for it the confidence of the people.

You will note, in the second place, that it was not addressed to the Congress of the United States or to any public official. Speaking of himself as an "old and affectionate friend," he addresses the people as "friends and fellow citizens." Therein lies the first great thought which Washington sought to convey by the Farewell Message. He believed that the only salvation of the people lay in themselves and not in parchment or red seals.

Shortly after the close of the Constitutional Convention and when the Constitution was undergoing the perilous process of ratification, Washington wrote, on September 7, 1788, to his friend and comrade in arms, Lafayette, and, after praising the Constitution as a wise instrument of government, he added that the new government would be in no danger of degenerating into a monarchy, oligarchy, or aristocracy, or any other form of despotism, "so long as there shall remain any virtue in the body of the people." He then continued:

> "I would not be misunderstood, my dear Marquis, to speak of consequences which may be produced in the revolution of ages by corruption of

morals, profligacy of manners, *or listlessness in
the preservation of the natural and unalienable
rights of mankind,* nor of the successful usurpa-
tions that may be established at such an unpro-
pitious juncture upon the ruins of liberty, however providently guarded and secured, as these
are contingencies against which no human prudence can effectually provide."

Washington regarded any form of government as but
a means to an end, and that it could never be better than
the people themselves.   Like Aristotle, he believed that a
constitution must correspond to the *"ethos"* of the people,
meaning thereby not merely the spirit of the people but
the aggregate of their habits, conventions, and ideas. These
obviously change from generation to generation.   If
there be any conflict between the Constitution and the
genius of the people, it is not the will of the people that
is broken but the Constitution.   Therefore, to insure vitality, there must be a reasonable correspondence between
the Constitution, as interpreted, and the spirit of the
people.

He reminded them that—

"It is of infinite moment that you (the people) should properly estimate the immense value
of your National Union to your collective and
individual happiness."

To him the surest foundations of that unity were sentiment and interest, and of the sentimental tie he spoke
first, as follows:

"Citizens by birth and choice of a common
country, that country has a right to concentrate
your affections. The name of America, which belongs to you in your national capacity, must always exalt the just pride of patriotism more than
any appellation derived from local discriminations.   With slight shades of difference you have
the same religion, manners, habits and political
principles.   You have, in a common cause,
fought and triumphed together; the independ-

ence and liberty you possess are the work of joint
counsels and joint efforts, of common dangers,
sufferings and successes."

Thus he sought to impress upon successive generations
the noble memories of the heroic days of our colonial
development, culminating in our struggle for independence. He bade them remember the "rock whence ye are
hewn." He knew that no nation can be truly great without an heroic past and a conscious remembrance of it.
He realized, as Lincoln did, that, in times of strife and
disunion, these "mystic chords of memory" would yet
"swell the chorus of the Union, when touched, as they
will be, by the better angels of our nature."

You will note his use of the word "America," instead
of the "United States." He generally spoke of our Nation as the "Union," and by it he meant the sympathetic
and sentimental bond that bound the Colonies together
long before the War of Independence. To him the American Commonwealth dated, not from the Fourth of July,
1776, but from the first Virginia settlement. In Washington's eyes America was born of those "spacious days"
which gave Shakespeare and Bacon, Raleigh and Drake,
Jonson and Spenser to an astonished world.

Having thus emphasized the binding ties of those "mystic chords of memory," struck by the blood-comrade-
ship of arms, Washington next passes to a practical consideration, which he regarded as greatly outweighing even
the sentimental tie. He addresses himself to the indissoluble wedlock of economic interests, which, far more than
the theories or formulas of lawyers, had welded the inor-
ganic union of the Colonies into the organic Government
of the United States. In a passage of great length and
equal wisdom, he dwells upon the inevitable interdepend-
ence of the North and the South and the West, and to
this end advocates "the progressive improvements of interior communication of land and water." These, he predicted, would bring about an "indissoluble community
of interest as one nation."

Time has vindicated his prophecy. The Union has
been held together for nearly a century and a half, not

by the Constitution alone, but by an ever-developing economic unity. I have always believed that the Union was safe when the last spike was driven in the Union Pacific Railroad. Even if the Civil War had terminated differently, and the sections had been divorced by a decree of the sword, they would have been long since reunited by steam and electricity in a lasting wedlock.

That the Union must largely depend upon an economic solidarity was a long-cherished belief of Washington. Even when our country was a feeble congeries of straggling and separated Colonies on the Atlantic seaboard and its statesmen regarded the Appalachian Range as their inevitable western boundary, Washington had the sagacity to look beyond the Alleghenies and to see in the undeveloped wilderness to the west a great future for America, if convenient trade routes could be provided.

Denied the vision of the railroad and the telegraph, he interested himself in the construction of canals. He was the first colonial statesman to advocate the linking of the Atlantic coast with the Mississippi Valley, then seemingly impossible. His correspondence shows that the possibility of water routes to develop and cement the union of the Colonies was constantly in his mind. As early as 1774 he introduced a bill in the Virginia House of Burgesses for the improvement of the navigation of the Potomac for 150 miles beyond tidewater. On his victorious return from the war he again plunged into the subject which had fascinated him from the time when, on horseback, he had penetrated into the unknown wilderness beyond the Alleghenies as a great explorer and pathfinder. Writing to Lafayette after the Revolution, Washington tells him that he is planning to leave Mount Vernon and find his way through the trackless forest to Lake Erie, thence by the Great Lakes to a point near the present city of Chicago, thence down the Des Plaines and Illinois and the Mississippi Rivers to New Orleans, and thence back to Mount Vernon. Even in these days such a trip would be an arduous journey, but in those days it would have taxed the strength and skill of the most ardent explorer, and Washington was then an old man. While he never carried out this ambitious plan, he did make extensive journeys to New England and the South.

In a letter to Edmund Randolph, in 1785, he said:

"The great objective for which I wish is for the navigation of the rivers James and Potomac extending to connect the western territory with the Atlantic States.   All others to me are secondary."

Always a broad-minded American, his interest was not confined to the transportation route for his native State, for he advocated long before Clinton the practicability of a water connection between Lake Erie and the Hudson River.

Writing on October 10, 1784, to the Governor of Virginia, Washington, having traced out the different routes and distances from the Potomac to Detroit, and having emphasized the economic value to Virginia of some connection with the "fur and peltry trade of the Lakes and for the produce of the country which lies within" added:

"But in my opinion there is a political consideration for so doing, which is of still greater importance.   I need not remark to you, sir, that the flanks and rear of the United States are possessed by other powers, and formidable ones, too; nor how necessary it is to apply *the cement of interest to bind all parts of the Union together by indissoluble bonds,* especially that part of it which lies immediately west of us, with the middle States."

In another letter to David Humphreys, dated July 25, 1785, Washington wrote:

"My attention is more immediately engaged in a project which I think big with great political, as well as commercial, consequences to these States, especially the middle ones; it is by removing the obstructions and extending the inland navigation of our rivers, to bring the States on the Atlantic in close connection with those forming to the westward by a short and easy transportation. Without this, I can easily conceive they will have different views, separate interests, and other connections. I may be singular in my ideas, but they are these: That, to open a door to and make easy the way for those settlers to the westward (which ought to progress regularly and compactly) before we make any stir about the navigation of the Mississippi, and before our settlements are far advanced toward that river, would be our true line of policy.

His belief in waterways justifies us in assuming that nothing today would interest him more than the proposed waterways from the Great Lakes to the Gulf and to the Atlantic Ocean.

It is of this empire builder, whose foresight was exceeded by none of his contemporaries, unless we except Franklin, that the college professor spoke as "slow witted."

Having thus developed the moral and economic argument for a union, Washington proceeds to discuss the importance of the Constitution. He says:

"Sensible of this momentous truth, you have improved upon your first essay (meaning the Articles of Confederation) by the adoption of a Constitution of government better calculated than your former for an intimate union and for the efficacious management of your common concern. This Government, the offspring of our own choice, uninfluenced and unawed, adopted upon full investigation and mature deliberation, completely free in its principles, in the distribution of its powers, uniting security with energy and containing within itself a provision for its own amendment, has a just claim to your confidence and your support. Respect for its authority, compliance with its laws, acquiescence in its measures are duties enjoined by the fundamental maxims of true liberty. The bases of our political systems is the right of the people to make and alter their constitutions of government; but the Constitution which at any time exists, till changed by an explicit and authentic act of the whole people, is sacredly obligatory upon all. The very idea of the power and the right of the people to establish government presupposes the duty of every individual to obey the established Government."

Has anyone better stated the moral sanction of constitutionalism?

He was not so foolish as to believe that any written document could lastingly hold successive generations within its wise restraints, and he, therefore, proceeded to warn his fellow countrymen against any destruction of this Constitution. He said:

"Toward the preservation of your Government and the permanency of your present happy state, it is requisite not only that you steadily discountenance irregular oppositions to its acknowledged authority, but also that you resist with care the spirit of innovation upon its principles, however specious the pretexts. One method of assault may be to effect, in the forms of the Constitution, alterations which will impair the energy of the system, *and thus to undermine what cannot be directly overthrown*."

If only the later generations had remembered that wise counsel, we today would not be appalled at the unceasing erosion of the Constitution and the vanishing rights of the States! The Constitution has withstood outward attacks, but it has been, and is still being, slowly undermined.

Washington continues:

"In all the changes to which you may be invited, remember that time and habit are at least as necessary to fix the true character of governments as of other human institutions; that experience is the surest standard by which to test the real tendency of the existing Constitution of the country; that facility in changes, upon the credit

of mere hypothesis and opinion, exposes to perpetual change from the endless variety of hypothesis and opinion."

I again interrupt to say that time and habit have done
more to interpret the Constitution than all the learned
decisions of the Supreme Court.

Nor did Washington believe that the chosen officials of
the Government, even though they acted under the sanctity of solemn oaths to support and maintain the Constitution, would always respect its wise restraints. To them,
by anticipation, he also gives his wise advice:

"It is important, likewise, that the habits of
thinking in a free country should inspire caution
in those intrusted with its administration, to confine themselves within their respective constitutional spheres, avoiding, in the exercise of the
powers of one department, to encroach upon
another. The spirit of encroachment tends to
consolidate the powers of all the departments in
one, and thus to create, whatever the form of
government, a real despotism. A just estimate
of that love of power and proneness to abuse it,
which predominates in the human heart, is sufficient to satisfy us of the truth of this position.
The necessity of reciprocal checks in the exercise
of political power, by dividing and distributing
it into different depositories, and constituting
each the guardian of the public weal, against invasions by the others, has been evinced by expe-
riments, ancient and modern; some of them in
our own country and under our own eyes. To
preserve them must be as necessary as to institute
them. If, in the opinion of the people, the distribution or modification of the constitutional
powers be in any particular wrong, let it be corrected by an amendment in the way which the
Constitution designates. But let there be no
change by usurpation; *for though this in one instance may be the instrument for good, it is the
customary weapon by which free governments*

are destroyed. The precedent must always greatly overbalance, in permanent evil, any partial or transient benefit which the use can at any time yield."

Washington thus foresaw the menace to our institutions of an undue exaltation either of Congress or of the Executive. There is little danger of the former, for Congress is a many-headed body, and, as such, has little appeal to the imagination of the people.

The tendency is to disturb the balance by an undue exaltation of the Executive. The framers of the Constitution wisely intended to create a strong Executive, but they never intended to assimilate him to a king. He is the first servant of the people and his great powers and heavy responsibilities require that he be respected as the First Servant of the people,—*primus inter pares.* The tendency, however, is to go further and to incarnate the majesty of the Republic in the individual who is temporarily the Chief Executive and that is the essential idea of kingship. There is a growing tendency to regard the President as the "Great Father" of the people and the Congress as little more than his "faithful Commons." Thus, in almost every controversy between the Executive and Congress, the sympathies of the people are with the former, for they can visualize him and make a legend of him, but Congress is impersonal.

Washington foresaw this, and in his earnest plea for a due equilibrium between the Executive and the Congress, which I have just quoted, he warned America against the evil of one-man power, for Washington knew that the love of power, like jealousy, "grows by what it feeds on." Fortunately, our Presidents have generally been men of the people—true democrats—but if the day shall ever come when we have an inordinately ambitious and unscrupulous Executive and a subservient Congress, we may then realize the wisdom of Washington's solemn warning that such undue exaltation of the Executive "is the customary weapon by which free governments are destroyed."

O wise old counsellor! How well he foresaw in the

last two sentences of the portion of the Farewell Address, which I last quoted, that spirit of political pragmatism, which is willing to sacrifice an eternal principle to gain some immediate good, an imponderable for a ponderable!

Time would not permit me to pursue further his wise counsel as to the public credit, the diffusion of education to insure an intelligent electorate, and, finally, the necessity of keeping our country free from any foreign entanglements that would impair its liberty of action. He never claimed that ours should be a hermit Nation. Independence, and not isolation, was his ideal of our foreign relations. To quote his own words, he would have us "independent of all and under the influence of none."

It is evident from the Farewell Address that he viewed with alarm the development of political parties, especially when formed on sectional alignments, and greatly feared that, in the heated collision of their passions and interests, the bonds of unity would be severed. The Civil War was a fearful vindication of this prophecy.

Washington believed in our dual form of government, and today his concern would be to defend the reserved rights of the States against the undermining forces of centralization.

Nothing more strikingly illustrates the profound changes in our constitutional idea, due to the "ethos" of the people, than the question of centralization. When the Constitution was adopted, the States had a very real consciousness of their own sovereignty. The success of the National Government and the immense moral influence of George Washington slowly developed the idea of a powerful Union. But even more potent have been the changes brought about through mechanical inventions. The Union is held together today, not so much by the Constitution as by the shining pathways of steel, over which our railroads run, and the innumerable wires, which, like antennae, coordinate the mighty energies of the American people.

To these must now be added one of the most potent unifying forces of all—namely, the radio. While the press served as a consolidating influence, yet the influence of a newspaper is limited to the zone of its circulation. To-day, however, any responsible leader of thought may, on occasion, speak to 20,000,000 people. Thus, both time and space have been annihilated, and the people have been irresistibly drawn into the consciousness of a central government, which far overshadows the consciousness of the States. This has caused a profound change in the "ethos" of the people in this respect, and our institutions have become so unified that the old struggle against centralization has largely passed away. Each of the old political parties, when in power, vie with the other in consolidating the Union by multiplying bureaucratic agencies and as a result many matters hitherto within the power of the States are now controlled from Washington. To the extent that this is the result of economic forces it is irresistible, even if not always desirable; but to the extent that it is the result of the greed for bureaucratic power, it is a grave peril. The difficulty in combatting the trend towards centralization is that while the men who framed the Constitution thought in terms of abstract political rights, this generation thinks only in terms of concrete economies.

The problem of the future is to hold this centripetal tendency measurably in check; for it is as true today as when the Constitution was adopted that our Government will not always continue if the planetary system of the States be absorbed in the central sun of the Federal Government.

Our Nation is too vast in area and our people too numerous to be governed altogether from Washington. The safety of the Union depends upon the preservation of the rights of the States, and the difficulty is to preserve these rights, when the elemental forces of steam and electricity continue to weld the country into a powerful unity and to reduce the political consciousness of the States almost to the vanishing point. The problem of the future will be to preserve, so far as is now possible, the just equipoise, which the Constitution vainly sought to maintain, between the power of the Central Government and the power of the States.

We are still a young country. In my youth I might well have known a distinguished lawyer of Philadelphia, Horace Binney, then over 90 years of age, who as a young boy had seen Washington and Franklin conversing in front of Independence Hall during the sessions of the Constitutional Convention. This measures the brief span of our existence. Centuries are still before America, and who can safely say, if it becomes too centralized for efficient government, that one day there may not be a powerful movement toward disintegration, especially if there develop between the sections powerful economic conflicts of policy? The history of nations is an unending cycle of integration and disintegration, of consolidating and then redistributing the powers of governments. Human institutions, like the globules of mercury, tend to scatter and unite. For more than a century the tendency of America has been to consolidate; but let us remember that, if the movement proceeds too far, the tendency to disintegrate will begin. The ideal of every patriotic American should be "the indestructible Union of indestructible States." To-day that ideal is fast becoming little more than a rhetorical phrase.

And this suggests a final thought.

The salvation of our form of government, in the last analysis, rests with the people, as Washington so clearly said, and the most discouraging sign of the times is their indifference to constitutional questions. What I have elsewhere called "constitutional morality" was never at a lower ebb. This is largely due to the overshadowing importance and grandeur of the Federal Government. Like the central sun, it blinds our vision, and—at least in popular consciousness—the States are gradually fading in importance, even as the planets cann't be seen by day because of the omnipresent rays of the sun.

At the beginning of the Republic there were thirteen self-conscious States which had behind them a century or more of traditions. But the Union is now composed of forty-eight States, many of which are but the creation of yesterday and which have no such background of tradition to stimulate the consciousness of the people. Most of them are the creation of purely artificial boundaries and, while there is local pride, yet they naturally regard themselves as the children of the Federal Government, whereas the historic thirteen Colonies had, at least at one time, the proud consciousness that they created the Federal Union and that the Federal Union did not create them. I confess I cannot see the way to combat this changed consciousness of the American people, largely due to mechanical forces, which no written constitution can wholly overcome.

The loss of the sense of constitutional morality, without which it is difficult for any constitution to survive, is also due to a subtler cause and one that is too little appreciated. Our very dependence upon a written constitution and our belief in its static nature and its self-executing powers have tended to deaden the political consciousness of the American people. We live in an age of specialization, and the people, forgetful that, in the last analysis, they must save themselves, feel that a constitution will execute itself and that the special and exclusive method of determining all constitutional questions is by resort to the courts.

This is especially perceptible in our legislative bodies. Time was when Congress felt that it had the primary duty of determining whether proposed laws were within its constitutional power. Many of the greatest debates upon the meaning of the Constitution took place in the halls of Congress and not in court rooms. Next January a full century will have elapsed since Daniel Webster, of Massachusetts, and Robert Y. Hayne, of South Carolina, engaged in their momentous discussion as to the true nature of the Government. Today such a closely reasoned debate would be impossible. In this age of specialism we unwisely believe that these questions are only for the judiciary. A century ago, the controversy over the power to create a United States bank and later the power to make internal improvements were questions which Congress had no disposition to shift to the judiciary, but which they preferred in the first instance to decide for themselves. This is as it should be, for every member of Congress takes an oath, as a judge, to support and maintain the Constitution of the United States.

In recent years there has been no disposition to argue the constitutional phase of any proposed law in Congress. Such a debate would be regarded as a loss of public time as the question must ultimately be determined by the Supreme Court. Laws are frequently passed of very doubtful constitutionality and their validity left to the processes of litigation. This might be a satisfactory division of governmental work if the Supreme Court had unrestricted and plenary power to disregard a constitutional statute or Executive act, but it has not this power. Many laws are *politically anti*constitutional without being *judicially un*constitutional.

The fact is that the Supreme Court does not have, as so many believe, plenary and unrestricted power to nullify unconstitutional legislation. On the contrary, there is a vast sphere of political activity in which the true construction of the Constitution is involved but on which the judiciary, *ex necessitate rei,* cannot possibly pass judgment, as, for example, censoring appropriations; for appropriations, as we all know, can be made for unconstitutional as well as constitutional objects, and in a constitutional sense no governmental activity is more destructive. The unlimited power to appropriate money is the "wooden horse" which may yet make a future America say of our dual form of government: *"Ilium fuit."*

The distinction between a law which is politically anticonstitutional and one juridically unconstitutional is somewhat subtle and is not one that readily occurs to many who study our form of government. Leaving aside the wide sphere of legislation in which, if a litigated case ever arises, the Supreme Court can correct our errors, the fact remains that there is still a large sphere in which the Supreme Court is powerless to act, either because of the necessity of the case or because the question, to use a lawyer's phrase, is essentially political, and not justiciable. The Supreme Court, with a conservatism that certainly cannot be called too moderate, has said it will invalidate no law unless it be indisputably repugnant to the Constitution, with the result that we pass many laws about which you and I are at least doubtful as to their constitutionality. Then when the constitutionality of such a law is argued before the Supreme Court, perhaps a quarter of a century after it has been in force, the court may not determine the unconstitutionality of the statute, for when such legislation is supported by the breath of popular opinion and has the pragmatic advantage of some supposed good, the court is human enough to conclude that it is not so indisputably repugnant to the Constitution as to justify the court in annulling it. Through that breach in the dike a great volume of legislation flows for which there is no sanction in the Constitution, and such laws are not nullified by the judiciary because either of their doubtful character or because they are unconstitutional by reason of the motive of Congress or by some powerful political consideration, and thus those laws become precedents for another law and gradually, like the ocean in front of my summer home at Sea Bright, N. J., the high tide sometimes seems to reach a farther mark and sometimes to recede, but in the long run, taking it by years and not by months, there is the steady erosion of the true coast line of our Government.

Thus the Constitution itself is slowly "undermined," even as Washington predicted.

Therefore I plead for an awakened conscience on the part of our legislators and the people themselves in the matter of constitutional morality. They should primarily determine these grave issues of constitutionality for themselves. Unless they do so they are in grave danger of losing the benefits of the wisest instrument of statecraft that the wit of man has yet devised. "Eternal vigilance is the price of liberty."

Washington died shortly before Napoleon won his great victory on the plains of Marengo. We can imagine the old soldier in his retirement at Mount Vernon following with eager vision the extraordinary developments in the Old World and the rising sun of the new Caesar. I can picture him in that last autumn of his life, seated on the porch of his beloved Mount Vernon in the gathering twilight—emblematic of the dying day of his life—and silently gazing upon the Potomac as it moved to the sea, a symbol of the infinite mystery of time.

It was on such an October evening, a few months before he died, with the autumn leaves falling from the trees upon the green lawns of his much loved home, that he retired to his study and wrote his last expression of opinion as to the affairs of the world, and what he thus wrote can be applied to the conditions of the present hour as expressing his opinion if he were alive today.

> "The affairs of Europe have taken a most important and interesting turn. * * * My own wish is to see everything settled upon the best and surest foundation for the peace and happiness of mankind, without regard to this, that, or any other nation. A more destructive sword never was drawn, at least in modern times, than this war has produced. It is time to sheathe it and give peace to mankind."

Thus spoke and still speaks the world's noblest citizen, and to that ideal of peace mankind is steadily marching. In the progress of humanity the character of Washington is a great factor, for "the path of the just is as a shining light, that shineth more and more unto the perfect day."

Let us today reverently thank the God of our fathers that Washington's influence is still a shining light. It illuminates as none other the soul of America. It is today, as it has ever been, a vital force. From his grave in Mount Vernon he still guides the destinies of the American people. When the seas are smooth we little feel his presence, but when the ship of state plunges into a storm and is threatened by angry seas his mighty shade is again our helmsman.

The Arthurian legend tells us that King Arthur sleeps at Avalon, but that he will come again and unsheathe his sword, if ever England were in desperate need.

Our Arthur, bravest of the brave and knightliest of the knightly, sleeps at Mount Vernon, but whenever disaster menaces our institutions the American people again become conscious of his potent influence, and while that influence remains the Republic will endure.

IV

THE LAWYER AND SOCIAL PROGRESS

In the year 1915 the Bar of Canada determined to form
a Canadian Bar Association on the lines of the American
Bar Association. The association was formed in Montreal
on March 19, 1915, and Mr. Beck was invited to deliver
the first of a series of annual addresses. He discussed the
relations of the Bar to the community and especially the
time-worn attacks upon the legal profession which have
marked the literature of almost every nation. The speech
was delivered during the World War and it is not unnatural that Mr. Beck, at the conclusion, made reference
to the epoch-making events which were then in progress.
—EDITOR.

*Mr. President, Gentlemen and Guests of the Canadian
Bar Association:*

I appreciate more than I can express the great and un-
deserved honor that you have done me in selecting me to
deliver this address. I wish sincerely that I could justify
the compliment. Especially do I appreciate the gracious
introduction of the presiding officer and the kind references to my contribution to the voluminous literature of
the present world-wide controversy.

In this connection I am reminded of the story which
Boswell tells of Dr. Johnson. The learned doctor had
been given a special audience by his Majesty, King George
the Third, and the author of the great dictionary, in relating the details to the ever-faithful Boswell, dwelt with
pardonable complacency upon the fact that the King had
been pleased to commend very highly the merits of his
dictionary.

> "And what did you say to the King when he
> thus praised your dictionary?"

asked Boswell, and the old doctor replied, with some
warmth:

> "Am I the man to bandy words with my sov-

ereign? If he said that my dictionary was the
best in the English language, it must be so."

The present crisis suggests my theme. What has the
lawyer done and what is he doing in the evolution of
human society? How far is he accelerating or how far
has he retarded the slow progress of mankind "to that
far-off divine event toward which the whole creation
moves"?

Possibly the theme may seem to some inopportune, as
this is the hour of force and not of reason.

"Inter arma silent leges" is an old maxim and in the
midst of arms perhaps even the lawyers should also remain
silent.

In this prodigious catastrophe, when the reign of law
seems for the time being to have given way to international anarchy and the passions of men are at flood tide,
the voice and authority of a lawyer are almost as incon-
gruous as that of the burgess of the town of Gettysburg
who, when he found the armies of Meade and Lee con-
verging upon the historic village, felt that it was his duty
to assert in some way the majesty of law. He consulted
the ordinances of the town and found that it was forbidden to fire off firearms within the county limits under
a penalty of $50. He communicated these regulations
to the commanders of the two armies and possibly it was
for this reason that the greater part of the battle was
fought just outside the borough limits.

Speaking seriously, this is a time of sifting, a time when
all truths and laws are being challenged and tested and
the comparative influences of different elements of human
society revalued. At such a period of revaluation it seems
not inappropriate to take a retrospective view and to in-
quire what the relations of the lawyer have been to social
progress and what part the law plays in the complicated
machinery of society.

The question is the more appropriate as President Hadley of the University of Yale said a few years ago that
there were but three masterful professions—journalism,
finance and politics. The exclusion of the law as a mas-

terful profession, together with the soldier and the educator, justifies serious doubt as to the accuracy of Dr. Hadley's estimate, and the pertinent query arises, what contribution the lawyer has made to social progress and whether his profession can justly be regarded today as among the masterful professions.

This last question might be answered by stating that justice, which is as deep as the foundations of society and almost as wide as human thought itself, has been in all generations, as Daniel Webster once said, "the great interest of man on earth." If so, then assuredly those who make it an especial study and by whose efforts its great ends are measurably attained must occupy in our infinitely complicated society a position of pre-eminent usefulness, power and honor.

The relative influence of any profession must be determined by the aggregate of the units. The individual lawyer, as such a unit, may in the course of his life influence only a comparatively narrow circle and yet in that narrow circle he is apt to play the part of legislator, executive and judge. The aggregate work of these units constitutes the elaborate machinery of law, without which society would be a self-destructive and uncoordinated force.

Even the units of our profession have in exceptional instances rendered conspicuous service, which is nothing undervalued to even the meritorious service of the greatest journalists, financiers and politicians whom Dr. Hadley has selected as members of the masterful professions. Let me, for example, take a few instances from my own country, but with which lawyers throughout the English speaking world are reasonably familiar.

What journalist ever contributed so much to the unification of my country as did Daniel Webster, by his great argument in *Gibbons v. Ogden,* and his even more impressive assertion of Federal authority in his great reply to Hayne?

What financier more potently affected the economic development of my country than the same great lawyer, when in the great case of *Dartmouth College v. Wood-word* he established the stability of corporate rights?

Between the statesman and the lawyer comparison is more difficult, for the statesman has generally been a lawyer, and his great achievements those of a lawyer who pleads at the great bar of public opinion and to posterity as the court of last resort. Thus it would be difficult to say which did more to precipitate the American Civil War, the decision in the *Dred Scot* case or the great debates of the lawyer-statesman, Abraham Lincoln, with his distinguished adversary, Senator Douglas.

Without further extending the comparison, it is enough to say of the law, in the language of a great judge and even greater philosopher, Lord Bacon, that—

> "it is the great organ through which the sovereign power (of society) moves."

Mr. Justice Blackstone, in his noble introduction to his commentaries, speaks of it as—

> "a science which distinguishes the criterion of right and wrong; which teaches to establish the one and prevent, punish or redress the other; which employs in its theory the noblest faculties of the soul, and exerts in its practice the cardinal virtues of the heart; a science which is universal in its use and extent, accommodated to each individual, yet comprehending the whole community."

These, however, are but the enthusiastic tributes of lawyers. Let me then quote one of the broadest and sanest of philosophers, Dr. Samuel Johnson, who said with equal terseness and felicity:

> "Law is the science in which the greatest powers of the understanding are applied to the greatest number of facts."

On another occasion when in the bluff old doctor's presence a superficial critic reflected upon the law and lawyers, Dr. Johnson brusquely said:

> "Let us have no general abuse. The law is the
> last result of human understanding acting upon
> human experience for the benefit of the public."

A government of law is the supreme manifestation of civilization. Both its creation and efficient operation are usually the result of the lawyer in his triple capacity of legislator, judge and practitioner. His power is exerted over the entire range of human thought and action. No human being is exempted from his commands and prohibitions. It is the lawyer who as judge pronounces in the name of society its judgments and commands. It is the lawyer as legislator and constitution builder who sets limits to the arbitrary powers either of princes or majorities, and it is the lawyer as practitioner who puts into operation the complicated machinery of human society in order that justice shall be done between man and man. The crude law of the savage is better than unrestrained license. Roman law established the "Roman peace" in all the vast territory which the Eternal City dominated and protected the weak against the strong. When the Centurion ordered the great Apostle to be scourged to compel him to testify, Paul said:

> "Is it lawful for you to scourge a man that is
> a Roman and uncondemned?"

The Centurion reported this to the Chief Captain, and said:

> "Take heed what thou doest; for this man is
> a Roman."

Thus in a ruder age military arrogance, seeking to scourge a man without trial or condemnation, was arrested by the puissant majesty of the law.

During the first three centuries of the Roman Empire the great work of framing the law fell entirely upon the jurists, and so fully did they vindicate their ability that the great body of the Roman law, which still governs civilized man, shares with the culture of the Greek and the religious conception of the Hebrew the distinction of being the greatest intellectual heritage of man.

It was the lawyer in the Middle Ages who broke the iron rigor of the feudal system and constructed the modern principles of equity. The lawyers of France voiced the aspirations of their oppressed countrymen and led the successful assault upon monarchical absolutism and class privilege. Of the National Assembly, which precipitated the French Revolution, three hundred and seventy members were lawyers.

Indeed the comparative civilization of a country can be measured by the relative power and influence of its Bar.

Finally to lawyers like Grotius and Puffendorf we owe international law, that fair rainbow of hope which foretells the coming of the day when the deluge of blood shall cease.

Possibly no country more admirably illustrates the masterful character of the legal profession than my own, for it was the American lawyer who precipitated the American Revolution by his agitation for unwritten constitutional principles of liberty. "No taxation without representation" was a lawyer's phrase. The Federal Constitution, which brought order out of chaos and has made it possible for this great people to govern itself, was the work of American lawyers, and it has been the American Bench, sitting since the adoption of the Constitution as a *quasi*-constitutional convention, which has for more than one hundred and twenty-seven years builded upon the foundation of the Constitution of 1787 that great and noble superstructure which we call our federal system. Henry, Jefferson, Madison, Marshall, Hamilton, Webster, Clay, Lincoln and others of potent achievement, whose name is legion, acquired much of their power and influence as members of the American Bar.

Masterful as it is, the law nevertheless is not a popular profession. As individuals, lawyers are generally respected and honored. Perhaps no class of men is the recipient of greater social and political distinction. The lawyer's versatility, due to the wide range of his observation, and his *savoir faire*, due to his intimate knowledge of human nature, have ever made him welcome as a friend, guest and adviser. But this does not affect the prejudice which some men feel towards the profession as such. Indeed there has been a constant and humorous identification of the lawyer with his Satanic Majesty. The analogy has had almost endless variations. A century ago, when Napoleon was apparently planning an invasion of England, all classes and professions of Englishmen sprang to arms, and amongst others the lawyers of the Temple organized a regiment. The King deigned to review this regiment. At the conclusion his Majesty sent for Erskine, its honorary Colonel, and asked him what he called his regiment, and Erskine replied that it as yet had no name, to which His Majesty replied, 'Call it the Devil's Own."

The greatest of all poets and the profoundest judge of human nature seems equally hostile to the profession. We recall for the moment Harry Hotspur's contemptuous remark:

"For in these nice sharp quillets of the law,
Good faith, I am no wiser than a daw."

The supposed avarice of the profession is referred to by Mercutio, when he says of his dream fairy, Queen Mab, that she gallops:

"O'er lawyers' fingers who straightway dream
of fees."

You may remember the satirical and altogether delightful parody upon the scholastic refinement and judicial Bunsbyism of the Elizabethan Bench, which Shakespeare, with remarkable audacity, inserted in the graveyard scene in "Hamlet." A case had been tried, involving the question as to whether the estate of a suicide escheated. The court did indulge in some very supersubtle reasoning as to when the crime of suicide, which worked the escheat, was consummated and whether the estate passed to the heirs before such consummation.

The suicide in question was Sir James Hales, who drowned himself while insane, possibly induced by the fact that he had been one of the Judges who condemned Lady Jane Grey. Suicide was a crime, which worked a forfeiture, and the question was when the crime was consummated. The subtlety of the arguments both of counsel and of the court approached the verge of absurdity, as thus—

> "Sir James Hales was dead, and how came he
> to his death? It may be answered, by drowning;
> and who drowned him? Sir James Hales. And
> when did he drown him? In his life time. So
> that Sir James Hales being alive caused Sir
> James Hales to die, and the act of the living
> man was the death of the dead man. And then
> for this offence it is reasonable to punish the
> living man who committed the offence, and not
> the dead man. But how can he be said to be
> punished alive when the punishment comes after
> death?"

In discussing Ophelia's chances of Christian burial, the gravedigger thus parodies the opinion of the court:

> "If the man go to this water and drown him-
> self it is, will he nill he, he goes, mark you that;
> but if the water come to him and drown him,
> he drowns not himself. Argal, he that is not
> guilty of his own death shortens not his own
> life."

The question arises how he came to parody the language unless he had some knowledge of the law, for the case, which is reported by Plowden, was decided before he was born. Plowden's Commentaries were not translated into English until towards the end of the Eighteenth Century.

This certainly justifies the suggestion that Shakespeare might have been, as tradition says, apprenticed at some time to a lawyer and thus picked up the jargon of the Elizabethan bench.

In this connection it is interesting to note in passing that the most recent and valuable find in Shakespeareana deals with Shakespeare as a witness. In searching the Hall of Records some years ago, an American professor discovered the record of a case in which the deposition of Shakespeare appeared and in which he was the principal witness. It seems that he at that time boarded with a wigmaker, presumably of French Huguenot extraction, named Mountjoy, in Little Silver Street, London. The wigmaker had a daughter and it was alleged that Shakespeare induced an apprentice to marry the daughter on condition of a marriage dot being settled upon her by her father. The young husband claimed that his father-in-law had broken his promise and accordingly sued, and the question turned upon what promise, if any, was made as a condition of the marriage.

Some of the witnesses deposed that Shakespeare had said that he had arranged the marriage with such an understanding, but his own deposition states that while he had arranged the marriage and the young people were a worthy couple, he himself did not recall any such arrangement with respect to a dowry. Thus early did witnesses find resort to the "I don't remember" statement.

In Hamlet, which represents the poet in the full flower of his matchless genius, when the gravedigger tosses up a skull, Hamlet, with biting sarcasm, says:

> "Why may not that be the skull of a lawyer? Where be his quiddits now, his quillets, his cases, his tenures and his tricks? Why does he suffer this rude knave now to knock him about the sconce with a dirty shovel and will not tell him of his action of battery? Hum! This fellow might be in his time a great buyer of land, with his statutes, his recognizances, his fines, his double vouchers, his recoveries. Is this the fine of his fine and the recovery of his recoveries, to have his fine pate full of fine dust?"

And then he asks Horatio the question:

> "Is not parchment made of sheepskins?"

To which Hamlet replies:

> "Aye, my lord, and of calfskins."

And the princely misanthrope replies:

> "They are sheep and calves which seek assurance in that."

Shakespeare forgot to say, however, that many of these technicalities and fictions were the method by which the lawyers emancipated society from the iron rigor of the feudal system, and the fact is that almost the only autographs we have of the great poet are those attached to these same sheepskin parchments for the better "assurance" of Shakespeare's title to his lands, and about the only business transactions in which he engaged, of which we know, were lawsuits in which he benefited by the services of counsel. It is with lawyers as with doctors, men criticize them in health, but run to them in time of need.

But it is the dramatists and the novelists who have given the severest caricatures of the profession. With few exceptions the lawyer of the stage is either a knave or a mountebank. The literature of the green room can be searched almost in vain for lawyers who can prove a good moral character. Instead we have a veritable rogues' gallery. Many generations of men have been influenced by a misinterpretation of the invective of the great Teacher:

> "Woe unto you, ye lawyers! for ye lade men with burdens grievous to be borne, and ye yourselves touch not the burdens with one of your fingers."

The theologian knows, but, alas!, the congregation is generally ignorant, that "the lawyers," who taxed too sorely the patience of the gentle Master, were simply the clerical copyists of the Mosaic Law, and, as such, we of the legal profession willingly resign them to our brethren of the clergy.

Let me play the part of *advocatus diaboli* and briefly show that this prejudice has in part its roots in causes which are not wholly the moral or intellectual deficiencies of our profession.

A prejudice which has persisted for so many generations and which is so deeply rooted in popular feeling must have its original source in some primitive trait of human nature. I find it in the elemental jealousy which the muscle has always felt for the brain. In primitive times physical prowess was the great source of power. Might was right, and the rule of society was that of Rob Roy:

"Let him take that hath the power
And let him keep that can."

Slowly, however, there emerged from ruder times a class whose strength consisted, not in their physical strength, but in intellectual cunning — "cunning" then meaning, not craftiness, but knowledge. The very deterioration in the meaning of "cunning" illustrates the truth of which I speak. It was not unnatural that the man of physical prowess should look with contempt, envy and fear upon the physically weaker man who triumphed through the subtle, but potent, power of thought.

The mythologies of prehistoric times clearly represent the views of life entertained by primitive human nature, and it is significant that the two systems of mythology with which our race is most directly connected both manifested this feeling of depreciation. In Greek mythology the gods symbolized various phases of physical power or beauty, but among them, although occupying a lesser station, was Mercury, the symbol of swift intelligence. He was the patron god of subtle men, of poets, lawyers, orators, and the depreciation of intellectual ability is shown by the fact that he was also accounted the god of liars and thieves. For him was reserved no high place on Olympus. He was lower in the scale of precedence than Vulcan, the symbol of brute strength, of Mars, the god of war, or of Venus, the goddess of beauty.

An even more striking illustration of this primitive estimate was the conception of the Norse analogue of Mercury. He was Loki, the god of fire, and therefore of intellect, argument and reason. His was not the thunder hammer of Donner, nor the burning sunshine of Balder, but whenever the gods were confronted with circumstances over which mere physical might could not triumph it was to Loki that they turned to suggest a way of escape.

You remember the Norse myth of "The Ring," as glorified by both the literary and musical genius of Richard Wagner. Wotan, the supreme god, desired to build the castle of Valhalla. He turns to Loki for guidance, and is advised to employ the giants, Fafner and Fasolt, under a promise that to them shall be given as their wage, Freia, the goddess of immortal youth. Loki promises when the work is completed to find some method of avoiding performance of the contract, and when Valhalla is built, and the giants claim Freia, it is to Loki that the gods turn to save them from the loss of eternal youth. Loki tells them that he has searched the world in vain for any worthy substitute for immortal youth, but that he might persuade the giants to take, in lieu of Freia, the gold ring, giving immeasurable power, which Alberich, the spirit of evil, had wrested from the Rhine maidens. By intellectual cunning Loki overcomes the dwarf, obtains the ring and persuades the giants to accept it in lieu of Freia, but when the gods, thus rescued from fatal disaster by Loki's cunning, proceed over the rainbow bridge into Valhalla they leave Loki behind, who, looking down into the waters of the Rhine, whence the gold was ravished, and then upward to the rainbow bridge to the stately procession of the gods, sarcastically exclaims of those, whom he had rescued and by whom he is now ignored:

"To their end they fleetly are led
Who believe themselves founded forever;
Almost I shame
To mix in their matter."

How often lawyers have thus expressed themselves after saving clients from their own folly!

This prejudice of primitive man has long outlived its original causes and finds its illustration today in the jealousy of which the legal profession, together with all purely intellectual occupations, is the subject.

This feeling of jealous admiration is probably intensified by the fact that with the growing power of law in the evolution of society the mass of men, who are too often hostile to its restraints, dislike the lawyer because he pre-eminently stands for the enforcement of law and the consequent limitation of license. It was this consideration which doubtless led Jack Cade, as he summoned his riotous followers to revolt, to endorse the sentiment:

"Let us kill all the lawyers first."

This worthy demagogue was philosophically correct, for if it is desired to destroy the fabric of human society, the natural beginning would be to kill those who stand as vigilant guards at its outer portals. These are and ever have been the men of the law.

Again, there is an unconscious feeling in the community that the legal profession is parasitic in its nature. In a Utopian state of society there might be no occasion for lawyers. Similarly in a state of society where perfect health existed, as it theoretically should, there would be no occasion for doctors. When the ideal commonwealth was founded on the banks of the Delaware, an enthusiastic promoter rejoiced that it contained neither doctors nor lawyers, as there was no need either "of the pestiferous drugs of the one or the tiresome loquacity of the other." Notwithstanding this Jeremiah, as the whole structure of human society rests upon the administration of law, and justice is, as Webster said, "the supreme interest of man on earth," the legal profession is no more parasitic than any other.

Another reason for this popular prejudice is the widespread and erroneous belief in the insincerity of the lawyer. No error is more persistent or widespread than that which asserts that the lawyer will sell his voice to any client, however base, or to any cause, however bad. Thus no question is more constantly asked of a lawyer than his ethical justification for defending a man whom he knows to be guilty. This question, like Banquo's ghost, will never down. The ethical question thus suggested has never been settled, and probably never will be settled to the satisfaction of all.

To discuss this mooted question adequately would take more time than is at my command. It is enough to say that the question rarely arises in the experience of the ordinary practitioner, and the reason for this is obvious. The great bulk of a lawyer's practice does not relate to litigated cases, as to which he is obliged to take a public position, but in explaining to his clients what they may lawfully do and how they may do it. As law is essentially applied morality, the lawyer in enforcing its principles without litigation does more to promote justice between man and man than any other profession. He rarely can secure absolute right, because absolute right in a complicated state of human society is rarely attainable. Life is an eternal compromise, and the lawyer cannot rise superior to the conditions under which he works. Many a disappointed litigant has had a poor opinion of the law, and therefore of lawyers, either because he has not obtained absolute justice, or because he is a victim of those general rules of human society, such as the statutes of limitations, which, though they work hardship in individual cases, are most necessary and salutary as rules of general application. The public, before condemning the legal profession, should appreciate that the administration of justice is necessarily but an approximation toward that ultimate and absolute justice which may come with the millennium, but never before. There is between the justice of the courts and absolute justice a "twilight zone," which the genius of man has not yet succeeded in spanning. Moreover, the average case is a tangled skein of disputed facts, in which the lawyer generally must accept his client's version. In the average litigated case, no side is wholly right. Upon the court, and not upon the lawyer, rests the ultimate responsibility of determining the law and the facts, and even then it must be said of legal justice, as George Eliot sadly said, in the great climax to "Romola":

> "Who can put his finger on an act and say
> 'this is justice'? Justice is like the kingdom of
> God: it is not without us as a fact, but within
> us as a great yearning."

The belief in the lawyer's insincerity has arisen largely from the least important feature of his professional life, his duties as an advocate. Unquestionably in former times there was much cheap acting in courts of justice, and the "chops and tomato sauce" style of argument of Sergeant Buzfuz, while somewhat of a caricature, has not wholly passed away:

> "The blustering artifice of a rhetorical hireling availing himself of the vile license of a loose tongued lawyer,"

as Disraeli once styled an attack which a lawyer made upon him, is generally out of fashion, and today candor, lucidity and sincerity are the most forceful elements in advocacy.

In his work as an advocate, the lawyer is apt to make his client's enemies his own. The latter is not apt to distinguish in the heat of a legal battle between his opponent and the opposing lawyer. In cases where human passion is excited and great interests are at stake, the lawyer is too apt, in winning a case, to add to his personal associations a life-long enemy and sometimes an ingrate.

Again, the lawyer is unjustly held responsible for all the defects of the law, for most of which he is not responsible. The nobility of law makes but little appeal to men, but its inevitable limitations—owing to the fallibility of human nature, and to the necessary limitations of organized society—have never failed to escape their attention. Thus the "law's delay" has been the fruitful theme of the poet and the satirist. Dickens, in *"Bleak House,"* preferred a terrible indictment against the Court of Chancery, but wholly failed to state in the preface to his novel that most of the defects, which he had so graphically illustrated, had been abolished by act of Parliament before *"Bleak House"* was printed. *Jarndyce v. Jarndyce* would be an impossibility today, and was an impossibility at the time *"Bleak House"* was written, but the entire legal profession could not with all its eloquence correct the popular impression to which the genius of Dickens had given rise. *"Bleak House"* was published in August, 1853, and Dickens in the preface asserts the substantial truth of his indictment against the Court of Chancery, but he fails to state that three years before his novel was written, Romilly, Lord St. Leonards and Lord Lyndhurst had secured an investigation of Chancery abuses and that subsequent legislation by Parliament put an end to many of the defects of the Chancery system so vividly and powerfully illustrated in *Jarndyce v. Jarndyce.*

Similarly, Dr. Warren in "Ten Thousand a Year," the masterpiece of fiction with reference to law and lawyers, bases the argument of his story upon defects of legal procedure which had long since passed away.

The law is and must necessarily be a reflex of contemporaneous society. It is no better, and it is no worse. Given a corrupt and cruel state of society, such as existed in the Eighteenth Century, and you necessarily have a corrupt and cruel system of laws. Especially in these days of triumphant democracy, the law is what the mass of men make it, and yet the great public, primarily responsible for the defects of the law, condemns the legal profession for whatever defects larger knowledge from time to time discloses. The laws of former times reflected the corruption and cruelty of the times and it is not surprising that the mass of men, who groaned under such burdens, regarded law as a kind of witchcraft or black art. The prejudice has long outlived its cause.

The chief reason for the unpopularity of the lawyer is due to the fact that men get their impressions of law and of the lawyer through the medium of fiction, and not from any personal observation, and it has always been the tendency of the poet, the novelist or the dramatist to select unfavorable and exaggerated types to give dramatic intensity to their productions. An honorable lawyer is too prosaic for literary portraiture. The lay figure of the dramatist and the novelist must be the worst type of the profession, and he so readily lends himself to "treason, stratagems and spoils" that it is not strange that the type of lawyer most familiar to the popular mind is the picturesque villain who cunningly thwarts virtue and promotes evil. While Shakespeare gives no portrait of a lawyer, unless we except the fair Portia, who somewhat perverted the law of Venice, yet, as previously noted, he has made many scornful references to the "law's delay," and to its technicalities and fictions. Next to Shakespeare, the average man of our race gets his first and strongest impressions of human nature from Charles Dickens. Although Dickens served his apprenticeship in the Middle Temple, and was himself for a time a lawyer's clerk, he had an intense hatred of the profession. This was partly due to the fact that he saw more of its shady side in the criminal courts than of its better side, but it is also due to the fact that his personal experiences in litigation with some literary pirates, who had published copies of the "*Christmas Carol*" and "*Martin Chuzzlewit*," were so unfortunate that when his books were again pirated he wrote to his counsel:

> "It is better to suffer a great wrong than to have recourse to the much greater wrong, the law. I shall not easily forget the expense and anxiety and horrible injustice of the '*Carol*' case, wherein, in asserting the plainest right on earth, I was really treated as if I was the robber instead of the robbed."

According to Dickens in "*Bleak House*":

> "The one great principle of the English law is to make business for itself. There is no other principle distinctly, certainly, and consistently maintained through all its narrow turnings. Viewed by this light it becomes a coherent scheme, and not the monstrous maze the laity are apt to think it. Let them but once clearly perceive that its grand principle is to make business for itself at their expense, and surely they will cease to grumble."

Bitter satire, and like most satire an exaggeration!
On the other hand, Sir Walter Scott, himself a lawyer of experience and no mean judge of human nature, puts in the mouth of the Antiquary this truer estimate of a lawyer:

"In a profession where unbounded trust is
necessarily imposed, there is nothing surprising
that fools should neglect it in their stupidity,
and tricksters abuse it in their knavery. But it
is more to the honor of those, *and I will vouch
for many,* who unite integrity with skill and
attention and walk honorably upright where
there are so many pitfalls and stumbling blocks
for those of a different character. To such men
their fellow citizens may safely entrust the care
of protecting their patrimonial rights, and their
country the more sacred charge of her laws and
privileges."

One further and most potent reason for the unpopularity of the lawyer remains to be considered. He is the
great conservative force in a nation, and is constantly
called upon to defend the individual against the tyranny
of the majority. He must frequently defy and defeat
public opinion by protecting the individual from its unreasonable demands. You will remember the splendid
exhibition of professional loyalty when Louis the XVI
was arraigned before the National Convention during the
Reign of Terror, and it was clearly understood that any
advocate who defended him would forfeit his own life
with that of his client. The great advocate, Malesherbes,
in volunteering his services, nobly said:

"I was twice called to the council of the King
when all the world coveted the honor and I owe
him the same service now when it has become
dangerous."

He gave to his royal client the sacrifice of his own life
and perished with him on the guillotine.

Erskine sacrificed his social popularity and political
prestige by accepting a retainer to defend the then despised Tom Paine, while Brougham in the teeth of royal
displeasure and social persecution espoused the cause of
the unfortunate Queen Caroline. One of the finest chapters in the history of the American Bar is the fact that

after the Boston massacre and amid all the tumult which culminated in the Revolution, two leaders of the popular party, John Adams and Josiah Quincy, offered to defend the British soldiers, who were charged with murder, and it is to the greater credit of a Boston jury that it so far arose above popular passion that the soldiers were acquitted.

The lawyer must sometimes share with his client public odium, and stand between a relentless public opinion and its victim. In defending the rights of the individual, he must often contravene the interests of the many. In thus appealing from "Philip drunk to Philip sober," the lawyer necessarily runs counter to public opinion, which, balked of its prey, visits in the blind passion of the hour its wrath upon the Bar and Judiciary.

The lawyer, if he respects the exalted nature of his profession, will be indifferent to the passing passion of the hour. He has no more right to betray the cause of justice because of the unpopularity of his client than the judge on the Bench has to pronounce judgment against him for like reason. Mr. Justice Cresswell, when once charging a jury, uttered some sentiments that caused a wave of applause to go through the court room. He quickly stopped, and sharply and sternly said:

> "The administration of justice is in great danger when the applause of a court is agreeable to a judge's ear."

The remark could be applied with almost equal force to the lawyer, who, if he regard his profession as something more than a trade, must not be affected by popular passion or personal interest. It thus not infrequently happens that the duties of a lawyer call for the greatest courage and the finest moral heroism. Lord Mansfield, in pronouncing a most unpopular judgment in the face of threats not only of royal displeasure and social ostracism, but of assassination, well said:

> "I wish popularity, but it is that popularity which follows, not that which is run after. It is

that popularity which sooner or later never fails
to do justice to the pursuit of noble ends by
noble means. I will not do that which my conscience tells me is wrong upon this occasion to
gain the huzzas of thousands or the daily praise
of all the papers which come from the press. I
will not avoid doing what I think is right
though it should draw upon me the whole artillery of libels, all that falsehood and malice can
invent or the credulity of a deluded populace
can swallow."

Such should be the spirit of every lawyer, and in these
days, when trial by newspaper has nearly supplanted trial
by the courts of law, such spirit is sorely needed.

Thus far my view of the lawyer in relation to social
progress has been rather retrospective and perhaps I have
unnecessarily defended the profession against some of the
criticism to which it has been subjected.

It remains to consider very briefly the future and here
I must, for lack of time, restrict my discussion to a single
thought.

Although the present system of justice has been painfully evolved by centuries of experience and needs but
little amendment and that chiefly in the detail of procedure, yet the greatest constructive work of the lawyer
still remains to be done. This crisis in the history of
nations has shown that international law largely existed
in name and has yielded too quickly and abruptly to a
condition of international anarchy. International conventions are little higher than comity or etiquette. It
may be doubted whether international law in the proper
sense of the term ever did exist, for a law implies not
merely a commandment but a paramount authority to
enforce that commandment and to punish its violation.

While the work of the jurists and diplomats had prior
to the first day of last August built up a system of jurisprudence, in which it is plain we put exaggerated confidence, and to which it gave the euphemistic title of international law, yet as its observance was voluntary with

each nation and existed only by comity and as there was no paramount authority to enforce its vital obligations, it may be doubted whether the word "law" was ever used with any degree of accuracy.

After this terrible war is over there will arise from every part of the globe an insistence that its repetition shall be prohibited and that the relations of the different States shall be fixed by some permanent and enforcible laws. We lawyers know that this of necessity will require an international legislature to enact such laws, an international judiciary to interpret them and above all some co-operative effort to enforce them. This does not mean necessarily the creation of a universal State, in which the present States of the world would be submerged, but it does mean that, with which modern times have made us familiar, a league of States, such as your great British Empire and the great American Republic of which I am a citizen. These noble commonwealths have pointed the way to the establishment of collective responsibility tempered by local autonomy.

To the rest of the world this cure for international anarchy may seem in the highest degree visionary, but to the lawyer, who has studied the slow evolution of centuries in the development of the reign of law, it is not altogether a dream, although the world is probably centuries behind its realization.

Had all the signatories to the Hague Convention agreed that they would unite to suppress the attempt of any member or of any nation to disturb the peace of the world by an unnecessary appeal to force, and had they all last July fulfilled their respective obligations, this great war would never have been. With the audacity of a madman, Germany and Austria challenged the greater part of Europe, but assuredly they would never have precipitated a war if there had been sufficient solidarity in civilization to make all civilized nations collectively responsible and mutually helpful for the suppression of the Dual Alliance's attempt to impose force upon a weaker State without resort to negotiation, mediation and arbitral justice.

The magnitude of this war, with its burden of losses to the entire world, demonstrates as no other war has done the absolute necessity of some system of co-operative effort and collective responsibility for the enforcement of international customs, which would then become laws in the truest and highest sense.

Every war ought to be regarded as a civil war, for civilization does exist as an organic entity, even though it has as yet no adequate political organization. The time will come when there will be in truth and fact "the Supreme Court of Civilization," of which I have elsewhere written, and that day may be sooner than any of us anticipate. Let us hope and pray that this war may be the travail of mankind, of which a better era will be born.

God speed the day when, not as a poet's dream but as the crowning achievement of the jurist and the statesman, there may be in fact and not merely in fancy, "The Parliament of Man and the Federation of the World."

Gray's Inn Hall, London.

V

HOW LAWYERS WORKED AND PLAYED IN TUDOR TIMES

What Mecca is to the devout Mussulman the Inns of Court should be to the English-speaking lawyer, for these "noblest nurseries of humanity in the Kingdom," as Ben Jonson called them, are the true fountain-head of our Anglo-Saxon jurisprudence.

As a master of the Bench of Gray's Inn, Mr. Beck has taken a peculiar interest in its history and the following address, which he delivered before the Ohio Bar Association at Cleveland on January 24, 1929, tells a fascinating story about the Christmas Revels at Gray's Inn in the winter of 1594-5. The editor believes that the preparation of this address must have been a peculiar gratification to Mr. Beck, for it enabled him to connect his beloved Inn with Shakespeare, a subject no less dear to his heart than the law. He has been a life-long student of Shakespeare and is a member of the Board of Governors of the Stratford Memorial Theatre and a member of the Shakespeare Society of Philadelphia, which is believed to be the oldest Shakespearean society in the world. Mr. Beck's conjecture that Shakespeare, in the so-called "missing" years (1585-92), may have been a student of Gray's Inn and thus gained the friendship of the Earls of Southampton and Pembroke, both members of the Inn and subsequently patrons of the great poet, is very interesting.

The whole address develops an unwritten and remarkable chapter in the history of the English-speaking Bar.

—EDITOR.

Mr. Chairman and Gentlemen:

I greatly appreciate the compliment of your invitation. It is always an honor to a lawyer to be invited by his brethren of the Bar to address them and, whenever opportunity offers, it gives me special satisfaction to do so.

On these occasions I have generally tried to lead my auditors from the broad, but somewhat arid, highway of the practice of the law into the fascinating by-paths, which deal with its historic background. To-night I shall take you into an almost forgotten by-path and it may seem so far removed from the dusty highway of our profession that you may think my speech ill-adapted to a meeting of the Bar. If so, I shall have to imitate the bland candor of the Southern lawyer who was arguing a writ of error from the highest court of a state in the Supreme Court of the United States. Twice a member of the Court asked him as to what federal question was involved in the case which would justify the writ of error. He ignored the question twice and proceeded calmly to discuss the merits of his case, when the same Justice, somewhat testily, said: "I have asked you twice, what is the federal question in this case, and now I want an answer." The lawyer looked up to the Bench with smiling assurance and said: "Who said there was a federal question in the case?" and, before the Court had recovered from its astonishment, he added: "I come from a section of the country where the surest way to lose a case is to say there is a federal question in it."

Perhaps, therefore, you may feel that the historic narration, which I am going to give you, is far removed from that class of legal topics which are generally discussed on occasions of this character. If my speech was, as indicated in my title, on the Inns of Court, its appropriateness could scarcely be questioned, for these historic law guilds remain today as they were in Elizabeth's time, to quote Ben Jonson, "the noblest nurseries of humanity in the Kingdom." However, my speech deals only with one of these Inns of Court, and the Inn which honored me by calling me to the English Bar and of which I am very proud to be a Bencher.

I do not know how many of this audience have actually visited Gray's Inn. The very name, to the layman, would suggest some kind of a hotel of an old-fashioned character, but the word "Inn," as applied to these Inns of Court, refers rather to the four law guilds in which London lawyers for many centuries have lived together to study and practice law. Of these, the oldest is either Gray Inn's or the Middle Temple.

The next time you are in London, whether you are a lawyer or a layman, go down Holborn and just before you reach Staple Inn, one of the last relics of Tudor England on the broad highways of that great city, and before you come to its junction with Chancery Lane, you may perceive, if your eyes are acute, an ancient gatehouse. If you enter and thread a narrow alley, you will suddenly find yourself in the Sixteenth Century and, indeed, in the centuries that are before. To the tumult and confusion of the great city an almost Sabbath serenity has succeeded. You are transported back to an era centuries before the railroad, or the telegraph, or the steamship. "Nothing else in London," Nathaniel Hawthorne wrote, "is so like the effect of a spell as to pass under one of these archways and find yourself transported from the jumble, rush, tumult, uproar, as of an age of week-days condensed into the present hour, into what seems an eternal Sabbath. It is very strange to find so much of ancient quietude right in the monster city's very jaws—which yet the monster shall not eat up—right in its very belly, indeed, which yet in all these ages it shall not digest and convert into the same substance as the rest of its bustling streets."

It is not strange that we must resort to literary men, rather than to lawyers, for the best descriptions of these Inns, for many of the masters of English literature either were originally students of the various Inns, or, at least, had chambers adjacent to the Inns and lived in close association with the lawyers. During the Renaissance and, indeed, even in feudal times, the Inns of Court included the leading men of the social world. The inmates of the Inn were as intimate with the Royal circle and the great nobles as with the men of affairs of the city. In former days, after leaving Oxford or Cambridge, the sons of the well-to-do turned to the Inns, whether they intended to study law or not, and it was a kind of common ground on which the different classes of society met.

Thus, between the commercial adventurers of the London Company, which founded Virginia, and the young noblemen of Gray's Inn, there was a very close connection, as there was between the lawyers of the Inn and the men of the theatre. There evidently was an intimate connection between the young Earl of Southampton and Shakespeare, and some think that the marvelous sonnets of the latter were addressed, in part, to this young Earl, and it is not improbable, as I shall hereafter point out, that Shakespeare's acquaintance with the Earl of Southampton and later with the Earls of Pembroke and Montgomery, to whom the First Folio was dedicated, commenced in Gray's Inn.

As I cannot visualize the Inns for you, unless you have seen them, the next best thing is to quote Thackeray, who himself was a student of the Middle Temple and who was simply narrating his own experiences in those charming chapters of *"Pendennis,"* where he describes the association of Arthur Pendennis (Thackeray himself) and George Warrington. It is believed that George Warrington was not a fictitious character and it is said that the original of this character was a man by the name of Venables. Let me, therefore, simply quote a passage from *"Pendennis,"* which seems to give the best picture of an Inn and which illustrates the close association which existed in Victorian days between the journalist and the lawyer.

"Nevertheless, those venerable Inns, which have the lamb and flag and the winged horse for their ensigns, have attractions for persons who inhabit them, and a share of rough comforts and freedom which men always remember with pleasure. I don't know whether the student permits himself the refreshment of enthusiasm, or indulges in poetical reminiscences as he passes by historical chambers, and says: 'Yonder Eldon lived; upon this site Coke mused upon Lyttelton; here Chitty toiled; here Barnewall and Alderson joined in their famous labours; here Byles composed his great work upon bills, and Smith compiled his immortal leading cases; here Gustavus still toils, with Solomon to aid him'; but the man of letters can't but love the place which has been inhabited by so many of his brethren or peopled by their creations, as real to us at this day as the authors whose children

they were; and Sir Roger de Coverley walking in
the Temple Garden and discoursing with Mr.
Spectator about the beauties in hoops and
patches who are sauntering over the grass is just
as lively a figure to me as old Samuel Johnson
rolling through the fog with the Scotch gentlemen at his heels on their way to Dr. Goldsmith's
chambers in Brick Court; or Harry Fielding,
with inked ruffles and a wet towel round his
head, dashing off articles at midnight for the
'Covent Garden Journal,' while the printer's boy
is asleep in the passage."

As you enter the first quadrangle of Gray's Inn, you
will see on three sides buildings not more ancient than the
time of Queen Anne and the Georges, and they are the
most recent constructions; facing you, as you come
out of the alley, is an old hall, built in the year 1555 under
the direction of Sir Nicholas Bacon, the father of Francis
Bacon and the Lord Keeper of the Seal under Elizabeth.
Indeed, the building itself is much more ancient than 1555,
for Nicholas Bacon himself said that he simply "reedified"
it and that this old Tudor hall, which claims to be the
oldest of the four Inns of Court, was formerly an
old manor house that had stood there for many centuries,
the origin of which is veiled in the mists of obscurity. This
old manor house, at that time far beyond the built-up
portion of London, was called the Manor of Portpool, and
was owned by a Justice of the town of Chester, whose
name was Gray, and in that way it became "Gray's Inn."
There he lived, in his feudal manor with its great hall, of
which probably the present Gray's Inn Hall is simply a
modern form, his windmills, barns and various *etceterae* of
a medieval manor.

As you know, prior to the time of Edward I there was
no Bar of England. Strange as it may seem, no litigant
was then permitted to have counsel to plead his own case,
except the King, who, because of his superior dignity, was
represented by an Attorney-General. The Bar itself was
a child of the Church and originally its functions were
discharged almost wholly by ecclesiastics. When, in the

reign of Edward I, a cleric was forbidden to practice law in the civil courts, and when, with the coming of more modern times and usages, a litigant, especially if a woman or child, was allowed to employ some one to plead his or her case in court, a group of men, called "common law" lawyers, were accustomed to group themselves around the portals of St. Paul's Cathedral, somewhat in the manner of the ambulance-chaser of the present day, to seek employment from any litigant who needed a lawyer. That was the origin of the Bar of England.

The theatre, then the most popular social institution of the day, was, like the bar, the child of the Church, for the modern theatre had its origin in the "Miracle" plays that were given in the churches in medieval times. Thus, the theatre and the Bar are, in a sense, twin children and, like twin children, there are many resemblances between them, for courts, lawyers and even judges have a histrionic character. Shakespeare suggests this in his "Seven Ages of Man," when he describes the learned justice, "with eyes severe and beard of formal cut; full of wise saws and modern instances," and then he slyly adds, with a touch of sarcasm, "and so he plays his part."

Gradually the itinerant lawyers formed themselves into groups to study law and, finally, they formed what are now called the four "Inns of Court." One group, in the Thirteenth Century, leased from the Knights of St. John what is now called the Middle Temple. From that came the offshoot of another group that formed the Inner Temple; another group formed Lincoln's Inn and, as we of Gray's Inn fondly believe, anterior to all three of those Inns was a group of lawyers who, preferring to go beyond the city walls, rented, some time in the Fourteenth Century, from Justice Gray this manor house, in order that, in the seclusion of rural life, they could study law.

Men at that time could only study law if they were "well born," not merely because of a certain social caste that prevailed, but also because it was no inexpensive process to qualify for the Bar, as you will presently see. They were, for the most part, the younger sons of the nobility of England. "The younger sort," says Stow, "are either gentlemen, or the sons of gentlemen, or of other most welthie persons." They would go to Oxford and Cambridge and, having graduated at one or the other, they could, if they intended to practice law as a profession, enter the subordinate Inns that were called the "Inns of Chancery," which were not connected with courts of equity but were preliminary schools to one of the four Inns of Court. Their novitiate over, they attached themselves to one of the four Inns. They assumed a garb appropriate to the Inn and were obliged to submit to almost monastic discipline. They must attend chapel at stated times and have their three meals with their associates. They were obliged for seven years, originally eight, to study law in the Inn before they could qualify for the Bar. "For the space of seven years or thereabouts," says Stow, "they frequent readings, meetings, boltinges, and other learned exercises, whereby growing ripe in the knowledge of the lawes, and approved withal to be of honest conversation, they are either by the general consent of the Benchers or Readers, being of the most aunctient, grave and judiciall men of everie Inn of the Court, or by the special privilege of the present Reader there, selected and called to the degree of Utter Barristers, and so enabled to be Common Counsellors and to practise the law, both in their Chambers and at the Barres."

As such students, they were called Inner Barristers, meaning, as we would say, merely law students. Their studies, of course, included not merely the reading of the comparatively few textbooks that at that time existed, but, above all, they had the practical training of going to Westminster Hall and hearing the various courts of law and equity in the practical administration of justice.

When they returned to the Inn, after a meeting at Westminster Hall, and had dinner, which was generally about one o'clock in the afternoon, these students were submitted to what was called "boltings," meaning simply the "sifting" of their knowledge by oral examination. The older lawyers—because a man did not leave his Inn when he became a senior member of the Bar—would take these students in hand during this seven years' probation and each veteran systematically sifted the knowledge of the student to ascertain whether he really knew what he pretended to know.

Then, as the afternoon wore along and evening came, the horn sounded for dinner and they came again into the old Tudor Hall—its floor covered with rushes and in the center a great fire on the rather cold nights of an English fall and winter—and would find, as Dugdale says, "a paper containing notice of the Case which was to be argued after dinner laid upon the salt." "Then," he continues, "after dinner, an Inner Barrister advanced to the table and propounded in Law French some kind of an action on behalf of an imaginary client. Another Inner Barrister replied for the defendant and thereupon two Utter Barristers argued the question and the Reader and the Benchers then gave their opinions in turn."

Thus the evening would wear away and, as Mr. Pepys long afterwards would say, "and so to bed."

But the work of the day, from morning to night, was not wholly that of hard work, because, as we will see, young students of the Inn, when they were supposed to go to Westminster Hall, in the truant spirit of youth, probably often went down to the River Thames, which at that time was not a great avenue of commerce, but was virtually, as the Grand Canal of Venice, the great promenade of fashion in Elizabeth's time. If you could imagine the London of Shakespeare's day, you would see a great and noble river lined with splendid palaces, of which only Somerset House remains, up and down which the fashion of London went in boats and stately barges. Or, these same students, if they did as we can well believe they did, might play truant and cross London Bridge to the Globe Theatre. Or, if they did not cross the Bridge, to the Blackfriars Theatre, or any one of the eleven theatres of London of that time. Thus, the student of Gray's Inn, at the time to which I refer, could have had the inestimable satisfaction of seeing "Hamlet" or "Macbeth" or "Othello" performed for the first time on any stage; he could even have mingled with the actors after the play

was over and have seen Shakespeare go to his home in
Little Silver Street, or Heminge or Burbage to their homes;
or any of the other idols of the day, for the theatre was
the great interest of Elizabethan England, out of which
grew the most splendid drama that the modern world has
known.

After a student had had seven years of this preliminary
training, he was then admitted to the Bar and became
what was called an "Utter Barrister." The origin of this
name is very doubtful. Doctor Johnson explains the word
"utter" to mean that he was a complete barrister; that is,
a full-fledged lawyer. The other explanation is that these
Utter Barristers sat in a post of honor away from the
Benchers' table, whereas, the Inner Barristers sat below
them and in a place of less dignity. No one could become
an Utter Barrister unless he had taken parts in the Moots
and there was a proviso that "anyone who procured letters from any great person to the Treasurer or Benchers
in order to be called to the Bar, should forever be disqualified from receiving that degree within that House."

Then, after a man had been an Utter Barrister for a
certain number of years, he became an Ancient, or what
we would call the "Senior" Bar, and, from the Ancients,
the Benchers, who were the great governing body, would
each year select two Readers.

The first function of the Reader was to give a costly
banquet, because the men of that time had gargantuan
appetites and the burden of expenses was so great that
finally, in one of the Inns, they had to provide that a
Reader should not spend in his inaugural banquet more
than a sum that, in modern purchasing money, would
be $8,000. Up to that time they had spent a great deal
more.

These two Readers would, on stated nights during the
sessions, deliver lectures, selecting some statute, like the
Statute of Uses, which Bacon, when he was a Reader,
selected, and would expound the theory of the statute,
the questions arising under it and the decisions of the
courts with respect to it.

After the Reader had finished, although he had reached

the august dignity of being selected from the Ancients, the Benchers would sit in judgment upon the lecture and dissect it.

The final Order was, of course, to be a Bencher. When a man had been an Ancient a sufficient number of years he was then elevated to the Bench and dined upon the platform a little above the rest of the hall, as today, and there he was privileged to sit at the table as the authority, or, at least, as one of the body who had the exclusive right to call to the Bar and to disbar.

Perhaps I could best illustrate all that I have said upon this point by taking the case of Francis Bacon, of whom I shall speak a little later. It was an age of remarkable precocity. Men entered college at an age which seems to us almost inconceivable. Bacon entered Cambridge in his thirteenth year and graduated in his sixteenth. Remember that all the academic instruction of Cambridge was in the Latin tongue. After leaving Cambridge he became a student of Gray's Inn and by thirty-three years of age —a period, therefore, of about seventeen years—he had become an Ancient of Gray's Inn. He finally became a Bencher and, indeed, the treasurer of the Inn, which is its highest office.

One would think, from the description that I have given, that these young men of the Elizabethan period, of such tender years as compared with students of law of our time, would have had a hard and grueling time in qualifying for the Bar, but, as a matter of fact, they had many sports and revels to mitigate the severity of their studies. Fortescue, who wrote in the Fifteenth Century, says:

> "There is both in the Inns of Court and the Inns of Chancery, a sort of an Academy or Gymnasium fit for persons of their station, where they learn singing and all kinds of music, dancing and revels."

Of their festival days, the same writer says:

> "After the offices of the Church are over, they employ themselves in the study of sacred and

profane history; here everything which is good
and virtuous is to be learned, all vice is discouraged and banished. So that knights, barons, and
the greatest nobility of the Kingdom often place
their children in these Inns of Court to form
their manners and to preserve them from the
contagion of vice."

Beyond the Tudor Hall, of which I speak, is a noble
garden, which Francis Bacon himself laid out. You know
it was Bacon who said: "God Almighty first planted a
garden. And indeed it is the purest of human pleasures."
He found his purest pleasure in laying out this garden
of Gray's Inn and, if you will go there, you will see the
stump of an old tree, a catalpa, which is said to have
been promised to Bacon by Raleigh when the latter parted
from Bacon in this same garden, and began his last trip
to South America in search of "El Dorado."

For seventy-five years before the events that I shall
narrate, the Inn at Christmas had some kind of a play,
or masque; a masque being the nearest approach to what
we would call "comic opera," except that it was allegori-
cal in character. These fanciful extravaganzas, with music
and acting, were forms of dramatic entertainment fifty
years before there was a theatre in London. Gray's Inn,
as all the Inns of Court, therefore, had their original plays and produced them, especially at Christmas time,
before the theatre had grown as a professional institution
in England.

The custom seems to have been an old one and I imagine
it has its obvious explanation in the rather unfortunate
climate of England and, especially, London. The autumns
and winters are apt to be cold, rainy and foggy and the
Briton's exceptional love of summer and sunshine and
the consequent love of sport can thus be explained, as
well as the fact that your Englishman, with the gloom
of long winter nights and the desire to raise his spirits
above its influences, is dependent upon the spirits, which
in this country are forbidden, although not prevented, by
the Eighteenth Amendment.

When the turn of the year comes and the days commence to lengthen, the Englishman, both as a Christian and a pagan, desires to celebrate the event by some joyous festivities and thus, in the King's Court, as well as in the rudest hovel, there has always been a desire at Christmas time to have a season of revelry. The great English nobles, as late as Shakespeare's day, had their own special companies of actors to enliven the winter months, and the King himself had his Master of the Revels for the same purpose. The Universities of Oxford and Cambridge indulged in the same seasonal pastimes. It would have been strange if the lawyers, living in monastic seclusion, had escaped this tendency and, as far back as the records are preserved, one finds the evidence of this spirit of revelry at Christmas tide. The records of the Inner Temple show revels, of the kind that I shall describe, as early as the year 1505, while the first account of these revels describes those which took place at Christmas, 1561, in the Middle Temple, in honor of Robert Dudley, Earl of Leicester. It did not differ in kind from the revels that I shall presently describe and the only reason why I select the revels of the Christmas season of 1594-5 for this address is that we have a full and comprehensive account of them written by one who was clearly an eyewitness.

Another feature of the revels was the fact that, while engaged in them, all distinction between the Bench and the Bar was forgotten. A Judge was only a lawyer, and this is true today of the Inns of Court, where, as I have had frequent occasion to notice, the Judges, at the recess for lunch, leave the Bench and join their fellow-barristers of their Inn and forthwith all distinction is forgotten and the most frank and joyous *camaraderie* prevails. I am inclined to think that the English Judge, except when he has his wig and gown, is not so austere as his brethren of the American Bench. One of Queen Elizabeth's Lord Chancellors, Christopher Hatton, was called "the Dancing Chancellor," and it was of his manor house that Gray wrote:

"Full oft within the spacious walls
  When he had fifty summers o'er him,
The grave Lord Keeper led the brawls,
  The seal and maces danc'd before him.

"His bushy beard and shoestrings green,
  His high-crowned hat and satin doublet
Moved the stout heart of England's Queen,
  Though Pope and Spaniard could not trouble it."

There was, however, a special reason why the Christmas Revels of Gray's Inn in 1594 were especially notable and may have far surpassed any of their predecessors.

It so happened that the Christmas of 1594-5 was one in which there was a special reason for an expansion of human spirits. Prior to that there had been for two years a plague in London that had driven most of its inhabitants away, had caused the grass to grow in the streets and had caused thousands of deaths. Whether it was cholera, yellow fever, or typhus fever we do not know, but it was like one of those dreadful epidemics of the Middle Ages.

You will see a reference to this plague if you will take your "Hamlet" when you go home tonight. You will find that when Hamlet is told the players are coming to Elsinore to entertain him, he at once said: "How do they come here? How does it happen that they are traveling? Is it by reason of the recent inhibition?"

The "recent inhibition" was the order to close all theatres, because they feared the contagion of the plague.

When the plague of 1594 finally passed, with the resilience of human nature, there was a desire on the part of the barristers and students of Gray's Inn to have Christmas Revels that would far surpass any revels theretofore had. And this they did, because, so far as we know, nothing ever had equaled the revels of that year and it may be doubted whether anything ever subsequently surpassed them, unless we except the joint revels of the four Inns of Court that were given in honor of King Charles I and which cost, in the money of that day, 24,000 pounds, which I imagine, in the purchasing value of our day, would be nearly a quarter of a million dollars.

It is important that I should now give the documentary justification of this account; otherwise you may think I am indulging in fiction.

In the year 1688 there was printed in London a book, at present very rare except in the form of reprints, which was entitled *"Gesta Grayorum."* It purported to give the revels at Gray's Inn in the year to which I refer, as narrated by those who had not only witnessed them, but had actually taken part in them. It states that these accounts were written because the revels were so exceptionally noteworthy that it was felt some record should be left to posterity. While 1688 is a long time afterwards and the narration at that time of events that took place in 1594—a period almost a century before—might seem open to doubt, we have, fortunately, ample confirmation of the revels elsewhere.

In the first place, in the Pension Book of Gray's Inn, of which I am very happy to have a reprint, there is recorded in the April and May sessions of the Benchers the efforts to raise money to pay the deficit caused by the revels.

In the second place, in the course of these revels, there having always been terms of peculiar friendship between Gray's Inn and the Inner Temple, it appears that Gray's Inn invited the Inner Temple to send an ambassador to participate in the revels. We find in the Pension Book of the Inner Temple, before the revels took place, the appropriation by the Benchers of twenty marks to enable the ambassador and his retinue to proceed in due state to Gray's Inn on the occasion of these revels.

But we have an even more interesting and suggestive confirmation of the authenticity of the revels. About fifty years ago there was discovered in the library of the Duke of Northumberland an ancient folio manuscript in Elizabethan script. Originally the title page was a table of contents and that table discloses that the folio volume originally contained seven essays of Bacon's that were first printed in the year 1597, an essay by Sir Philip Sidney and the plays of Richard II and Richard III. On this table of contents some unknown scribbler, in Elizabethan script, has scrawled again and again, as though his hand was idly following the musings of his brain, the names "Francis Bacon, William Shakespeare"; in all sorts of variance: "W. Shakespeare," "Wm. Shakespeare," "Will Shakespeare," and so forth. In the table of contents, to which I refer, in addition to the seven essays already described, there is this entry: "Orations of Francis Bacon at Gray's Inn Revels." *"Gesta Grayorum"* contains these orations and the authoritative biographer of Bacon, Spedding, and other students of Bacon have always said that these orations clearly bear the indicia of Bacon's style.

Thus you have here the old Northumberland manuscript specifically referring to a given number of orations delivered at Gray's Inn Revels and you have the Revels themselves, containing the same orations, so I conclude that, while the Chronicler may have enlarged the story a little, nevertheless, we are dealing with documentary history. I may add that the supposition is, of which there is no adequate proof, that the "Gesta Grayorum" was printed from a manuscript that was taken from the Northumberland folio volume.

The account begins by reciting that "the great number of gallant Gentlemen that Gray's Inn afforded at Ordinary Revels, betwixt All-Hollantide and Christmas" had suggested and wished to have some Christmas Revels and for that purpose desired to select "an head answerable to so noble a body and a leader to so gallant a company." "After many consultations had hereupon by the youths and others that were most forward herein, at length, about the 12th of December (that is, 1594), with the consent and assistance of the Readers and Ancients, it was determined that there should be elected a 'Prince of Purpoole,' to govern our state for the time."

Of course, "Purpoole" was taken from the old manor house of Port Poole.

They thereupon selected one of their youngest students, who, according to the records of the Inn, had only entered in the preceding June, a young man named Mr. Henry

Holmes, a Norfolk gentleman, who apparently was of such rare accomplishments that one could almost apply to him the words that Ophelia applied to Hamlet. I quote the Chronicler: "Mr. Holmes was thought to be accomplished with all good parts, fit for so great a dignity; and was also a very proper man of personage, and very active in dancing and revelling."

Thereupon they constituted an imaginary kingdom within Gray's Inn. They selected Holmes as the Prince and assigned him, in the rooms about the old hall, royal chambers and a council chamber and all the *etceterae* of royalty. They divided up between all the students of the Inn, who probably numbered as many as two hundred, the various offices that would ordinarily go to a great court like that of Queen Elizabeth: Lord Chancellor and Lord Keeper of the Seal and Attorney-General, Solicitor-General, Speaker of the House, and so forth.

Having thus created this imaginary kingdom with every student assigned to a part, naturally the first thing to do was to raise money because it required very expensive stage settings, elaborate costuming, if it were to be well done, and, as a consequence, the Prince of Purpoole sent out a writ in legal language commanding all upon whom the writ was served, to subscribe.

As the first writ of assistance was not wholly successful, there was an *alias* writ issued and apparently the latter also failed to raise the necessary funds and they, thereupon, appealed to their friends at court, a number of whom contributed. Among these was Sir William Cecil, afterwards Lord Burleigh, who gave ten pounds and curiously enough, "a purse of fine needle-work." The significance of that gift passes my comprehension as the revels were not intended to be adapted to a ladies' sewing circle, as will presently appear.

Having thus financed the enterprise, Gray's Inn determined to invite their ancient friends of the Inner Temple. The next time you go to London, if you go to the Inner Temple, you will find over a portal the griffin, which is the emblem of Gray's Inn. And if you go to Gray's Inn, on an old gate that leads into Gray's Inn Lane,

you will find Pegasus, the flying horse, the emblem of
the Inner Temple. The ancient friendship of the two Inns
is indicated by the compliment that each permanently paid
to the other.

Gray's Inn did not want the Inner Temple to be lacking in these rare festivities and the Prince of Purpoole
thereupon dispatched an embassy to the Inner Temple,
which he called "The Kingdom of Templaria," and asked
them to appoint an ambassador with a full retinue to attend the great festivities that were about to be held. As
we will presently see, an ambassador, in gorgeous costume
and with twenty-five attendants from the Inner Temple,
came on the first of the great nights.

Upon the 20th of December, the Prince of Purpoole
was ready for his coronation. With all his train and in
splendid array, he marched from his lodging house, his
royal palace, so-called, and, as the chronicle says, "there
took his place on his throne, under a rich cloth of state;
his Counsellors and great Lords were placed about him;
and before him, at a table, sate his learned Council and
Lawyers; the rest of the officers and attendants took their
proper place."

Upon all being seated—mark you, there were one hundred men representing the different functionaries of a
royal court—the trumpets were commanded to sound
thrice, and the King at Arms, in a rich surcoat, stood forth
and proclaimed the title of the Prince. The chronicle says:
"After that the King at Arms had thus proclaimed his
style, the trumpets sounded again and then entered the
Prince's Champion, all in compleat armour, on horseback,
and so came riding round about the fire and in the
midst of the hall stayed and made his challenge, in these
words following:

> " 'If there be any man, of high degree or low,
> that will say that my Sovereign is not rightly
> Prince of Purpoole, as by his King at Arms
> right now hath been proclaimed, I am ready
> here to maintain that he lieth as a false traitor;
> and I do challenge in combat, to fight with him,

either now or at any time or place appointed;
and in token hereof I gage my gauntlet, as the
Prince's true Knight and his Champion.' "

Thereupon, the horseman slowly rode out of the hall,
and, there being none to challenge the right of the Prince
of Purpoole, the King was proclaimed with a great fanfare
of trumpets.

I must take from the first page of the *"Gesta Grayorum"* the titles of the Prince, because an Elizabethan
would have heard them with a broad grin, for reasons that
will presently appear. This is the title page of the book:

"The History of the High and Mighty Prince
Henry Prince, Prince of Purpoole, Arch-Duke
of Stapulia, Duke of High and Nether Holborn,
Marquis of St. Giles and Tottenham, Count
Palatine of Bloomsbury and Clerkenwell, Great
Lord of the Cantons of Islington, Kensing-
town, Paddington and Knightsbridge, Knight of
the Most Heroical Order of the Helmet, and
Sovereign of the same, Who Reigned and Died
A. D. 1594."

Any Elizabethan would have laughed at this recital, as
they did laugh that night, because all the places were dis-
reputable neighborhoods in the City of London.

The Prince having been duly crowned, the Attorney-
General arose and made a speech of congratulation and
the Prince made a gracious reply. Then the Solicitor-
General did the same, with a like reply.

Thereupon, the Homagers and Tributaries of the Prince
made obeisance, each one of them being a take-off on
some of the less reputable parts of London, as I have said.
Then a Parliament was held and a subsidy granted by the
Commons toward the support of his Highness. The King,
thereupon, pardoned everybody for all offenses and proceeded to give twenty exceptions, which comprised every
possible crime that any man could commit, so that at the
end of the pardon no one was really pardoned. The chronicle then says:

"Then his Highness called for the Master of the Revels, and willed him to pass the time in dancing; so his gentlemen pensioners and attendants very gallantly appointed, in thirty couples, danced the old measures, and their galliards, and other kinds of dances, revelling until it was very late; until it pleased his Honour to take his way to his lodging with sound of trumpets."

That was only a curtain-raiser to what was to follow.

When that first night's revelry was held, a great many ladies of the court were in attendance, and evidently there was dancing. The fame of the first night passed through London so that when the second night was about to be held, the crowds became so great as to be unmanageable and it was then that the incident occurred which brings us to the interesting grouping of the two most illustrious names of the Elizabethan age, namely, Francis Bacon and William Shakespeare.

Bacon at that time was about thirty-three years of age, and Shakespeare was thirty. After the birth of Shakespeare's twin children (Hamnet and Judith), he left Stratford, in 1588. Nothing more is known of him until the year 1592, when he is assailed by Greene, a rival dramatist, and charged with plagiarism.

In 1593 we know that he astonished the London world with the first of his love lyrics, "*Venus and Adonis*," and in 1594, the very year of these revels, he wrote the second of his great poems, "*The Rape of Lucrece*." There have been many conjectures, but the nearest approach to anything like evidence is the fact that among Shakespeare's companions there was a man by the name of Beeston. Beeston had a son whose name was Christopher Beeston. The son followed his father as a theatre manager and, in the time of the Restoration, the younger Beeston, was the veteran of the theatrical world of London. No one knew more than he about the lore of the stage. He could well have known and seen Shakespeare when he was a boy and was the son of a father who had known Shakespeare well. Beeston says that Shakespeare, after he left Stratford, was a school teacher in the country for about five years. That is all we know.

There are two mysteries about Shakespeare. The first is that the man who wrote the plays evidently knew a great deal about the stage. There are over three hundred references in the plays to the theatre, generally used, of course, only metaphorically, but the theatre in all its details was always in the mind of the writer of these plays. Upon the other hand, the law was in his mind also, and while he occasionally used legal terms inaccurately, his familiarity with current legal phrases cannot be questioned. Might not Shakespeare, between 1588 and 1592, have been a student at Gray's Inn? This would explain a great deal. How did the country boy become so quickly the protege and friend of the Earl of Southampton, also a student at the Inn and a little younger than Shakespeare, so that he could dedicate these two marvelous poems to him and make him his patron? How could he have better met him than if he had gone to the Inn as a student and in that way gained the friendship, which undoubtedly existed between one of the proudest nobles of the court and this country lad from Stratford, who amazed the whole world of London, as he has amazed the world ever since with the most stupendous imagination the world has ever known?

Shakespeare was then in London and we know that he was in the year 1594 a member of the Lord Chamberlain's Servants. That was a theatrical company. These students determined that, as a part of the second Night, they would have the Lord Chamberlain's Servants give one of the plays of their repertory in the hall of Gray's Inn and on the second night of the Revels, "*The Comedy of Errors*" was produced.

It may have been written especially for the occasion; one thing that would bear out such a suggestion is that it is the shortest of all Shakespeare's plays and it was apparently written for an entertainment which required some degree of brevity. Certainly, there is no mention of the "*Comedy of Errors*" before that time and its first printed appearance was in the First Folio seven years after Shakespeare's death. So it is quite possible that the "*Comedy of Errors*" was especially written for Gray's Inn and that the editors of the First Folio printed it from the Gray's Inn copy of the play. This of course, is conjecture.

The next Grand Night was intended to be upon Innocents-Day, which is three days after Christmas. The fame of the first night brought to the old Inn "a great presence of Lords, ladies, and worshipful personages," but, unfortunately, the crowd overtaxed the Inn. Here the incident occurs, as I have said, which gives historic interest to the occasion. I quote from the chronicle itself:

"When the Ambassador from the Inner Temple arrived in full state and very gallantly appointed and attended by a great number of brave gentlemen, about nine of the clock at night—when the Ambassador was placed, as aforesaid, upon the dais where the Prince of Purpoole sat and there was something to be performed for the delight of the beholders, there arose such a disordered tumult and crowd upon the stage that there was no opportunity to effect that which was intended; there came so great a number of worshipful personages upon the stage that might not be displaced, and gentlewomen, whose sex did privilege them from violence, that when the Prince and his officers had in vain, a good while, expected and endeavored a reformation, at length there was no hope of redress for the present."

The Ambassador of the Inner Temple and his twenty-five courtiers, "discontented and displeased," left the hall. The brave spirits of the Inn were not discomfited by this unfortunate *contretemps*, however, for the chronicle says:

"After their departure, the throngs and tumults did somewhat cease, although so much of them continued as was able to disorder and confound any good inventions whatsoever. In regard whereof, as also for that sports intended were especially for the gracing of the 'Templarians' (that is, the Inner Temple), it was thought good not to offer anything of account saving dancing and revelling with gentlewomen; and after such sports, a *Comedy of Errors* (like to Plautus) was played by the players, whereupon it was ever afterwards called "The Night of Errors."

While the play, I suppose, was a failure in the midst of all the confusion and there was much ill feeling, this did not daunt the ingenuity of these brave young spirits of Elizabeth's time. To turn the current of dissatisfaction into good feeling, they proceeded a few nights later to hold a mock trial. They indicted many retainers and Lords of the Prince of Purpoole and arrested them for having permitted "by sorceries and enchantments," the disorders of the preceding occasion. A formal trial was then held and among the charges against the defendants was that they had "foisted a company of base and common fellows to make up our disorders with a play of Errors and Confusions; and that that night had gained to us discredit and itself a nickname of Errors." This referred to Shakespeare's company, but was merely ironical. The defense was that no such confusion had taken place, but that it was "nothing else but vain illusions, fancies, dreams and enchantments."

In other words, it was in the nature of a plea of emotional insanity.

The Prince of Purpoole was the judge and, on the theory that the whole preceding night was an illusion, discharged all of the defendants and thus the mock trial ended.

The chronicle then says: "When we were wearied with mocking thus at our own follies, at length there was a great consultation had for the recovery of our lost honour. It was then concluded that first the Prince's Council should be reformed and some graver conceipts should have their places, to advise upon those things that were propounded to be done afterward."

On the 3rd of January the Revels continued, this time with a watch of armed men to guard the entrances and to prevent over-crowding and confusion.

In the meantime the fame of these Revels became the talk of London. It was then a town of less than 200,000 people and, naturally, an event of this kind interested so many important personages that it attracted a great deal of attention among all classes. On this next night it is said that "a great number of knights, ladies and very worshipful personages" attended, and "when they were all thus placed and settled in very good order," the chronicle continues, "the Prince came into the Hall with his

wonted state and ascended his throne at the high end of
the Hall, under his Highness' arms; and after him came
the Ambassador of the Inner Temple." Then followed
what in those times was called a masque, written by a
rival of Shakespeare, a poet called Campian, and to which
it is believed Bacon contributed a part. The masque dealt
with the great friendships of history and the two final
figures were representatives of Gray's Inn and of the Inner Temple in classic costume. This beautiful masque, in
honor of the ancient friendship between the Inns, was
evidently effective, for the chronicle adds:

"Thus was this shew ended, which was devised to that
end that those that were present might understand that
the unkindness which was growing betwixt the Templarians (the Inner Temple) and us, by reason of the former
Night of Errors and the uncivil behaviour wherewith they
were entertained, was now clean rooted out and forgotten,
and that we now were more firm friends."

Thereupon, the Prince, as a token of the reconciliation,
conferred upon the Lord Ambassador of the Inner Temple
the Knighthood of the Helmet. The Prince, coming down
from his chair of state, took a collar and put it around
the Lord Ambassador's neck and upon his twenty-four
associates. The Prince then stated the conditions of this
new Knighthood, some of which are of Rabelaisian humor,
and the final covenant of the Order contained a compliment to Elizabeth, who may possibly have been present:

"Lastly, all the Knights of this honorable Order, and
the renowned Sovereign of the same, shall yield all homage,
loyalty, unaffected admiration, and all humble service, of
what name or condition soever, to the incomparable Empress of the Fortunate Island."

A compliment not quite so beautiful as Shakespeare's
tribute to the Virgin Queen in "The Midsummer Night's
Dream" but having a little of the ring of Shakespeare's
imagery. Even the old Queen must have smiled when this
reference was made to the "incomparable Empress of the
Fortunate Island."

Then, after this conferring of the orders of knighthood,
there was a "variety of concert-musick" and what was

called a "running banquet," by which I suppose was meant a stand-up collation. A table was then set in the midst of the stage and six of the Lords of the Privy Council made communications on matters of state. These were the orations which all students of Bacon agree that he wrote and were, presumably, those which were at one time a part of the Northumberland Folio.

After this entertainment, the Prince arose from his seat and "made choice of a lady to dance withal; so likewise did the Lord Ambassador, the Pensioners and courtiers attending the Prince, and the rest of that night was passed in those pastimes."

The chronicle adds:

"The performance of this night's work did so delight and please the Nobles and other auditory that thereby Gray's Inn did not only recover the lost credit and quite take away all the disgrace that the former 'Night of Errors' had incurred; but got, instead thereof, so great honour and applause as either the good reports of our honourable friends that were present could yield or we ourselves desire."

The students now determined to branch out into the city, and having advised the Lord Mayor of London, who at that time lived at Crosby's Place, that the Prince of Purpoole desired to visit him in state, the Prince, with some seventy or eighty of the men on horseback, made a journey through the streets of London to the Lord Mayor's house. Every cavalier had a feather in his cap to distinguish his Inn—the "Grayans" using a white, and the "Templarians" an ash-colored feather.

"Thus they rode very gallantly through Chancery-lane, Fleet Street, and so through Cheapside, Cornhill and to Crosby's Place in Bishopsgate Street; where was a very sumptuous and costly dinner for the Prince and all his attendants, with variety of musick and all good entertainment."

After dinner, the Prince and his cavalcade returned in the same order to Gray's Inn, "the streets being thronged and filled with people to see the gentlemen as they passed by; who thought there had been some great Prince, in very deed, passing through the city. So this popular shew through the streets pleased the Lord Mayor and his Commonalty so well, as the great Lords and others of good condition and civility, were contented with our former proceedings."

The next night in the Revels was January 12th and again before a "worshipful company of Lords, Ladies and Knights." First came six Knights of the Helmet, with three whom they led as prisoners and were attired "like monsters and miscreants." The Knights said that these people were captured in the war against Russia.

After their departure, "six Knights entered in a very stately masque and danced a new devised measure; and after that, they took to them Ladies and Gentlewomen and danced with them their galliards, and so departed with musick."

Upon the dancing being ended, there appeared an Ambassador from the Mighty Emperor of Russia and Muscovy. Upon being received, he made a long address and the Prince a corresponding reply. Thereupon came a post-boy with "letters of intelligence concerning the state, from divers parts of his Highness' provinces," one of them being a letter from the Prince's Lord Admiral, which gave an account of a great naval action and which was audacious even for Tudor days. It is a masterpiece of witty Rabelaisian obscenity.

After the Ambassador had retired, the Prince took "a lady to dance withal, and so did the rest of the Knights and Courtiers; and after some time spent in reveling, the Prince took his way to his lodging and so the company dissolved and made an end of this night's work."

Evidently the students needed a little interval to devise some new revels, so the Prince of Purpoole announced that he intended to visit Russia and would not be back for some time. In the meantime, the students determined to make preparations for even more elaborate revels, but by this time the older lawyers were revolting at the use of the hall for such tom-foolery and the chronicle says, that on account of their objections "very good inventions, which were to be performed in public at his en-

tertainment into the house again, and two Grand Nights
which were intended at his triumphal return, were by the
aforesaid Readers and Governor made frustrate, for the
want of room in the hall, the scaffolds being taken away
and forbidden to be built up again."

On the 28th of January, when the members of the Inn
sat at dinner with the Readers or Benchers—I suppose
this was not welcome to these latter, who evidently wanted
to get back to work—the sound of a trumpet was heard
and the Prince's King at Arms entered and, in the name
of the Prince of Purpoole, commanded attendance upon
His Majesty "at the port of Black-wallia on the 1st of
February."

This summons contemplated a visit to no less a person
than Queen Elizabeth—not a mock visit, but a real one.

The chronicle says:

"The Prince and his train were met at Blackwall; from
whence they came up the River of Thames in a very
gallant shew." He and his retinue filled fifteen barges,
bravely furnished with standards, pendants, flags and
streamers; "there was also in every barge music and trumpets; and in some ordnance was shot." (I suppose small
cannon.) "Being thus gallantly appointed, we came on
our way by the Stairs at Greenwich (where Queen Elizabeth was in residence), where the ordnance was shot off
and the whole navy made a sail round about" for the
entertainment of the Queen.

The revellers sent a message asking permission to visit
the Queen. Elizabeth took the message in the best of
humor, although, of course, the whole thing was a mock-
ery, and made the following gracious answer:

"That if the letter had not excused his passing by, he
should have done homage before he had gone away,
although he had been a greater Prince than he was: yet,
she liked well his gallant shews, that were made at his
triumphant return." And the Queen added: "That if
he should come at Shrovetide, he and his followers should
have entertainment according to his dignity."

The Prince having received this invitation from the
Queen to return to Greenwich at Shrovetide, the

chronicler states that he and his retinue continued their course until they came to the Tower; where, by Her Majesty's commandment, he was welcomed by a volley of great ordnance by the lieutenant of the Tower.

"At the Tower-hill, there waited for the Prince's landing, men attending with horses, very gallantly appointed, to the number of one hundred and all very bravely furnished with all things necessary."

When the Prince and his retinue had mounted, they rode "very gallantly through Tower Street, Fenchurch Street, Gracechurch Street, Cornhill, Cheapside, and so through St. Paul's Church Yard."

To show the precocity of the boys of the times, they stopped at St. Paul's School—a school for little boys—and evidently all the students were released from class to see the parade. One of the boys had composed a Latin oration, in the nature of a greeting to the mighty Prince of Purpoole. This oration, which is in the *"Gesta Grayorum,"* is an extraordinarily clever piece of writing. "The oration being ended, the Prince rewarded the boy very bountifully and thanked them for their good will."

Then the riders continued their way to Ludgate and through Fleet Street, "where, as all the way else, the streets were so thronged and filled with people that there was left but room for the horsemen that were to pass."

In this state they returned to Gray's Inn, where the Prince was received "by a peal of ordnance and the sound of trumpets and all the good entertainment that his loving subjects could make." Then followed more dancing and reveling in the Inn on that and the following nights, but nothing else for want of the stage and scaffolds that had been taken down.

The end of the Revels was the visit to Queen Elizabeth and on this occasion another masque was given in honor of the Queen. After it had concluded, the chronicler says:

"For the present, Her Majesty graced everyone; particularly she thanked his Highness for the performance of all that was done; and wished that their sports had continued longer, for the pleasure she took therein; which may well appear from her answer to the Courtiers, who danced a measure immediately after the masque was ended, saying, 'What! Shall we have bread and cheese after a banquet?' "

Her Majesty willed that the gentlemen should be invited on the next day and that he should present them to her. Which was done and "Her Majesty gave them her hand to kiss, with most gracious words of commendation to them, particularly, and, in general, of Gray's Inn, as an House she was much beholden unto, for that it did always study for some sports to present unto her."

Upon the conclusion of this masque, they engaged in the sport of "tilting." This was a form of competition on horseback, in which the horses were separated by barriers or hurdles. Once again, young Holmes became the hero of the hour, because he tilted on horseback against the Queen's favorite, the Earl of Essex, and evidently discomfited Essex in the matter of horsemanship, for it is recorded that Holmes "behaved himself so valiantly and skillfully that he had the prize adjudged due unto him, which it pleased her Majesty to deliver unto him with her own hands, telling him that 'it was not her gift; for if it had, it should have been better; but she gave it him as that prize which was due to his desert and good behavior in those exercises; and that hereafter he should be remembered with a better reward from herself.' "

Holmes was subsequently knighted by James I and became a prominent noble in his court.

Thus, on Shrove Tuesday, on the eve of Lent, the Revels of Gray's Inn came to an end.

The chronicle quaintly ends with a compliment to Queen Elizabeth by saying that, while the Court of the Prince of Purpoole shone bright, "yet, at the royal presence of Her Majesty, it appeared as an obscured shadow; in this, not unlike the morning-star, which looked not cheerfully in the World, so long as the Sun looked not on it; or, as the great rivers that triumph in the multitude of their waters, until they come unto the Sea."

This seems to me so graceful that Shakespeare, himself, might have written it.

The fertility of imagination, the literary skill and the taste for beautiful pageants, which enabled these law stu-

Mr. Beck before the Privy Council

dents to invent and carry on these Revels can be explained
by the fact that there never was an age in which the imagination of man was so expanded as in the age of the Virgin
Queen. It was the climax of the Renaissance.

Three things had caused it. In the first place, the discoveries of astronomy had revolutionized all ideas of the
celestial universe. Through Keplar, Copernicus and Gali-
leo there dawned upon men this stupendous conception of
abysses of space.

Then, in the second place, there had been rediscovered
the classic treasures of Greece and Rome, which had caused
an immeasurable flowering of the human intellect.

And, finally, there had come the discovery of America.
America was only discovered about seventy years before
Shakespeare was born and about a century before the
events of which I speak and Shakespeare could have known
men who first heard the news that Columbus had discovered a new world. This discovery had immensely stimu-
lated the imagination of men in the Sixteenth Century.

Of this unprecedented flowering of the human intellect
the joyous sports of the law students of Gray's Inn in
1594-95 are one, but by no means an inconspicuous, example.

VI

ELIHU ROOT—LAWYER AND STATESMAN

This tribute to Elihu Root is a good example of the felicity of the style of Mr. Beck's after-dinner speeches. The occasion was a dinner given on February 13, 1925, by the Union League Club of New York City to Mr. Root on the eightieth anniversary of his birth.

Charles Evans Hughes, formerly Governor of New York and associate Justice of the Supreme Court of the United States, and later Secretary of State, now Chief Justice of the United States, was the first speaker of the evening, Mr. Beck followed with this address and Elihu Root responded in a reminiscent vein.—EDITOR.

Mr. President, Mr. Root, and Fellow Members of The Union League Club:

It is a privilege to participate in this tribute of respect and affection for a distinguished member of this Club, and I regard it as a great honor that I should be selected as one of the interpreters of your good will.

Speaking between the present Secretary of State and a past Secretary of State, I feel very much as a little minnow attempting to breast the vasty deep between two great whales; or if I can vary the metaphor, I may liken myself to a small elephant attempting to keep pace between two larger members of the herd. I recall in my reading of the classics that the great Roman naturalist, Pliny, records the interesting fact that whenever a herd of elephants is about to cross a stream, the older ones send the smaller elephants first, and for this the great naturalist of antiquity gave two reasons. The first was that the older elephants wished to see whether the river was full of crocodiles, and the second and more charitable explanation suggests some solicitude for the smaller elephant, for if the larger elephants crossed first they were likely to deepen the bed of the stream with their mighty feet and thus the little elephants would be in danger of getting beyond their depths and drowning. Tonight, the smaller elephant neither precedes nor follows, but is placed between two leaders of the herd in order that he may be as inconspicuous as in such distinguished company he should be.

It is a tempting opportunity to pay a tribute to each of these distinguished public servants, but this is Mr. Root's night, and I am very much in the position of *Macheath*, in The *Beggar's Opera*, when he said, or rather sang:

> "How happy could I be with either,
> Were t'other dear charmer away!"

After the very eloquent address to which we have just listened, mine must be an anti-climax, as it will also be an undesirable postponement of the pleasure that is to follow in hearing from the distinguished guest of tonight. One remark of the Secretary prompts me to say that, if Mr. Hughes, as he tells us, first saw Mr. Root with a "long procession of retainers" pressing forward to congratulate the new United States district attorney, then I confidently predict that the retiring Secretary of State, when he resumes his practice at the New York bar, will, at no distant period, have another and a different "long procession of retainers" crowding upon him. (Laughter and applause).

This occasion is as unique as it is interesting. It is not often that eighty years finds a distinguished publicist, who has known the dust of the arena, still in the fighting armor of public service, with his eye undimmed and his natural force unabated. To look at Mr. Root is to wonder whether we are not tonight the victims of a practical joke and whether he has really arrived at fourscore years. As a French courtier once said of Madame de Maintenon, we prefer to say that Mr. Root is only twenty years of age four times. (Laughter and applause). Today finds Mr. Root still in the arena of public affairs and still giving his masterful intellect to a wide variety of useful causes.

When Benjamin Franklin had attained the age of eighty years—and how much more this ripe age then made a man a venerable sage than it does today—the great philosopher, in writing his will, wrote himself down simply, "I Benjamin Franklin, printer, of Philadelphia;" and this notwithstanding the fact that he had retired from the craft of printing when forty years of age and had received honors which in variety and splendor have never had a parallel in the history of this country or of any country.

I imagine that if Mr. Root should have occasion to make a similar characterization of himself, he would be content tonight to write himself down as "I, Elihu Root, lawyer, of New York," for that designation not only suggests the foundation of his great career, but constitutes his greatest field of service.

He has been a very great lawyer — few, if any, greater in this generation. For many years he has played a conspicuous role in the most masterful of professions. As all great lawyers, he has not lacked enemies, but these attacks, considering their source, are to be accounted as only an added honor to the many which he has received.

There are different kinds of lawyers. Some have had in very high degree the qualities of the advocate. Such was Rufus Choate. Others have had less of the fiery passion of the advocate and more of the judicial mind and the well-poised brain. Such was John Marshall. Few like Mr. Root have been rich in both qualities. He has been both a great advocate and a great legal philosopher; but, if I am at liberty to estimate his professional career tonight, I would say that the judicial quality of his mind impresses me more than even his forceful qualities as an advocate.

In this connection, may I suggest that those who gave him in baptism his Christian name must have had something of the gift of prophecy. I shall venture now upon a Biblical reference, which Bishop Manning will understand, but I cannot hope that all the members of the Union League Club will follow. (Laughter and applause). In my judgment the noblest poem in all literature is the Book of Job. I do not think that any Greek dramatist, or even our own English-speaking Shakespeare, ever reached the height of sublimity as did the unknown writer of that masterpiece of ancient literature. It was in that wonderful drama that we first hear of the character of Elihu. You will remember, or at least Bishop Manning will, that

Job had a long debate with his three friends — doubtful comforters at best — as to the origin and explanation of evil in the world. The debate was not purely an intellectual debate; at times it was highly emotional. The participants from time to time lost their temper, and the argument proceeded not so much as a reasoned exposition of an insoluble problem as an emotional and passionate discussion of the relative positions of the disputants. The three comforters, Eliphaz, Bildad, and Zophar, bitterly upbraided Job for his passionate protest against the justice of God in inflicting suffering upon an innocent man; while Job, in turn, arraigned his friends for lack of sympathy and cried: "Miserable comforters are ye all."

When the debate had spent its force, the writer of this dramatic poem, or possibly some later writer, introduced the character of Elihu, who was a younger man than the others, but who was a man of crystalline intellect. He became the moderator of the greatest controversy on the greatest subject that has ever perplexed the world, namely, the existence of evil. Elihu, with his finely-poised intellect, felt that Job was neither wholly right nor wrong, and that his friends had equally seen but one side of the great problem. Elihu was thus the judicial mind in the great debate.

Was it not an unconscious prophecy when, eighty years ago, a little child lay in his cradle and was named Elihu, for no more appropriate name could be given to describe the crystalline character of his intellect; for, as I have followed that career for many years with the admiration that a junior should have for a masterful senior, I have always found that, while other men in discussing great questions are swayed with emotion and are led to extremes because of some reaction either to their own personal interests or their past prejudices, Mr. Root has approached the problems of the day as Elihu, in the Book of Job, approached his problem, with calm reflective intellect, that was not swayed with emotion, or led astray with selfish interest, but saw the question with the pellucid clarity of a mountain spring. (Applause).

I can better express this quality of both Elihus if I

may use the beautiful tribute that Hamlet paid to Horatio on the eve of the play scene:

"Since my dear soul was mistress of her choice,
And could of men distinguish her election,
She hath sealed thee for herself. For thou hast
    been
As one, in suffering all, that suffers nothing;
A man, that fortune's buffets and rewards
Hast ta'en with equal thanks; and blessed are
    those,
Whose blood and judgment are so well co-
    mingled,
That they are not a pipe for fortune's finger
To sound what stop she please."

Mr. Root has never been "a pipe for fortune's finger" or time or circumstance to sound what stop they please, but he has been one who, with judicial clearness, weighed the *pros* and *cons*, and when he had deliberately reached his conclusion it was generally a judgment that commended itself to the thoughtful and the discerning.   (Applause).

Lawyers may be classified into two other types. One is the class of which Mr. John G. Johnson, of Philadelphia, and my old partner, Mr. John W. Sterling, of this city, were conspicuous examples. To them the law was such a jealous mistress that they gave all their devotion to her, although it should not be forgotten that, in the case of each of them, while in their lifetime they restricted their energies to the practice of the law, in dying they bequeathed the accumulation of their toil to noble philanthropic purposes.

There is, however, another class of lawyers who are not content with merely being a lawyer. They believe, to use the fine phrase which I think is Lord Bacon's, that they are "indentured to the public service"; and just as Franklin, when he was forty years of age, gave the next forty years of his life to the service of his country and mankind, so it seems to me that the credit of Elihu Root's career is that, having gained a competence, nevertheless, with unlimited pecuniary possibilities before him, he dedicated, in the middle of his life and the prime of his power, the rest of his energies to the public service. What a service that has been!

Mr. Root has been something more than a lawyer. He has been a lawgiver, and, as such, has rendered service of such conspicuous usefulness that, by common consent, he is ranked as one of the great statesmen of an extraordinary age of human history.

One unhappy consequence of our "express-train" civilization is that the great achievements of unselfish public servants sometimes fail to receive that continuing appreciation which to men of noble mind is the richest reward of public service.

I could readily recall tonight many of Mr. Root's achievements as Secretary of War, Secretary of State, and Senator of the United States which were of exceptional and permanent value and yet in the mad rush of a feverish age are almost forgotten. Let me content myself with one.

A quarter of a century ago our nation was confronted with a novel responsibility, which was more pregnant with future consequences than any since the Civil War. One could say of it as Jefferson wrote Monroe at the time of the promulgation of the Monroe doctrine:

> "The question is the most momentous since that of independence. That made us a nation. This sets our compass and points the course which we are to steer through the ocean of time opening on us."

Admiral Dewey's victory had placed us in possession of islands in the Pacific Ocean. To return them to Spain was to disavow the justice of the war; to abandon them to other powers was unthinkable and might have then precipitated a world war, and yet to annex them to our country as permanent possessions was to cross a fateful Rubicon which might well give us pause. Fortunately for the American people, William McKinley was President and Elihu Root was Secretary of War. Of the former I shall say nothing, except to apply to him the tribute of an American historian to another William, the Silent:

"As long as he lived he was the guiding star
of a whole brave nation, and when he died the
little children cried in the streets."

To Washington is the glory of independent America.
To Jefferson that of continental America. To Lincoln
that of united America. To McKinley that of cosmopolitan America.

In the wise and noble solution of that great problem,
Elihu Root played a great part. As President McKinley's
Secretary of War, possibly no one contributed more to its
administrative details. Of many of the great public documents and measures, to which that fateful period in our
history gave rise, it can be said that while the signature
is that of William McKinley the text is that of Elihu Root.

To Cuba was given independence, and yet, under the
masterly guidance of Secretary Root, a beneficent circle
in the nature of a protectorate was drawn about the new-
born nation, which gave Cuba the opportunity of working out its own destiny, free from European interference.
To Porto Rico and the Philippines was given the measure
of self-government that was adapted to their capacity,
and no one can read the great principles of government
which the then Secretary of War prescribed for the administration of the Islands without wondering which is
the more admirable — their wisdom or their nobility.
These policies were fully vindicated by the results, and
if there be a Philippine problem today, it is not due to
the wise statesmanship of Root and Taft, but to the impracticable idealism of a later Administration, for which
neither Mr. Root nor his party is responsible.

If Mr. Root had done nothing more for his country and
mankind than to draw the chart and give the course to
the Ship of State in this turning point of our history, when
America became not only a power in the Orient but, potentially, the first power of the world, he would have
written his title clear to the admiration and gratitude of
his fellow men. In Cuba, Porto Rico, and the Philippines,
we fed the starving, clothed the naked, subdued the lawless, extirpated disease, opened hospitals and schools, made

the courts of justice free and impartial, and gave freedom to oppressed peoples.

It was a wise and noble policy that blessed those who gave as well as those who received, for while America may not have derived material advantages compensatory to its sacrifices, yet its vision was so broadened that it became possible sixteen years later, with a larger conception of her destiny, to take a decisive and heroic part in the greatest war in history.   Who shall say that a liberal civilization would not have perished in Europe if it had not been for the intervention of the United States in 1917?   Such intervention might not have been possible if it had not been for the wider vision of America's duty and destiny, which is due in part to the enlightened policy of President McKinley and the administrative statesmanship of Elihu Root.

I am weak enough to recall a fact which Mr. Root has doubtless forgotten.   It was my great privilege as Assistant Attorney General to co-operate with him in the great work which he then did.   It was not enough to prescribe a wise administration for these newly-acquired territories — it was essential to find justification in the Constitution for an unprecedented exercise of governmental powers. The application of certain clauses of the Constitution to countries which we were occupying under the war power became the subject of litigation, and it was my privilege as Assistant Attorney General to defend in the Supreme Court of the United States, in the case of *Neely* v. *Henkel,* the constitutionality of some of Mr. Root's acts.   This case became the forerunner of the later *Insular Cases.*   I only mention the fact to show a kindly trait of Mr. Root's character, for when the Supreme Court vindicated his policies, I received one day an envelope with the superscription of the War Department.   Opening it, I read with great delight a letter of appreciation from Secretary Root for my work in the argument of these cases.   It was a gracious act of a great lawyer to a young lawyer, and I have no doubt is only one of many similar kindnesses which he has shown to his juniors in the profession.

I must not postpone the pleasure that we all anticipate

in hearing Mr. Root, but there is another thought, to which I want very briefly to allude, because it seems to me the inspiring lesson of Mr. Root's career.

We are endeavoring in this country to solve on a scale of unprecedented vastness the great question of popular self-government. It is not by any means certain that we have solved it, but let us hope that we have. Time will tell. Certainly the experiment has not lasted so long that we can say, looking into that future with all its infinite possibilities, that the government, with so vast and heterogeneous an electorate, will always be workable in the absence of adequate leadership. After all, the successful career of the Republic has not been a very long one.

When I was a boy of fourteen years of age I might well have known in my native city of Philadelphia, though such was not my privilege, Horace Binney, the eminent lawyer, who was ninety-four years of age in the year 1874. He had seen Washington and Franklin engaged in conversation in front of Independence Hall.

I am persuaded that the problem of self-government in America will not be lastingly solved unless we can develop a leadership that is adequate to its great necessities. It is the greatest of all prerequisites to the successful working of democracy; for was it not well said by Cicero:

"Such as are the leading men of the State, such is the State itself."

Without such leadership, the future is, at best, doubtful, for I imagine that Mr. Root, who is a philosopher as well as a lawyer, will agree with me that, if our only reliance is upon the written limitations of a constitution, we may one day find that we have relied upon a bruised reed. Without adequate leadership, popular government is likely to become a failure.

One of the most discouraging symptoms of our time is the lessening interest of educated men in public affairs, and the decreasing disposition on their part to assume any responsibility in public life. One of the kindest foreign critics of our institutions, Lord Bryce, in his classic book, *The American Commonwealth*, has said:

"The proportion of men of intellect and social eminence who enter public life is much smaller in America than in each of the free countries of Europe."

I have discussed in my recent book, "The Constitution of the United States," the reasons that Lord Bryce assigns for this regrettable phenomenon, and have added some of my own. Two of the greatest of these reasons are the decay of representative principle as an ideal in our political life and the malicious attacks to which public men are too easily and unfairly subjected. Many proud and self-respecting men have much sympathy with Shakespeare's Coriolanus, who, in standing for the consulship, was disinclined to show his wounds to the gaping mob in the market place.

These and other reasons, while they afford some explanation of the reluctance of many men to go into the public service, do not excuse such failure. If the Republic is to survive, it can only be by the participation in public service of the best men of the nation — the "saving remnant," to use Matthew Arnold's phrase.

To me, the great lesson of Mr. Root's career is that he has given to every man of this generation a lustrous and inspiring example of unselfish consecration to the public service. If there were more Elihu Roots, there would be less ground for fear that one day the Republic may be found, like many strong men, to have died from the head downward.

We are privileged to have at this table tonight two great servants of the people, each of whom, in the very prime of his life, put behind him the great rewards of a lucrative profession and gave the best of his energies to the public service; but in all this country, how many men of the type of Mr. Hughes and Mr. Root can be found who are willing to make such a sacrifice?

In England the son of a father who has distinguished himself in the public service regards it not only his duty but his privilege to follow in his father's footsteps. The young English boy, who goes through Eton or Harrow, and then to Oxford or Cambridge, regards as the natural objective of his life an entry to Parliament or the public service; and far from there being, as in this country, sneering reflections on the man who either seeks office or holds office, to seek either is regarded in England as the normal manifestation of patriotism. In our country, with our preoccupation in its more material development, few men go into public life, and some of them do not even take the pains to vote on election day.

Mr. Root has always regarded the public service as the great aim of his life. How unselfishly, how magnificently, he has given the very best that is in him, every energy of his mind, every passion of his soul! He truly has been "indentured to the public service."

While he lives, his ambition is to serve the public, and, like old Stephen Girard, the banker of Philadelphia, Mr. Root could say:

"If I thought I was going to die tomorrow, I would plant a tree nevertheless today."

This is Mr. Root's spirit; and if there were other Roots in this country, if there were more men willing to work and die in the harness, there would be less occasion to talk of the deterioration in our public life or of the real and substantial dangers that threaten the Republic.

Mr. Root, you must know, because you are among lifelong friends, how much we honor you tonight! It was said by Shakespeare that the just rewards of an honorable age are: "Love, honor, obedience, troops of friends." You have them all.

"Love?" You have the love of family and friends.

"Honor?" You have the honor not of New York alone nor of the United States, but of the whole thinking world, for nowhere in the civilized world, where men of intellect and character work out the great problems of human existence, is the name of Elihu Root unknown.

"Obedience?" Why there are thousands who tread the paths of public usefulness that you have trodden and who owe much, very much, of the little success they have had in the public service to the fine inspiration of your example.

"Troops of friends?" Why those who are here tonight

are an infinitesimal minority of your host of friends. They are everywhere.

What a thought at eighty years of age to feel that you have not lived in vain; that you have fought a good fight; that you have kept the faith; that you have won the respect and esteem of men whose esteem and respect are indeed worth having.

Interpreting the views of all here about you and of many who are not privileged to be here, I know no better way to conclude my tribute to you than that prayer of the genial old pagan, Horace, when he said: "*Serus in coelum redeas.*"

VII

THE NATION AND THE STATES

On February 4, 1901, the centennial anniversary of the day when John Marshall took the oath of office as Chief Justice of the United States, a notable commemorative celebration took place in the city of Chicago, under the auspices of its bar. Mr. Beck was then Assistant Attorney General of the United States and was invited to respond to the toast, "The Nation and the States." At the time there had been much discussion throughout the United States as to the centralization of federal power. The acquisition of colonial dependencies, as a result of the Spanish-American war, had given rise to many new questions as to the power of the federal government to govern such dependencies. Furthermore, the immense and rapid growth of large interstate corporations had raised new problems as to the constitutional powers of the federal government. As Mr. Beck had been assigned, on the occasion of the centennial banquet, the subject, "The Nation and the States," it was inevitable that he should refer to these questions and the thesis of his speech was that the Constitution was a living organism and therefore susceptible of indefinite development.—EDITOR.

Mr. Chairman, Ladies and Fellow Members of the Bar:

You will permit me to acknowledge most gratefully the distinguished honor that you have done me in assigning me to any part in the exercises of tonight and in permitting me to share in your generous hospitality. I wish that it were within my power to repay in any manner so great a compliment. I must, however, throw myself upon your indulgence and ask you to bear with me in the generous spirit with which the young Prince of Denmark bade Polonius welcome the players who had come to Elsinore to entertain his lordship. Said the young Prince:

"Use them after your own honor and dignity.
The less they deserve, the more merit is in your
bounty."

Two considerations alone seem to give to my selection as one of the speakers of the evening any propriety. At a banquet in memory of John Marshall it is not inappropriate that a representative of the Philadelphia bar should be present, for Marshall's undying fame rests securely upon his marvelous exposition of the Constitution, and Philadelphia is the city of the Constitution as well as of the great Declaration. Within the shadow of her State House, from which, as from Pharos, the light of liberty has streamed to the uttermost part of the world, the great Chief Justice died. It was the historic bar of Philadelphia which, within twenty four hours of his death, started the movement to erect a suitable monument to his memory, and the result of its labors is that noble piece of bronze at the foot of the Capitol, which, by a happy coincidence, was fashioned by the artistic genius of a Story.

One other circumstance connecting Marshall with Philadelphia is of epic grandeur. The old bell, which, from the tower of her State House had rung for many years, was silenced forever in tolling for the passing of his mighty soul. It had for more than a decade sounded to the mother country its warning notes. It had summoned the First and Second Continental Congresses to their solemn sessions. Later, its reverberations had rolled over the waters of the Delaware to signalize the birth of a new nation, and to "proclaim liberty throughout the land and unto all the inhabitants thereof." Its iron tongue had mourned the brave men who had fallen at Germantown and Brandywine, and had rung joyfully to announce the culminating triumph of Yorktown. It had welcomed the delegates to the Constitutional Convention as they entered the historic city of Philadelphia and had signalized the commencement of the new republic when the first sessions of its congress met at its deep-toned call. It had welcomed Marshall on his return to the seat of government from France, where he had so nobly upheld the honor of the Republic against the arrogant assaults of the corrupt Directory. As, one by one, the great characters of that epic struggle for independence passed away, the bell tolled mournfully. On July 6, 1835, John Marshall, after sixty years of public service, of which thirty-five had been spent upon the bench of the Supreme Court, died in Philadelphia, and as his body passed, a few days later, through the streets of Philadelphia to his Virginia home, the bell again sent forth its mournful reverberations across the waters of the Delaware. And as it tolled, its iron side was rent in twain, and the full tones of the Liberty Bell became mute forever. A mere coincidence, you say? Yes, —but it is such coincidences that give to a nation's life dramatic significance; and if it is desirable that the sound of this bell should only be associated with the heroic age of the Republic, then its tongue could not have better sounded its final note than in lamenting the passing of John Marshall.

One other circumstance seems to give some propriety to my selection. It seems to me fitting that a member of the junior bar should speak on this occasion, for John Marshall, greatest of justices of the greatest of courts, was the contribution of the junior bar to the judiciary of the United States, for he was comparatively young when appointed to the supreme bench and his years at the bar were still those of a junior. Our admiration for the colossal figures of the heroic age, the stupendous character of their achievements when seen in the perspective of time and results, have created an impression that the great men of the Revolution were venerable in years. We call them the "Fathers" of the Republic and think of them as patriarchs. The trick of costume also contributes to this illusion. The powdered hair and stately costume, of which we get some faint conception in the portraits of the period, convey to this prosaic age the idea of advanced years. The fact is that this Republic was called into being by young men, largely members of the junior bar, but for whose brave and revolutionary spirit the United States of America had not been. Think, for example, of the three young lawyers of Virginia, who, shortly before the Revolution, entered the bar from the law office of Chancellor Wythe. One, Thomas Jefferson, who at twenty-five years of age, procured the honor of an attainder by the British Parliament by publishing his "Summary Views of the Rights of America," and who, at thirty-three years, was selected, because his was the masterful pen of the time, to give to mankind its title deed to liberty in the Declaration of Independence. Think of James Madison, who, at twenty-nine years of age, was a member of the Continental Congress and who was only thirty-six when he participated in the deliberations of the Constitutional Convention and won his immortal title as "The Father of the Constitution."

No less wonderful was John Marshall, who was but twenty-two when he helped drag the artillery over the frozen hills of Valley Forge, who became the leader of the Virginia bar when little more than thirty years of age, and Chief Justice of the United States at forty-six after having filled at an earlier age some of the most exalted positions in the gift of the American people. In Massachusetts it was the young lawyers who were the revolutionary spirits of the times. John Adams was but thirty years of age when he commenced to champion the rights of the colonists. Josiah Quincy was twenty-nine when, on the eve of the famous tea party, he addressed the crowd in front of the old South Church, while John Hancock was then but thirty-seven years of age. In Pennsylvania it was John Dickinson, not over thirty-five years of age, who was educating the good people of the colonies by his "Pennsylvania farmer" letters, while Thomas Mifflin and Robert Morris had not yet turned forty. Or shall I speak of that marvelous boy, the "Admirable Crichton" of his time, Alexander Hamilton, who was but thirty when he sat in the Constitutional Convention? Or of John Jay, who was but thirty-two when he became Chief Justice of New York? Or of Joseph Story, who at thirty-two was an Associate Justice of the Supreme Court? With such names as these on their roll of honor, the right of the junior bar to have a voice in the deliberations of this evening need not be questioned. My only regret is that a more fitting representative of that militant branch of the bar is not here in my place to express in fitting language the deep respect which every lawyer feels when he recalls the achievements of John Marshall of immortal memory.

You have, however, assigned to me the toast, "The Nation and the States," a very large subject for an after-dinner speech. Its discussion at the present day fills most of the pages of one hundred and seventy-nine volumes of the official reports of the Supreme Court, for, under our

peculiar system of government, which makes the nine justices of that court a quasi-constitutional convention, which
is always in session, few constitutional questions can ever
be said to be at rest. It is well that this should be so, for
nothing that has vitality is at rest. Stagnancy is death,
and when the people of the United States cease to deliberate upon the meaning of the great compact, and, what
is more, when they cease to develop it by fair interpretation, or, when necessary, adapt it by formal amendment
to the ever-changing needs of one of the most progressive
peoples on the face of the earth, then it will no longer
have justification for its existence and will cease to be.
Mr. Gladstone's oft-quoted statement that the Constitution of the Fathers was the "most perfect work ever struck
off by the brain and purposes of man at a given time" is
erroneous to the extent that it conveys the idea that the
Constitution sprang from the brains of its framers like
Minerva from the brain of Jove. It was the fruition of
the ages, the result of an evolution which has been pro-
gressing through unnumbered centuries. Much of it,
in fact, nearly all of it, was the adaptation of old principles of government to a new nation. But while this is
true, yet the Constitution did make one distinct contribution to the science of government in creating a Supreme
Court as a co-ordinate branch of the government, with
exclusive power to declare the meaning of the written
compact and to nullify any law or act repugnant thereto.
This was a novelty in 1787 and it is a novelty today, for
neither in the German Empire, closely as it approximates
the Federal Constitution in many respects, nor in England,
with whose political institutions we are most in sympathy,
has there yet been constituted any court with similar
powers.

It would be interesting, in passing, to speculate as to
what might have been, had there been such a tribunal in
England at the time of the American Revolution. The
chief grievance of the colonists was the assertion on their
part that Parliament had no right to tax them except
through their colonial legislatures and, therefore, with
their consent. Under the English system, while the acts
of the Crown have at times been questioned in the courts

of justice and arbitrary acts of monarchs have been set aside by intrepid judges, yet Parliament is the last judge of what may be enacted into a law. If the English judiciary had been an independent, although coordinate, branch of the government, and the colonists could have argued the constitutional questions involved in their grievances before a tribunal of judges, it is possible that the Revolution would never have been. If we are to believe Earl Rosebery in his recent address at Glasgow, the inevitable effect of that would have been that the sceptre of power of the united English-speaking race would have passed from Westminster to some western capital and England would have become but a portion of the American Empire. We need not, however, regret this, but may say in the spirit of Dr. Franklin at the close of the Constitutional Convention, that if a sparrow does not fall unnoticed by the Supreme Ruler of the Universe, an empire cannot rise without His design; and we can therefore believe that the Ruler of the Nations had a wise purpose in dividing the English-speaking race, destined to be dominant in the world, into two great political divisions. The mere division in their political government cannot destroy the united force which their common laws, literature and language exert throughout the world.

The theory upon which the Constitution was formed was likewise a novel experiment in the science of political government. It breathed the spirit of home rule for the state and personal rights for the individual. It was designed to restrain, as well as to promote, the will of the majority. In the ceaseless conflict between the individual and the state it sought to reconcile the liberty of the citizen with the authority of the state. It therefore created a government of enumerated powers, and prescribed as well what the servants of the people should not do as that which they should do. Both grant and prohibition were expressed in words of extraordinary brevity and simplicity. It was reserved for John Marshall to interpret this marvelous compact with reference to its tremendous objects and it has been well said of him that "he found the Constitution paper and he made it power; he found it a skeleton and he clothed it with flesh and blood." In nicest equipoise he held in the scales of justice the tremendous issues of state and national sovereignty and today his opinions are the living oracles of the law. Even his fugitive expressions are the subject of graver debate and are often given greater weight than the solemn decisions of many later judges.

In the ceaseless struggle between the delegated sovereignty of the central government and the reserved sovereignty of the states, the stern logic of events and the constitutional evolution of our country have not only vindicated most of the decisions of John Marshall, but it may be truly said that he gave a definition of national sovereignty which time will not make obsolete.

At a banquet given in honor of the centennial anniversary of the adoption of the Constitution, Mr. Charles Francis Adams, the lineal descendant of a federal and a whig President, uttered these remarkable words:

> "Steam and electricity have in these days converted each thoughtful Hamiltonian into a believer of the constitutional theories of Jefferson. Today everything centralizes itself. Gravitation is the law. The centripetal forces, unaided by government, working only through scientific sinews and nerves of steam and steel and lightning, this centripetal force is nearly overcoming all centrifugal action. The ultimate result can by thoughtful men no longer be ignored. Jefferson is right and Hamilton is wrong."

I may not be deemed presumptuous if I partly dissent to this sentiment of this eminent publicist of our day and generation. I think it is more accurate to say that neither Jefferson nor Hamilton was wholly right or wrong. They were the complement of each other and to the conflict of their theories is due in part the freedom and efficacy of our institutions. Jefferson, on the one hand, had been betrayed by the visionary sentimentalism of the French doctrinaires into excesses which impaired his otherwise sagacious foresight. His passionate love of individual freedom blinded him to the necessities of government and yet, without his lofty idealism, many important safeguards of individual liberty and the saving spirit of freedom would not have been. Hamilton, on the other hand, had the greatest genius for constructive statesmanship of any American statesman, but his temperament was so lacking in sympathy with the people, or with popular government, that the government of Hamilton would have been the negation of individual freedom and little better than a monarchy. Between these two extremists stood John Marshall. Before he ascended the bench he had been a federalist, but as Chief Justice he was the far-seeing, sagacious and inspired patriot. The best thought of America now sees that John Marshall was more nearly right than either of his distinguished contemporaries, for it was he, who, utilizing the best of each political system, constructed on foundations more enduring than granite the "indestructible union of indestructible states."

Marshall saw more clearly than his contemporaries the nature of the Constitution. He saw that it was little more than a working plan for an edifice that was to endure forever, and that, while it must guide the master builders, who in the future would erect the superstructure, it could not express the various means by which the design was to be carried out. To quote his own language in the great case of *McCulloch v. Maryland*: "This provision is made in a constitution intended to endure for ages to come, and, consequently, to be *adapted* to the various crises of human affairs. To have prescribed the means by which government should in all future times execute its powers would have been to change entirely the character of the instrument and to give it the properties of a legal code. It would have been an unwise attempt to provide by immutable rules for exigencies, which, if foreseen at all, must have been seen dimly and can best be provided for as they occur."

He thus clearly stated the truth that the Constitution does not pretend to anticipate all the contingencies which must arise in the ages which await America. It is important that we should remember this at this time, when the Republic is entering upon a new and most important phase of constitutional development. While this development can only proceed under and within the Constitution and in accordance with the methods prescribed by that instrument, the people of the United States, independent of their form of government, either state or national, have, as a collective body of individuals, political ideas and tendencies which are bounded only by their high aspirations and their God-appointed destiny. Constitutions, both state and federal, proceed upon the principle that only a portion of the power inherent in the people should be vested in a government, and that a residuum of freedom should forever remain in the citizen. Because of this spirit of individualism, you can no more "crib, cabin and confine" for all time the growth of aspiration and possibility of achievement of the American people within any traditional policy than you could dam up the waters of the Mississippi.

In a recent utterance of the Supreme Court, Mr. Justice Brown says:

> "This court has not failed to recognize the fact that the law is, to a certain extent, a progressive science; that in some of the states the methods of procedure which at the time the Constitution was adopted were deemed essential to the protection and safety of the people or to the liberty of the citizen have been found to be no longer necessary; that restrictions which had formerly been laid upon the conduct of individuals or of classes of individuals, had proved detrimental to their interests.
>
> Of course, it is impossible to forecast the character or extent of these changes, but in view of the fact that from the day the Magna Charta was signed to the present moment amendments to the structure of the law have been made with increasing frequency, it is impossible to suppose that they will not continue, and the law be forced to adapt itself to new conditions of society."

Do not understand me as suggesting that the Constitution of the United Staates is insufficient for the needs of the present hour. Far from meaning that, I believe that in nothing is it so marvelous as in the fact that it has been found sufficient hitherto for every emergency which the American people have been required to meet. The fifty provincial gentlemen, with their powdered queues and knee breeches, who, in less than one hundred working days, framed the form of government, dealt with a little group of scattered colonies, which at that time were of less importance to civilization than is the Congo Free State at the present hour. And yet, the product of their labors, which so far as the mere structure of form of government is concerned, has been practically unchanged, has been found sufficient for a nation whose development has been among the miracles of history. Although the last two years have witnessed epoch-making events, and the flag of the Republic has been carried into the Eastern Hemisphere and new problems have confronted the American people, yet it is the belief of the Administration that there are none for whose solution the Constitution, fairly interpreted, is not sufficient. It is possible that such a contingency as that presented in our occupancy of Cuba, or the cession of Porto Rico and the Philippine Archipelago never presented itself to the minds of the framers of the Constitution.

But it is no answer to any constitutional contention that the application of a general principle to particular facts was not in their contemplation. Of these master builders it may be said in truth that "they builded better than they knew." As an obvious illustration, let me suggest that, when in twenty-one words they gave to Congress the power to regulate interstate commerce, they dealt with almost primitive conditions. Little could the Fathers have dreamed of an age when the United States, from ocean to ocean, would be covered by a very network of railroads, telegraph and telephone lines. And yet, the interstate commerce clause has been found broad and elastic enough to enable Congress to control the vast interstate traffic of the United States, which to-day exceeds the foreign commerce of any other nation in the world; and this invaluable grant of power, without which the Republic could not have continued, has been applied to subjects, of which the Fathers did not even dream, as for example, the regulation of the machinery of transportation.

If, therefore, we find ourselves, in the strange sequence of events, treading unbeaten paths (and when did nation ever achieve greatness except along such paths?) and facing conditions and problems unknown and undreamed of by the Fathers, let it not be said that we are doing violence to their spirit in applying, or even adapting, their principles to such new conditions.

The Constitution pretends to be nothing more than a frame of government. As such it answers every present need. While it was marvelously great in what it provided, it was wise to the point of inspiration in what it left unprovided, and the mere political policies, with which given powers are executed, must not be confused with the exercise and scope of such powers, as delegated by the great compact. As to the manner in which, and the object for which, these powers shall be exercised, this generation, while paying due heed to the past, must not forget the present. As Jefferson aptly said: "The Constitution was made for the living, not for the dead."

In nothing was John Marshall so surpassingly great as in the fact that he reached his wonderful conclusions, not by slavish and exclusive resort to precedent or analogy, but by reasoning which was both independent and logical. In many of his decisions he could in the nature of the case have no precedent to guide him, and perhaps their surpassing greatness may be in some measure due to this consideration. I do not mean that every judge should disregard precedent, for not every one can "bend the bow of Ulysses." But self-respect bids us remember that the Almighty never intended that wisdom should die either with one man, one generation, one race, one century or one epoch. Least of any people should America doubt the increasing purpose of the ages and the widening of thought with the process of the suns.

I mention this because, as I have said, our country is unquestionably entering upon a new phase of constitutional development. Problems which are entirely novel are confronting us at the beginning of the twentieth century as they confronted John Marshall at the beginning of the nineteenth. The United States is destined to be the dominant power of the world. Already the shadow of its coming greatness envelops the globe, while its flag waves tonight as a symbol of dominion in two hemispheres and is illumined with the glory of unending day. The traditional policy which confined us to a single hemisphere has been discarded forever. We must meet these questions with the same breadth of view and independence of thought with which John Marshall met the questions of his day. Our duty as a nation is to be determined by present and not by past conditions. We cannot stand still; we must move onward. From civilization we derive inestimable rights; to her we owe immeasurable duties, and to shirk these would be cowardice and moral death. The greater the power, the greater the responsibility, and therefore no nation owes a greater duty to civilization than the United States.

If our people and those temporarily charged with authority have but the spirit of John Marshall, no problem to confront us will prove too great for our solution and no work too great for our achievement. To faintly grasp the future of this country is to bewilder and exhaust the imagination. East and west from the Father of Waters, north and south of Mason and Dixon's line, we are one today, my fellow countrymen, one, in the proud possession of a glorious past, one, in a resolute purpose to meet the duties of the hour, and one, in an abiding faith in the future of our beloved country. The spirit of America is that voiced by Montalambert, when he said, "Bowing respectfully to the past, and doing justice to the present, we salute the future and true progress."

VIII

THE HIGHER LAW

At the annual meeting of the American Bar Association in 1918, Mr. Beck was invited to address its Judicial Section. As the World War was then apparently nearing its end, the nature of the peace was becoming of paramount interest, and possibly with this in mind, Mr. Beck selected as the subject of his address, delivered at Cleveland, Ohio, on August 28th, "The Higher Law." It is now a matter of history that the Treaty of Versailles, which terminated the World War, was a compromise treaty, and that international tranquility and peace has not been its result.—EDITOR.

Gentlemen of the American Bar Association:

In inviting your patient attention to a necessarily brief consideration of the higher law, I must first anticipate the question as to whether the higher law exists except as a metaphysical abstraction of generous idealists.

In addressing myself to this preliminary inquiry, I must first define what I mean by a "higher law." If it have any existence, it must mean something more than the sense of moral obligation which each normal human soul, as an individual, owes to the Supreme Being under any form of religion. A law, in the sense in which jurists use the term, must mean a clearly recognizable regulation, which imposes upon men collectively definite obligations and to a greater or less extent compels compliance therewith. It seems to me, however, a narrow view to hold that nothing can be a social law unless it is promulgated by the authority of a political state and is cognizable in its courts of justice. In a narrower sense this may be so, but the laws which regulate human conduct are not restricted to those of the political state.

To the eye of the imagination, as Proudhon saw as early as 1845, human society, as developed by civilization, is a "living being, endowed with an intelligence and activity of its own, and as such an organic unit."

Long before Proudhon, a greater jurist and philosopher, Francis Bacon, wrote that in human society there was a

160

reign of law beyond that effected by union of sovereignty or pacts of states. He added, "there were other bands of society and implicit confederations," and if my auditors will start with the conception of human society as an organic unit more comprehensive than the political state, which is only one of its organs and subdivisions, then it will be clear that, outside of the circle of political laws and to some extent overlapping the domain of positive state-made law, there is a large body of human regulations having their origin in the common conscience of mankind and possibly affecting human conduct even more vitally than the regulations of the political state.

I am quite aware that the school of political jurists, such as Austin, Hobbes and Bentham, have disputed the application of the word "law" to this great body of regulations, to which Austin gave the term "positive morality" and which German jurists designate as "Sittlichkeit" and "Moralitaet." I have no disposition to enter into this controversy and to make another fruitless attempt to distinguish between various shades of meaning suggested by the word "law." In this time of "blood and iron," such metaphysical subtleties are of little value. Indeed, I should not have selected the subject if I had not been deeply impressed with the belief that the maintenance of this higher law is in the last analysis the supreme issue of this titanic war and that its vindication should and probably will have a potent influence upon the great problems of a just and durable peace. Let me content myself by justifying my application of the word "law" by a single illustration.

When the Titanic went down, all its passengers became immediately and instinctively conscious of a regulation that, in saving their lives, women and children should have preference. Who made this law? No legislature ever enacted it and no sovereign state ever gave it sanction. It was not the result of any contractual agreement, for probably few of the ill-fated passengers ever considered the question until the terrible exigency suddenly confronted them. It did not arise from utilitarian consideration, for it is probable that the lives of the male passengers were at least as pragmatically valuable to human society as those of the women and children. The law was something more than a sense of individual morality. It had compelling power. All were conscious of its obligation and all obeyed it. Its instantaneous recognition and the loyal acceptance of its results, which meant death to many of the passengers, shows that it was due to a great primal instinct which, notwithstanding the biologic law of natural selection and the struggle for existence, requires the strong to have compassion on the weak.

Assuming that the word "law" can be properly applied to such recognized regulations of human conduct, it remains to consider in what respect its characterization as the "higher law" can be justified. And here again the illustration of the Titanic helps our reasoning, for the rule of conduct which was then put into effect was regarded as a fundamental decency of human life greater even than the powerful instinct of self-preservation. Such laws are higher, in the sense that they are primal and fundamental laws. They constitute the great unwritten Constitution of human society. They are antecedent to all laws of the State and indeed the latter are but the imperfect expression of the higher law of morality. As the planetary worlds are evolved out of the nebulæ, so the laws of the State, especially such as are based upon moral rather than utilitarian considerations, are evolved out of these fundamental decencies of human conduct, and, as I will presently attempt to show, the systems of jurisprudence with which we are most familiar, the Latin and English, have always taken into account in the development of legal institutions the primary claims of the higher law.

Let me next attempt to show the evidences of the higher law, as they have existed in human thought and institutions, time out of mind.

If there be one thing upon which the wise and just of all ages and of all nations have been agreed, it is that there is, distinguished from the law of political state, a higher law which in a very potent way affects and controls the destinies of men.

We find abundant evidences of it in the great mythologies of the ancient world, which represent in the truest form the moral philosophy of the primitive races. The mythology of Greece saw the influence of the gods in all phenomena, physical, social or moral. Any uniform sequence was regarded by them as due to the law of the gods. Among these deities in the Homeric times was Themis, the goddess of justice. Her decree, "themistes," was the result of a primal law, to which not only men, but even gods were compelled to conform.

The sturdy and virile mythology of the Norsemen represented the same truth and in the great Saga of The Ring, it is to be noted that the theft of gold brought a curse to all into whose hands it came, even though the recipient of stolen goods was the supreme god, Wotan; and it was not until the gold, in the form of the ring, was restored to the Rhine-maidens, that the curse was lifted from gods and men alike. Thus the great moral truth of retributive justice was taught from the earliest ages.

Passing mythology, as evidencing the moral conscience of prehistoric ages, and turning to the sacred writings, which still dominate the conscience of mankind, we shall see an even more striking recognition of the existence of a primal law, which existed independently of the regulations of the political State and was paramount thereto. No nobler recognition can be instanced than the sacred writings which constitute the supreme contribution of the Jewish race to the world. While in the Mosaic writings God was only a tribal God—one of many—yet later on in the times of the Chaldean and Assyrian invasions, the noble conception dawned upon that race of a single God, Who ruled all mankind with infinite justice and patience and compassion. Whether we turn to the Lamentations of Jeremiah or the Psalms of David, or the fiery invectives of Isaiah and the other prophets, we find again and again the assertion, in language of infinite beauty and power, of a supreme law-giver and a supreme law, to which all men and all political states must conform their conduct.

The supreme recognition of this higher law came later from the Great Teacher, whose beatitudes remain its most perfect expression. The golden thread, which runs throughout the teachings of Christ, was the superiority of the higher law to the laws of the Jewish state. His constant protest was against that too-rigid adherence to state-made law, which sacrificed the spirit to the letter and failed to recognize the primal truths of the higher law. Rarely did He speak in terms of invective. His bitterest reproaches were addressed to those too-rigid lawyers of an ecclesiastical state, who regarded state-made laws as ends in themselves, and not as means to an end. He was careful to emphasize that His kingdom was not of this world and that His system of morals was based upon a higher sanction than that of the State. The prayer we lisped in childhood, "Thy kingdom come, Thy will be done," is the recognition of this higher law. While the Great Teacher, Himself, made no laws and founded no kingdom, yet His appeal to the higher law was of such potent influence in shaping the destinies of man, that, as Richter has said, "with His pierced hands, He lifted the gates of the centuries off their hinges and turned the stream of the ages into a new channel."

In all history there is no greater manifestation of the higher law than the fact that the Galilean Teacher has more powerfully influenced the destinies of men than has the universal Roman Empire, of which He was but a citizen, and which was the greatest governmental embodiment of law that the world has ever known.

Turn from the sacred writings of the Jewish race to those of the most intellectual race in recorded history, Greece. We here see the higher law vindicated with incomparable power in the moral philosophy of the three great dramatists, Æschylus, Sophocles and Euripides. These were the Greek prophets. The constant theme of their tragedies is that all men and all political institutions are subordinate to the operations of the higher law, whose retributive justice was called Nemesis. The terrible character of this retributive justice is illustrated by Sophocles in his great Theban trilogy, for he teaches us especially in Œdipus that even an unintentional violation of the higher law by an innocent man must be atoned for. The argument reaches its greatest height in the noble play of

Antigone, where the conflict between the law of the state and the higher law is emphasized. The brother of Antigone had committed a crime against the State of Thebes, and by its laws his body was denied the final dignity of burial. In defiance of the laws, Antigone buries her brother, in obedience to the call of affection and the dictates of humanity. The king, who incarnated the power of the State, demanded of her whether she had transgressed its sovereign laws, and to that Antigone nobly replied:

> "Yes, for that law was not from Zeus, nor did Justice, dweller with the gods below, establish it among men; nor deemed I that thy decree— mere mortal than thou art—could override those unwritten and unfailing mandates, which are not of today or yesterday, but ever live and no one knows their birthtide."

The Greek conception thus assumed that there existed above all state-made laws a higher law of retributive justice, eternal, immutable and from whose workings neither god nor man could escape.

Five centuries later one of the greatest of the Roman jurists, orators and essayists, Cicero, spoke in the same terms of a higher law,

> "which was never written and which we are never taught, which we never learn by reading, but which was drawn by nature herself."

In Rome this was the especial teachings of the Stoic school, and of the great moralist, Seneca, and it exercised, as we shall presently see, a profound influence upon the development of the noblest body of law, the civil law, and, through it, upon our Anglo-American system of jurisprudence.

Now turn from the classic Tiber to the lovely Avon. We find again that the supreme genius of all poets and dramatists accepted in his great tragedies the same theme. Nowhere does he illustrate it more beautifully than in the Merchant of Venice, for in the trial scene he takes great pains to emphasize that, as a matter of strict law, Shylock was right in his contention.   Venice was a commercial state.   Its material welfare depended upon the sanctity of contracts and the stability of precedents.   Therefore, Portia, having sustained the legal justice of Shylock's contention, turns to him and says:

"Then *must* the Jew be merciful."

To emphasize the significance of the word, "must," Shylock repeats it and thus challenges the existence of the higher law:

"Upon what compulsion *must* I, tell me that."

Portia does not suggest that mercy is a matter of grace, but that its mandate is greater than that of a Venetian Doge or the Council of Ten.   The usurer has his legal right to the penalty, but the higher law compels him to surrender that right.   Portia thus announces the higher law:

"'Tis mightiest in the mighty; it becomes
The throned monarch better than his crown,
His sceptre shows the force of temporal power,
The attribute to awe and majesty,
Wherein doth sit the dread and fear of kings;
But mercy is above the sceptered sway,
It is enthroned in the hearts of kings,
It is an attribute to God himself."

With incomparable insight, Shakespeare put this vindication of the higher law into the mouth of a woman, one of the noblest of his heroines, for in the permanent differentiation in the social office of the sexes, which no law or constitutional amendment can ever wholly override, the woman is the peculiar advocate and high-priestess of the higher law.   In her care peculiarly rests the ideal and the abstract.   To man, as the constructive agent of human society, is given the concrete and practical.

Turning from the doctrines of these great teachers, to the legal institutions of mankind, we find the most striking evidence of the higher law.   While analytical jurists of the Austinian school may deny its existence or its relation to the laws of the State, the fact remains that as the rocks show unmistakable evidences of the glacial movements, so our state-made institutions and laws bear equally striking evidence of those mighty moral movements which, like the glaciers at the beginning of the world, have swept over its surface and determined the form and shape of continents and oceans.

In States which, like the Jewish state, were a combination of church and State, the influence is naturally more evident, but if we take Rome, the greatest of all secular States in history, and examine its body of law, the noblest that man has ever developed, we shall find there the clearest recognition of the higher law as an organ of society, of which courts can and should take cognizance.

Thus arose the distinction between the *jus civile* or the law of the State, and the *jus naturale,* or the law of nature. The Roman jurists recognized that while the local law of the State was of value within its own scope, yet there was on occasion the necessity of applying a system of laws which it conceived to be common to all mankind. "All nations," says the institutional treatise written under the authority of the Emperor Justinian, "who are ruled by laws and customs, are governed partly by their own particular laws and partly by those laws which are common to all mankind. The law which a people enacts is called the civil law of that people, but that which natural reason points for all minkind is called the law of nations, because all nations use it."

This was the Law of Nations, but it must not be confused with international law, for the latter, so far as it arises from the agreement of nations and regulates their mutual intercourse, is one manifestation of the higher law, but only a part of it. To the Roman jurists the Law of Nations represented something more than any code of nations. They conceived of human society as a single unit and they assumed the existence of a universal law, which was both antecedent and paramount to the law of Rome. In this the jurists of the Empire were powerfully influenced by Seneca and his school, and out of it grew the great conception of *aequitas,* or Equity, which, in its last analysis, is the most concrete manifestation of the higher law, either in the civil or in our own system of jurisprudence. The essence of equity was that the necessarily rigid laws of the State would at times work injustice and that in such cases certain primal truths must be invoked to moderate the rigor of the law. These primal truths were never wholly codified but were summed up in the word, "equity" or justice. We all know how profoundly the Roman conception of equity influenced the development of law in England and the United States. Our system of equity jurisprudence began in the reign of Edward III and assumed that there was in the king a residue of power which enabled him to overrule the usages of common law, or even the statutes of Parliament by resort to certain primal principles and fundamental decencies, epitomized in the word "equity." The great maxims of Equity are but expressions of this higher law. As in the famous case cited from the Merchant of Venice, the creditor was entitled to the penalty of his bond, yet equity would forbid it when the penalty was unconscionable.

"He that asks equity must do equity." What is this but the command of the Great Teacher that we must love our neighbor as ourselves.

In the time of Edward III, the Lord Chancellor would permit nothing, the laws of the State to the contrary notwithstanding, that was inconsistent with *"honestas"* or honesty. Thus the idea of an abstract justice, something higher than the letter of the law, became lodged in our system of jurisprudence and thus we can fairly claim that both our system of equity jurisprudence with its invariable emphasis upon abstract justice and the equity system of the civil law, from which we in part derive it, form the clearest recognition by legal system of a higher law.

Another recognition of this higher law could be given, if time permitted, in the relation of the Roman church to the political states of Europe, up to the time of the Reformation and in some instances since then. Naturally the church asserted itself as the greatest organ of the higher law, as the German emperor recognized when he stood barefooted in the snow-covered courtyard at Canossa awaiting an audience with Hildebrand. Chivalry, that fairest daughter of the mediæval church, which so profoundly affected the destinies of mankind, owed its direct inspiration to the higher law. This wonderful institution was not only international, but also supernational. It paid little heed to the law of the State. Its object was to vindicate certain fundamental decencies in life and in its best estate it sought to meet the requirements of the higher law as voiced by the Prophet Micah:

"What doth the Lord require of thee? but to do justly, and to love mercy and to walk humbly with thy God."

The allegiance of the young knight, when at the altar of God he knelt and received his sword and spurs, was to a higher law than that for which his or any political State stood.

In the jurisprudence of France there was until the time of the Revolution the same manifestation of the higher law. Those who believe the principle of *Marbury vs. Madison* to have been a novel contribution to the science of jurisprudence, may well remember that for at least two centuries before, no law of France acquired validity until it was "registered" by the judiciary, and if it appeared to the French courts that the proposed law was against common reason and justice, the courts would refuse to register it. If the law-making power then refused to withdraw, the king summoned a *lit de justice,* in which he heard and considered the objections of the judges, and if he refused to yield the judges would often refuse to enforce the law; and if they in turn refused to register the law, it at times happened that the king, to compel registration, would send the judges to the Bastile with a *lettre de cachet.* Generally, however, the courts prevailed.

It is interesting to Americans to remember that the same plan was embodied in the first draft of the Constitution of the United States, which proposed that the executive and the national judiciary should constitute a "Council of Revision" with the power of vetoing all legislation, both in the Federal and State legislatures. It is probable that in this suggestion, Mr. Randolph, the author of the first draft of the Constitution, followed the French plan, but it was wisely rejected by the Constitutional Convention, and was restricted to a qualified veto of the President. In this connection let me add that the recognition of a higher law should not carry with it any confusion between the executive and judicial branches of the government, or between the functions of a political State and those of organized society, which operate outside the sphere of political government and could not be confused therewith without moral anarchy. Human society as well as the political State has its limitations and the scope of each is determined by the good sense and common conscience of mankind. Indeed the true genius of government is in the nice determination of those regulations of human conduct which should be left to the political State and those which should be left to the potent influence of society in general.

Another striking recognition of the higher law in our legal institutions is found in constitutional limitations, whether express or implied. The idea of a restraint upon the power of the political State, to compel its conformity to certain fundamental verities, is as old as civilization, as continuous as its history, and has its origin in the axiom of the higher law, that any state-made law grossly repugnant to natural justice violates the unwritten social contract and is null and void. Locke, Montesquieu and Rousseau all base their political philosophy upon an assumed State of Nature, and an implied contract, under which individuals surrendered their freedom to organized government with a reservation of certain inalienable rights. Those rights constitute the great unwritten constitution of human society. I need hardly remind you how potent was the influence of this school of philosophy upon Thomas Jefferson when he drafted the Declaration of Independence. He expressly asserts the existence of the higher law, when he says that "a decent respect to the opinions of mankind" requires a nation to justify its acts by the fundamental and universal principles of morality.

This idea was much older than either Locke, Rousseau or Jefferson. It is older than the English law. Traces of it can be found in the Roman law, even during the autocratic power of the emperors. Every system of jurisprudence which is derived in part or in whole from the civil law, shows some evidences of this implied restriction upon arbitrary power, whether of kings or majorities. The doctrine of the omnipotence of Parliament, as we understand it today, was not an accepted principle of English constitutional law when Jefferson wrote the Declaration of Independence. On the contrary, the Great Masters of the common law, including the four Lord Chief Justices, Coke, Hobart, Holt and Popham, all supported the doctrine of the common law, as laid down by Lord Coke (Bonham's case, 8 Coke Reports, 114), that the judiciary had the power to nullify a law, if it were "against common right and reason."

While this theory has long since yielded to the omnipotence of Parliament in English jurisprudence, yet the doctrine was accepted by the constitutional lawyers of the Colonies in our struggle for independence, for when they sought to invalidate an act of Parliament, which imposed a tax on tea, they could not reasonably pretend that the invalidity of taxation without representation was a recognized part of the constitutional system of England, but they did contend that such taxation was tyranny because it violated a fundamental principle of the "higher law" of liberty, that no man could be compelled to pay tribute except when granted by his representatives. Neither then nor even at the present day does the principle of the invalidity of taxation without representation admit of literal application. The United States has always taxed its territories and colonial dependencies without any voting representation.

The Pilgrims, who signed the famous compact in the cabin of the Mayflower, did not covenant to obey any laws that the majority might dictate, but only such as were "just and equal."

When the founders of the Republic framed the Constitution of the United States, they took good care to write the higher law into that Constitution in order that the restraints upon arbitrary power, which in England were real, although unwritten, should in the new Republic be evidenced by a written contract. The great restraints upon legislation, both of Federal and State governments, are clear recognitions of a higher law. Thus the fifth and fourteenth amendments, with their prohibition of any legislation which takes away life, liberty and property "without due process of law," are but repetitions of the prohibition of the great charter, as to "the law of the land." The Barons at Runnymede did not attempt to define that law. What they had in mind were certain primal verities of personal liberty, upon which their freedom depended, and similarly the framers of the Constitution never pretended to define what they meant by "due process of law."

Daniel Webster, in the famous Dartmouth College case, gave the classic definition of the "law of the land," the phrase from which "due process of law" was derived, as follows:

> "By the law of the land is most clearly intended the general law; a law which hears before it condemns; which proceeds upon inquiry, and renders judgment only after trial. The meaning is that every citizen shall hold his life, liberty, property and immunities under the protection of the general rules which govern society."

Almost contemporaneously with this historic argument, the Supreme Court, in the opinion by Mr. Justice Johnson, gave a more felicitous definition, when it said:

> "As to the words from Magna Charta, incorporated into the Constitution of Maryland, after volumes spoken and written with a view to their exposition, the good sense of mankind has at length settled down to this, that they were intended to secure the individual from the arbi-

trary exercise of the powers of government, unrestrained by the established principles of private
rights and *distributive justice*."

This last expression was significant, for "distributive"
justice was one of the definitions of the higher law as expounded by great jurists in times past.   Thus Puffendorf
defines it as the species of justice which gives to each member of society his rights under the social contract—the
social contract referring to the state of natural justice
from which all legal institutions were presumed to evolve.
The essential idea of such distributive justice was expressed
in the opening words of Justinian's Institutes:

"*Justitia est constans et perpetua voluntas jus
suum cuique tribuere.*"

If this be somewhat vague, yet justice is also so indefinite
as to be undefinable.

Among our formal legal institutions, the greatest concrete manifestation of the higher law is that which we call
international law. This international code, which to some
extent impairs the sovereign power of nations and which,
until this war, had brought them measurably nearer to
the "parliament of man and the federation of the world,"
is a striking manifestation of an authority to which even
sovereign nations must yield. A greater part of this law
has consideration for those fundamental decencies of human life which cause the strong to respect the weak and,
therefore, seeks to save women and children and all non-
combatants from the horrors of war. Under this "higher
law," even the vanquished has his rights as against the
victor, and the mighty spirit of justice and compassion
which breathed through the two Hague Conventions
marked the high-water mark of human progress, until
Germany ruthlessly destroyed the dikes and flooded the
world with a torrent of primitive barbarity. While the
higher law is something more than international law, yet
the latter is its most noble manifestation, for it points the
way to that "far-off divine event, toward which the whole
creation moves," when the rules of justice, as formulated

by the common conscience of mankind, shall have complete sway throughout the world.

This leads me to a graver inquiry. Are all these teachings of the spiritual leaders of mankind and its ripened institutions mere rhapsodies of words? Were the wise and good of all ages cheating themselves with empty visions or, treading the mountain ranges of human observation, did they see the dawn of the perfect day more clearly than we who dwell in the darkened valleys of this working-day world?

History replies that the greatest evidence of the higher law is to be found in its records. Through the long drama which has been enacted on the boards of this "wide and universal theater of man," are as clearly seen the workings of retributive justice as in the tragedies of Sophocles or Shakespeare.

Time does not permit me to demonstrate the truth of this observation. I must content myself with two instances. Let me take one especially within our knowledge. In the year 1850, a very notable debate took place in the Senate of the United States.

The three greatest leaders of thought of the middle period of the republic—Clay, Webster and Calhoun—all of whom were then approaching the end of their careers, participated in it. The subject of the debate was the geographical restriction of slavery and the extension of the fugitive slave law. That the Constitution recognized slavery could not be gainsaid, and that its maintenance as an institution within certain geographical restrictions had been solemnly agreed to by all political divisions of the United States was equally undeniable. The two great parties and nearly all responsible leaders of public opinion were then opposed to the abolition of slavery, and yet parties and statesmen were subconsciously aware of a mighty power, driving them to an inevitable end. In a vain attempt to maintain the *status quo*, Clay proposed his great compromise of 1850. Webster favored the compromise in the speech of March 7, 1850, and the maintenance of slavery was further supported by that most acute and profound constitutional lawyer, Calhoun. In the course of the great debate, the young Senator from New York, William H. Seward, said:

> "The Constitution devotes the national domain to union, to justice, to defense, to welfare and to liberty; but there is a higher law than the Constitution."

The expression the "higher law" was not original with Seward. He had borrowed it almost verbatim from an address which Channing had made eight years before, on "The Duty of the Free States." The suggestion of a law higher than the Constitution quite naturally convulsed the nation and yet, within thirteen years, Seward had countersigned the Emancipation Proclamation and a year later Lincoln, who, at the beginning of his administration, had disclaimed any intention to interfere with the institution of slavery, proclaimed in his second inaugural his solemn belief that the fratricidal war was but the inexorable working of a "higher law" which set at naught the plans and expedients of statesmen and parties.

The inescapable judgment of the Nemesis of history is even more strikingly manifested in the titanic war now in progress, the greatest drama ever enacted on the stage of the world. The first act of that tragic drama began in 1740, and the curtain is now rising on the last act. When it finally falls it will be seen that the higher law has again overridden the purposes and plans of Chancellors and Prime Ministers, of Presidents, Czars, Kings and Emperors and made of them mere pawns upon the chessboard of history.

To appreciate this, it must be remembered that the roots of the present titanic war go much farther back than the tragic deed at Sarajevo. The true root of this upas-tree was the indefensible seizure of Silesia by Frederick the Great, in 1740. Had there been no condoned rape of Silesia there might have been no rape of Belgium. In that year a robber king had ascended the throne of a robber state, who, as Macaulay said, was "without fear, without faith and without mercy." Like a thief in the night and in violation of his solemn promise, he invaded Silesia and stole it from Austria. The act was the most naked and wanton challenge to the higher law in modern times, and the leading European nations sprang to arms. Had the Hohenzollern then been defeated and deposed, the present world war might never have been. But unfortunately at the very moment of the Allies' triumph, Russia in 1762, as again in 1917, not only crumbled, but deserted to the enemy. Weary with the terrible slaughter, the Allies compromised the great ideal of justice, made peace with Frederick the Great and confirmed his wicked seizure of Silesia.

Here were two ideals, each false but differing greatly in degree.

One was that of Frederick the Great, that the State was above morality and the only limit to its aggressions was that of physical power.

The other was the false pacifism that taught that it were better to condone a wrong, even though the higher law were sacrificed, than to inflict upon mankind the scourge of war.

The ideal of Germany was "power at any price," that of the Allies, "peace at any price."

These two principles profoundly impressed the whole course of European politics, until the inexorable workings of the higher law, seemingly moving with a leaden heel, but striking with an iron hand, wrought in our time the terrible expiation of the most destructive war that history has recorded.

Frederick the Great, encouraged by the condonation of the Silesian crime, made common cause with Russia and Austria, in the three partitions of Poland, at the end of which that noble kingdom was destroyed.

Then came the French Revolution and the Napoleonic Wars, in which the perverted ideal of physical power was invoked by an even greater master of the art of war than Frederick the Great. Napoleon wantonly invaded nation after nation and again and again, to secure peace at any price, his ruthless violations of the higher law were condoned, but each condonation only whetted his appetite for universal dominion. Finally the greatest of the Caesars fell from exhaustion and died at St. Helena, "the mighty somnambulist of a shattered dream of universal empire."

For a few decades civilization had a breathing spell and then the Hohenzollern dynasty, again entered upon its career of rapine and again the civilized world, in the supposed interests of peace, condoned its shameless felonies. It violently wrested Schleswig-Holstein from Denmark and no nation lifted a hand to protect that helpless power. Austria was next assailed and then a quarrel was deliberately picked with France, and after her defeat Alsace and Lorraine were arrogantly demanded by the ruthless conqueror.

France then appealed to the leading nations of Europe. M. Thiers vainly besought the governments of France's present Allies, to prevent this great wrong. All turned a deaf ear. It was not their quarrel. France could be left to perish. Our country, still pursuing a policy of isolation, which though admirably adapted to its period of infancy was unworthy of our maturity, gave no heed to our ancient ally, without whose generous aid the United States might never have become an independent nation. The world deserted France in her hour of extremity and the world is now paying the penalty. Had the civilized states of Europe and America, in 1871, compelled Prussia to respect the higher law in her dealings with France, this world war would probably never have been.

A new problem had now arisen with the development of commerce in southeastern Europe. Acting upon the spirit of false pacifism, the European nations preferred to tolerate Turkish cruelties to Christians to the vindication of Justice by the sword. Turkey had consistently tortured and almost destroyed the Christian nations of southeastern Europe. The cries of the butchered Armenians in Asia Minor and tortured Serbs in the Balkan Peninsula called aloud for vengeance, but Europe in the supposed interests of peace turned a deaf ear.

In 1877, Russia took up the fallen standard of humanity and in defense of the victims of Turkish misrule advanced to the gates of Constantinople. Had the European nations at that time had as much concern for justice and humanity as they had for the material ease of a false peace, this world war would have been prevented. But, unfortunately, England, contrary to the counsel of many of its noblest statesmen, such as Gladstone, Earl Derby and John Bright, intervened to serve Turkey, and Disraeli took his "thirty pieces of silver" by guaranteeing the perpetual integrity of Turkish territory in Europe in return for the cession of Cyprus.

To preserve a false peace, the Congress of Berlin was called in 1878, and at the head of the council table the most sinister personality of the nineteenth century, Prince Bismarck, sat in the role of an "honest broker," to use his own expression. These distinguished diplomats and statesmen vainly thought that they could preserve the peace of Europe by a sordid exchange of territory, even though the adjustment stifled the cries of the dying Christian states in southeastern Europe. Disraeli returned to London in triumph and was acclaimed for bringing back "peace with honor," but we now know that he only brought the seeds of a terrible war. If England could have foreseen the conditions forty years later and beheld the very flower of British youth perish at Gallipoli, the thoughtless acclaim which welcomed the return to Disraeli would have frozen on her lips.

It was solemnly covenanted in that treaty of 1878 that the *status quo* as then established should not be altered, except with the consent of all the participating nations, and yet in 1908 Austria boldly annexed Bosnia and Herzegovina and when the other European nations attempted to intervene, the German Kaiser ostentatiously ranged himself by the side of his imperial cousin, as a "knight in shining armor." The counsels of cowardice prevailed. Again a false pacifism induced the European nations to accept this denial of the good faith of treaties and again their statesmen in a spirit of smug complacency felt that they had preserved the peace of the world by sacrificing justice.

This constant condonation of offenses against the higher law in the supposed interests of peace, emboldened Germany and Austria to plot their treacherous and cowardly *coup* of 1914. The "wheel had come full circle." Russia and France sprang to arms and when the Hohenzollern crossed the frontier of Belgium, Great Britain abandoned its policy of peace at any cost, by staking the existence of its empire in defense of Belgium.

Had the other leading nations of the world followed their course, the war would either never have begun, or would have abruptly ended. This greatest catastrophe of the world, as it is the greatest crime since the crucifixion of Christ, would never have happened, with its loss of the lives of ten millions of men, women and children, if the leading civilized nations of the world had intervened when Germany and Austria sought to violate the fundamental decencies of the higher law by condemning Servia to a living death without a hearing. We all sinned against the light and we are now all paying the penalty.

This war has written in letters of blood the great truth of the necessary solidarity of civilization and the collective responsibility of all nations for the peace of the world. The fact that the war has not been localized, as the neutral nations of 1914 vainly hoped, but has become a world-wide conflagration of immeasurable proportions, must bring home to all nations the great truth of the higher law, that they cannot selfishly and complacently stand aside when the world is in flames, with the sneering remark of Cain, "Am I my brother's keeper?"

A nation is more than a political State. It is an historic entity. Prussia has contributed little or nothing to the German people, except its military martinets and subservient statesmen. Lessing, Fichte and Wagner were Saxons, Holbein and Durer were Bavarians, Goethe was from Frankfort, Wieland, Schiller and Hegel were Swabians, Beethoven was a Rhinelander of Belgian ancestry, Bach a Thuringian.

When the obscure causes of this war are fully revealed, it may be found that the Prussian dynasty precipitated it for one reason, among many, that the rising democracy of Germany, as expressed in the ever-increasing and predominating socialistic vote and the steady widening of the breach between Prussian and other German states, made the future of the Empire uncertain, unless it could again, as in 1871, rivet the chains by a victorious war.

This condition of internal disunion, which preceded the war, will be infinitely increased when the bitter chalice of defeat is commended to the lips of the Hohenzollern Emperor and he fully realizes that this calamity, which has lost his dynasty the respect and goodwill of the world, was caused by a wholly unnecessary and unjust war brought by the Imperial Government upon the most false of false premises.

We must check the present tendency, born of war weariness, to eliminate Justice as a vital factor and to treat the problems of Peace as mere questions of political power and economic value. The folly of statesmen in all ages has been to regard Justice as a mere abstraction of impracticable idealists. They and we must realize that Justice is the dominating factor in human progress and that its ultimate vindication is as certain as the existence of God and as infallible as His judgments. To sacrifice uncounted billions of treasure and uncounted millions of lives for a lame and impotent conclusion, such as a peace by compromise and shifty accommodation, would mark the high tide of human folly. It would be to crucify the cause of Justice afresh and to put it to an open shame.

All other considerations must be subordinated to the primal requisite of Justice. Only thus will the nations "rise to the height of the great argument and vindicate eternal Providence and justify the ways of God to man."

IX

THE TRIUMPH OF DEMOCRACY

The Sesquicentennial of the Declaration of Independence was celebrated in Philadelphia in 1926, where it was written and promulgated out of "decent respect to the opinion of mankind." Though Mr. Beck had recently concluded approximately five years of an arduous service as Solicitor General, he was offered by President Coolidge and accepted the Chairmanship of the National Advisory Committee to the International Exposition. The following address was made at the invitation of the City of Philadelphia on July 4, 1926, in Independence Hall at the approximate hour when, one hundred and fifty years before, that great document was signed by the members of the Continental Congress.   EDITOR.

Mr. Chairman, Ladies and Gentlemen:

The place and the hour are alike of moving eloquence. On July 4, 1776, when the shadows of evening were lengthening and the sun was descending in the direction of Valley Forge, a little band of fifty-five men met within these four walls and issued to the world a statement of their grievances and a declaration of the birth of a new republic. The imagination would indeed be dull, if it were not stirred by the reflection that today one hundred millions of people, constituting the most powerful nation of the modern world and potentially one of the most powerful of all time, are now forgetting for the moment the vivid and vital day, in which they are privileged to live, to recall that other day, one hundred and fifty years ago, when the Fathers created a new nation and dedicated it forever to the cause of human freedom. The flame then lit on that little altar in this Hall still illuminates the world.

Well might Mirabeau say of the great Declaration that, "tried by its standard of liberty, every government in Europe was divested of its sanction." To the masses of men in every part of the world, struggling to escape from the house of bondage and into the promised land, the great Declaration has been as a pillar of cloud by day and a pillar of fire by night. This little group

181

of heroic men "lifted the gates of empires off their hinges, turned the stream of the centuries into a new channel, and still governs the ages."

Well did Tom Paine say in his stirring manifesto, "Common Sense," to which the event we celebrate owes almost as much as to Jefferson's inspired Declaration:

> "We have it in our power to begin the world over again. The birthday of a new world is at hand, and a race of men, perhaps as numerous as all Europe contains, are to receive their portion of freedom from the event of a few months."

Prophetic as was the author of "Common Sense," he did not and could not appreciate the full implications of his statement that "the birthday of a new world is at hand." Although the Fathers little perceived it, the greatest revolution in the history of human thought and social conditions was then in progress. While the imagination of men has taken the Fourth of July as the central fact of the American Revolution—even as the imagination of the French people has taken the Fall of the Bastile as the beginning of the French Revolution—yet to both incidents a disproportionate significance has been attached. Both were only stirring scenes in an epic drama. The Declaration did not create us a people. We were a great people before it was adopted. Declarations, Constitutions and governments do not create peoples, but peoples create governments and ordain constitutions.

France did not begin its great career with the fall of the Bastile, and the attempt of the French Convention to revise chronology by declaring the date of its constitution the year "One," proved abortive. Similarly, the American Commonwealth antedated the United Colonies and later the United States of America. It began with the landing of the first English pioneers upon the coasts of Virginia.

As such, the American Republic is the noble child of the greatest revolution in human thought of an earlier age, namely, the Renaissance. It was born in the "spacious days of Queen Elizabeth" and came into being

through the same great impulse that gave to the world
Frobisher and Raleigh, Drake and Spenser, Sidney and
Coke, Bacon and Shakespeare. Never did human imagination rise to greater heights, and the finest flower of its
genius was the birth of democracy in the new world, of
which the American Revolution was but a single, although
a very noble, chapter. Of Plymouth Rock, which shares
the glory with the shores of Virginia of the great adven-
ture, a New England poet has well said:

"Here on this rock, and on this sterile soil,
Began the kingdom, not of kings, but men;
Began the making of the world again.
Here centuries sank, and from the hither brink,
A new world reached and raised an old world link,
    When English hands, by wider vision taught,
And here revived, in spite of sword and stake,
Their ancient freedom of the Wapentake.
Here struck the seed—the Pilgrims' roofless town,
Where equal rights and equal bonds were set;
Where all the people, equal-franchised met;
    Where doom was writ of privilege and crown;
    Where human breath blew all the idols down;
Where crests were naught, where vulture flags were
        furled,
And common men began to own the world!"

In the Eighteenth Century, humanity was in labor and
of that mighty travail a twin birth resulted. One was
industrial and the other was spiritual, one, the birth of
the machine and the other the birth of democracy. Twin
children are not more inseparably united. While heroic
souls in England, France and America were valorously
fighting for greater freedom for the masses, Watt was developing his steam engine and Ramsey and Fitch were
applying it to transportation. The dynamic power of
man was about to be increased a thousand-fold. A day
was to dawn when he would out-fly the eagle in the air,
out-swim the fish beneath the surface of the waters, and
speak with the rapidity of light itself. Like Prometheus,
man was about to storm the hitherto inaccessible ramparts

of divine power, and, measured by dynamic strength, he was about to become a superman.

It was inevitable that such an infinite expansion of physical power should be accompanied by a struggle for greater freedom. No two facts in all history are of more tremendous and inestimable importance, or of more pregnant consequence to the future,—for good and ill,—than the seemingly indefinite expansion of man's dynamic power, and his invincible demand for the full right to pursue his own true and substantial happiness. The democracy of the hand and the democracy of the soul are, in the last analysis, but one manifestation of the same unconquerable spirit, whose ultimate claim is that man shall be in truth, as well as in theory, "master of his soul and captain of his fate."

De Tocqueville, that extraordinarily keen and prophetic intellect, well said, nearly a century ago:

> "The gradual development of the principle of equality is a providential fact. It has all the chief characteristics of such a fact; it is universal, it is durable, it constantly eludes all human interference, and all events, as well as all men, contribute to its progress. Would it be wise to imagine that a social movement, the causes of which lie so far back, can be checked by the efforts of one generation?"

I have said that the Declaration of Independence did not constitute us a people; it is equally true that it did not constitute us a nation. Inchoate sovereignty as a nation began with the first shot of the "embattled farmers" at Concord Bridge. Months before the Declaration of Independence, the colonies had, to a greater or less extent, become independent and assumed full sovereignty. The Declaration of Independence simply recognized an accomplished fact, and its purpose was not to create a new nation, but to justify its existence to the world.

This does not lessen either its dignity or nobility. On the contrary, its dominant purpose, when rightly conceived, ennobles the great Declaration and has given it due place as one of the noblest documents in the annals of statecraft. The American nation could have contented itself either with facts that spoke more eloquently than words, or, at least, with the formal proposal of Richard Henry Lee, which had been adopted on July 2nd and which declared "That these United Colonies are, and of a right ought to be, free and independent states." This resolution had been proposed as early as June 7th by Richard Henry Lee, under instructions from the mother commonwealth of Virginia, and its passage was then so certain that on June 9th a Committee of Five was appointed to draft a declaration to the world of both the existing fact and its moral justification. This committee consisted of Thomas Jefferson, John Adams, Benjamin Franklin, Roger Sherman and Robert R. Livingston. To Jefferson was assigned the immortal honor of drafting the Declaration, and it is to his undying glory that that Declaration, with a few changes by Franklin and John Adams, was his exalted utterance.

What then was the purpose of the Declaration of Independence? As clearly set forth in its noble Preamble, it was an appeal to the conscience of the world in support of the moral justification of the Revolution. It commences, "When in the course of human events, it becomes necessary for one people to dissolve the political bands which have connected them with another * * * *a decent respect to the opinions of mankind requires that they should declare the causes which impel them to the separation."*

Possibly no state paper ever contained a nobler sentiment than this. It assumed that there was a rule of right and wrong that regulated the intercourse of nations as well as individuals. It believed that there was a great human conscience, which, rising higher than the selfish interests and prejudices of nations and races, would approve that which was right and condemn that which was wrong. This approval was more to be desired than national advantage. It constituted mankind a judge between contending nations, and, lest its judgment should temporarily err, it established posterity as a court of last resort. It placed the tie of humanity above that of nationality. It solemnly argued the righteousness of the separation at the bar of history, solemnly prefixing its statement of grievances with the words: "In proof of this, let facts be submitted to a candid world;" and finally concluded its appeal from the judgment of the moment to that of eternity, in the words: "Appealing to the Supreme Judge of the world for the rectitude of our intentions."

The great Declaration was more than an eloquent plea for the favorable judgment of the world. Another great purpose was to give to man new title papers to liberty. For thousands of years, man had lived under conditions, which justly provoked the cynical remark of Rousseau, with which he began his immortal book, "man is born free and is everywhere in chains." Prior to the middle of the Eighteenth Century, the conception of the sovereignty of the people was almost unknown. Even in France, where the ideas of liberty were then germinating, the people had so little conception of their own rightful sovereignty that, thirteen years after the Declaration of Independence and at the beginning of the French Revolution, the only claim that the French people made was that they should share equally with the clergy and the nobility in the constitution of the legislative body. In 1789 that body had not been convened for over 150 years and there was no novelty in Louis XIV's arrogant boast, "L'etat, c'est moi." The state was conceived as a sacred institution, which existed apart from the people, and had its sanction, not in their will but in some inherent claim. In nearly every nation, the fountain-head of all power and justice was an hereditary monarch, whose power was absolute except as he graciously gave immunities to the people, which were called "liberties." Even in those nations, where the soil had been broken and the seeds of liberty planted, the utmost claim of the masses was for some participation, by the grace of the king, in the legislative councils of the nation. A few inspired spirits, like Locke, Burlamaqui, Montesquieu and Rousseau, were suggesting the then wholly revolutionary idea that, in the origin of human society, sovereignty had originally rested with the people and that it was only by their consent, given by a mythical social contract, that the state, as a separate entity, had been created and its sovereign power vested in an hereditary king.

The mighty shadow of the greatest of the Caesars still rested upon the earth and a century and a half ago Caesarism was the political religion of nearly every people.

Even the men of the Revolution, at its beginning, fully accepted this theory of government. Until the Declaration of Independence, the foremost spirits of the Revolution insistently claimed that they had no quarrel with the King, to whose intervention in their behalf they appealed as suppliants, but solely with the Parliament. It was not until Jefferson drafted the Declaration that the American people denied that there was a "divinity that doth hedge a king." It is noteworthy that the Declaration says nothing whatever about the Parliament and even refrains from mentioning it by name, and that this terrific indictment was preferred against a stupid and obstinate King.

If the Declaration today gives us a quickened pulse, it is not because of the counts of the indictment against the misrule of George the Third, but because Jefferson, at heart an idealist and with all the enthusiasm of youth, challenged this universal conception as to the nature of government and asserted in eloquent phrase, the sovereignty of the people.

He drew for all mankind, without distinction of race, condition or creed, a title deed to liberty, so broad and comprehensive that "time cannot wither nor custom stale" its eternal verity. As with the blast of a mighty trumpet, the Declaration asserts that all men are created equal; that they have a right as the gift of God, and independent of government, to life, liberty, and the pursuit of happiness; that governments derive their just powers from the consent of the governed; that the people have the inherent right to alter or abolish their government when it has ceased to answer their necessities, thus constituting the people the first and only estate. These far-reaching principles satisfy the highest ideals of liberty.

By the much quoted and much misunderstood axiom, that "all men are created equal," Mr. Jefferson did not mean either a natural equality or even an equality of natural opportunity, for either would contradict the common observation of men. He was simply defining the province of government, and he was contending that all men were politically equal and that the government, therefore, should not give to any man an artificial and lawmade advantage over another. "Equal and exact justice to all men, special privileges to none." When asked fifty years later, and nine days before his death, to write a sentiment for the forthcoming fiftieth anniversary of the Declaration—the day of jubilee on which, by a singular coincidence, he was destined to die—he wrote:

"The eyes of men are opened and opening to the rights of man. * * * The mass of men are not born with saddles on their backs nor a favored few booted and spurred, ready to ride them legitimately by the grace of God."

In the noble preamble Jefferson was not attempting to discuss a *form* of government. The Declaration of Independence is no more a treatise on the science of government than the book of Genesis is of natural science. Jefferson's only purpose was to hold up to the imagination of men the great ideals of liberty. He was not appealing to the cold reason of men, as much as to their imagination. Many of the eloquent phrases in the preamble can be as little reconciled with existing realities as some of the Beatitudes with practical Christianity. It can be said of liberty, as George Eliot, in the great climax to *Romola*, finely said of justice that it "is not without us as a fact, but only within us as a great yearning."

Shortly before his death, Jefferson said:

"This was the object of the Declaration of Independence. Not to find out new principles, or new arguments, never before thought of, not merely to say things which had never been said before; but to place before mankind the common sense of the subject, in terms so plain and firm as to command their assent, and to justify ourselves in the independent stand we are compelled to take. Neither aiming at originality of principle or sentiment, nor yet copied from any particular or previous writing, it was intended to be an expression of the American mind, and to give to that expression the proper tone and spirit called for by the occasion."

Due to this fact, few, if any, political documents have more profoundly influenced the struggling masses throughout the world. It remains the classic definition of democracy, if not of liberty, and its noblest echo was the speech of Abraham Lincoln over the new-made graves at Gettysburg, when, inspired by Jefferson, he solemnly said that "government of the people, by the people, and for the people shall not perish from the earth."

It is no mean event, therefore, in the annals of mankind that brings us together today to recall in grateful memory the great event of a century and a half ago. It is interesting to note that if a great Virginian, Thomas Jefferson, drafted the Declaration, yet no one in the Continental Congress supported it more eloquently than John Adams of Massachusetts. Each became a subsequent President of the United States, and there is beauty in the fact that, precisely fifty years later and almost at the same hour on July 4, 1826, Thomas Jefferson and John Adams, great yoke-fellows in the struggle for liberty, were gathered to their fathers. Each had been a storm center of a political conflict, which, in intensity and virulence, has had few equals in our history. Time healed the scars and a mellow age soothed the asperities of political strife, and few incidents in our political history are more beautiful and pathetic than the affectionate intercourse of these two venerable sages—once such bitter enemies—in their later years. If each of them had his temperamental defects, yet each of them had great and noble qualities.

While each has a great claim to our affectionate remembrance, yet as we especially commemorate the Declaration of Independence and as that was largely the work of Thomas Jefferson, we naturally consider him more today than his great rival in fame.

It would be interesting to contrast what the Declaration of Independence would have been, if Franklin, Hamilton or Marshall, instead of Jefferson, had been its draughts-cussion of the practical advantage to foreign nations of as-man. Franklin would have restricted it to a utilitarian dis-

sisting in the creation of a new government and thus weakening the power of the British Empire. He would have invested it with a touch of humor which would have caused the whole world to laugh. Hamilton or Marshall would have restricted the Declaration to an analytical statement of the constitutional principle involved in taxing the colonies without the consent of the local legislatures. Jefferson, although a lawyer, threw away his law books and with flaming imagination wrote the gospel of liberty. An ardent soul, his was also a great intellect. No one of his time, with the exception of Franklin, ever gave so much of a life to intellectual pursuits. From early boyhood until his latest hours, he remained the unwearying and zealous student of the great subjects which challenge the attention of the human intellect. A valued correspondent of four great colleges, the successor of Franklin as President of the American Philosophical Society, he crowned his most useful life by founding the ancient and honorable University of Virginia upon lines so broad and catholic as to anticipate many of today's most valued improvements in education. Art, music, literature, history, politics, science, agriculture, philosophy, religion, all engaged his thoughts, and when his great library, which in the days of his poverty he was compelled to sell to the government, was transported to Washington, it required sixteen wagons, and it was found that they were written in many languages and comprised in their sweep nearly every department of intellectual activity. Here was a man who could supervise a farm, draw the plans for a mansion or a public building with the detail of a capable architect, study nature like a scientist, make useful inventions, play a Mozart minuet on the violin, ride after the hounds, write a brief or manage an intricate law case, draft state papers of exceptional importance, and conduct correspondence with distinguished men in many languages upon questions of history, law, ethics, politics, science, literature and the fine arts.

How did he, the student and recluse, become, in the apt language of one of his contemporaries, "the most delightful destroyer of dust and cobwebs that his time has ever known?" I find that secret primarily in his sturdy optimism, in the fact that he believed in the work which he attempted to do, in his own ability to do it, in its significance in the predestined advancement of humanity, and in the ability and disposition of his fellow men to follow a true leader. He believed passionately in the people. In that lay his great strength.

It would be flattery of the dead to claim that Jefferson was the "Father of Democracy." "There were great men before Agamemnon" and there were great democrats long before Thomas Jefferson. The Elizabethan dramatist, Dekker, said of Christ that he was "the first of gentlemen," and it could be added that the gentle Teacher of Nazareth, who loved the plain people and sympathized with their sorrows, was the first and greatest of democrats. Jefferson was like that noble idealist of Rostand's fancy, Chanticleer. While his clarion voice, of which the great Declaration was the noblest note, did not cause the Sun of Democracy to rise, it did proclaim in the Eighteenth Century more truly than any other human note, the "reddening morn" of the present democratic era.

I am tempted, if only briefly, to discuss the interesting question as to the present state of democratic institutions. When the greatest war of history had ended, and the roar of the last gun on the long battle line had died away in distant echoes, it seemed indeed that Jefferson's political faith had received its most impressive vindication, that "government of the people, for the people, and by the people" had been vindicated and the world had been made "safe for democracy." Not in a thousand years had there been such a dissolution of ancient forms. Crowns had fallen "thick as autumn leaves that strew the brooks of Vallambrosa." Hohenzollern had followed the Hapsburgs and Romanoffs into the night of exile. Ancient dynasties perished; kingdoms fell and empires of a thousand years vanished. Indeed, as President Wilson passed through Europe and the masses arose to acclaim him with hysterical enthusiasm, it seemed as if the existing governments of even the victorious nations were crumbling.

And then a mighty change came over the world's dream of democracy. Russia, Turkey, China, Italy, Poland, Portugal, Spain and even Greece which gave us the word "democracy," are today in the grasp of dictators. A reaction, swift and terrible, against parliamentary government, through which alone institutional democracy can function, swept over the world like the shadow of a huge eclipse. Today everywhere throughout Europe there is a remarkable trend toward a form of government, which is not dependent upon parliamentary majorities.

It is a curious paradox that this does not necessarily mean a revolt against democracy in its ultimate meaning, for a government can be democratic, if it is *of* the people, even though it is not functionally *by* the people. Mallock, in his book, "The Limits of Democracy," accuses Lincoln of tautology in speaking of government "of" and "by" the people, but such is not the fact. A people may themselves authorize a dictatorship and, if so, it as truly represents democracy in its sanction as a parliamentary majority, which too often represents the minority.

But, while a dictatorship may be democratic in the source of its authority, it is never democratic in its machinery, and it is by the method of government, rather than by its sanction, that men commonly judge whether a government is democratic or undemocratic. Thus judged, many dictatorships in Europe are undemocratic, just as Rome was undemocratic when, probably with the consent of the majority of the people, all power was concentrated in Julius Caesar.

The great fact today is that while democracy as a form of government is at low ebb, as a social spirit it is at high tide. Let us not be discouraged if there is a temporary reaction against democratic parliamentary institutions. Human progress moves in a constant series of ascending and descending curves, or, to change the metaphor, its forces are at times centripetal and at times centifugal. Man has, throughout all history, passed through a ceaseless cycle of integration and disintegration. Every age that has been marked by the concentration of power in the hands of a few has been followed by a redistribution of that power among the many and, in turn, every democratic movement, when it has spent its force, has been succeeded by a period of integration.

Take English history. The autocracy of William the Conqueror was followed by the comparative democracy of Magna Charta, and that was, in turn, succeeded by the absolutism of Edward the First, only, in turn, to be supplanted by the democracy of the Peasants' Revolt. When that had spent its force, there came the absolutism of the Tudors, only to be followed by the execution of Charles the First and the democratic Commonwealth. Then came the Restoration and later the absolutism of the earlier Georges, only to be followed by the Chartist movement, in turn succeeded by the early Victorian reaction towards absolutism. In our time democracy in England has triumphed in the virtual destruction of the political power of the Crown and the House of Lords.

No present fact is more significant than the reaction in many nations against parliaments and in favor of one-man power. It matters not whether the one man be called a czar, emperor, king or dictator—the essential fact is his power. Today many of the oldest nations of Europe are in the grasp of dictators. The revolt is not against democracy as a social ideal, but against the inefficiency and venality of parliamentary institutions.

At no time within the memory of living man has Lincoln's ideal of a government of and by and for the people been more openly denied and flouted. The World War revealed, as in a vast illumination, the fact that democracy as a governmental institution is not workable, unless there be a people, who are politically capable of self-government. The founders of our nation recognized this. Washington, Franklin and Hamilton all said that the success of popular government depended less upon its form than upon the moral and intellectual capacity of the people. If they fail to take an intelligent interest in their government, and if they are unprepared to show the spirit of self-restraint, which in my recent book on the Constitution I have called "constitutional morality," there can be no successful democracy. Let us not lay the "flattering unction to our souls" that we have finally and completely solved the great problem of popular government. It is still, to use the words of Lincoln, "an unfinished task," and to it the living, from generation to generation, must still dedicate themselves. "Eternal vigilance is the price of liberty."

In this connection, it must be remembered that a democratic government, as any form of government, is but a means to an end and not, in itself, an end. It must be judged by its fruits. It is not necessarily a final truth, but may prove to be only an inspiring prophecy. President Wilson's eloquent call to arms that "the world must be made safe for democracy," while most effective for its immediate purpose, incorrectly assumed that democracy was an end, of which the world was simply the means, whereas, in truth, the welfare of the world is the end and democracy is but the presently accepted means. Even as the greatest of all teachers said that the "Sabbath was made for man and not man for the Sabbath," we can say that democracy is made for man and not man for democracy.

Our political philosophy has changed the divine right of a king to the divine right of King Demos, and one theory is as untenable as the other. The right of a majority, often mistaken, to impose its will upon the minority, who are only too often in the right, is not by divine ordinance, but is based upon the purely utilitarian consideration that the common welfare requires a temporary subordination of the minority to the majority in the interests of peace. Law is only the reasoned adjustment of human relations and its authority consists only in its reasonableness and service to the common weal. A democracy slowly realizes this. When a majority impose upon a minority some oppressive law, which transcends the fair province of government, the minority revolt as they would against the tyrannous edict of a King. This is not lawlessness, but a true love of liberty. If democratic institutions should prove more prejudicial to the common welfare than other forms of government, to it will come the stern challenge of the great Woodman, "Why cumbereth it the ground?"

Moreover, all forms of government must depend upon the character, or as Aristotle expressed it, the "*ethos*" of the people. It was well said by Lord Morley, one of the most scholarly publicists of our day, that "the forms of government are much less important than the force behind them. Forms are only important as they leave liberty and law to awaken and control the energies of the individual man."

I fear that the founders of the Republic recognized this more clearly than we of this later generation. Even after the adoption of the Constitution,—the best form of government that the wit of man has yet devised,—Washington, on February 7, 1788, wrote that it would only be effective "as long as there shall remain any virtue in the body of the people," and on the last day of the Convention, Franklin said—

"There is no form of government but what may be a blessing to the people, if well administered for a course of years, and can only end in despotism, as other forms have done before it, when the people shall become so corrupted as to need despotic government, being incapable of any other."

Were Franklin alive today, he would see an extraordinary verification of his prophecy in current European developments, where great, historic peoples, who are also liberty-loving, have willingly acquiesced in the despotism of a dictator rather than endure further the incapacity of parliamentary government that will not function.

In weighing the political institutions of a democracy in the scales of a candid judgment, care must also be taken to distinguish between the ponderables and the imponderables. Judged simply on the ponderables, the judgment on democracy, as a form of government after a century and a half, would not be wholly favorable. Its inefficiency, wastefulness and, at times, venality shock the judgment. The believer in democracy is only comforted by the reflection that undemocratic governments have also been wasteful, inefficient and dishonest, and have added tyranny to these vices. Possibly the most repellant feature of democratic institutions is the coarse flattery of the mob, that, by degrading manhood, tends to destroy true leadership. With the destruction of the representative principle, the average politician becomes a mere flatterer of the many and, sometimes, even of the minority, who, under the party system, hold the balance of power. To a democratic age the spectacle is as repellant as that Gallery of Mirrors in the Palace of Versailles, where three thousand courtiers would crowd upon the so-called "Sun-King" to crave the servile honor of handing His Majesty his napkin at dinner. But in a democracy three hundred thousand politicians equally become the obsequious flatterers of King Demos. To flatter the many is no more creditable than to flatter a king.

When, however, the imponderables are taken into consideration, it is easier to defend democracy, for its theory satisfies the noblest aspirations of men. It not only educates them, but gives them hope.

Referring to that great democrat, Abraham Lincoln, Lowell finely said in his classic address on democracy:

> "Democracies have likewise their finer instincts. I have seen the wisest statesman and most pregnant speaker of our generation, a man of humble birth and ungainly manners, of little culture beyond what his own genius supplied, become more absolute in power than any monarch of modern times through the reverence of his countrymen for his honesty, his wisdom, his sincerity, his faith in God and man, and the noble humane simplicity of his character."

Again, Mr. Lowell, himself an intellectual aristocrat, but a democrat by instinct, well said:

> "The democratic theory is that those constitutions are likely to prove steadiest which have the broadest base, that the right to vote makes a safety-valve of every voter, and that the best way of teaching a man how to vote is to give him the chance of practice. For the question is no longer the academic one, 'Is it wise to give every man the ballot?' but rather the practical

one, 'Is it prudent to deprive whole classes of it any longer?' It may be conjectured that it is cheaper in the long run to lift men up than to hold them down, and that the ballot in their hands is less dangerous to society than a sense of wrong in their heads."

Let us today remember that democracy is something more than a form of government—it is a great spirit. Whatever may be said in this temporary ebb-tide of democracy, as to the fate of parliamentary institutions, democracy as a social ideal is as dominating and beneficent today as it has ever been. The equality of man, properly interpreted, is still our ideal, but we mean thereby not an enforced equality, which would standardize man to the level of mediocrity, but, in its last analysis, his right to his own hard-earned inequality. In other words, the inalienable right of man to pursue his own true and substantial happiness, as proclaimed in the great Declaration, means his right to be unequal, for there can be no career open to talent, or any natural justice, if each man is not entitled to the fair fruits of his superior skill and industry. Social democracy asserts the right of every man to make the best of his life, and wars eternally against any form, whether it be of hereditary privilege or class legislation, that would handicap a man in the competition of life, or level him to the plane of his inferiors. This great conception of a "career open to talent," as Napoleon expressed it, or of "the square deal," to use Theodore Roosevelt's effective expression, remains the most dominant and vitalizing influence in life today.

To it we owe the greatness of the Republic. The ideal that every man has a right, free from governmental interference, to make of his dead self the stepping stone to a higher destiny gives to the masses that hope, which has made us the most virile nation the world has ever known. In many other lands, a man is forever identified with his class or caste. Once a coal-miner, he and his children and his children's children can never hope to be anything else. Thus, lacking an incentive to achievement, he sullenly identifies himself with his class and is deaf to the calls of social justice.

In America the democratic spirit gives to every man the hope of rising. To this we owe our illimitable energy and our inexhaustible strength. It is the great imponderable of the subject, and while there is much in democratic institutions today which, judged by the ponderables, would cause our faith to waiver and our minds to be clouded with despair, yet, judged by this great imponderable, we know that the march of man, wherever democracy has led him, is steadily forward. He may, at times, sink into a "slough of despond" or a morass of difficulty, but that eternal hope, which the spirit of democracy has planted in his breast, gives him the strength to struggle out of the morass and march resolutely forward to the "delectable mountains." Such was the spirit of Washington, Jefferson, Franklin and Lincoln, and it is this invincible faith, triumphing over fear, that has made them the great leaders of the American people. As long as democracy can produce such leaders, it vindicates itself.

I fear I have detained you far too long, but I cannot refrain, before concluding, from suggesting the fact that democracy has hitherto had its most effective and noblest expression in the Constitution of the United States. It is true that that great charter is not in method or even theory wholly democratic. On the contrary, it marked a salutary reaction against the extreme claims of democracy. Its essential spirit was finely expressed by Edmund Burke, when he said:

> "Liberty, to be enjoyed, must be limited by law, for law ends where tyranny begins, and the tyranny is the same, be it the tyranny of a monarch, or of a multitude—nay, the tyranny of the multitude may be the greater, since it is multiplied tyranny."

While the Constitution does set limits to the power of the majority and, to this extent, negatives the extreme claims of democracy, yet, as it was adopted by the American people and has now been maintained by them for over one hundred and forty years, that Constitution, with its salutary restraints upon majority rule and its defense of the rights of the individual, is broad-based upon the more permanent general will and is, therefore, in the truest sense of the word, democratic. It is significant that, in all the violent changes of this changing world, our form of government has been the most stable. It has been in the past, and will increasingly be in the future, the model for democratic governments, and upon its maintenance and perpetuity the future of democratic institutions may depend.

Let me recall the proud prophecy of John Bright, one of the noblest democrats of our time:

"I see from the East unto the West, from the rising of the sun to the going down thereof, in spite of what misled, prejudiced, unjust and wicked men may do, the cause of freedom still moving onward; and it is not in human power to arrest its progress."

Part II

ARGUMENTS

X

THE REVOLT AGAINST PROHIBITION

Few speeches in Congress in recent years have attracted more general attention and been the subject of more extended comment than the speech which Mr. Beck delivered in the House of Representatives on February 7, 1930, on the fundamentals of the prohibition controversy. Dealing with a highly controversial subject and addressing a House which is predominately in favor of the Eighteenth Amendment, Mr. Beck had the close and undivided attention of the House and of a crowded gallery for more than an hour and on the conclusion of his address the House rose as a tribute to the speaker. Since its delivery there has been a wide-spread demand for it and it has been characterized by many leaders of opinion as one of the most notable speeches made in Congress in many years.

As the several reprints of this notable speech have been incomplete, it is a satisfaction to the editor to print herewith the full speech with Mr. Beck's final revisions. Whatever the reader may believe as to the merits of prohibition, it can, at least, be said that this speech raised the discussion to a higher plane and challenged the attention of the American people to the fundamentals, not merely the incidentals, of the great controversy.—EDITOR.

Mr. Speaker and my Fellow-Members:

As it will not be easy for me to compress my credo on the subject of prohibition within the limits of the time alloted to me, I must ask my brethren of the House not to interrupt me with questions until I have finished. If time then remains, or if the House is pleased to extend the time for the purpose, I am quite willing to submit myself to the flight of Parthian arrows, which many of my esteemed colleagues may wish to aim at me, for I am quite aware that the views that I am about to express are not shared by a majority of this House. Fortunately, this is a free forum and no parliamentary body in the world is more tolerant in listening to any views that any member may wish to express than the House of Representatives. Therefore, it is not necessary for me to say, as Brutus:

"Hear me for my cause, and be silent, that

203

you may hear; believe me for mine honor, and
have respect to mine honor, that you may believe; censure me in your wisdom and awake
your senses, that you may the better judge."

I ask the indulgent attention of the House to a brief
and inadequate discussion of one phase of the preliminary
report of the Law Enforcement Commission. While I
may have occasion, in the course of my address, to make
some references to the interesting and eloquent address
which our distinguished colleague from New Jersey (Mr.
Fort) delivered last Friday, yet I have no present intention to make a full reply to his argument. I leave that
to abler colleagues, but cannot refrain, in passing, from
expressing my admiration for a speech which has justly
made a deep impression, due largely, I think, to its admirable diction, its faultless delivery and the transparent sincerity and courage of the speaker.

I may further say, in passing, that, notwithstanding his
brilliant argument, I am not convinced that the cause of
temperance would be promoted by making every house-
holder a vintner and every cellar a brewery. I believe
that the greatest evil of our age is the slow destruction of
the home. I am not impressed that either its dignity or
welfare as the greatest asset of civilization is promoted
by the manufacture of intoxicating liquors within the
home.

Nor is it my intention to discuss the entire so-called
"Wickersham Report," nor even the remedial provisions
which this report recommends. As to the latter, my course
is easily charted. The Eighteenth Amendment is undoubtedly the law of the land. It is the duty of the President
to execute it. His great mandate under the Constitution
is to see that the laws are "faithfully executed." It is
ours to determine what laws shall be enacted. He has
taken an oath and can say with a famous litigant in a
celebrated case:

"An oath, an oath, I have an oath in heaven:
Shall I lay perjury upon my soul?
No, not for Venice."

I am, therefore, prepared to vote for any reasonable enforcing measure, which the President may ask, provided always that it is not inconsistent with the Constitution. On some future occasion I may discuss the question whether one recommendation of the President's Commission does not, in substance, deprive the American people of the most ancient right of the English-speaking race, namely, trial by jury.

I restrict my discussion this morning, however, to the opening paragraphs of the preliminary report, which are well titled "Scope and Size of the Problem." I do so because this portion goes to the very fundamentals of the great controversy. Unfortunately, it is expressed in somewhat cryptic phrases, as though the learned Commissioners were consciously walking on very thin ice. I doubt whether the American people have yet fully realized the significance and prophetic character of the inevitable implications of this portion of the report.

I confess to some curiosity as to its author. I suspect that its draftsman was Professor Roscoe Pound, than whom there is no abler student of the philosophy of law. When I read his writings, I recall the lament of Palmerston, who once wished that he was as certain of any one thing as Lord Macaulay was of everything.

Whoever be the author, this is the significant prelude to the Preliminary Report, to which I invite your close attention and upon which it is my purpose to make some comments:

> "It is impossible wholly to set off observance of the prohibition act from the large question of the views and habits of the American people with respect to private judgment as to statutes and regulations affecting their conduct. To reach conclusions of any value, we must go into deep questions of public opinion and the criminal law. We must look into the several factors in the attitude of the people, both generally and in particular localities, toward laws in general and toward specific regulations. We must note the

attitude of the pioneer toward such things. We must bear in mind the Puritan's objection to administration; the Whig tradition of a 'right of revolution'; the conception of natural rights, classical in our polity; the democratic tradition of individual participation in sovereignty; the attitude of the business world toward local regulation of enterprise; the clash of organized interests and opinions in a diversified community; and the divergencies of attitude in different sections of the country and as between different groups in the same locality. We must not forget the many historical examples of large-scale public disregard of laws in our past. To give proper weight to these things, in connection with the social and economic effects of the prohibition law, is not a matter of a few months."

To many this preliminary explanation of the Commission may be as enigmatic as the Delphic oracle, but if the prohibition leaders had caught its full significance, they would have rent their garments, sat themselves down in sackcloth and ashes, or possibly have had resort to the wine which on high scriptural authority "maketh glad the heart of man." The obvious meaning of this cryptic deliverance of the President's Commission is that the collective experience of the past and the time-honored traditions of the English-speaking people constitute a damning indictment of the Eighteenth Amendment. It is a pity that the Commission did not say so in words that "he who runs may read," for it would have cleared the present foggy atmosphere. While it should not require "a few months" for the learned members of the Law Enforcement Commission to convert their plain implications into positive statements, yet it should be a matter of gratification to the wets and of apprehension to the drys that this Commission, composed of able and learned men, will at some appropriate time pass from the mere incidentals of the great controversy and discuss the very heart of the problem. They have by fair implication made a solemn promise to do so and they will not break faith with the people.

The fanatical dry leaders are at the moment enjoying a Belshazzar's feast, as they view the fat and juicy majorities which they have in this Congress and in other legislative bodies. But upon the wall now appear the words, "*Mene, Mene, Tekel, Upharsin*"—for the sentences that I have quoted, when translated into common speech, mean that the prohibition amendment has been "weighed in the balances and found wanting."

I do not profess to be a Daniel, although at the moment, surrounded by a largely preponderating majority of the drys, I may be in a "lion's den," but I shall venture to explain the real significance of these pointed allusions to the ancient traditions and experiences of the English-speaking race and their application to the present situation.

The profoundest intellect of antiquity, Aristotle, said two thousand years ago that, if a constitution—by which he meant the aggregate of the laws prescribed by the State—conflict with what he called the "ethos," namely, the spirit or genius of a people, the result of the conflict would not be uncertain, for laws can have no lasting vitality save in the spirit of a people. We must distinguish this "ethos," or spirit, of a people from the mere results of the polling booth, or fluctuating votes in legislative assemblies, for these only register the temporary opinions of fleeting majorities, and at times even minorities, while the "ethos" of the people is a quality born with the individual and persisting unto his death. "The shallow murmur but the deep are dumb."

If this be true, then it is especially true of a race of individualists, who have never been disposed to place upon the brow of King Demos a crown, which they had taken from autocratic kings. Hence, the significance of the phrase in the report, "We must note the attitude of the pioneer toward such things." We are still a race of pioneers. It is true that we have cleared a continent of its once virgin forests, but the American people did something far greater than that. They cleared the mind of America from the obsession of past ages that a State had an unlimited and divine power to regulate, in all respects, the conduct of the individual. A race of individualists does not deify the State. It refuses to believe that the oil of anointing, that was once supposed to sanctify the head of the monarch and clothe his utterances and acts with infallibility, has now fallen upon the multitudinous tongue of the majority. The individualist at all times, and never more than in this country, has said to the State: "There is a limit to your power; thus far and no further, and here shall thy proud waves be stayed." The ten-year revolt against the oppressive regulation of private conduct prescribed in the Eighteenth Amendment is a most encouraging sign. If many Americans had not thus risen in protest, we would not be worthy descendants of a freedom-loving ancestry. It proves that, no matter how powerful the State is, and no matter how great its appeal to the imagination, the American people have not yet lost the spirit of individualism which has made them the greatest nation in the world.

It may be, as the gentleman from New Jersey argued, that prohibition has been a great economic advantage to our industrial society, although I confess it is hard to understand, if that be so, why Germany, France and England, three of the most efficient industrial states in the world, have managed for centuries to conduct their great industrial enterprises with unexampled efficiency without denying the laboring man the right to have a glass of wine or beer. But, assuming it to be the fact that prohibition has added an infinitesimal fraction of one per cent to the industrial output of America, the American people, and especially those who labor with their hands, are not disposed to sell their ancient birthright for such a mess of pottage.

The report goes on: "We must bear in mind the Puritan's objection to administration." That suggests an historical fact of great significance. When the Pilgrims of the Mayflower set forth on their momentous journey, fleeing as they were from oppressive laws whose sanctity they refused to admit, and were by chance of wind and wave brought to the coast of Massachusetts, instead of that fair land of Pennsylvania, to which they had intended to go, and when, having seen the rock-bound coast of Massachusetts, they preferred to put out again to sea, and when, that being impossible, they decided to land, they felt it necessary to enter into a compact of government, and it is interesting to note that, in that first rudimentary constitution written in the cabin of the Mayflower, these pioneers only agreed with each other to obey such "just and equal laws" as the majority might prescribe. In that lay the germ of our system of constitutional limitations upon the power of the State. Having had some experience with the abuses of legislation and believing that there was an unwritten law that prevented any State from exceeding the true province of government, they only agreed to obey "just and equal" laws.

The preliminary report further emphasizes its meaning by a most significant analogy. It says: "The Whig tradition of a 'right of revolution'; the conception of natural rights, classical in our polity; the democratic tradition of individual participation in sovereignty." What does this allusion to the great "Whig tradition" mean? The word "Whig" first became associated with the liberal tendencies of the free yeoman of England before the revolution of 1688. James II, an arbitrary monarch, believed that it was his divine right to impose his ideas of morality upon individuals and to enforce his mandates, he sent out his Lord Chief Justice Jeffreys on what was known as the "Bloody Assizes." Within four weeks Jeffreys had tried and convicted over twelve hundred men and women, and even children. Of course, this is not a record for efficiency, as compared with our government in the matter of prohibition, for last year, according to the report of our able Attorney General, there were terminated 56,455 criminal prosecutions under the Volstead Law. Jeffreys, therefore, only converted free Englishmen into criminals at the rate of three hundred a week, whereas our benign government is indicting the American people at the rate of one thousand a week!

This significant reference to the Whig tradition may refer to the use of the name in American politics and this suggests an analogy of profound interest and significance. The Whig Party from 1830 to 1860 was a great party. It had such leaders as Henry Clay and Daniel Webster. Its weakness was its disposition to adjust questions of profound morality in the spirit of compromise and surrender. Clay was the "great compromiser" of American politics. Webster yielded to the spirit when, eighty years ago next March, he arose in the Senate and, in the interests of the Union, which he loved so truly, advocated a drastic extension of the Fugitive Slave Law. It must be remembered that the Fugitive Slave Law was also based on the Constitution, but the attempt to make the people of the North involuntary slave-catchers provoked such an intense moral revolt that Webster did not avert the Civil War by his speech of March Seventh, but simply destroyed himself in his honest attempt to save the Union by making the Fugitive Slave section of the Constitution more obligatory.

The result is a sinister omen for the Republican Party even in this day of its great power. The Whig Party perished and the Republican Party came into being. Our history gives an earlier instance of the danger of violating this "higher law" of human freedom, even though its pretended justification is the maintenance of the Constitution. The Federalist Party believed that Jefferson and his party were attempting to destroy the Constitution and in its defense passed the alien and sedition laws. These oppressive laws destroyed the Federalist Party. The Republican Party may well profit by these two great lessons. I say it with regret, but I say it as a necessary warning, that the Republican Party cannot longer afford to sell its soul to the fanatical Drys and if it does, and thus becomes the party of Prohibition, it may have a like fate. The party did not emancipate the slave to put the white man in the chains of an intolerant policy. The Democratic Party can retain its hold upon its rank and file by the *vis inertiae* of invincible prejudices, but the Republican Party cannot hold forever a large number of self-respecting men and women to whom the intolerance of prohibition is a moral affront. It cannot forever be half-wet and half-dry.

And what is the meaning of this "conception of natural rights classical in our polity," to which the draftsman of the preliminary report refers? To understand it, we must go back to the epic days of our Republic. In the colonial period, the sturdy yeoman of America believed, as all their ancestors had before them, that the State was a thing separate and apart from the people and that its authority to impose its will without restriction upon its subjects was only secondary to that of God. In the middle of the Eighteenth Century, the new conception of the sovereignty of the people and the reserved rights of the individual became the great ideal. It gave the burning significance to the great preamble of the Declaration of Independence, which has given, not only to us, but to all mankind, a definition of liberty which "time cannot wither, nor custom stale."

Even as the pathfinders of the Mayflower limited the power of government to the imposition of "just and equal" laws, so there is in the hearts of all generations of Americans a profound instinct that, whether safeguarded by constitutional limitations or not, there is a moral limit to the power of government to regulate private conduct.

I do not construe this right of personal liberty as narrowly as did the gentleman from New Jersey last Friday. He said: "What is the American's right of personal liberty? Well, first, he may think as he pleases, and when he has done that, there is not another thing he can do as he pleases." I cannot accept such a definition of liberty. I commend to my distinguished colleague a rereading of the Bill of Rights, as set forth in the first nine amendments to the Constitution. If the utterances of the living ever reach the dead, then my colleague's definition of liberty must have made George Mason, and Thomas Jefferson and George Washington turn in their graves. Such a definition of liberty is so amazing that I prefer to think that our colleague did not mean the literal import of his words. He simply meant that there was no liberty that was absolute and in this I agree. But there are ancient liberties of a free people, protected by constitutional limitations, or by this "ethos" of the people, of which Aristotle spoke, or by ancient customs and the collective experience of free nations which, when invaded by the State, cannot find any moral justification, even in a constitutional amendment.

No one who knows me will challenge my deep reverence for the Constitution. I have given much of the best energies of my life to its defense. If I have rendered to my day and generation any service, it has been in calling attention, by pen and words, to a noble compact of government, which, I fear, is more respected than read. But I am not prepared to say that even an amendment to the Constitution forecloses controversy upon any subject, or that it is unpatriotic to challenge its wisdom. Certainly the fact that there was constitutional authority for the Alien and Sedition Laws and for the Fugitive Slave Laws failed to stifle the revolt of the people against these laws which were found to be undue interferences with personal rights and beliefs—and thus contrary to their "ethos." The Constitution is a living organism and finds its strength and vitality in its adaptability to changed conditions and a wider vision.

We are constantly reminded by the fanatical drys that to question the wisdom of the Eighteenth Amendment is a challenge to the Constitution itself. I deny it. They would not think so if the conditions were reversed. Suppose—and it is a fanciful supposition—that the Eighteenth Amendment read that the manufacture and use of alcoholic beverages should be encouraged and that every citizen was commanded by its terms to drink an alcoholic beverage once a day. Would the fanatical Dry, in that event, have the same feeling as to the sanctity of the Constitution and its infallible wisdom? Would he not argue, as the wets now argue, that such an amendment goes beyond the fair province of government? Would those, to whom any alcoholic beverage is distasteful, take their daily portion out of respect to the Constitution?

Certainly, the leaders of prohibition showed scant respect for the Constitution when they wrote this illegitimate amendment into that noble instrument and thus destroyed its perfect symmetry and turned a wise compact of government into a mere police code. Certainly, they had scant respect for the Constitution when they thus destroyed its basic principle of local self government and in this matter of daily habit, relegated the sovereign States to the ignominious position of mere police provinces. The Constitution has suffered many changes, some of which have impaired its symmetry and beauty, but none that is comparable to the Eighteenth Amendment in its destructive effect upon the proud consciousness of the once sovereign States.

The preliminary report goes on to say: "We must not forget the many historical examples of large-scale public disregard of laws in our past." The report might have added, in the past of the whole human race, for the political progress of civilization has always been marked by revolts against unjust and oppressive laws and it is significant that, in the long run, the spirit of the individual has been triumphant. Two thousand years ago, the greatest Empire that the world ever knew tried for three centuries to stamp out a little group, who were proposing to the world a new religion, and it is interesting to note that the most sacred ceremonial of that religion involves the use of wine. After three centuries of the most ruthless oppression known to antiquity, the Roman Emperor Constantine not only abandoned the policy as futile, but actually raised the Cross as the conquering symbol of the Roman Empire.

A thousand illustrations could be given from intermediate history, but a present one should suffice. Before the Great War the most powerful and ruthless despotism in Western civilization was Russia under the Czars. It attempted to stop the use of alcoholic beverages and when an even more powerful government supplanted the rule of the Czars, the attempt was continued. In the whole history of the world, there has never been anything more ruthless, despotic and cruel than the Russia of the Soviet regime. To the leaders of this organized system of cruel oppression, Marat, Danton and Robespierre are as innocent Sunday School children. No rights, in our conception of the word, are given to any Russian when he finds himself in conflict with the small coterie who rule that vast country.   And yet, neither the iron hand of the Czars, nor the ruthless power of the Soviet regime, has ever made prohibition effective, even in a country where for centuries the people have in other respects accepted despotic rule as of course.   It must be said in candor that the Soviet Regime at least had the wisdom to abandon the futile attempt.   Shall our nation be less wise?

It was Edmund Burke who said that he did not know how to frame an indictment against all the people, but he might have gone further and said that you cannot indict a substantial portion of the people.   The fact that, after ten years of enforcement, with the expenditure of hundreds of millions of dollars and a ghastly sacrifice of many lives, the prohibition law is still largely unenforced, damns it beyond any defense, and the only remedy suggested by the gentleman from New Jersey proves its futility.   The great argument for prohibition was the injury to the home from excessive drinking and our colleague well said, "there is not a man who does not know, even the moderate drinker, that his use of liquor never added anything to the happiness of his family or the comfort of his home," and yet our esteemed colleague, as a last attempt to enforce the unenforceable, would make every home a potential brewery or wine press.   It is enough to say of that argument that, even if it were desirable, which, in my opinion, it is not, it can find no justification in the Volstead Law, which expressed its own intent to prevent the further "*use*" of alcoholic beverages.

The only explanation that our colleague can give for the present situation is his suggestion that "the truth is that we Americans do not obey laws when it serves our purpose not to.   We hate to be told we must do anything."   This, is of course, an echo of the oft-quoted statement that we are the most lawless people in the world. I deny it.   Excluding the slums of our cities and judging the nation as a whole, we are the most patiently law-abiding people in the world.   I doubt whether there is a nation in Europe, outside of Russia, in which such a policy could have been received with so much good humor, and obeyed by millions to whom it seemed a gross violation of individual liberty. Imagine the passage of such a law in France! In 1916 it was my melancholy privilege to witness the bombardment of Rheims and, in that scene of desolation and ruin, I shall never forget the sight of the vineyards of France, extending around the destroyed city and almost to the battlefront, in which the women and children worked while their fathers, husbands and brothers died in the trenches. To me the wine pressed from that vintage might be regarded as distilled in the tears of the French women and children. Who can say that France has suffered by the enjoyment for a thousand years of the delightful light wines of that country and who could say that a law, which would seek to prevent them from enjoying this fruitage of that fair garden of France, would not cause a revolution?

If a law have any reasonable justification, or is even within the reasonable province of government, then the American people are as loyal to it as any other people, but they refuse to believe that a law is either infallible or omnipotent. They know better. To the American the law is but the reasoned adjustment of human relations and its true sanction is largely in its reasonableness and not in the fiat of the State. It is ever-lastingly true that you cannot make the American people respect a law in the intellectual sense unless it be worthy of respect. In this respect, at least, they have still the liberty of thought, which our colleague from New Jersey regards as our one remaining liberty.

A law, to be enforced, must find its justification in the conscience of the American people. They know full well that they do not make the laws, except indirectly. The laws are made, under our system of representative government, by men whom the people select for this purpose, but the people know little or nothing of nine-tenths of the laws which the representatives of the people enact in their behalf. The American people themselves directly never placed the Eighteenth Amendment in the Constitution. It was "bootlegged" into the Constitution in a period of stress by a combination of misguided moral forces led by fanatics, and by a few manufacturers, who, with their own wine cellars well filled, were quite content to increase their output to sell the liberty of the American citizen for "thirty pieces of silver." It was proposed to the people by a portion of five hundred Senators and Representatives in Congress and it was ratified by possibly five thousand votes in the legislatures of the States. The people never had an opportunity to pass upon the question, except in Ohio, where on a referendum the people rejected the Eighteenth Amendment, although it had already been ratified by the Legislature. I do not mean to intimate that a majority of the people might not favor this law. Perhaps they would. It matters not to me if they would, for the reserved rights of the individual under the higher law of human liberty are not dependent upon fleeting majorities.

An increasing number of Americans, who once advocated prohibition, no longer believe in it after the practical test of ten years. They have seen some disadvantages in the policy, which apparently escaped the attention of our esteemed colleague from New Jersey, when last Friday he entered upon his audit of the advantages and disadvantages of prohibition. I will give you one, to which he paid no attention, and that is the effect of this policy upon the moral fiber of the American people. We all remember the famous poem of another century as to what constitutes a State. It is not the form of government— it is the character of the people. When the great work of the Constitutional Convention was ended, Washington wrote to his comrade-in-arms, Lafayette, that it would last as long, and no longer, "as there was any virtue in the body of the people."

What effect, then, has prohibition had upon the American people? That it has not increased their respect for law, which is the vital spirit of any government, must be conceded, but it is of far greater consequence that prohibition has organized our country upon a vast scale of collective hypocrisy, and, like a cancer, this spirit of double-dealing is eating away the moral fiber of the American people. The more you try to enforce it, the greater the spread of hypocrisy. The proposed additions to the Volstead Law will have as little effect as putting a mustard plaster on a cancer. It will not cure the cancer—it will only intensify its activity and cause it to spread more rapidly through the body politic. From their pioneer forefathers the American inherited a spirit of sincerity, but now we witness a general hypocrisy and double-dealing, which is fast destroying the character of our official life and even the morale of the people.

The spiritual leader of Christendom was the patient Nazarene. He could forgive almost any form of transgression. About him he found everywhere human errors and yet he had no harsh words for human weakness. The one exception was the vice of hypocrisy, and, be it noted, the hypocrisy of the Scribes and Pharisees, the lawgivers of the Jewish commonwealth of that time. In all literature there is possibly no more biting invective than that which the patient and forgiving Nazarene uttered against the scribes of the law, as set forth in Chapter 23 of St. Matthew's Gospel:

> "Woe unto you, scribes and Pharisees, hypocrites! for ye pay tithe of mint and anise and cummin, and have omitted the weightier matters of the law, judgment, mercy and faith: these ought ye to have done, and not to leave the other undone.
>
> "Ye blind guides, which strain at a gnat and swallow a camel.
>
> "Woe unto you, scribes and Pharisees, hypocrites! for ye make clean the outside of the cup and of the platter, but within they are full of extortion and excess.
>
> "Thou blind Pharisee, cleanse first that which is within the cup and platter, that the outside of them may be clean also."

I commend these verses to the distinguished Bishop of Virginia, whose sincerity and high motives I do not question, that if in his militant efforts for prohibition he will only regain the spirit of the twenty-third chapter of St. Matthew he will moderate his activities and he will then become more like the bishops of the early Christian Church, of whom it can be said that they never provoked a political revolution and never tried to impose morality by state law. They never felt that was any part of the true functions of the Church. To "render unto Caesar the things that are Caesar's" and to the church its moral functions and activities was their ideal.

If the spirit of these verses makes no appeal to the distinguished prelate, then may I pass from sacred to profane literature and say to him, as Sir Toby said to Malvolio, "Dost thou think, because thou art virtuous, there shall be no more cakes and ale?"

We were told that prohibition would empty the jails and we have just voted millions to build more Federal prisons to accommodate the thousands who are being driven there by the law, many of whom might have been useful citizens. I refuse to believe that any system that indicts a thousand American citizens a week in our Federal courts, and in many cases destroys their self-respect, is of any real advantage to the development of American manhood.

The prohibition controversy presents an irrepressible problem, which has two grave aspects for the American people.

One is the relation of the Nation to the States.

The States had been losing their powers through the inevitable results of steam and electricity, but Federal prohibition so destroyed their moral consciousness as States that they are fast becoming little more than police provinces and their rights as States are rapidly vanishing. The "indissoluble union of indestructible states" has become little more than a rhetorical phrase. To those of us who loved the old Union, whose basic principle was local self-government as to all matters that did not require a uniform rule of national regulation, it is tragical that, in less than one hundred and fifty years after the adoption of the Constitution, its very foundation, namely, Home Rule, has been thus undermined.

But, apart from the effect of prohibition upon our dual form of government, there is the greater and more ancient struggle between the man and the State. Our esteemed colleague from New Jersey, towards the close of his very eloquent remarks and after offering the wets the consolation that they could make their own wine and possibly beer in their own cellars, suggested to them that they "be content with what they make, but, above and beyond all, that they be good sports." Let me remind him that the English-speaking race have never taken tyrannical laws lying down. Their conception of sportsmanship is to continue to fight until it is won. They believe, with Lincoln, that no question is ever settled until it is settled right, and they are no more afraid than Lincoln to be temporarily in a minority. They are not afraid of temporary defeat. Their spirit in this matter is an earnest one and has more to do with the human spirit than with physical appetite. To many—and I am one—the use of such beverages is a matter of indifference. It has never been a habit with me, although, when I leave the Statue of Liberty behind me on my Summer holiday, I occasionally enjoy a glass of wine or beer. The only appetite, of which I am conscious, is to restore the institutions of a once self-respecting people.

The direct way to end this system of tyranny and hypocrisy would be to repeal the Eighteenth Amendment and thus leave to the States the adjustment of the problem, in accordance with their local conditions and several necessities. The only function of the Federal government should be to tax heavily all such beverages to discourage consumption and to utilize its power over interstate commerce to prevent the nullification of State laws by interstate shipments.

I appreciate the present and insuperable difficulty of securing such a repeal. The shadows of life are fast lengthening with me and I may never live to see the day when the Eighteenth Amendment is formally repealed. Fortunately, the American people are not so impotent that they cannot undo this gigantic folly without first securing the consent of three-fourths of the States. To make a formal addition to the Constitution, such consent is necessary, but the enforcement of any clause of the Constitution, which is not self-enforcing, depends upon the preponderating will of each living generation, for, as Jefferson well said, "the Constitution is for the living and not for the dead."

A clear distinction must be made between the clauses of the Constitution that in themselves are a mandate to Congress, on the one hand, and a mere delegation to Congress of power to do a thing. For example, the Constitution, by a specific mandate, required a census every ten years and the recent lamentable failure of Congress to comply with that imperative mandate admits of no excuse, for our duty was largely ministerial, but the Constitution also gives to Congress "the power" to regulate commerce. The method of regulation is a matter of political discretion, and if Congress is of opinion, as it was for the first century of the Republic, that the interests of commerce were best subserved by the absence of any federal regulation, this would not constitute any violation of the Constitution. The Constitution gives to Congress the sole power to declare war but to maintain peace is not a violation of the Constitution. Congress has always had "the power" to levy an income tax but refused to do so until the Sixteenth Amendment made apportionment unnecessary.

In other words, the Constitution grants to Congress many powers, and states many objectives, but often leaves to the political discretion of Congress the question as to the manner of their exercise, or, indeed, whether they shall be exercised at all. Chief Justice Marshall well expressed this in *Gibbons* v. *Ogden,* when he said:

> "The wisdom and the discretion of Congress, their identity with the people, and the influence which their constituents possess at elections, are, in this, as in many other instances, as that, for example of declaring war, the sole restraints on which they have relied, to secure them from its abuse. They are the restraints on which the peo-

ple must often rely solely, in all representative governments."

It must be conceded that the first section of the Eighteenth Amendment does contain a prohibition, which, however, is a mere *brutum fulmen* without enforcing statutes. But the second section shows that the Eighteenth Amendment is not self-enforcing, for it vests in Congress and the several States concurrent power "to enforce this article by appropriate legislation." The means, therefore, of enforcing this statute, or, indeed, the duty of enforcing it at all, rests in the political discretion of Congress and its members are only responsible to the American people. Therefore, while the Constitution is a "sacred compact between the dead, the living and the unborn," as Burke said, yet the living generation can determine whether such grants of power shall be exercised, and if so, in what manner. For a century, as stated, they were satisfied that the commerce power of the Constitution should not be exercised by affirmative legislation and similarly each living generation can determine for itself whether they will pass affirmative legislation to enforce the Eighteenth Amendment, or leave it without federal enforcing statutes.

Even if this were not so, Congress could, without any violation of the Constitution, reach the conclusion that the methods of enforcement and the actual enforcement of the Eighteenth Amendment were best left to the States, even as the States may without any violation of the Constitution leave all enforcing measures to the federal government.

I shall probably be stigmatized by thoughtless men, who have possibly not read the Constitution in years, with being a "nullificationist."

Such is not the fact. The discretion, which I claim for Congress, is vested in it by the Constitution itself. That great compact was formulated after our mother country had firmly established the supremacy of Parliament as the great Council of the Realm. Within the sphere of federal power the Fathers intended to make the Congress the great council of the Republic, with this difference that even within that sphere of federal power, the Constitution limited the powers thus delegated by imperative "shalls" and "shall nots." Except as thus directed, the exercise of other "powers" was in the discretion of the Congress as the truest representative of the American people. This gives to the Constitution the "elasticity in detail," which Lord Bryce so much admired in his classic work. It makes the Constitution serve the living, as well as the dead.

Section 2 of the Eighteenth Amendment clearly lodged in the Congress of the United States and the legislatures of the several States "power" to enact enforcing legislation. It is significant that the Eighteenth Amendment did not say that they "shall" do so. It simply gives them the "power."

Whenever a political discretion is lodged in Congress, the Constitution uses the expression "the Congress shall have power" and when no such discretion is vested in the Congress, the Constitution, with its characteristic precision, says Congress "shall" do a thing or Congress "shall not" do a thing. It thus wisely discriminated between matters which required an imperative mandate and matters which were left to the political discretion of Congress. The logical order of the Constitution clearly indicates this. The first seven sections of Article I, consist almost wholly of imperative "shalls" as to which Congress has no discretion whatever. As, for example, the mandate that Congress "shall" enumerate the people by a decennial census for the purpose of apportionment.

Then by section 9 there is provided a long series of "shall nots," as to which Congress has no political discretion whatever. For example, the provision that no bill of attainder shall be passed, or any preference given to the port of one State over the port of another State, or that no title of nobility shall be granted by the United States. These imperative "shall nots" leave no political discretion whatever to Congress.

Section 10 then provides for a number of "shall nots" with respect to the States. As, for example, the statement that no State shall lay any impost or duty on imports or exports.

Having thus provided with an emphasis worthy of the Ten Commandments, what the Congress shall or shall not do, and what the States shall not do, section 8 of Article I is a lengthy statement of matters which are committed to the political discretion of Congress, and such grant of power is uniformly in the words, "the Congress shall have power," etc.

Undoubtedly the first section of the Eighteenth Amendment does operate to prevent any *affirmative* legislation, either by Congress or the States, which would legalize what that section expressly prohibits. If, for example, Congress or any State Legislature should pass a law to permit the sale of ardent liquors, the Supreme Court could declare such a statute void, but, if the Congress failed to pass any enforcing statute whatever, the prohibition of the first section is unenforceable in the federal courts.

In other words, Congress has a political discretion as to whether it will pass enforcing statutes or not, but if it passes an enforcing statute, it must be consistent with section 1 of the Eighteenth Amendment. In exercising this discretion, Congress has a right to define what an "intoxicating liquor" is and, within reasonable limits, the judiciary would accept such definition. In other words, the judiciary would not declare a beverage intoxicating which Congress refused to class as an intoxicating beverage, unless the fact of such intoxicating quality was clear beyond reasonable doubt.

When the American people thus recognize that the non-exercise of such a power is not necessarily a challenge to the Constitution, they will in due time wholly sweep away that monstrous compound of iniquity and folly, the Volstead Law, and upon its ruins build afresh. They will recognize that the normal use of light wines and beer not only does not lead to intoxication, but promotes temperance by preventing hard drinking and the use of narcotics. When that happy day comes, our colleague from Mississippi, who delighted us this morning with his discourse on ancient books, can add the Volstead Law to his valued incanabula of human folly.

However, it is not my purpose to discuss remedies, but to suggest that the living generation, without any violation of the Constitution, can mitigate the intolerable evils under which we are suffering. If we continue to submit to the graft, corruption and violence brought about by the Volstead Law, then it can be said of us, "The fault, dear Brutus, is not in our stars, but in ourselves that we are underlings."

The American people often think slowly, but, in the long run, surely. They are too wise not to acknowledge a demonstrated error. Above all, they have not lost their love of individual liberty and their jealousy of governmental power and if they do not, in their own good time, end the "Witches' Sabbath" of moral demagoguery, hypocrisy and corruption, then I have much misjudged the character of the American people.

I have made no attempt to follow our distinguished colleague from New Jersey in his attempt to assay the relative economic advantages and disadvantages of prohibition. These are but the ponderables of the question. The great imponderable is the right of every man in a true democratic commonwealth to live his own life, always provided that he does not injure the equal right of others to pursue their own true and substantial happiness. In applying that basic principle of democracy to the problem of prohibition, we must not generalize from exceptional cases. A drunkard can be both a nuisance and a menace, but our past history and the history of civilization have shown that uncounted millions can enjoy the kindly juice of the grape without any injury, either to themselves or to others. Unless we are prepared to vindicate that primal liberty of a man to order his own life, we should tear down the Statue of Liberty in New York harbor, for at the moment and in this respect, it is little more than a brazen lie.

My colleagues of the House, I cannot conclude, as my time has expired, without assuring you how deeply I appreciate the consideration and patience with which those who differ with me have listened to my inadequate argument. To my mind the House of Representatives—and I do not say it to be ingratiating—is not only the most efficient parliamentary body in the world, regard being had to the unparalleled burdens that are cast upon it, but I think it has the noblest spirit. You would not find, I believe, in any other parliamentary body, in a moral issue in which there is such acute feeling as prohibition, that a speaker, representing but a fraction of the House, would have the patient, courteous attention, with which you all have honored me, even those to whom my argument is worse than "foolishness and a stumbling block."

Such tolerance is in this Chamber,—thank God for it,— and may it always be so, but it does not exist in equal measure outside of this Chamber. Since I announced five days ago my intention to make this speech on prohibition, I have had many letters, one of them threatening me in the most emphatic way, that if I dared to make this speech, I need not expect to return to Congress.

My fellow Members of Congress, when the time comes that in a great fundamental moral problem like this, I compromise my convictions to save my seat in Congress, may "my right hand forget her cunning and my tongue cleave to the roof of my mouth."

XI

THE END OF A CENTURY-OLD CONTROVERSY

Few constitutional questions have ever been the subject of such continuous discussion during the existence of the Republic, or have led to more striking developments in the political life of the Nation than the one that is herein discussed.

The Constitution was silent as to the power to remove executive officials and in the First Congress of the United States the question arose as to whether the President had this power of removal by virtue of his executive prerogative, or whether it existed by either an express or implied grant from Congress. A debate of many weeks ensued, in which many participated who themselves had formulated the Constitution in the great Convention. Few abler debates have ever taken place in Congress. The champion of the executive prerogative was James Madison and never was his clarity of reasoning and foresight more in evidence. Hamilton at first was of the opinion that Congress was the source of the removal power, but later in life he is said to have changed his opinion.

The Act of July 12, 1876 (19th Statutes 80), had provided that a Postmaster could only be removed "with the advice and consent of the senate." President Wilson removed the Postmaster of Portland, Oregon, without such consent and, in a suit brought by Myers, the Postmaster, against the United States for his salary, the question was finally raised in the Supreme Court in a form that imperatively required a decision of this century-old controversy. The opinions of the Court, which will be found in 272 U. S. 52, are among the lengthiest of constitutional opinions. The report of the case comprises 242 pages of that volume. Unquestionably, this case will always rank in the judicial history of the country as one of the great leading cases on constitutional law.

As the case involved a distribution of power between the executive and the Congress, the Court invited the Honorable George Wharton Pepper, the senior Senator from Pennsylvania, to argue the case in behalf of Congress. The Honorable Will R. King, former Justice of the Supreme Court of Oregon, argued the case for the Postmaster. As Solicitor-General of the United States, Mr. Beck argued it in behalf of the President. The final decision of the Court, which sustained the executive prerogative, will always rank among the great decisions of the Court and hardly less noteworthy than the comprehensive opinion of the Chief Justice, who spoke for a majority of his brethren, were the powerful dissenting opinions of Justices Holmes, McReynolds and Brandeis.—EDITOR.

If the Court Please:

I agree with opposing counsel that, if this statute is constitutional, the appellant has a good cause of action. The statute of limitations, which Congress prescribed, gave Mr. Myers six years within which to assert his rights. While this Court has held that a less time can result in a waiver of an office by virtue of acquiescence in the act of removal, yet such acquiescence must be shown by circumstances that clearly justify the conclusion that the man thus unlawfully removed never intended to assert his just rights in the premises.

In this case, I am frank to say, I can find no evidence of any waiver or acquiescence. I do not know what more Mr. Myers could have done in asserting his rights. The pertinacity, with which he asserted his title until his commission had expired, is worthy of the legendary boy on the burning deck. He stood by his guns in respect to the alleged unlawfulness of his dismissal and awaited an opportunity to serve in an office, of which he consistently asserted he had been unlawfully deprived, until his commission had expired and within a few weeks thereafter commenced his suit.

Therefore, if the Government is to prevail in this case, it must be on the ground that the statute, in so far as it required the consent and approval of the Senate to his removal, is unconstitutional.

I therefore address myself to this great constitutional question—a question which has been repeatedly submitted to this Court, but which the Court up to the present hour has found it unnecessary to decide; a question of great delicacy, because it affects the relative powers of two great departments of the Government; and a question, the decision of which, I venture to say, cannot long be postponed. I quite concur in the concluding statement of the distinguished Senator from Pennsylvania that, as this great question is squarely presented in a concrete case, this Court should now determine it for the benefit of both departments of the Government.

I am glad that the case was not disposed of on the preceding *ex parte* argument, and that the Court has now had the benefit of the argument of the appellant's counsel, formerly a distinguished member of the Supreme Court of Oregon. The wisdom of inviting the senior Senator from Pennsylvania to represent the views of Congress has been amply vindicated in the scholarly and powerful brief that he has filed, and in the very interesting and eloquent argument that he has orally made. I take a just pride in his brief and argument; for I share with him the great privilege of having been called to the bar by the historic bar of Philadelphia; and I think that Senator Pepper's oral argument and his very able brief are worthy of the best traditions of that bar.

His scholarly research and the earnestness with which he has pressed the argument are only equaled by his courage; because he has not shrunk from the logical implications of his argument; and I shall try to show, *in limine*, that that argument, if applied by a hostile Congress to the President, might make our Constitution little more than a house of cards.

For, if I understand Senator Pepper's contention, it is this: That the President's power of removal is not a constitutional power; that he derives nothing from the Constitution, under which the "executive power" was vested in the President of the United States. That he gains nothing by reason of the solemn obligation imposed upon him by that Constitution to "take care that the laws be faithfully executed." That he gains nothing by the oath which the Constitution exacts from him that he will support, maintain, defend, and preserve the Constitution of the United States. That his only power in this vital matter of administration of removing officers is derived from the inaction of Congress, which has plenary power over the subject of removals from office. So I understand the Senator to contend.

It seems to me an amazing proposition. I had not so

understood his brief; but I do so understand his oral argument of yesterday. As I read the brief, he said that the power of removal is "an executive act"; he did not say "an executive power"; and perhaps he had in mind that fine shading of expression in the Constitution, to which he attached a significance which I do not think it deserved, between the "*power*" to negotiate treaties and the *duty* imposed merely to nominate. I think there is no practical distinction between the two grants of power.

But he did not in his brief challenge the fact that, from the beginning of this Government to the present hour, and by the sanction of this Court in the *Parsons case* and the *Shurtleff case* the power to remove has been recognized as an executive power; that it exists in the President by force of the Constitution; that it is a part of the "executive power" granted to him in words, and that it is a part of the necessary means to carry out the great objective of his duties. What he did not challenge in his brief, he now challenges in oral argument, for I understand him to argue that the power of removal as exercised by the President is only by the sufferance of Congress.

The one question that this Court has never decided has been whether Congress, under its limited grant of legislative power, may restrict, limit, or modify the executive power of removal. If so, and the contention is carried to its logical conclusion, then it can destroy the executive function of removal altogether.

Senator Pepper has argued—and I want to show the Court the grave implications of his contention, not merely suggesting fanciful illustrations, but by illustrations that have their basis in reality—that the power to create an office is legislative in its nature—I grant that—and that in thus creating an office Congress may impose as an inherent condition of the continuance of that office whatever conditions it pleases, even if those conditions, as in the instant case, involve a transfer of the executive power of removal from the Executive to the Congress.

He would sustain the law on the ground that Congress was not obliged to create the position of Postmaster of Portland, Oregon, and therefore could create it upon such terms as it pleased, and if so, those conditions are beyond judicial review. In other words, Congress can provide—as it has provided in the statute under consideration—that the Postmaster at Portland, Oregon, should serve during the pleasure of the Senate. If this be true, then the executive power of removal, hitherto supposed to be granted by the Constitution to the President, is no longer in the President, but when Congress creates the office it may grant executive powers with respect thereto to the Senate.

But the grave implications of that doctrine—and I venture to say that no more surprising one has been addressed to this Court for a long time—are further illustrated by the fact that the Senator and Judge King champion, as an illustration of their argument, the law with respect to the Comptroller-General; and while that law is not before this Court, yet it does so illustrate the extent to which Senator Pepper's argument can be carried as to the paramount authority of Congress to redistribute powers, in the guise of creating an office, that I want to read that act to the Court. It provides:

> "There is created an establishment of the Government to be known as the General Accounting Office, *which shall be independent of the executive departments*"—

If this law be valid there is nothing to prevent the Congress from saying that postmasters of the first, second, and third classes are also to be "independent of the executive branch of the Government"—not merely with respect to removal, but for all purposes of administration.

The Budget statute continues:

> "and under the control and direction of the Comptroller-General of the United States"—

Not a word of the power and duty of the President of the United States, to whom it has hitherto been supposed the executive power had been granted by the Constitution. This fiscal agency, properly a part of the Treasury Department of the Government, is not only affirmatively made independent of the executive branch of the Government, but in order to exclude the possibility of any power of the President, we are told that it is to be under the control and direction of the Comptroller-General of the United States.   And then it provides—

> "Except as hereinafter provided in this section, the Comptroller-General and the Assistant Comptroller-General shall hold office for fifteen years. The Comptroller-General shall not be eligible for reappointment. The Comptroller-General or the Assistant Comptroller-General may be removed at any time by joint resolution of Congress after notice and hearing, when, in the judgment of Congress"—

You see, there is not the shadow of executive power left.

> "the Comptroller-General or Assistant Comptroller-General has become permanently incapacitated or has been inefficient, or guilty of neglect of duty, *   *   * and for no other cause and in no other manner except by impeachment."

Its purpose was to take the office out of the doctrine of the *Shurtleff case,* in which this Court recognized that, even if Congress prescribed some grounds of removal, yet, unless it clearly indicated to the contrary, the President's power to remove for other causes still remained.

If Senator Pepper's argument be a sound one, Congress, in creating the offices of the Government—and through what other means does the Government function except through offices?—can create them in such manner and upon such conditions as it may think proper, even if those conditions involve a portentous transfer and shifting of power from one department to the other. If that be true, then where does the power to alter the form of our Government stop? Congress, like Warren Hastings, might well marvel at its own moderation; because it could have added to this clause with regard to the Comptroller-General's office, that it should be independent of the judicial department of the Government also.

Because, if the Congress can create an office, upon such conditions as it may think proper, and if it can make such an office, essentially executive in character, independent of the Executive, then obviously, it can make it equally independent of the judiciary. Possibly the Comptroller-General may have had this idea of the independence of his office. Let me read from his decision of February 7, 1924, in which he says:

> "Under the act of June 10, 1921, responsibility to settle and adjust claims against the United States and to determine the availability of appropriations for their payment is upon this office and while opinions of the Court are given most careful consideration, especially where it appears that the merits or legal principles involved have been fairly presented to *and fully considered by the Court,* it is not believed that this office would be justified in applying the decision in the Quinn case to the case here under consideration."

In other words, the Comptroller-General judges not only whether the case has been properly presented to the Court, which might well be within his power, but also whether the Court has fully considered the question; and, if he reaches the conclusion that the Court has not done so, his independence would be justified on Senator Pepper's theory.

Let me again suggest to the Court the grave implications of the contention made by the distinguished Senator. If Congress has this thaumaturgic power by reason of its legislative duty to create offices, then this power is not exhausted in the act of creating the office; because, obviously, Congress can abolish an office whenever it sees proper; and therefore, not merely in the original creation of the office but at all times during the continuance of the office, Congress always, according to the contention, has the power to impose upon the office such conditions with respect to the manner in which governmental power shall be divided as it sees proper.

Let us see, then, where that would lead us. Our Government has over 556,000 civilian employees. If you add to that the Army and the Navy, the employees of the Judicial Department, and of the Territories and of the District of Columbia, there are over 800,000 employees of the United States.

Logically this court must pass upon this question as though the act included all these officials. If this law be valid on the grounds submitted by the distinguished Senator, the law which I am about to suggest would be equally valid. Suppose that Congress passes an omnibus law, whereby it is provided that all civilian officers of the State shall hold their offices during the good pleasure of the Senate, or of Congress; that they shall be independent of the executive departments of the Government; and that they may never be removed by the President, no matter how culpable their conduct may be, even though it may amount to disloyalty or treason, unless the Senate or the Congress (whichever the law might state) should so provide.

Eliminating offices created by the Constitution, as to which this Court could find a limitation upon the power of Congress to extend this statute, yet as to every other civilian employee of the State, Congress could effectually take them out of the control of the executive department of the Government and even of the judicial department.

And if that be so, you might as well put out a sign "To let" at the White House, because the President would be *functus officio*. His great power would be diminished to a shadow.

[Mr. Justice McReynolds: I would not say that. Congress could cut off every civilian employee of the Government by cutting off his salary.

Mr. Beck: Certainly.

Mr. Justice McReynolds: Congress could absolutely stop the wheels of the Government from turning if it wanted to, so I do not see why you should be drawing a picture like that. Suppose Congress should say tomorrow, "We will not appropriate a dollar for the support of the Government"; it could do that, could it not?

Mr. Beck: That would be by virtue of an express constitutional grant which gives to Congress the power to appropriate money——

Mr. Justice McReynolds (interposing): But it would stop the Government?

Mr. Beck: Undoubtedly, Congress has the power to stop the Government, if it sought to work a revolution by bringing the Government to a standstill.

Mr. Justice McReynolds: So that I do not see that it will help us very much for you to say that it would stop the Government if the President had not the power to remove officers.

Mr. Beck: But stopping the Government through the power of Congress over the purse; or by abolishing all offices whatever—either of which, of course, would be an essentially revolutionary step—may be within the power of Congress. To provide, with respect to all officers, that they shall no longer be a part of the executive department of the Government, and, above all, that they may not be removed, except with the consent of the Senate, is quite another thing, which would seem to be a portentous transfer of the principal Executive power from the Executive to Congress.]

Of course, no one pretends that any such omnibus legislation would be suggested; but nevertheless, the fact remains that, if this law is constitutional, such an omnibus law would likewise be constitutional. And in that event it would necessarily follow that there would be two executive departments, one the executive department of the Constitution, which would be shorn of its powers and its halls like the poet's "banquet hall deserted," which the President would tread alone, with "all but him departed," and the other, a congressional executive department, which would function independently of the President and be responsible only to Congress and removable only by Congress.

But if Congress has this power to delegate to one branch the determination as to whether the President shall exercise his right of removal, then it has equally the power —and, if applied to all the officers of the State, it would be a stupendous undertaking—to delegate to any part of itself the executive power or function of removal. For, after all, that is what Congress has done in this act. The Congress has not itself assumed the power to remove this postmaster. It has delegated it to the President of the United States, by and with the advice and consent of the Senate. If it could do that, it could then delegate the approval of the President's removals to the Speaker of the House and the President of the Senate as the representatives of the two branches of Congress. And thus you would have revived the old triumvirate of Rome, for you would have three great officers of the State sharing that which is vital in the practical administration of the State, that which requires hourly exercise in the administration of the State, namely, the removal of unworthy, incompetent, or inefficient officials from the public service. The Constitutional Convention rejected a triumvirate when they refused to have an executive of three individuals.

I have, I trust, sufficiently stressed what seemed to me to be the necessary implications of Senator Pepper's far-reaching claim that the President only enjoys his power by the inaction of Congress, that is, by the sufferance of Congress, and that Congress at any time may apply conditions to the right of removal.

I come to what I suggested in my revised brief, with respect to the question whether there may be a middle ground in this matter between the absolute power of the President to remove and the absolute power of Congress to dictate the method of removal.

I shall suggest to this Court (and I want to stress it, because it may be of some value to the Court in its deliberations), that it is not necessary in this case to determine the full question that is involved in this record. In other words, this Court can say that this particular act is unconstitutional, without denying wholly to the Congress the power to create legislative standards or public policies which have a legitimate relation to the nature and scope of an office. Let me illustrate what I mean:

Suppose a law is passed that an office is created and that the incumbent may be removed for inefficiency or dishonesty. I take it that no one would have any difficulty in reconciling such a statute with the Constitution; because the executive power of the President is in no respect impaired; his exercise of his duty is guided by a legislative standard which prescribes efficiency and integrity as a condition of the tenure of office. The President, however, applies the standard. He determines whether the officer in any given case is efficient or inefficient, dishonest or honest; and he removes upon his ascertainment of the facts.

But suppose the law does not provide that. Suppose it says that an office is created and that the incumbent may be removed for inefficiency or dishonesty, but *for no other reason whatever.*

It would be far more difficult, if I am right, to reconcile that with the Constitution of the United States, if the President has as a constitutional prerogative the power of removal. Because that does say to the President, "You can remove for the two causes; but for all other causes we forbid you to remove."

But in this case it is not necessary for this Court to pass upon that class of cases. For even as to such a law, even though it involves an undoubted impairment of the full freedom of the Executive to remove, the Court might still say that such an act merely prescribes a legislative standard, or declares a public policy with respect to tenure of office, which was an inherent part of the office, and left to the President, as an executive function, the duty of applying it to a concrete case.

I am not conceding that such a law, which limited the President to only two causes of removal, would be a constitutional law; but I simply say that it is not necessary to decide that in this case.

Why? Because this law differs, *toto caelo,* from the kind of law to which I have just referred. This law prescribes no legislative standard. It declares no public policy with respect to any inherent attribute of an office. It simply says, "We create this office, provided that you allow the Senate and President to remove, and not the President alone." In such case, there is no legislative standard of efficiency; it is a mere redistribution of power—a giving to one branch of Congress some of the power which belongs to the President.

And, therefore, as you have here the naked assumption of Congress that it can transfer the Executive power from the President to the Senate, you have it in your power to say: "Without now deciding how far the President's power of removal can be guided, or modified, or controlled by laws that are inherently part of the nature and the scope of an office, Congress cannot, under the guise of creating an office, transfer a constitutional prerogative of the President to the Senate of the United States, when the Constitution gave no sanction to any such transfer."

I contend that the power of the President is not a mere implication from the Constitution and existing only from the inaction of Congress. That is a new theory which the Senator has advanced; and, so far as I know, it finds no countenance in any previous discussion of this great question.

The power to remove is based on a just interpretation of the language of the Constitution; an interpretation that has had the sanction and confirmation of unbroken usage; except to the extent that the question has been raised whether there can be such an interdependent exercise of the legislative power as to control and regulate this power of removal.

But the power of removal is constitutional in its origin.

Let us first take the background of the Constitution, and let us recall what it was that the framers were trying to accomplish.

The great defect that called the Constitution into being was that under the confederation all judicial, executive, and legislative powers were vested in the Congress of the confederation. And it was because the old Congress exercised executive power that there came the tragedy of the Revolution, and especially the dark and terrible days of Valley Forge, when Washington's little army starved in a land of plenty, because of a headless Government that had no Executive whatever, but which, under the guise of a legislative tribunal, attempted to exercise both legislative and executive powers.

The result was that, when the Constitution was formed, quite apart from the teachings of Montesquieu as to the distribution of power as a safeguard of liberty, the one thing that they were anxious to create (and my brief supports this by contemporaneous allusions) was a strong independent Executive, who, carrying out the laws of Congress, would yet have sufficient inherent strength to preserve his department against the creation of a parliamentary despotism.

In the debates of the Constitutional Convention, it must be admitted that there is very little to be found on this subject. They discussed nearly every other subject relating to government, but they did not discuss this. They did discuss the question of removal, so far as the President is concerned, because he could not remove himself, and so far as the judiciary is concerned they intended to give the justices a life tenure and necessarily made some provision for removal for extraordinary reasons.

They did assert—and this is the answer to Senator Pepper's charge of executive absolutism — that if the President, in the exercise of his executive functions, failed in his duty; if he tolerated dishonest, inefficient, or disloyal men in the executive department, he or any other officer of the State could be impeached by the House of Representatives and tried by the Senate and removed from office. And that was the great reservation of power by the legislative branch to prevent any absolutism by the Executive. But with that exception, there was no suggestion in the debates with respect to the question of removal.

And from that I draw a conclusion favorable to my contention. Why? Because at that time, in the science of government, according to the custom of the nation from which we drew out institutions in great part, and according to the custom of every country, so far as I know, the power to appoint and the power to remove had always been regarded as executive functions. I examined the other night a book which contained the constitutions of nearly all the great modern States at the present day. My examination was cursory and may not be wholly accurate; but as far as it went, with the exception of the Argentine Republic, there is not a clause in any one of the constitutions that specifically confers the right of removal upon anybody; but it has always been regarded as an inherent attribute of the executive branch of the government, where there is any division of the powers of government into the great trinity of the legislative, the executive, and the judicial.

[Mr. Justice Brandeis: Mr. Solicitor-General, if the power of removal is an inherent prerogative of the President, why is not the power of appointment without the advice and consent of the Senate an inherent prerogative of the President?

Mr. Beck: Because the Constitution says otherwise.

Mr. Justice Brandeis: I beg your pardon?

Mr. Beck: Because the Constitution says otherwise.

Mr. Justice Brandeis: Well, does it say otherwise in respect to every office?

Mr. Beck: Every office.

Mr. Justice Brandeis: Regardless of whether they are named——

Mr. Beck: Every office. The President "shall nominate, and by and with the advice and consent of the Senate, shall appoint" such-and-such officers, "and all other officers of the United States"; except that Congress may vest such appointments *as it thinks proper* in somebody else than the President; but it need not vest a single one in any other body.

Mr. Justice Brandeis: But it says Congress may vest the appointment to an office such as this office in some one other than the President?

Mr. Beck: Well, if it did it would not make any difference for the purpose of my argument, as I shall try to show.

Mr. Justice Brandeis: I am not referring to the constitutional officers, of course; but I am referring to the offices which are created, not by the Constitution but by the Congress itself.

Mr. Beck: In my judgment, on this question of the scope or nature of the constitutional power of the President to remove, the nature of the office is important only in this respect: That no one questions that the Congress, if it vests in the Postmaster-General the appointment of a postmaster, can restrain the Postmaster-General from removing his subordinate. Congress has control over those upon whom it confers the mere *statutory* power of appointment. But it has no such power as against the President; because the President's power is not statutory; it is *constitutional*.

Mr. Justice McReynolds: Do you mean that every officer appointed by every source in the United States is subject to removal by the President?

Mr. Beck: Yes; every officer in the executive department of the Government.

Mr. Justice McReynolds: Take the marshal of this Court: Can the President remove him?

Mr. Beck: If he is part of the executive department of the Government, yes.

Mr. Justice McReynolds: He is provided for by Congress, and paid by Congress, and the method of his appointment is provided by Congress. Can the President remove him?

Mr. Beck: In my judgment, the President can remove anyone in the executive department of the Government.

The employees of the judicial branch of the Government and the special and direct employees of the Congress, like the Sergeant-at-Arms, may not be officers of the executive branch of the Government, and, if so, are not within the grant of executive power to the President.

That is one theory. The other theory is the one I first suggested, that the executive power is even more comprehensive. But it is not necessary for me to press the argument that far.]

When the Constitution was adopted, therefore, what were the provisions with respect to powers?

In the first place, there was the division of the Government into three great branches: The legislative, the executive, and the judicial.

[Mr. Justice Brandeis: I do not know, Mr. Solicitor-General, that you have fully answered my question: Assuming that this is an office—and I presume it is—which is wholly within the control of Congress as to its existence; and that Congress chooses to have the President make the appointment to this office: Why, having created the office, if this is a prerogative of the President, cannot the President disregard altogether the provision as to the advice and consent of the Senate, and say that an office has been created which is not a constitutional office, and that the appointing power exists in him as to that office?

Mr. Beck: You say, why could the President not do that?

Mr. Justice Brandeis: Yes.

Mr. Beck: Simply because the Constitution says explicitly that the President "shall nominate, and, by and with the advice and consent of the Senate, appoint" certain officers therein named—constitutional officers and all other civil officers — leaving it to Congress to determine the extent to which it will waive the question of the senatorial confirmation.

Mr. Justice Brandeis: You are undertaking, therefore, to limit this by confining the term "officers"?

Mr. Beck: It says, "and all other officers of the United States, whose appointments are not herein otherwise provided for, and which shall be established by law; but the Congress may by law vest the appointment of such inferior officers, as they think proper, in the President alone, in the courts of law, or in the heads of departments."

Mr. Justice Brandeis: Well, I mean, why the distinction as to inferior officers? There does not seem to be anything particularly inherent in the office of one who is a postmaster; I do not know why a distinction should be drawn between first, second, third, and fourth class postmasters and any other officer of the United States, except so far as the Congress chooses to give them a certain kind of appointment.

Mr. Beck: Well, I do not know whether your honor has in mind the theory that the sole source of the power

to remove is the power to appoint, and therefore that
Congress, having the power to vest the appointment of
an inferior officer in the heads of departments or the courts
of law, instead of in the President—that therefore, the
President's right of removal is gone, because he has lost
the only source from which he derives his power, namely,
the original power of appointment.

If it were true that the sole source of the President's
power to remove is the power of appointment, there would
be great force in that argument.

But, as Mr. Madison showed in the first great debate
on this subject (and I have quoted at length from it in
the brief), the power to remove is not a mere incident
and is not solely attributable to the power to appoint. It
has a much broader basis.

To assume that the only source of the power to remove
is the power to appoint is to put the pyramid on its apex;
whereas I put the pyramid on its base when I argue
that the power to remove is part of that which, in sweeping and comprehensive and yet apt phrase, is denominated
the "executive power," coupled with the explanation that
the executive power is to "take care that the laws be
faithfully executed," a mandate of tremendous significance and import.]

I was about to say that the Constitution, in addition
to this division of the Government into three great
branches, draws this significant distinction between the
grant of legislative power and the grant of executive
power:

In the grant of legislative power it said (and it never
uses a word idly):

> "All legislative powers *herein granted* shall be
> vested in a Congress."

And when you come to look at the "powers herein
granted," you will search in vain for any suggestion of
a power to remove by the Congress. The most you can
say is that, under the general power, the omnibus clause
of the legislative grant, namely, the power to make laws
"for carrying into execution the foregoing powers," there

is the implied power to create offices, and according to the theory advanced by opposing counsel, the resultant power to step over the dead line into the executive department and assume the right of removal.

When you come to the executive branch of the Government, it is significant that the framers omitted the words "herein granted."

Why? They could specify the nature of and classify the legislative powers with reasonable precision. But the executive power was something different. And therefore they simply said "the Executive power"—not "the Executive powers." It was not only in the singular number; but it was intended to describe something that was very familiar to them, and about which they did not believe men could disagree; and therefore they said, remembering the innumerable ills of the old confederation, "the executive power."

It was not granted to an executive department. That is, again, a very significant thing. They might have limited it. But they said:

"The executive power shall be vested in a President of the United States"—

distinguishing him from all other servants of the executive department, and making him the repository of this vast, undefined grant of power called "the executive power."

Then they went on to say what that power was—not in any way attempting to classify or enumerate it; but they simply gave its objective, and that was "to take care that the laws be faithfully executed."

It was common sense in the days of the Fathers, when our country was a little one; it is common sense today, when we are the greatest nation in the world; when we have, as I say, 800,000 employees of the State—that the President cannot take care that the laws are faithfully executed, unless he has the power of removal, and the summary power of removal, without any interference or curb upon him. And that has been shown again and again in our history.

But it did not stop there. There is a clause to which very little significance has been attached in the discussion on this question, but which I submit has great significance.

It says that the President shall "commission" officers. The Constitution never descends to details. You cannot find in the whole document any other case where they descended to what might otherwise be regarded as a mere mechanical or clerical detail. And there was special significance in the minds of the framers when, in this broad grant of "executive power," they said that the President should commission. Not that Congress should commission. The Congress of the old confederation commissioned; and Washington's experiences during the seven years of warfare were the bitterest experiences of his life. He trod his *via dolorosa* because he could not control the men that were under him; because they owed their commissions to Congress and not to the President.

And therefore, sweeping aside the attempt to have a many-headed Executive (which never has worked in history), in order to emphasize what they meant by the executive power, they provided that the President shall commission the officers of the State.

And that is very significant; because just before the Constitution was adopted there was a great crisis in the Government from which we are sprung. The Crown (and I use the word "crown" as distinguished from "the king" because it answers to our executive department) dismissed Fox as Prime Minister, although he had the support of a majority of the House of Commons. Pitt was substituted for him. There was a great debate in Parliament; and that must have had its reflexes in this country. It was then determined that the ministers, although they are members of the House of Commons, at that time drew the source of their authority from the Crown.

And so today the commission which any of the members of this Court has, and which I have as Solicitor-General —each would read, if it were the appointment of the present administration—

"I, Calvin Coolidge, reposing special trust and

faith in the integrity, etc., do commission and authorize and empower, etc."

The commission comes from the President.
The Constitution also provides:

"The President shall nominate."

The Committee of Detail, when it reported to the Convention of 1787 before the last revision, had provided that the Senate should appoint all officers, if my recollection serves me correctly. At all events, it was either that the Senate should solely appoint, or that the President and the Senate should appoint.

And then these wise men, who were not muddled dreamers, in the last revision by the Committee on Style, said:

"The President shall nominate, and, by and with the advice and consent of the Senate, shall appoint."

And then they said he "shall commission."

Thus there are four steps—nomination; confirmation; appointment; commission.

What did nomination mean? Nomination implies in its very essence the power of removal. What is the power of nomination? It is the power to select at all times and at all places the best man for a position. I do not say that great ideal is always realized; but that is not the question. But that ideal is the objective.

The President must at all times, if he is to nominate—if nomination be selection—determine, having regard for the public interests, who is the best man for a particular position.

An office may be filled. It may be filled by a man who is neither inefficient nor dishonest; it may be filled, however, by a man who is not as good a man as another man whom the President has selected. Therefore, before the President can nominate, he must first displace. The power to nominate does not include the power to remove, so far as the original creation of an office is concerned. But in the matter of an existing office, the power to nominate is always the power, if necessary, to remove an existing incumbent, to make way for a better man.

In President Arthur's administration Congress passed a law that it would create an office, provided that the President named a certain man to fill it. President Arthur vetoed the bill, on the ground that Congress could not create an office and name the incumbent.

So that the power to nominate as given in the Constitution carries within itself, as an essential ingredient, the power to remove.

Then comes the one qualification of the Constitution: That as to all offices which the Congress may think sufficiently important, no one can be appointed except with the advice and consent of the Senate.

The framers of the Constitution recognized that, in the matter of appointment, the President would require local knowledge. If he attempted to distribute, even with the country as small as it then was, the offices of the State throughout the country, as presumably he would, it was desirable for him to have the advice and the consent of the local representatives, who would be a kind of a jury of the vicinage, and who would better know whether or not the appointment was in all respects desirable.

But is it not significant that there is no suggestion that he cannot remove except by the advice and consent of the Senate? It is true, as I have said, that the power of removal can only be given to the President—or to anybody—by attributing it to the proper grant; and the proper grant is the executive power. But it is significant that, while the power of nomination, the power of appointment, is subject to the confirmation of the Senate, nowhere is there a suggestion in the Constitution that in the power of removal, as an executive power, any such limitation has been put upon it.

The power of appointment required local information. At all events, it was a matter in which the framers might well say that the ambassadors of the State desired to be consulted before a man was taken out of their vicinage to be made a part of the civil service of the United States.

But when a man has been taken from his locality and has become a part of the Federal machinery; when he has been for one or more years under the supervision of the President, who knows best whether that man is faithfully or unfaithfully discharging his duties? How can the Senate know? Preoccupied in its work of legislation (and that is enough of an undertaking), how can it know whether employees of the executive branch of the Government, scattered from Manila to Alaska, deserve removal?

Please observe that the senatorial privilege of confirmation was a departure from the doctrine of Montesquieu, to which they otherwise attached great importance; it was an interblending of the executive and legislative; and as Mr. Madison pointed out, such interblending must be confined to its fair terms; you cannot interblend the executive and the legislature by putting a curb on the Executive through the powers of the legislature, unless you can find in the text of the Constitution some warrant for it.

From those grants of power; from the nature of the Government; from the division into three different departments; from the sweeping grant of executive power; from the power to nominate; from the duty of taking care that the laws be faithfully executed; from the power to commission, importing a continuation of that confidence which the President, in the very text of the commission, reposes in the appointee—from all these grants, I assert that it is a just interpretation of the Constitution, and not a mere implication, that the power to remove is a part of the executive power granted to the President.

If it be a part of his executive power, does it not throw the whole machinery of our Government into cureless confusion, if you assume that the Congress can take that power from him and transfer it to itself, or to one branch of the Congress, at its discretion and for its purposes?

This question was discussed very ably about 136 years ago. It was one of the great debates in Congress. Senator Pepper has tried to minimize the force of that great discussion. Not so those who have considered it, including those who did not favor the executive prerogative of removal.

Mr. Webster, who in his antipathy to President Jackson did take advanced ground in that direction — but not going to the great lengths of Senator Pepper—still recognized the tremendous force of the judgment that was reached in the First Congress of the United States. And it cannot be quite so idly dismissed or minimized as is indicated in the briefs of opposing counsel. And remember what that First Congress was. They were starting the wheels of the Government into operation. Of the Senate, one-half of them had sat in the Constitutional Convention. Possibly, as they met there in the first Senate of the United States, it was the first time since they had parted company in the historic State House in Philadelphia on that fateful 17th day of September, 1787.

In the House of Representatives not a majority, but a considerable number, had also sat in the first Constitutional Convention. They were creating the first of the departments of the Government, the Department of State and the Secretary of State.

And at once, in this first Congress under the Constitution, the question arose: Is the power to remove in the Congress or in the President? If it is in the Congress, can the Congress delegate the power to the President; or if it is in the President, can the Congress limit or restrict that power?

Why, to show the immensity of the subject as it dawned upon those supremely great men, I read the words that James Madison used in the course of the debate:

"The decision that is at this time made will become the permanent exposition of the Constitution; and on the permanent exposition of the Constitution will depend the genius and character of the whole Government. It will depend, perhaps, on this decision whether the Government shall retain that equilibrium which the Constitution intended, or take a direction toward aristocracy or anarchy among the members of the Government."

And it was in that spirit that they proceeded to discuss the very subject we are now considering.

I have not the time to read excerpts from what Mr. Madison said in that great debate. He took the lead in favor of the proposition that the grant of power was a constitutional grant to the President. He repudiated the suggestion that it was a mere incident to the power to appoint. On the contrary, he said that it was the just derivative of the executive power and the power to execute the laws, and that the power to appoint was a mere incident. He reasoned it out on the ground that the separation of the Government into three departments would be quite impracticable, unless this power to remove was in the President.

I say I have not time, because there is so much else that I want to say. But I do want to read what was not in my first brief, two very practical suggestions made by two of his colleagues, Mr. Boudinot of New Jersey and Mr. Sedgwick of Massachusetts.

Says Boudinot, who was taking Madison's side:

> "If the President complains to the Senate of the misconduct of an officer, and desires their advice and consent to the removal, what are the Senate to do? Most certainly they will inquire if the complaint is well founded. To do this, they must call the officer before them to answer. Who, then, are the parties? The Supreme Executive officer against his assistant; and the Senate are to sit as judges to determine whether sufficient cause of removal exists. Does not this set the Senate over the head of the President? But suppose they shall decide in favor of the officer, what a situation is the President then in, surrounded by officers with whom, by his situation, he is compelled to act, but in whom he can have no confidence, reversing the privilege given him by the Constitution, to prevent his having officers imposed upon him who do not meet his approbation?"

Sedgwick says this:

"How is the question"—

that is, as to whether a man is properly to be removed—

"to be investigated?   Because I presume there
must be some rational rule for conducting this
business.   Is the President to be sworn to declare the whole truth, and to bring forward
facts? Or are they to admit suspicion as testimony? Or is the word of the President to be
taken at all events?   If so, this check is not of
the least efficacy in nature.   But if proof be necessary, what is then the consequence? Why, in
nine cases out of ten, where the case is very clear
to the mind of the President that the man ought
to be removed, the effect cannot be produced,
because it is absolutely impossible to produce the
necessary evidence.   Are the Senate to proceed
without evidence?   Some gentlemen contend
not.   Then the object will be lost.   Shall a man,
under these circumstances, be saddled upon the
President, who has been appointed for no other
purpose but to aid the President in performing
certain duties?   Shall he be continued, I ask
again, against the will of the President?   If he
is, where is the responsibility?   Are you to look
for it in the President, who has no control over
the officer, no power to remove him if he acts
unfeelingly or unfaithfully? Without you make
him responsible, you weaken and destroy the
strength and beauty of your system."

And that is just as true today as it was when Mr. Sedgwick said it.   If the contention of Senator Pepper were
adopted by this Court and the Congress acted upon it,
you would destroy the beauty and the strength of our
system of government.

What was the result of the debate? The House of Representatives sustained Mr. Madison. The Senate equally
divided; but Vice President Adams in the chair voted for

the law in the form that would sustain the President's prerogative. And George Washington, the first President of the United States, the presiding officer of the Constitutional Convention, added his concurrence to the view thus expressed, and would have acted upon it if he had had any occasion to exercise the power of removal.

Let me say in passing that whenever the question has arisen every President of the United States has taken this view. I do not mean to say that every President has had occasion to take it. But I do say that no President has ever disaffirmed his executive prerogative to remove; and wherever it has been challenged the President has always maintained what he believed to be the great mandate given to him.

But there is one quotation from a President so striking, and recalling events of such tragic memory, that I venture to say that if I read no other declaration of the many declarations of the Presidents (even up to and including the present President) which have asserted the President's prerogative in this matter, I should read this.

President Johnson, who had lived with Lincoln through the tragic days of the Civil War, took up the scepter of power which had fallen from the hand of the martyred President; and a hostile Congress attempted to put President Johnson in a strait-jacket by making it impossible for him to remove any officer, even his Cabinet; and then impeached him for removing a member of his own Cabinet. And this is what President Johnson said — and I think it will be his ample vindication for all time:

> "The events of the last war furnished a practical confirmation of the wisdom of the Constitution as it has hitherto been maintained in many of its parts, including that which is now the subject of consideration"—

namely, the tenure of office act.

> "When the war broke out, rebel enemies, traitors, abettors, and sympathizers were found in every department of the Government, as well

in the civil service as in the land and naval military service. They were found in Congress and among the keepers of the Capitol; in foreign missions; in each and all the executive departments; in the judicial service; in the post office and among the agents for conducting Indian affairs. Upon probable suspicion they were promptly displaced by my predecessor"—

Who? Abraham Lincoln. Did the men who impeached Andrew Johnson, led by Thaddeus Stevens, ever question Abraham Lincoln when he displaced men who he thought were plotting to destroy our Government?

"Upon probable suspicion they were promptly displaced by my predecessor, so far as they held their offices under executive authority, and their duties were confided to new and loyal successors. No complaints against that power or doubts of its wisdom were entertained in any quarter. I sincerely trust and believe that no such civil war is likely to occur again. I cannot doubt, however, that in whatever form and on whatever occasion sedition can raise an effort to hinder or embarrass or defeat the legitimate action of this Government, whether by preventing the collection of revenue, or disturbing the public peace, or separating the States, or betraying the country to a foreign enemy, the power of removal from office by the Executive, as it has heretofore existed and been practiced, will be found indispensable."

Can anybody challenge the force of that reasoning, as you apply it to the tragic episodes of the Civil War?

My friend, the distinguished Senator from Pennsylvania, enjoyed a little pleasantry at the expense of my James Madison illustration. Let me supplement his retort to my original argument.

Let me say, before doing so, that James Madison lived to be a Cabinet officer and to be twice President of the

United States; and he lived until some time after 1835. He witnessed the bitter attack of the great triumvirate of Senators, Webster, Clay and Calhoun, upon Andrew Jackson, when, for the first time since the question was settled in the first Congress, the question arose whether the President could remove against the opposition of Congress. And old Madison, nearing eternity—he was far advanced in the eighties—thereupon wrote three letters that are in my brief, in which he reaffirmed what he had said in 1789, that not only was it a fair construction of the Constitution that the President's executive prerogative of removal was beyond the control of Congress, but, in addition to that, as he argued, the unity of the system, the symmetry of the Constitution, the equilibrium of the three great departments of the Government would be fatally shattered if the paramount power of Congress in the creation of offices to prescribe any condition that it saw fit with respect to those offices was accepted as a true construction of the Constitution.

I was about, in a very amiable and not at all offensive way, to reply to Senator Pepper's retort to my Madison illustration in my brief. The Senator regarded it as amusing that I should instance the fact that James Madison tardily discovered that he had a very incompetent Secretary of War—an aged officer who had apparently outlived his usefulness; namely, Armstrong. He had taken no steps to defend the Capital; he had left our gates open to the enemy. And unfortunately, after this Court was destroyed and the House of Representatives taken and the Capitol partly burned, and Madison and the Congress were in flight and the British Army in possession of our Capitol —that is important for the purposes of my reply—it was then that Mr. Madison removed General Armstrong as Secretary of War. "And," says the Senator, "is that any argument for your position, when the Congress could have more effectively removed him?"

Suppose this law that we are now considering had applied at that day, and Madison, with the smoke rising from the ruins of the Capitol; with the country in such mortal peril that he could not even borrow $20,000,000

to save the country until old Stephen Girard, of Philadelphia, came forth and, with a sublime faith, took the
whole loan—suppose that Mr. Madison should then have
been unable to remove his Secretary of War until he had
the consent of the Senate, would there have been any
improvement in the situation? The Senate could not be
convened; they were in full flight. It would have been
very difficult, in the panic that then raged in Washington,
to have secured a quorum of that august body.

But assuming that the Senators could, in some convenient place other than the Capital—because the British
were then occupying Washington—have met, and that
thereupon the Senators had said, "Well, you may think
General Armstrong is an unfit Secretary of War; but we
do not share your opinion; and before you remove General
Armstrong we would like very much to have you give us
substantial reasons." And thereupon the President would
say, "I told him to fortify Washington and he failed to
do it."

In the meantime, while they were discussing the matter
—and you cannot discuss matters of that import in the
midst of war—for all we know the country might have
fallen into cureless ruin. And I think my Madison illustration was far from weakening my argument, and that
on the contrary it strengthens it. For, while Madison
may have been injudicious in not sooner exercising his power of removal, the duty of summary removal remained just
as important after the British had entered Washington as
before.

Let me read the last of the three letters of Madison;
because, coming as it did from him at that time, at the
great eminence of his age, the words have peculiar force;
and they were spoken with reference to the great political
struggle that was then in progress:

"The claims for the Senate of a share in the
removal from office, and for the legislature an
authority to regulate its tenure, have had powerful advocates. I must still think, however, that
the text of the Constitution is best interpreted
by reference to the tripartite theory of govern-

ment to which practice has conformed, and which so long and uniform a practice would seem to have established.

The face of the Constitution and the journalized proceedings of the convention strongly indicate a partiality to that theory, then at its zenith of favor among the most distinguished commentators on the organizations of political power. * * *

If the large States could be reconciled to an augmentation of power in the Senate, constructed and endowed as that branch of the Government is, a veto on removals from office would at all times be worse than inconvenient in its operation, and in party times might, by throwing the executive machinery out of gear, produce a calamitous interregnum."

Some weight must be given to the almost unbroken usage in this matter.

The first Congress of the United States, which one might almost call an adjourned session of the Constitutional Convention, so determined it. And from that day until it was challenged in Jackson's time, a period of nearly half a century, there never was a question as to the power of the President, nor any attempt by Congress to regulate or curb it.

When that great controversy was determined in Jackson's favor—not merely by the continued adherence to the existing theory of government, but by the popular mandate of the people, that in the period of great financial distress first re-elected him and then elected Van Buren, his residuary legatee or political heir—I say in both respects he had the support of the people.

And then the question never arose again until the "tenure of office" acts in President Johnson's administration, and these acts resulted—if I may use a pragmatical argument—in one of the most discreditable chapters in the history of this country. I do not believe, if those who participated in the impeachment of Andrew Johnson, could again come to life, that any of them would feel any pride in their conduct; and on the contrary, I believe that the great body of opinion of posterity would, without any hesitation, say that, with respect to the question now under consideration, President Johnson was right. Certainly, the Congress repealed all those laws, except this law, in 1876.

And now, more than a half century later, as a part of the "irrepressible conflict" between the Congress and the Executive, Congress again raises the question in its most offensive form in the Comptroller-General act, which President Wilson vetoed on that ground, and which I am satisfied that President Harding would have been glad to veto if he could have separated it from the other provisions of the Budget law, in whose welfare he had taken a very deep interest. I am very confident that President Harding's signing of the Budget law was never intended to deny that which nearly all his predecessors—and all of his predecessors so far as they have ever made any public declaration on the subject—had consistently affirmed; namely, the inability of Congress to curb the power of the Executive to remove his own subordinates.

But Congress passed the law, not merely taking wholly from the President the power of removal, but making the office independent of the executive departments and putting it peculiarly under the tutelage of Congress.

I would repeat what I said at the beginning of my argument, if it were not idle repetition, and I want to avoid that: That if this Court is prepared to sustain this law, then the door is opened, and an unlimited opportunity is given to Congress to strip the President of nearly every essential power.

If you take my middle ground, that Congress may guide and direct the discretion of the President by such statutory qualifications as are properly inherent in the nature of an office, but without disturbing the power of removal as the Constitution vested it, Congress cannot destroy the independence of the Executive.

But if you take Senator Pepper's view and that of his colleague, the power of Congress to put the President in a strait-jacket is unlimited.

This is a grave question. The men who framed the Constitution honestly believed that we could never succeed through a legislative despotism. I am quite willing to concede also that they believed that our Nation could not endure an executive despotism. I am not contending for an executive absolutism; but I am protesting against a legislative absolutism.

[The Chief Justice: Mr. Beck, would it interrupt you for me to ask you to state specifically what your idea is in regard to the middle ground to which you referred? What kind of a method did you mean?

Mr. Beck: Well, I instanced one case, Chief Justice. I will now try to give two or three illustrations: Take, for example, the kind of law I first cited, a law that says that an office is created and that the President shall appoint somebody to the office, and that he shall be removable for inefficiency and dishonesty. That largely leaves the President's prerogative untouched.

The Chief Justice: Do you mean that he still would retain the power of absolute removal without having any such cause as that mentioned in the statute?

Mr. Beck: Exactly. And he would apply the legislative standard that had been given to him, viz., whether the incumbent was inefficient or dishonest. In other words, the execution of the law is left to him. All that Congress has done in that case is to prescribe a certain standard of the office; and if it be a legitimate ingredient and not merely the assumption of a power that is not authorized, I am not prepared to say that it would be unconstitutional.

Let me give another illustration that is far more to the point: Suppose the Congress creates an office and says that it shall only be filled by a man learned in the law; and suppose it further provides that, if a man ceases to be a member of the bar, he shall be removed. I think that can be reconciled with the Constitution. The office itself, by reason of its nature, may call for a man with legal qualifications. The Congress may be quite indisposed to create such an office if a layman were to be appointed to it. Therefore, it first limits the character of men from whom the President may select; he must be a lawyer. It then says, as a part of the tenure of office, that if he ceased to be a member of the bar, *ipso facto,* his tenure shall cease. Of course, they could abolish the office and provide for it in that way; but they might say that the President shall remove in that case. Now, I am not prepared to say that such a law cannot be reconciled with the Constitution.

What I do say is that, when the condition imposed upon the creation of the office has no reasonable relation to the office; when it is not a legislative standard to be applied by the President, and is not the declaration of qualifications, but is the creation of an appointing power other than the President, then Congress has crossed the dead line, for it has usurped the prerogative of the President. In vain does he have the power to remove if he cannot remove without the advice and consent of the Senate. What he does have, if such a law is possible, is the power to nominate for removal; and only that is left of a prerogative which hitherto has distinguished an American President from "figurehead" Presidents.

Mr. Justice Brandeis: Has he not the power to suspend, and has that power been questioned?

Mr. Beck: No. And yet the power to suspend, within the interpretation of the Constitution, is only part of the power to remove. The suspension may be a temporary one or it may be a permanent one; but it is a part of the same power to determine who shall fill that office.

Mr. Justice Brandeis: Well, it seems to me that many of the dangers to which you call attention of such an interpretation of the Constitution could be met by the power of suspension by the President.

Mr. Beck: Do you mean until the Congress has acted?

Mr. Justice Brandeis: Well, either until Congress has acted or otherwise. From what I understand, the power of the President to suspend is not infrequently used?

Mr. Beck: Yes, not infrequently. But the power to suspend is as much either a matter of correct interpretation of the Constitution or a matter of implication from it as the power to remove. Can you distinguish between them?]

You will recall that those who in the First Congress took the side against the President had two contentions: One was that the only way to remove an officer was by impeachment. And they had some slight sanction for that, because the Constitution said that all officers, from the President downward, could be removed by impeachment; therefore they argued that that was the only way. But no one contends now that impeachment is the only way; but all now agree that impeachment is only a paramount way of asserting the power of the people as against a negligent or recalcitrant Executive if he fails to discharge his duties.

The other argument of those who took that side was that whenever an officer was appointed by the President with the advice and consent of the Senate, in such case the removal must also be made with the advice and consent of the Senate.

Hamilton was at first of that view. He expressed himself to that effect in No. 77 of "The Federalist." But Lord Acton says, in his review of Bryce's "American Commonwealth"—although I have not been able to verify it—that Hamilton recanted from that view. I find this slight confirmation of it, that in the edition of 1802 of the "Federalist Papers," which Senator Lodge says was revised by Hamilton, there is a footnote to the effect that Hamilton's statement is no longer a fair statement of the Constitution, and that the concurrence of the Senate is not necessary to the President's power of removal.

At all events, there has never been since the First Congress a contention that, unless Congress affirmatively requires the consent of the Senate to a removal, the Senate concurrence is necessary. That has long since been settled by this Court and by the unbroken practice of the Government. For there is not a day, there is hardly an hour, that the power is not exercised. It may be that while I am speaking the President is removing somebody; it is not at all unlikely that he is. And it has never been from the time of George Washington down to the possible removal at this instant by the President of some one of the 800,000 officeholders a contention that, unless Congress affirmatively confirms the power of the President, he must go to the Senate and get its consent for the removal.

[Mr. Justice Sutherland: Your contention, as I understand it, is that Congress has authority to regulate or limit the power of removal, but it has no power to appropriate it?

Mr. Beck: Your honor has stated my suggestion of a possible middle ground between two extreme theories more felicitously than I fear I have. I am not conceding that any impairment of the power of the President to remove is constitutional. I am only suggesting to the Court that in this case it is not necessary for you to decide the full scope of the power. In other words, you need not determine in this case whether Congress may not reasonably regulate and control or guide the discretion of the President as to the act of removal, so long as it does not impair his essential power of removal. You do not have to decide that. It would be, in my judgment, unwise to decide it, for this reason; that if Congress passes a law such as I instanced before, that a man shall be removed for inefficiency or for dishonesty, and for no other cause, it might well be that the President would have the fullest justification for removing that man and yet neither of the statutory causes existed in the case. And I do not want to question any part of the great prerogative of the President by conceding, or by inviting this Court to say, that there is any power of control which would prevent the President, in a case properly within his discretion, from exercising the power of removal in the teeth of an act of Congress.

Mr. Justice Sutherland: You might concede that without conceding the validity of the statute in this case.

Mr. Beck: Yes, sir; that is correct. Under this law there is no control or regulation; you have simply a bald, naked, unquestioned, indefensible usurpation of the power of the Executive—unless you are willing to say that the Executive has no such power except by the sufferance of Congress.

The Chief Justice: Mr. Solicitor-General, how much of a concession is it that you make? You may have some machinery in your mind by which you are going to work it out. But if you say that Congress may provide reasons why a man shall be removed and the Executive may still retain the power to remove him absolutely, how much of a concession do you make? Is that a mere gesture by Congress or a mere suggestion of Congress?

Mr. Beck: Well, I apparently did not make myself clear to your honor. I simply conceded the possibility (though it is not involved in this case) that the President might be controlled in the exercise of his power of removal by some legislative standard that naturally and properly inheres in the nature of the office. I recognize that as a possibility.

The Chief Justice: How are you going to exercise that control and make it effective? What kind of a law would you suggest?

Mr. Beck: Well, I instanced the case of an office which could only be held by one learned in the law, and where the President is directed to remove the officer if he ceased to be a member of the bar.

The Chief Justice: Well, how are you going to put that through? Will the auditors refuse to pay him?

Mr. Beck: Well, assuming the constitutionality of an act which, in prescribing such an ingredient of the office as affects and guides the President in the exercise of his right of removal, then it is to be presumed that the President would respect that law and be guided by the policy of the Nation as declared by Congress. But if my friend answers——

Mr. Justice Sanford (interposing): How would you have him treat that? Would he only treat it as a guide entitled to some consideration, but not as being controlling?

Mr. Beck: No; I did not mean that it might not have the force of a legal regulation. I do not concede that it can; but I simply said that it is a debatable question whether this Court in passing upon such a law, and holding in nice equipoise the respective powers of the Presi-

dent and legislature, might say of a given regulation of
the nature of an office that that is not such an infringe-
ment of the essential power of removal as to be in violation of the Constitution.

Mr. Justice Van Devanter: Your contention is that
such a provision of law would be effective in so far as
your conception of the powers is concerned?

Mr. Beck: Yes, sir.

Mr. Justice Stone: Suppose Congress passed a law creating a board of commissioners, and provided that the
members of that commission should not be engaged in
any other activity, and made that a prohibition upon the
officers; that would not enlarge or diminish the President's
power of removal under your theory, would it?

Mr. Beck: No; not at all.

Mr. Justice Stone: It would suggest to him that the
officer ought to be removed if he engaged in other activities?

Mr. Beck: Yes.

Mr. Justice Stone: Suppose he did engage in other activities; would that be a ground for impeaching him under
the impeachment provision of the Constitution?

Mr. Beck: No; I should think not.

Mr. Justice Stone: Although he violates the provision
of the statute?

Mr. Beck: Of course, that was the question involved
in the Andrew Johnson impeachment. He violated an
act of Congress which forbade him to remove a member
of his own Cabinet. It is fair to say that the majority
of the Senate voted for impeachment——

Mr. Justice Stone (interposing): That is a different
question; that is as to the constitutional power. Now, a
member of this commission that I instanced would not
have the constitutional power to engage in any other
activities?

Mr. Beck: But your honor's proposition went further,
and questioned whether if the President refused to remove him for violation of an act of Congress the President could be impeached.

Mr. Justice Stone: Oh, no—the officer himself; whether he could be impeached.

Mr. Beck: Oh, I thought your honor meant whether the President could be impeached in that case. I think the officer clearly could be impeached.

Mr. Justice Stone: Well, does not that suggest the validity of your middle ground, namely, that it would be ground for impeachment if that was violated by the President?

Mr. Beck: Yes; in the case your honor mentioned, the legislative standard, if I may call it so, is plainly created as an ingredient of the office; it is not a thing outside of the office.]

I have only five minutes left; and if I may, I will close my argument in a very few words:

Suppose the Court sustains this law: You will have broken the uninterrupted flow of constitutional development in this country for 136 years.

Suppose you refuse to sustain this law: You will have maintained that unbroken flow.

Senator Pepper says in his argument that the genius of our race requires that the last hope of the people shall be reposed in the legislative branch of the Government. I do not think the last hope is reposed in either the legislative branch or the Executive. The last hope of the American people is reposed in the Constitution of the United States, which has seen fit to divide the powers in such a way that neither of these three great departments can monopolize the powers of government.

I have no love for one-man power. I am inclined to think that the two greatest dangers in this country are, in the first place, what I call "nullification by indirection"; that is, the perversion of Federal powers to accomplish objects that are beyond the purposes of the Federal Government, of which we have clearly had abundant evidences in the legislation of recent years, and the other is the steady concentration of power in one man, which does threaten the equilibrium of the Government.

Aristotle said, 2,000 years ago, that no constitution would long endure unless it corresponded to what he called the *ethos* of the people—that is, the spirit of the people—and when it ceased to correspond to the genius of the people, then it would not be the spirit of the people that would be broken; it would be the constitution.

I believe that is everlastingly true. And I believe that one of the most sinister signs of the times, in all departments of life — social, political, and economic — is that there is a strong centripetal tendency toward one-man power.

But see how wisely the Constitution preserves the equipoise; how it takes away from the President the temptation to remove any man without cause; because the moment he appoints a successor the Senate must be consulted.

Moreover, Congress has its power over the purse strings. Congress has the power of impeachment. Congress can abolish the office altogether. Congress can do anything except create an office upon conditions which change the fundamental nature of our Government. That is what it cannot do; and that is what it has attempted to do in this law, unless I am very much mistaken.

Again I assert solemnly, that if it is within the power of Congress to create offices in such a way and by such methods as to constitute a redistribution of the powers of government, by transferring this executive power to Congress (which, being human, is also naturally ambitious and glad to have a power superior to that of the President)—if such be the fact, then the Constitution will sooner or later become, by congressional usurpation, a mere house of cards.

Our form of government is a magnificent edifice today, erected by a hundred and thirty-six years of patient sacrifice and labor. It has its "cloud-capped towers"; its "gorgeous palaces"; its "solemn temples"—and this great Court is such a temple. But if the Court should sustain Senator Pepper's contention, this noble edifice of constitutional liberty might one day become an "insubstantial pageant faded," and posterity might then say that it was not the work of supremely great men, but of muddled dreamers, for it would be of "such stuff as dreams are made of."

XII

THE CONSTITUTIONAL RIGHT OF THE SENATE TO EXCLUDE A SENATOR-ELECT

One of the great compromises in the Constitutional Convention of 1787 was Article I, Section 3, that the Senate of the United States should be composed of two Senators from each State, chosen by the Legislatures thereof—and the compact in Article V that no State, without its consent, shall be deprived of its equal suffrage in the Senate. There was also the provision in Article I, Section 5, that the Senate, with the concurrence of two-thirds, might expel a member.

In the early days of the Republic, nearly all candidates for public office were selected at caucuses, but King Demos has provided in more recent years that such candidates shall be selected in party primaries and that the choice of candidates of the respective political parties shall be submitted to all of the voters at a subsequent election.

Frank L. Smith of Illinois offered himself in the Republican primary of that State in 1926 as a candidate of that party for the subsequent election of a United States Senator. He was successful in securing the nomination of the Republican Party, and at the ensuing election was elected over his Democratic opponent.

It appeared, however, that Smith's friends, including a utility magnate, had spent large sums of money in the primary campaign, though there was never any question that Smith possessed the qualifications for Senators named in Article I, Section 3, of the Constitution. The right of Smith to take the oath as Senator was challenged and denied by a majority vote of the Senate.

Mr. Beck took a great interest in the controversy because of the constitutional principle involved and wrote a book, "The Vanishing Rights of the States," which Senator Blease of South Carolina read almost entirely into the Congressional Record, wherein he denied the Constitutional right of the Senate by a majority vote to exclude from the Senate a person unquestionably elected by a sovereign State because of some alleged irregularity in the primary campaign.

Mr. Beck accepted as a public duty the burden of defending Mr. Smith's right to the office before the Senate Committee on Privileges and Elections, and on Saturday, January 29, 1927, made the following argument.

—EDITOR.

265

Mr. Chairman and Gentlemen of the Committee:

Senators, "hear me for my cause," and "censure me in your wisdom." I trust that there is no man on this committee who can feel anything but sympathy for a man who made a brave, valorous fight, both in the primary and the election, against seemingly overwhelming obstacles, and as to whose title, so far as the fairness of election, in both the primary and the general election in Illinois is concerned, no possible question has been or could be raised. I think it is due to Colonel Smith to say that, whatever may be the action of this committee or of the United States Senate hereafter, he has had his vindication at the hands of his party associates in the primary, and of the people of Illinois in the general election by great majorities. That is the verdict of the vicinage, of those who have known him from boyhood to manhood, and he comes here with the full approval of the people of Illinois.

There is a second reason why I know you will listen to me with patience, and with open minds, and that is the rights of a sovereign State are involved in this great question; and the rights of Illinois are the rights of every State of the Federal Union. The fate of Illinois today may possibly in future years be the fate of some other State.

And in the third place, and greater than all, there is not one member of this committee who can have other than a feeling of deep affection and veneration for the Constitution of the Fathers, and no matter how any of you may have voted hitherto, there is not one of you who would willingly pull down in a day what it has taken 140 years to construct. I do not want to indulge in verbal hysterics in relation to the Constitution, although the solemnity of the matter cannot be too strongly impressed. If you allow this fabric to be destroyed on this occasion in this or other respects, you have destroyed that which can never be rebuilt. There is not today the statecraft that could ever do again what the Fathers did in Philadelphia 140 years ago. One can say, as Othello said in that last act of Shakespeare's greatest drama, "Put out that light"

—the light of the Constitution—"and I know not whence is that Promethean heat that can that light relume." It will be extinguished forever, and with it will pass an experiment in democracy which hitherto the whole world has admired.

With this invocation to your indulgence let us consider what is the question before us. The Senate of the United States, without itself expressing any opinion, has asked this committee to consider and to report, first, whether upon any evidence before it there is any reason why the oath of office should not be given to Colonel Smith upon his undisputed credentials; and secondly, assuming that such oath of office were given, what should be the action of the Senate with respect to giving him his seat.

We are confronted with an unprecedented situation here. There is no accuser; there are no formulated charges; there is no contestant; there are no rival credentials, and all that the committee has and all the facts upon which any argument can be predicated, are these, that in an *ex parte* investigation—and by that I am not speaking invidiously, at all, because I think the Reed Committee rendered a great public service by calling the attention of the American people to the excessive use of money in politics, but nevertheless on an *ex parte* investigation—certain facts were developed, and as I understood this committee last Saturday, you desire to have me argue, upon the face of the report and upon the face of the testimony, whether there is any reason under the Constitution of the United States why the oath of office should not be administered to Frank L. Smith upon the undisputed credentials of his State.

Therefore, I must first address myself to what were the facts developed in the Reed Committee. If I took the bulky record, most of which has little reference to Mr. Smith—and there are other features for which he is not responsible and as to which he is not interested—and fumble from page to page, I would certainly tire the committee; and therefore I have carefully read all the pertinent testimony, and I have tried to summarize it, extenuating nothing, and obviously setting down naught in malice, in the form of a few typewritten pages, and if you will allow me to read the "evidence in the case," to use a term that I once made the title of a book, such recital will have the added advantage that for each reference I will quote the page of the record of the Reed Committee where it may be found, so that any member of the committee can verify it. With your indulgence, these are the facts that are disclosed by the testimony in the case:

Frank L. Smith is the president of a small bank in a town of 2,500 people. He has been in public life for over thirty years and against his reputation there has never hitherto been any imputation. In November, 1925, he determined to enter the Republican primaries, which were to be held in the following April, as a candidate for United States Senator against the late Senator McKinley. He was a man of small means, as compared with his opponent, who was a multimillionaire. Moreover, his opponent had the advantage of being the sitting member, which enabled him to frank his political literature to every voter and which gave him, to a considerable extent, the control of the Federal organization. The proof shows that until very late in the primary campaign, Mr. Smith had no factional or organization support except an improvised organization of his friends.

Mr. Smith required an organization and he requested his friend, Allen F. Moore, to form a campaign committee, of which Mr. Moore became chairman and treasurer. Mr. Moore "undertook the task of creating the organization and conducting the campaign, except in so far as Mr. Smith would make speeches and see the people." (1533.) Mr. Moore opened headquarters in the Congress Hotel, Chicago, and Mr. Smith departed on his speech-making campaign, during the course of which he made 300 or 400 speeches, "making as high as thirty-one towns in a week and fifty-six speeches a week." (1539.)

He was constantly moving from place to place and to one in public life that is full of meaning. Some years ago, being engaged in some litigation with John Philip Sousa, we were cross-examining him, and it developed that he had written two letters which had two contradictory statements in regard to the same matter. When we asked him how he could reconcile these statements he turned to the lawyer who was examining him, and said, "Mr. So and So, did you ever do one-night stands?" It was so appropriate that we did not bear too hard upon a man who in one letter had said one thing and in another exactly the opposite, when he was thus doing the hardest thing that a man can possibly do; namely, the driving, intense energy of a public man, shaking hands with thousands of people, addressing thousands more, and exerting every energy of mind and body and soul to the extreme limit in an attempt to overcome the desperate odds against which he was struggling.

This division of work required Moore to collect and disburse the money and Smith to meet and address the people. (1539.) Mr. Smith testified that he "had nothing to do with the collection of the money." (1535.) Asked by the chairman whether he had discussed with Mr. Moore "where he could get money," Mr. Smith replied: "No; I did not tell him where he could get money." (1539.) He further testified: "I have the information that Mr. Moore conducted the campaign, collected the money, and will be ready and glad to respond as a witness and tell where he got it. As to where the money came from, I did not see the money and know nothing as to the form in which it came to Mr. Moore." (1537.)

Mr. Smith further testified that he had instructed Mr. Moore to accept no contributions that would involve any obligation on his part. He did not know what contributions had, in fact, been made until after the primary, although he admitted that, during the campaign, he had knowledge that Mr. Insull, a utility magnate, had made contributions to his campaign fund and, as it had become an issue in the primaries, his only reply was "that if one who had made $38,000,000 reduction in utilities costs saw fit to support my candidacy, I could see no reason for objection."

Reading: "The Chairman: I take it, then, Mr. Smith, that you had information that put you on notice of the fact that Insull had contributed.

Mr. Smith: I would not put it that way, Senator. I had information that Mr. Insull was supporting my campaign. As to the amount or any specific donations, I had no knowledge at that time.

The Chairman: Did you not take up that matter with Mr. Moore?

Mr. Smith: I talked with Mr. Moore about the progress of the campaign and Mr. Moore indicated to me that he was getting along all right with managing the campaign and with finances. (1868)."

Mr. Smith himself contributed $5,000 and some small checks, aggregating a few hundred dollars, which his friends had given him.

Mr. Smith further testified upon his and Mr. Moore's activities:

"From the beginning there was a division of labor between us. I was to make the campaign throughout the State, attend meetings, meet the voters and in every way possible, by word of mouth, carry the message to the people of the State of Illinois. Mr. Moore was to effect the best organization possible under the circumstances, direct the campaign from central headquarters, and find the money to pay necessary expenses. * * * We had a clear understanding from the start about money. This understanding was that under no circumstances was I to be put under any obligation whatever to any one for contributions or other assistance. I have not violated that understanding at any time and I am firm in my belief that Mr. Moore has in no way violated it. I have never at any time or under any circumstances, either previous to this primary campaign, during the campaign, or after its close, in any manner, directly or indirectly, obligated myself to any person for,

or on account of, any assistance, whether mone-
tary or otherwise, that he or she might have contributed toward the success of my campaign. I
am just as sure of Mr. Allen F. Moore as I am of
myself in this regard. (1868)."

Please understand, Senators, that Mr. Smith, in this testimony, is not in any sense repudiating what Mr. Moore
has done. He accepts responsibility for that, and therefore he would not have me put him in the position of
repudiating it. The fact is, however—and there is no
contradiction of it—that the matter of financing the campaign was undertaken by Mr. Moore, a man of substantial
means; that Mr. Smith had departed and traveled from
one end of the State to the other; and the only knowledge that he had that Mr. Insull had made any contribution was the fact of the contribution: but the amount,
or the circumstances, were unknown to him until after
the primary elections.

Mr. Moore confirmed this testimony about the division
of the work, and testified that he himself, as a friend of
Mr. Smith, had contributed $75,000, and that other con-
tributions had been made which aggregated about $250,-
000. Of this sum about one-half was contributed by Mr.
Insull. In November or December of 1925 Mr. Samuel
Insull, a man of large wealth and varied enterprises, asked
Mr. Moore to call at the office; and, after indicating his
interest in the campaign, Mr. Insull contributed $50,000.
Early in March he contributed a second $50,000, and
shortly before the primary he contributed $25,000 more.
Mr. Insull gave as his reason that he did not like Senator
McKinley, and did not think that he had made a good
Senator. (1558.) No other reason was assigned for the
gift, except that one, and the principal avowed ground
of Mr. Insull's objection to Senator McKinley was the latter's approval of American participation in the World
Court.

Mr. Moore testified:

"Mr. Smith did not know anything about the

finances of this campaign. I handled that myself." (1566).

He gave a detailed account of his expenditures, which
aggregated $253,000; and be it remembered that there
never was any evidence whatever, or the pretense of evidence, that a single dollar was ever spent illegitimately.
Every dollar of it had been accounted for, for what was
not merely a legitimate object but quite a laudable object,
in acquainting the citizens of Illinois with the issues of
the campaign.

Mr. Insull testified that he had opposed Senator McKinley because of his deep-rooted convictions on the World
Court matter. He stated that, apart from the Smith
campaign, he had spent, through men of his own selection,
about $26,000 in propaganda against the World Court.
He specifically stated that the money he contributed
was wholly his own, and that none of it had been contributed by any public utility corporation. The only testimony on this subject is as follows:

"The Chairman: Where did you get the money
from?

Mr. Insull: My own personal resources. Every
dollar that I have contributed to Mr. Smith's
campaign and every dollar that I have contributed to this World Court campaign is the
money absolutely of Samuel Insull—of myself.

The Chairman: There was no arrangement
for any reimbursement?

Mr. Insull: Absolutely none whatsoever."
(1825).

Therefore the committee can at least start with the
fact—and it is an important fact—notwithstanding
the idea so generally prevalent throughout the country,
owing to the misleading headlines of some newspapers,
that no public utility corporation ever contributed a
penny to Mr. Smith's campaign. Of course you may say
that Mr. Insull, who is a very prominent corporation official and perhaps you could go so far as to say the control-

ling spirit, of public utility companies, did contribute it out of his pocket; but I do not want to argue the case now until I have completed my facts. Certainly, however, if Judge Gary makes a contribution to a political campaign, there is no necessary inference that the United States Steel Corporation gave it; and when a man like Mr. Insull, who is a type of citizen common in many cities, who takes an interest in everything, the opera, the art gallery, civic enterprises, the theater, public utilities, political movements, etc., exercises his undoubted right as a citizen of the United States, in the absence of any prohibitory law, to contribute to a party movement which has his sympathy, it is gratuitous—at all events it is without justification—to conclude that the money of the public utility corporation was contributed.

At the time these gifts were made by Mr. Insull to Mr. Moore for the Smith campaign fund, Mr. Smith was the chairman of the Illinois Commerce Commission. It is a body of seven men, each of them given an equal vote, which regulates utilities. Mr. Smith testified that during the World War the rates had been raised to meet extraordinary conditions, but after its termination the commission commenced investigations to reduce them. They first took up the Chicago surface lines and the Peoples Gas Light & Coke Co., an Insull concern. The street car company's rates were reduced and a saving effected to the patrons in four years to June 30, 1926, amounting to over $35,000,000.

As to the Peoples Gas Light & Coke Co., the chief Insull concern, an order was made, effective August 1, 1923, which reduced gas rates from $1.19 per thousand cubic feet to $0.96 per thousand cubic feet, resulting in a saving to consumers up to June 30, 1926, of approximately $25,000,000.

The Commonwealth Edison Co., another Insull concern, had its rates reduced on August 1, 1923, and this reduction to June 30, 1926, amounted to $5,800,000.

I may interject here that not only is there no evidence whatever that the public utilities commission—of which Mr. Smith was but one of the seven members, and whose orders were at all times subject to an appeal to a court by any interested party—ever raised the rates of any public utility company a penny, but, as a matter of fact, the reductions were substantial and deep-cutting; and after the primary and the election there never was a suggestion that the public utility companies received any possible favor at the hands of the public utilities commission.

If you can spell out from this testimony an inference or a presumption that Mr. Insull gave this money to Colonel Smith to influence him as chairman of the public utilities commission, then you have this very remarkable fact, that in that event the object of the gift and the inevitable use of the money was to make it impossible for Mr. Smith to continue to act as chairman of the public utilities commission, because the moment he was elected Senator, he could not continue as such chairman, and his opportunity of being useful (if he had been a serviceable tool of Mr. Insull) had altogether vanished with his election; so that the contribution of money was designed to take away the very effect which is sought to be imputed from these facts.

Such is all the pertinent testimony as to the Insull contributions, upon which was based the charge of impropriety or corruption.

Turning now to the partial report of the Reed Committee, it will be found that there is nothing inconsistent with the evidence already quoted. The report speaks of Mr. Insull's contributions, and gives the correct amount, and then specifies the various corporations with which he is identified; but the report does not find that the public utilities corporation, or any corporation, contributed anything whatsoever.

Without troubling the committee to read the report, it is enough to say that it simply states that this money was contributed by Mr. Insull, a public utility owner; but it does not say that it was contributed by any public utility.

The same is true of the smaller contributions which were made by two other wealthy men who were identified with public utilities corporations, namely, Mr. Copley and Mr. Studebaker.

From these facts it may be summarized that Mr. Insull voluntarily contributed from his personal resources $125,-000 to the Smith campaign fund, making the contributions in three payments to Allen F. Moore, the chairman and treasurer of said fund, and that, while Mr. Smith was not ignorant that Mr. Insull had made some contribution, he did not know until after the campaign was over what contributions had been made. The gifts, which were purely voluntary, were not made upon any promise or obligation; and the only action by the Utilities Commission upon the Insull properties of which there is any evidence was to reduce their rates, and presumably their profits, by many millions. All these orders required a majority of the Utilities Commission, and all of them were subject at the instance of any interested party to an appeal in the courts of Illinois. In every instance when the question of rates is involved, the officials of the municipality where the utility operate are, under the Illinois law, given notice of any hearing on the subject of rates.

The Reed Committee report is fair, and no just exception can be taken to it except that it does not dwell upon some of the disclaimers to which I have referred; but, so far as it goes, it is fair in simply stating the naked fact that a man who was identified with public-utility corporations, out of his own resources, as he testified, contributed to a party movement in which he was interested.

One further finding of the Reed Committee remains to be noted. It is this:

> "The State of Illinois has no statute restricting the amount which may be expended by any candidate, nor any law requiring the candidates or their committees to file a statement of such expenditures. The Federal corrupt practices act has been declared unconstitutional by the Supreme Court in the Newberry case in so far as the act applies to primary elections, and there is no duty imposed on the candidates or their committees to file with the United States Senate a statement of expenditures."

The report failed to notice the fact that there was a Federal statute of great significance in determining what conclusion you may properly draw from the fact that Mr. Moore, Mr. Smith's campaign manager, received from Mr. Insull, a man of many enterprises, a gift of money to use in a party primary. As a matter of fact—and I do not recall that in the debates in the Senate any reference was made to it—Congress, by a law passed on February 28, 1925, chapter 368, passed a Federal corrupt practices act.

[Senator King: What year was that?]

Mr. Beck: 1925. The act commences by stating that it is to be called the Federal Corrupt Practices act of 1925. The reference is 43 Statutes at Large, 1070. It commences with a definition of those with whom the act is going to deal, and I want to read one or two of those definitions.

Having defined what a candidate is, and given him a distinct status, it says:

> "The term 'political committee' includes any committee, association, or organization which accepts contributions or makes expenditures for the purpose of influencing or attempting to influence the election of candidates or presidential and vice presidential electors"—

It then goes on to say:

> "The term 'contribution' includes a gift, subscription, loan, advance, or deposit of money, or anything of value, and includes a contract, promise, or agreement, whether or not legally enforceable, to make a contribution."
>
>   *   *   *   *   *
>
> "The term 'person' includes an individual, partnership, committee, association, corporation"—

And so forth. Thereupon it starts to define what a party movement shall consist of, because it was intended to apply to the two old historic and other parties of America, and the act then provides:

"Every political committee shall have a chairman and a treasurer. No contribution shall be accepted, and no expenditure made, by or on behalf of a political committee for the purpose of influencing an election until such chairman and treasurer have been chosen."

It then prescribes what the treasurer shall do in the matter of taking receipts and making an account of expenditures.

Then follows Section 305, giving far more in detail the duties of the treasurer of the committee; but as, for a reason presently disclosed, they have no immediate application, I forbear to read them.

I beg your attention to the following language. It is referring to a Federal Corrupt Practices act in the matter of elections, and the section says:

"The term 'election' includes a general or special election, and, in the case of a Resident Commissioner from the Philippine Islands, an election by the Philippine Legislature, but does not include a primary election or convention of a political party."

Whether that was done in deference to the Newberry decision, which had theretofore held there could be no valid Federal legislation in respect to primaries, at least prior to the Seventeenth Amendment, or whether it was because of the historic policy of this country under all parties, except in grave intermittent crises of our national life, to leave the regulation of election and the details thereof to the States, I do not pretend to say; but the fact is that at the time Colonel Smith opened this campaign and arranged with Mr. Moore to attend to what might be called the executive management while Mr. Smith went through the populous State of Illinois and tried to reach two and a half million of qualified voters, there was no law of the State of Illinois that forbade Mr. Insull, out of his personal pocket, to give money to a political cause in any sum whatever.

Secondly, the Congress of the United States had specifically provided that it did not legislate with respect to primaries or political conventions, and that the act which I have quoted referred, only, to the general election.

Third, and most important—because I do say, with great respect, that if Colonel Smith is disqualified and denied his seat it will not be upon tangible facts, but upon innuendo from facts—at the time he made this arrangement with Colonel Moore, the law of the land, the Federal law, had recognized a party movement as a distinct entity, having a legal status as such, requiring every political committee to have a chairman and a treasurer, prescribing the duties of the treasurer, and making him responsible directly to the people for the proper collection and the proper disbursement of moneys in connection with elections.

Mr. Doyle suggests—and I am very glad he does—that the Willis resolution adopted in the Newberry case—which, of course, was nothing more than a declaration of the then existing sentiment of the Senate, because it could have no force of law, being but a statement of the opinions of the Senate as then constituted as to whether or not more than $25,000 could be properly spent in a senatorial election—that resolution, with no legal force as a statute, was prior to this act of Congress, which, passed under the Constitution, is the supreme law of the land, and which, therefore, did say that in respect to primary elections the Federal Government had and could have no possible concern, disclaiming it by the emphatic exception to which I have referred.

I know that it is easy to say in newspaper offices—I do not say this invidiously, but they work under terrific pressure from hour to hour, and cannot give that calm and sober consideration to any public question which a judicial body such as a court or this committee may give—that:

"Oh, well, if Mr. Insull is connected with a public utility corporation, and he gives money,

that is the money of the public utility corporation. If he gives it to Mr. Moore, that is given
to Mr. Smith."

As a matter of fact, when you are passing upon so
grave a matter as denying the right of the State of Illinois
to have her own choice in the United States Senate, you
must not determine a question upon innuendos or without recognizing the existing status under statutes of men
who occupy any relation to the activities of a campaign.

The treasurer was a legal officer, responsible as such;
and when, therefore, money was given to Mr. Moore by
Mr. Insull—a proper gift on the part of Mr. Insull, certainly forbidden by no law—when it was given, it was
not a gift to Mr. Smith, even though Mr. Smith was the
beneficiary of the political movement.

Gentlemen, such are the facts and Federal statute dis-
claiming any application to primary campaigns upon
which you are to base your recommendation. Perhaps I
should say, in candor, that there was a question involved,
which may be the subject of an inquiry in the Senate, as to
whether or not a contribution that Mr. Insull made to the
local Republican organization of Chicago should be the
subject of inquiry, and, if so, whether it had any reference
to Mr. Smith's campaign; but, whether it is added and
charged against Mr. Smith or not, I do not think that so
grave and highly punitive action by the Senate as the disqualification of a man on the ground of his lacking moral
character can proceed merely upon the amount of the
money.

In this connection, it may interest the committee to say
that since this great controversy began I have received a
letter from a distinguished judge in England, who for
thirty years was the party counsel for the Conservative
Party in all election petitions; and he wrote me that the
trend of the English decisions was to disregard the amount,
and to ask the other and more important question, "How
was it collected, and how was it disbursed?" The amount
is regarded as a matter of unimportance, and there is good
reason for that belief, and it is this:

The greatest evil that afflicts this country today—infinitely graver than the use of money in elections, and the thing that makes me, for one, despair of the future, is the fact that the people are no longer interested in politics.   They are interested in movies, baseball and so on; but unless we can revive an interest—and a militant interest—on the part of the people, our whole form of government will become unworkable, or else it will ultimately drift into an oligarchy.   Therefore, the legitimate expenditure of money to interest people in the issues of the campaign, and to educate them to vote rightly, to my mind is a beneficient use of money, and at all events cannot constitute any disqualification.

If the mere amount of money is to be regarded as cause to forfeit a seat on the part of a Senator and to forfeit the right of his State to choose him, then it is for Congress, if it have any constitutional power, to pass a statute so that we may know the rules of the game.   Congress not only has passed no statute to apply to party primaries but has expressly declared that the statute it did pass should not so apply.   In the absence of any statute in Illinois forbidding the expenditure of a quarter of a million dollars to interest and inform an electorate that numbered two and a half millions, and in the absence of any Federal statute, if such a one could be passed, limiting the amount of money to be expended in either primary or general elections, the rules of the game are that each side can spend such money as it can properly collect and properly disburse.

To say to a man, because he spends a quarter of a million dollars or more, when his opponent spends $500,-000, that he is thereby disqualified, is to invoke a rule which was not in existence when the game was played, and that seems to be a violation of the ordinary rules of fair play.   It is on all fours with an *ex post facto* law with this difference that the denial of the seat is no law at all but merely a majority vote of the Senate—a part of the law-making power.

Gentlemen of the committee, you have heard me with a patience that I expected, and have received what might be called the facts upon which you must predicate your action. I want now to lift the whole discussion to a much higher atmosphere, and one that I know will be far more interesting and perhaps more convincing, and that is, what are the rights either of this committee or of the United States Senate in the premises?

[Senator Goff: Mr. Beck, before you leave that subject, without interrupting your line of thought I want to ask you to bear in mind, please, a question such as this as you continue your legal argument.

Some States, as you well know, limit a Senator in his primary to $5,000. Other States have no limitation whatsoever as to what a Senator can spend. I know that personal illustrations are often inopportune; but the State of West Virginia, which Senator Neely, my colleague, and myself have the honor to represent, limits us to $75 a county. There are fifty-five counties in the State, and therefore we can spend in the primary $4,175, only. In the State of Pennsylvania, separated from the State of West Virginia by an invisible line, there is no limit, and in a campaign for Senator a million or two millions of dollars can be spent.

Now, I know it is in the minds of members of the committee that there should be some limitation, and that this unlimited expenditure makes not only for the corruption of the electorate but also for a disqualification of the ultimate beneficiary of such an expenditure. I trust that when you go on with your argument—because I have read your very interesting book upon this subject—you will kindly bear that in mind and discuss it, because I know that many members of the committee have such a thought in their minds, as well as members of the Senate.

Mr. Beck: The first part of your request, Senator— I do not know whether it was a question or a request— is purely a matter of legislative policy. It certainly is fair to say, "Let us know the rules of the game." Now, the Federal Government hitherto, from the very beginning— with, as I said, a few unfortunate intervals—has felt that that was one of the questions which had best be left to the States themselves, as a matter of home rule. All that the Constitution ever said in the way of a positive restriction was that the electors should have the legal qualifications of the electors for the most numerous branch of the State legislature. Such has been the policy of this country, never departed from except at a great loss to the country's peace and happiness. We have different conditions. We have different characters of people. They are materially different in number. These questions had better be adjusted by the States themselves, except in so far as the Federal Constitution provides otherwise.

Therefore, in the first instance, every State ought to be the judge of the necessities with respect to the amount of money which can be legitimately expended and this has been the historic policy of Congress. It is equally true, however, that if the Federal Government is to pass upon that question within the limits of its powers—and of course it has power to do it as to a general election, not as to a primary—then it follows necessarily that we ought to have a positive law passed by the House and Senate and duly approved by the President, so that those who enter the game may know the rules of the game, and not find out, after they have won the game, that they are disqualified for something which had never been a part of the rules of the game. That certainly is neither fair nor the law.

You invite a person to go in, as the State of Illinois does, and collect and spend money without limit in the primaries, and the Federal law disclaims any interference. Very well. When a man like Colonel Smith goes and spends a quarter of a million dollars, or his friends for him, against half a million dollars of his opponent, he suddenly finds he is disqualified, the door is shut in his face, although no statute had said, "Stop, look, and listen!" The only Federal statute in the matter said it was not concerned with primary campaigns.

Reference was made to the Newberry decision. I take it the Newberry decision amounts to this, in a very few words:

The majority of the court unquestionably found that prior to the seventeenth amendment there was no constitutional power on the part of Congress to pass any law in reference to primary elections and therefore the Senate had seated Newberry. There cannot be any doubt about that.

Senator Goff: None at all.

Mr. Beck: A majority of the court held, and they could hold in no other way, that primaries were a thing undreamed of when the Constitution was formed. Undoubtedly Justice McKenna did say in substance in his concurring opinion, "I do not express any opinion as to whether the power may not exist since the seventeenth amendment." Therefore the Newberry case cannot be cited to the effect that a majority of the court have held that Congress today may not legislate with respect to the primaries. It is an open question. The power cannot be affirmed, it cannot be disaffirmed, but it is a question as to which Congress can pass a statute and allow the Supreme Court to pass upon it.

Senator Neely: What do you maintain, that it does or does not have power to enact such legislation?

Mr. Beck: I do not see that the seventeenth amendment changes the nature of the Federal power. I do not think it was intended to do more than describe the method of electing a Senator. I do not think it was intended to confer upon the Federal Government a greater power in reference to the political activities within a State. That is my belief.

I may suggest, Senator, that there is force in the minority opinion in the Newberry case, that even though primaries were unknown to the men who framed the Constitution, yet the Constitution is a matter of continuing adaptation to new conditions as they arise; and inasmuch as the primary had become a part of the election machinery, and had acquired a legal status, Congress had power to regulate primaries. But the majority of the court have said otherwise, and Congress has not since attempted to do so, and why, then, should I discuss it?

Senator Smith: So far as the relations of the Federal Government to the States are concerned, did the seventeenth amendment in any way fundamentally change the relations? Did it not just change the power to elect from the legislatures to the people, and leave the relations of the Federal Government with the State practically as they were before?

Mr. Beck: Yes, Senator; you have stated my belief as I have tried to state it, a great deal better than I did. That is exactly it. It left the existing lines of demarcation between the Federal power and the State power just where they were before, except that it is no longer the legislature which elects. It is now the people.

Senator Smith: I ask that question because I was a member of the Senate when that amendment was ratified, and I do not think it would have been as easy to pass it as it was had it been contemplated that we were granting more power to the Federal Government to control the nominations of candidates who were to go into the general election than it had before.

Senator Caraway: If the Senator will stop and think a moment, it will occur to him that Congress could eventually take over all Federal elections. Since we provided for the elections by popular vote, of course the relations between the Federal Government and the States have been affected. While the Congress could not take over the election of the legislators who were to vote, the Constitution did give Congress absolutely the power to prescribe the qualifications of the members.

Mr. Beck: The fact is that Congress has not done so. On the contrary, by an explicit statute, it says that what it provides shall not apply to primary elections.

Senator Edge: Mr. Chairman, we have heard each other's views on this question for two days. I would like to hear Mr. Beck's views.

Mr. Beck: I have said that whatever you may say as to the power of the Seventeenth Amendment, the only exercise of the possible power was a disclaimer by Congress of any intention to regulate primary elections.]

Gentlemen of the committee, I want now to address myself to a great question, and it certainly is one of the greatest questions that ever confronted this generation, far greater than the question I argued two years ago as to the relative powers of the President and the Congress to remove an officer. And it is no disrespect to you, gentlemen, to say that I only wish I could get this question into the same tribunal that decided the case of Myers against the United States, because it is a pity there is not some way that a question which so gravely affects the due equilibrium between the rights of the Government and the rights of a State cannot in some way be passed upon by that judicial tribunal which is the keeper of the conscience of the American people in matters of constitutional morality.

I shall try to throw some light upon the origin and the meaning of the word "qualifications," which has not, I think, been thrown upon it in any previous discussions in this case, and it may, perhaps, be convincing to the members of the committee.

I take it that every member of this committee will agree with me that if the clause of the Constitution "Each House shall be the judge of the elections, returns, and qualifications of its members" were out of the Constitution, no one would contend for one moment that the Senate could refuse to the State of Illinois the right to send such person as she may choose; that the only possible doubt in this controversy is as to whether the ambiguous word "qualifications" may not confer some undefined and illimitable power on the part of the Senate to determine for itself whether a man the State thinks fit is, in the view of the Senate, unfit.

Before giving my own interpretation of the word "qualifications," based upon the political history of the country and of the nation from which we are sprung, I want to recall what happened in Philadelphia 140 years ago, when the Constitution was framed. It was no compact between the thirteen States and a new entity called the United States. The United States was not the creator, it was the created, and the Constitution is a solemn compact between thirteen sovereign States, to the full benefit and privilege of which other succeeding States have been admitted, as to the conditions upon which a new entity called "The United States" should be brought into being for certain general purposes, as to which the States did not regard themselves as competent to act.

In that constitutional convention, as all of us who have read its history know, there was a fight of unexampled bitterness upon two grounds, one of which is very pertinent to this discussion. The first was the claim of the larger States that they ought to be represented in some way relative to their population or wealth, and the second was as to the manner of choosing Senators. So bitter were the divisions, so keen the acrimony, that the small States finally said to the president of the convention, "You will take what we say, namely, equal representation both in the Senate and the House, or the convention is at an end."

It is one of the most dramatic incidents in our history. At that supreme moment Washington looked at Franklin —because the end of their labors had seemingly come; they had been in session six weeks, they were getting no nearer an agreement, they were in an irreconcilable conflict—and Franklin rose and suggested an adjournment for 48 hours, and made one of the most beautiful speeches—I think as beautiful as Lincoln's speech at Gettysburg—that marvelous speech in which he suggested that a chaplain be brought in so that they could all fall upon their knees and invoke Almighty God to help them.

After two days, and further debate, finally, on July 16, Benjamin Franklin's great compromise was effected. First, that in the House the States should be represented relatively to their population; that in the Senate each State should have equal representation. And as to the manner of choosing Senators, what was the compromise? The men who were in favor of creating a powerful, consolidated central government, of whom Hamilton was the great exponent, were not in favor of the States having any right to select the members of the powerful body, to be called the Senate, except the polite right of suggesting a list of eligibles, because the proposition first was —and it was the wish of the larger States, and especially of the advocates of a powerfully consolidated Union— that the States should suggest eligibles, and the House of Representatives should elect the Senate. They answered that with an indignant "No," and if they had not, the convention would have come to an end.

Then, not wholly defeated, the larger States proposed to create a Senate with these unique powers which make its members virtually the elder statesmen of the Republic, more powerful than the Members of the House, and peculiarly representatives of the sovereign States, and therefore they contended that the Nation should have some right to say something about the character of men, and therefore they asked: Why not allow the States to suggest eligibles, and then allow the President of the United States to select the Senators?

Again they said, "No; under no circumstances will we allow that."

Finally, as one of the compromises of the convention, they agreed to the proposition that the Senators should be "chosen" by the legislatures of the respective States.

Having given the States this unlimited and absolute grant of power to choose for themselves the kind of men they would have in the Federal council, it was suggested, "Well, suppose a State sends a boy here." It was a period when youth had tremendous vogue with Pitt a prime minister when only 21 years of age.

The men who were creating the Federal Government said, "We will restrict this absolute power by providing that a man to be a Senator must be 30 years of age."

They further decided to restrict the power of the States by stating that "he shall have been a citizen of the United States for nine years."

Then they decided further to restrict the right of choice by stating that a man must be an inhabitant of the State.

And, lastly, they said that Federal officeholders should not be chosen for manifest reasons.

When you thus have an almost absolute grant of power to the States to choose whomever they will, and then some partial restrictions, certainly it is true of this, as of any compact framed and signed by men, that you cannot carve into the absolute grant of power exceptions beyond those that have specifically limited the grant. That would be the natural construction, as I have said, and but for this final power over "qualifications," it would be the only construction you could put upon it; for if that were not so, if each house separately had unlimited power, to prescribe the kind of a man they wanted, then they could practically nullify and destroy the right of a State to choose anybody, because all they would have to do would be, by the process of exclusion, to say the kind of a man they wanted, and the power of the State would diminish to a vanishing point. There cannot, of course, be any question as to that. If Congress or each of the two Houses has unlimited power to limit the State's right of choice, the Federal Government could do as the man did who said, "I will take any color provided it is red." The Congress or each House could say, "I will take any kind of a man, provided he is this kind of a man, or that kind of a man, or the other kind of a man," and in that way the choice of the State would be limited to the vanishing point, especially as the final act of exclusion comes after the State has made its choice.

When you find in the words of the Constitution that a man is to be chosen—such is its word—by the State, what does it fairly mean? It means that as a part of the fundamental compact, without which the States would never have created the Constitution, without which the United States would never have been born, each State had a right to choose. To choose is to discriminate. To choose is to marshal the good and the bad in a man's character, to marshal his mental qualifications against his moral, to determine from a variety of complex conditions that enter into human nature whether a man is the particular man who will represent that State to advantage.

Daniel Webster was sent to the Senate by Massachusetts until he died. He did not have in all respects an admirable character. He was loose in his private life. He did not pay his debts. It did not affect him, when the United States Bank bill was before the Senate, to write to Nicholas Biddle, of the United States Bank, and ask for a retainer. Massachusetts had an entire right to say, "This man is the greatest intellect of his time, the greatest expounder of the Constitution since John Marshall, and no matter what his personal failings are, no matter how loose he may be in his money matters, no matter how slowly he pays his debts, no matter where he borrows his money, nevertheless, we of the State of Massachusetts have a right to select this man, because of all our citizenship, he is the man who will be Massachusetts' greatest contribution to the Federal Union and to the interests of Massachusetts."

One could amplify such instances an hundredfold; and, Senators, right in that connection, could any more powerful argument be used against the latitudinarian construction now sought to be given to the Constitution than that in 140 years of constitutional history, with party passion often running mountain high; with men in past times who were quick on the trigger, metaphorically and actually; with Benton, Webster, Clay and Calhoun at times at dagger's point; when sometimes the aisle of the Senate was the road to the dueling field; when there were the most bitter attacks upon the personal integrity of men; when the passions between men were powerfully excited, as they have never been in what may now well be called an era of good feeling, there never was a suggestion that the door of the Senate could be shut in the face of the Senator designate of a sovereign State.

I will test this question of qualification in a way which will admit of but one decision. One argument is historical, and the other is conjectural. The historical is this: Does any man on this committee who has read the debates of the constitutional convention, who has studied that history, who has known the animating motives of the different members, who knows of the struggle between Madison and James Wilson as against Hamilton and Gouverneur Morris, with those great old Democrats, George Mason and Benjamin Franklin, in the background—is there any one of you who would venture over his signature to avouch as a belief that if, in the constitutional convention, it had been proposed that Senators "shall be chosen by the legislatures of the States, by and with the advice and consent of the Senate," there ever would have been a Constitution?

I will go further, and suppose that the Congress of the United States would propose a twentieth amendment to-morrow—and it could have all the whereases that you might employ—reciting:

> "Whereas the growing use of money in politics is a serious menace to the perpetuity of our insti-tutions: Therefore be it
> *Resolved,* That the following amendment shall be submitted to the States, namely, that the States shall have the right to choose a Senator by and with the advice and consent of the Senate."

Gentlemen, there would not be one State in the Federal Union which would ratify any such amendment.

What did the framers of the Constitution mean on the subject of qualifications? Gentlemen of the committee, one thing we may agree upon in this discussion, I think, without hesitation, and that is that the members of the convention were master draftsmen. They never wasted a word. They never indulged in "weasel words." There are few documents of such exquisite and perfect clarity. There never was a document so free from the objection that one sentence destroyed another.

Is it possible that when they wrote in the very first section of the Constitution, at the head of it, over its very portal, that the Members of the House should be "chosen" by the people of the States, and that Senators should be "chosen" by the legislatures of the States, that they meant, by providing that each House should be the judge of the returns, elections and qualifications of its members, largely to impair, if not to potentially destroy, the power of choice? Yet there is no middle ground. If "qualifications" is to be whatever the Senate may for the moment regard as affecting the moral character of the Senator-designate, then the power of choice is subject to the paramount and changing view of the Senate as to whether they think he is a fit man.

What did this clause say? This clause said that each House shall be the "judge"—not that each House should fix, but that each House should be the judge—of the elections, returns, and qualifications of its members. To judge a qualification fairly implies some legal standard by which you can measure it. It is not an unlimited moral discretion. It is not to determine whether a man is intellectually of a certain capacity, or whether morally he is so deficient in the scale of conscience that you do not care to have his companionship in the Senate. To judge the qualifications is merely to determine whether certain qualifications which have been theretofore made the legal standard of eligibility have been complied with.

I have here—and I will not take the time of the committee to read it, although I am going to ask your permission, not only because of its distinguished source, but also because of its intrinsic value, to add it to my argument—a statement which has been very kindly furnished me by Mr. Charles Warren, a loyal Democrat, a distinguished lawyer and the historian of the Supreme Court of the United States, whose work on that great subject has never been equaled, and I question whether it will ever be surpassed, as a monumental history of that tribunal. Mr. Warren has gathered here all the clauses of the Constitution of the thirteen Colonies, which in various forms suggest the same power, except that in some they were very careful to say, "judge of the qualifications as herein prescribed." Mr. Warren proceeds—and I wish I had time to read it—to give his own opinion, which is quite in accord with the opinion I have advanced, that the word "qualifications" simply meant the qualifications prescribed in the Constitution, which were the sole restrictions upon the otherwise absolute right of the States to choose as they saw fit.

The Colonies did not evolve this expression, which is found in all the proposals, and which was carried into the Federal Constitution, out of their inner consciousness. They had borrowed it, as they had so many other expressions, from the great country from which we are sprung. It was a term of parliamentary practice.

What did it mean in English parliamentary history? It did not mean that the House as against the electorate, the people, should be the judge as to whether a man was a fit man for the particular district or borough to send, but the determination of a constitutional struggle between parliament and the Crown as to how disputed elections should be heard.

[Senator Caraway: Was not that very question involved in the Wilkes case?

Mr. Beck: Yes.

Senator Caraway: And Wilkes was excluded time and again for no other reason than that they did not approve his morals.

Mr. Beck: Exactly; and the result was that he was finally seated; and from the time that Wilkes was seated and there was vindicated the right of the people of Middlesex to send him even though he were an outlaw and a criminal—from that time until the time that Charles Bradlaugh was denied admission to Parliament because, being an atheist, he could not take the oath—it has never been contended in the Parliament of England that there was any power to disqualify a member-elect simply on the ground that he was ineligible for lack of moral character.

Senator Caraway: Can you tell us the date of the Wilkes case? Was it prior to the adoption of the Constitution?

Mr. Beck: It was; it was in 1769.

Senator Caraway: Shortly before the Constitution was adopted, that very qualification had been invoked by the English Parliament.

Mr. Beck: And it was decided in favor of the right of the people of Middlesex.

Senator Caraway: Oh, no; Wilkes was not seated until very much later than that.

Mr. Beck: Gentlemen, in the time of James I, that despotic king, desiring to be an absolute monarch, decided that in the future all disputed elections should be sent into the courts of chancery. Courts of chancery, of course, were king's courts. At all events, the judiciary was then subject to royal influence. The House of Lords acquiesced in this, but the House of Commons did not.

In Anson's Law and Custom of the Constitution, at pages 169 and 170, this assertion of the right of the House of Commons is described as follows [reading]:

"Sir Francis Goodwin, an outlaw, was returned for the county of Bucks. On the return of his election being made, it was refused by the clerk of the Crown on the ground of the outlawry. The clerk issued a new writ on his own authority, and Sir John Fortescue was returned.

The House inquired into the matter, and having examined the clerk of the Crown, resolved that Goodwin was duly elected and ordered the indenture of his return to be filed in the Crown office.

The Lords first took the matter up and asked an explanation of the Commons; the Commons refused to discuss the question. A message then came from the Lords that the King desired the two Houses to confer upon the election. The Commons thereupon demanded access to the King, and stated the grounds of their action. The King asserted that returns "being all made into the chancery are to be corrected and reformed by that court only into which they are returned," and he desired the House to hold a conference with the judges. This, after a long debate, the House determined not to do, but submitted an argumentative memorial to the King, meeting his objections and alleging precedents for the right they claimed. It is noticeable that of the five precedents set forth two only are cases of disputed returns, two are cases of disqualified persons being returned, and one a case of a member being returned for two places.

The King was not satisfied with the answer of the House; he still desired a conference between the Commons and the judges. To this the Commons reluctantly assented; a conference took place before the King and council, and the

King in the end admitted the right of the House
to be a court of record and judge of returns,
though he claimed a corresponding jurisdiction
for the chancery; and he suggested as a compromise that the elections of Fortescue and
Goodwin should both be held void and a new
writ issued. This was done, and the right of the
Commons was not afterwards questioned, nor
that of the chancery asserted."

Senator Caraway: The point there was the right of
the Commons to be the judge of the election and qualification of its own members.

Mr. Beck: Exactly, and the right was a right of the
House of Commons asserted against the King's claim to
determine such questions in the courts. As a matter of
fact, as I imagine Senators all know, the English Government in our time has gone back to King James' precedent, and, with the full consent of Parliament, all election
cases are now decided in the courts. I am not at all sure
that that is not the wisest disposition, but the point is
this, that from the time of that victory over the King—
not over the electorate, but over the King—it became the
established principle that the House of Commons did not
have to determine the election of a member in the courts;
that they themselves were to be the judge of the elections
and returns and qualifications of the members.]

What was meant by qualifications? I had intended—
but it would take too much time—to go back to Blackstone and show that in England there were qualifications,
just as there are in our Constitution, except that they
were much more elaborate. But there were qualifications,
stating, for example, that no one who is not 21 years of
age should be a member of the House of Commons; no one
who held certain public offices should be a member of the
House of Commons, etc.; but these were all statutory
regulations of Parliament as to eligibility. Parliament being omnipotent, there was no question of the right of
Parliament, vis-a-vis constituent States, as in our case;
but, it being purely a question of Parliament making the
constitutional form of government, that body described

by statute, certain conditions as to eligibility, and, outside of these every man is as of right eligible to a seat in the House of Commons, and he cannot be disqualified, unless there be some written disqualification in a statute, or unless there be some doubt as to whether the people actually elected him.

I think the first colony to adopt this phrase with reference to judging the qualifications, going back to the time of King James, did so in 1701. But, from the very beginning of our colonial history, this phrase was always in constitutions and charters, and it was always an assertion of the right of the legislative body of the colony as against the colonial governor, who was a Crown appointee, to determine who were the members of the house.

When, therefore, the Constitutional Convention met, they included this clause without any discussion or debate. Gentlemen of the committee, do you think for one moment that if they could have conceived as a possibility that 140 years later members of the United States Senate would be discussing whether the word "qualifications" might not include a latitudinarian power to disqualify the choice of the State for any reason that met the approval of the Senate—do you think that they would, without debate, have included an expression that was fatal to the rights of the States, that destroyed their power of choice, in a matter that was vital to their continued efficiency and integrity as sovereign States? No.

What they meant by it was plain, it seems to me, if you judge it from the background of English history. It was simply this. "We do not propose that the courts shall try elections. We are quite competent to decide these questions ourselves, and each House shall be the judge of the returns, the elections, and the qualifications," obviously meaning thereby the qualifications prescribed in the constitution and not left to the whim of a temporary majority as was the case of Wilkes. Whether a qualification can be added to the constitutional qualifications by a statute of the United States may be an open and debatable question.

[Senator George: Do you think it is open?

Mr. Beck: The best opinion is to the contrary, that no statute could superadd—

Senator George: Your view is that the weight of the opinions is that way, at least.

Mr. Beck: Yes.

Senator George: I think so.

Senator Shortridge: Against such a proposed law?

Mr. Beck: Yes, sir. It is against superadding by statute.

Senator Shortridge: When you say it is an open question, I take it that you mean it has not been decided by the courts.

Mr. Beck: It has not been decided by any court nor has Congress attempted to do so. You remember the national prohibition case, where the court upheld the constitutional provision that only legislatures of the states could ratify a constitutional amendment. Ohio adopted a provision that no constitutional amendment was valid without a referendum, and the Supreme Court very properly held that it was invalid; that they could not add to the methods of ratification prescribed in the Constitution. By analogy of reasoning, I believe that the Supreme Court would hold that it was intended as a part of the fundamental compact of the sovereign states that every state could send any man they pleased, always provided that the choice did not offend the few restrictions upon such power that the Constitution adopted and adopted, I repeat, with the example of Wilkes before the Fathers when no such, or similar qualifications had been fixed.

Senator Edge: Your view is that even if Congress added to the Corrupt Practices Act of 1925, to which you referred, a maximum amount which could be legally spent by a candidate—or nominee, rather—for the Senate, if that amount were exceeded and the matter taken to the Supreme Court, it would be declared unconstitutional.

Mr. Beck: I am not so sure that I would say that, Senator, because the power to regulate elections proceeds under another clause of the Constitution, which does give the Federal Government power to regulate the manner, places, and times of elections.

Senator Edge: I thought you were confining the qualifications to the qualifications in Article 2, and that Congress had no legal power to add additional qualifications.

Mr. Beck: There is a difference between the regulation of elections and the disqualifications as to eligibility. They are two different things. Eligibility is a prior status, and must be determined by some kind of a law. To regulate elections and to prescribe that only a certain amount of money can be spent is the exercise of a different power, as to which the Constitution has given some power.

Senator Deneen: Mr. Beck, the Senate has decided that very point in an Illinois case, the Lyman Trumbull case. It has decided that Illinois could not add to the qualifications.

Mr. Beck: Yes. That was the Trumbull case.

Senator George: But I think it is equally applicable to the Congress, as a congress.

Senator Shortridge: Mr. Beck, I presume you know it has been argued, in the consideration of the subject matter before the committee now, that the Senate or the House, as the case may be, has greater power than the Congress.

Mr. Beck: Yes.

Senator Shortridge: That each House is all-supreme in the matter of determining the qualifications of its members; wherefore it is argued that the Senate, for example, might reach a certain conclusion, and find that certain things were necessary to qualify for a seat in the Senate, and do, in effect, what the Congress could not do by way of a statute specifying the qualifications of members of Congress, or members of either House. Perhaps, sooner or later, that thought will be discussed by you or others. I throw it out now.

Mr. Beck: I am very glad to have it, and will discuss it. I can not think that the power of the Congress, whose laws are made the supreme law of the land when passed in pursuance of the Constitution, can be subordinate to the mere disciplinarian power of each House. But let me make this suggestion—

Senator Shortridge: I have not acquiesced in the views that were thrown out.

Mr. Beck: I know you have not acquiesced, but you suggested it as a theme for discussion. But, on this matter of qualification, have we all considered fully the terrific implications of the doctrine that "qualifications" is an elastic term, to be determined by this question? The great office of President has qualifications, and they are prescribed in the Constitution. The Congress is made the judge of the election of a President, for, it says that when the states certify the electoral votes, the Vice President shall open the votes and they shall then be counted. While it is not as clear as the other clause of the Constitution, yet to count a vote necessarily means to judge a vote, and I take it that, therefore, Congress has the power of judging of the vote as cast.

If so latitudinarian a construction be given to the word "qualifications" in the Senate clause of the Constitution as to enable it to determine for itself whether a man whom the state thinks fit is unfit, it might well be, in a disputed presidential election, there would arise the question of whether or not there are implied qualifications, either in respect of intellectual ability or moral fitness equally applicable to the presidential office.

I had that very much in mind, because as I came to the committee room I saw, on the other side of the elevator, a picture representing the Electoral Commission of 1876. That great crisis is very vivid in my recollection. I was a freshman at college at the time, and it left with me a very deep and permanent impression.

In that case, as we all remember, a contest arose over the counting of the electoral votes of three states, and the assumption of an authority to create an extraconstitutional commission in order to determine whether the votes of whole counties in three states should not be arbitrarily and abruptly disregarded, but I may say that even in that controversy it was never suggested there was any question of the qualification of the two candidates for presidential office, or any question of the right to bring the votes to the city of Washington and count them under Federal supervision. No such thought was ever in the mind of anyone even during that stormy period of our history. Thus far have we traveled in the 50 years intervening since 1876.

The term "qualifications" has a definite and well recognized legal conception, and if we apply it to the presidential office, as showing that the only qualifications which limit the eligibility of any man to be President, or the right of the people to select their own President, are those that are prescribed in the Constitution, then the same thing applies equally to all the governmental machinery, down to the humblest officer to be elected.

For example, if in the law of your state—and I assume we are all quite familiar with such laws—it is prescribed that the qualifications of a voter shall be such and such, and judges of elections are appointed to pass upon such qualifications of the voters, no one would seriously contend in such a case that the judge, having found that the voter is 21 years of age, has paid his taxes, and conformed to other features of the election laws, could say, "You are not fit to vote anyway; you are either intellectually or morally unfit to cast a vote in the public interest." No one would contend that.

Therefore you are asked to give a definition to the word "qualifications" which, in effect, subverts not only the express restrictions upon the otherwise absolute power of the states to select their own Senators, but gives to the Senate the right to substitute its conscience for the conscience of the several states, and to define who shall be a Senator upon provisions so broad and unlimited and so nebulous and vague that no one could possibly define them on paper. What might be the view of one Senate as to moral unfitness may not be the view of another, and thus, instead of the Senate being composed of men who come here with definite measures and conditions of eligibility, you would have none except those in the minds of the various Senators as they voted.

Fortunately, all this was very carefully considered in the Constitutional Convention. I believe it will profoundly interest the committee if I read—and it will not take more than five or six minutes—exactly what these superlatively wise statesmen of the convention of

1787 said when they had this precise question before them for discussion. Let me quote the record in *Madison's Debates* of August 10, 1787. By that time they had threshed out the abstract principles that were to govern the concrete document. They had gotten as far as a committee on detail and that committee had reported to the convention on that day. Now, as a committee of the whole, they were considering the report of the committee on detail. That committee had, curiously enough, decided that they would not prescribe the qualifications in the Constitution, but would leave them to the discretion of the National Legislature. Please remember what I said before, because it is an impressive background to what they did. They had previously rejected, first, the idea that the House of Representatives should select the Senators; secondly, the idea that the President should select the Senators, and now they were confronted with the very proposition before this committee, that it should be left to the National Legislature to define, from time to time, and from generation to generation, what kind of a man should sit in Congress, except that such definition should be in a statute and not in the resolutions of the Senate. So that there will be no doubt about it, let me read from Madison's Debates: [reading]:

> "Mr. Pinckney: The committee, as he had conceived, were instructed to report the proper qualifications of property for the members of the National Legislature; instead of which they have referred the task to the National Legislature itself. Should it be left on this footing, the first legislature will meet without any particular qualifications of property; and, if it should happen to consist of rich men, they might fix such qualifications as may be too favorable to the rich; if of poor men, an opposite extreme might be run into. He was opposed to the establishment of an undue aristocratic influence in the Constitution, but he thought it essential that the members of the legislature, the executive, and the judges should be possessed of competent property to make them independent and re-

spectable. It was prudent, when such great power was to be trusted, to connect the tie of property with that of reputation in securing a faithful administration. The legislators would have the fate of the Nation put into their hands. The President would also have a very great influence on it. The judges would not only have important causes between citizen and citizen, but also where foreigners are concerned. They will even be the umpires between the United States and individual states, as well as between one state and another. Were he to fix the quantum of property which should be required, he should not think of less than $100,000 for the President, half of that sum for each of the judges, and in like proportion for the members of the National Legislature. He would, however, leave the sums blank. His motion was that the President of the United States, the judges, and members of the legislature should be required to swear that they were respectively possessed of a clear, unincumbered estate to the amount of —— in the case of the President, etc.

Mr. Rutledge seconded the motion; observing that the committee had reported no qualifications, because they could not agree on any among themselves, being embarrassed by the danger, on one side, of displeasing the people by making them high, and on the other, of rendering them nugatory by making them low.

Mr. Ellsworth: The different circumstances of different parts of the United States, and the probable difference between the present and future circumstances of the whole, render it improper to have either uniform or fixed qualifications. Make them so high as to be useful in the Southern states and they will be inapplicable to the Eastern states. Suit them to the latter, and they will serve no purpose in the former. In like manner, what may be accommodated to the existing state of things among us may be very inconvenient in some future state of them. He thought, for these reasons, that it was better to leave this matter to the legislative discretion, than to attempt a provision for it in the Constitution."

Then the grand old man of the convention arose, the man for whom, next to Washington, I have the most profound respect, old Doctor Franklin, the first of American democrats, and probably the greatest in our history. [Continuing reading]:

"Doctor Franklin expressed his dislike to everything that tended to debase the spirit of the common people. If honesty was often the companion of wealth, and if poverty was exposed to peculiar temptation, it was not less true that the possession of property increased the desire of more property. Some of the greatest rogues he was ever acquainted with were the richest rogues. We should remember the character which the Scripture requires in rulers, that they should be men hating covetousness. This Constitution will be much read and attended to in Europe; and, if it should betray a great partiality to the rich, will not only hurt us in the esteem of the most liberal and enlightened men there, but discourage the common people from removing to this country.

The motion of Mr. Pinckney was rejected by so general a "no," that the states were not called."

The debate, however, had not ended. Now arose the man who is so well and justly called the "Father of the Constitution," the greatest scholar in politics in that convention, and incontrovertibly the best student of general government, James Madison. [Continuing reading]:

"Mr. Madison was opposed to the section, as vesting an improper dangerous power in the legislature. The qualifications of electors and elected were fundamental articles in a Republican government, and ought to be fixed by the Constitution. If the legislature could regulate those of either, it can by degrees subvert the Constitution. A republic may be converted into an aristocracy or oligarchy as well by limiting the number capable of being elected as the number authorized to elect. In all cases where the representatives of the people will have a personal interest distinct from that of their constituents, there was the same reason for being jealous of them as there was for relying on them with full confidence, when they had a common interest. This was one of the former cases. It was as improper as to allow them to fix their own wages, or their own privileges."

That is, leaving to the legislature the right to say who should sit in it was as improper as to allow them to fix their own wages or their own privileges. [Continuing reading]:

"It was a power, also, which might be made subservient to the views of one faction against another. Qualifications founded on artificial distinctions may be devised by the stronger in order to keep out partisans of a weaker faction."

Then Ellsworth arose, and he spoke as follows (continuing reading]:

"Mr. Ellsworth admitted that the power was not unexceptionable, but he could not view it as dangerous. Such a power with regard to the electors would be dangerous, because it would be much more liable to abuse.

Mr. Gouverneur Morris moved to strike out "with regard to property," in order to leave the legislature entirely at large.

Mr. Williamson: This would surely never be admitted. Should a majority of the legislature be composed of any particular description of men, of lawyers, for example, which is no improbable supposition, the future elections might be secured to their own body.

Mr. Madison observed that the British Parliament possessed the power of regulating the qualifications, both of the electors and the elected; and the abuse they had made of it was a lesson worthy of our attention. They had made the changes, in both cases, subservient to their own views, or to the views of political or religious parties."

Thereupon the Convention abandoned the idea of leaving qualifications to the discretion of the Congress, and wrote into the Constitution the only restrictions upon the absolute power of the sovereign states to choose their own senators.

That last reference of Madison's was, of course, to the matter that had been most in the people's mind at the time of the Revolution and at the time the Constitutional Convention met. That was the great constitutional crisis in England, whereby the King, through his subservient puppets in Parliament, had attempted in the Wilkes case to deny to the people the right to select their own representative. To that I shall refer in a few moments.

To show you that even after the convention had adopted it, it was clear to the greatest contemporary commentator upon the Constitution that this was so, let me simply read what Alexander Hamilton said.

This is in No. LXII of the Federalist papers [reading]:

"It is equally unnecessary to dilate on the appointment of Senators by the State legislatures. Among the various modes which might have been devised for constituting this branch of the government, that which has been proposed by the convention is probably the most congenial with the public opinion. It is recommended by the double advantage of favoring a select appointment, and of giving to the state governments such an agency in the formation of the Federal Government, as must secure the authority of the former, and may form a convenient link between the two systems.

* * * *

"In this spirit it may be remarked, that the equal vote allowed to each state, is at once a constitutional recognition of the portion of sovereignty remaining in the individual states, and an instrument for preserving that residuary sovereignty."

That is a great point. The right to select the Senators is the method of preserving the residuary sovereignty of the states. [Continuing reading]:

"So far the equality ought to be no less acceptable to the large than to the small states; since they are not less solicitous to guard by every possible expedient against an improper consolidation of the states into one simple republic."

The Constitution does not stop there. The Constitution, as drafted by the men of 1787, did stop there, but there came the most terrible chapter in our history as a Nation. We entered upon the most fratricidal and the most deplorable civil war of all history. Before it had ended 400,000 men had fallen on one side, and between the two sections there was the most bitter feeling, which persisted until a century had passed from the foundation of the Republic, when men of the North and South met in my native city of Philadelphia, the city of the Constitution, and there, in the common memory of the glories of the Republic, they ended their quarrel. The day of dreary reconstruction through Federal bayonets, ceased, as we may well hope, forever.

It was shortly after the last gun had sounded upon the battlefield, when the memories on both sides were filled with thoughts of sons who would never return, when the tragedy of the vanished hand and the sound of a voice that was still was causing aching hearts both in the North and South, when each side looked at the other across ravaged homes and desolated fields, that the question arose, "What about the men who took part in the war of secession? What about them? Are they to return, or is there to be a reasonable discretion on the part of the Federal Government as to who, of those who were recent enemies, but now, happily, again citizens, shall return to the halls of the national legislature?"

Gentlemen of the committee, if the latitudinarian theory of qualifications is correct, it was not necessary then to have amended the Constitution. The Republican Party was in dominating control of both Senate and House. Some of the Southern states, through the exigencies of war, had ceased to function. It was a simple thing for House and Senate, with masterful spirits like Thaddeus Stevens in the House, and men like Wade and Morton of Indiana, in the Senate, to have said, "We will see every man who comes to us from the South, and we will determine what his relations to the late Confederacy were, and, under our power to determine the qualifications, we may exclude them." But they never thought they could do this. In all the strife of the Civil War, the constitutional theory so recently discussed in the Senate was never regarded as a possibility.

On the contrary, they wrote into the Constitution an express authority to exclude, if they cared to exclude, because the fourteenth amendment said that no person shall be a Senator or Representative in Congress, or elector of President or Vice President, or hold any office, civil or military, under the United States or under any state, who, having previously taken an oath as a member of Congress or as an officer of the United States, or as a member of any state legislature, or as an executive or judicial officer of any state to support the Constitution of the United States, had engaged in insurrection or rebellion against the same, or given aid or comfort to the enemies thereof, but that Congress could, by a vote of two-thirds of each House, remove such disability.

Fortunately, that clause of the fourteenth amendment is a matter of no present importance to us in these days, because, in the happy accord that now unites us, the disabilities have all been removed. But the fact of the matter is that if Mississippi had sent Jefferson Davis to the Senate, under the clear theory of the men of that tragic period, the most stormy of our history, it was never dreamed he could be excluded without the direct authority of this fourteenth amendment, which put a new restriction upon the otherwise absolute power of the states to choose their own Senators in their own way, whether their choice were wise or unwise.

I return to something that was referred to before we took a recess, because it has a profound bearing upon this question. That is, what bearing does the great constitutional crisis in England between 1763 and 1782 have upon the meaning upon the Constitution?

It was suggested, by Senator Caraway, that the final vindication of John Wilkes came after the Constitution. Since the recess I have consulted the Encyclopedia Britannica. I find that such is not the fact. That confirmed my own recollection. The final triumph of John Wilkes was on May 3, 1782, or nearly five years before the Constitutional Convention met.

I do not want to go at length into the John Wilkes case, because I treated it in my monograph, with which the committee is familiar, but there are one or two salient features of it to which I do want to call your attention.

The fact is—which I did not know when I wrote last summer the "Vanishing Rights of the States"—that John Wilkes's triumph had come much sooner, and it had come in a very extraordinary way. If you want the verification of it and will get Trevelyan's History of Charles James Fox, you will read what is beyond question the most fascinating account of the John Wilkes controversy.

That controversy simply amounted to this in a very few words. John Wilkes was a member of Parliament at the time the controversy began in 1763. While a member of Parliament he wrote a pamphlet which was called the North Briton Number XLV, and it was conceived to be a libel upon the ministers of the Crown, and a direct insult to King George III. He, moreover, had unlawfully circulated some indecent literature, in the form of a parody on Pope's Essay on Man. John Wilkes was thereupon arrested, and at once pleaded his privilege as a member of Parliament.

Both the House of Commons and the House of Lords had passed what would be forbidden under our Constitution, namely, a bill of attainder. So, they declared the North Briton Number XLV, and the Essay on Woman, infamous and illegal libels, and thereupon the motion to expel was made, and the great debate took place.

Meanwhile Mr. Wilkes, as you know, had been seriously wounded in a duel with one of his political opponents. He was outlawed and fled to France. At the end of three years he came back, presented himself in the Court of King's bench; the outlawry was removed by a technicality, but another judge sentenced him to 22 months in prison. All that he subsequently did in that crisis, in which he had almost the general support of the people, was done by him in prison. So far as the libel against the King is concerned, that might be called a political offense, but the indecent essay was not a political offense at all. He was in prison and made his canvass from prison.

As you all recall, for several times the people of Middlesex returned him, every time with increased majorities, and every time he was returned he was promptly expelled.

In the course of that debate the elder Chatham, Edmund Burke, Henry Grenville, and others spoke, and if any of you have neglected, in the "Vanishing Rights of the States," to read Grenville's speech, please read it, because, apart from the dignity and splendor of that piece of parliamentary eloquence, the magnanimity and greatness of the man excite admiration.

Grenville was one of the men whom Wilkes had cruelly lampooned in the North Briton. Moreover, he was an aristocrat of the aristocrats, and very close to the King. Nevertheless, he believed that it was quite improper on the grounds suggested to expel Mr. Wilkes from the House. After the fourth election, the man who was second in the poll, was, under the orders of the King, declared the elected member.

This is the part that I do not think is generally known. When John Wilkes was released from prison he walked into the House of Commons. There was no motion to seat him; there was no motion to expel him on the ground that he had committed a crime. There was no motion to expunge the resolution that he was ineligible, but he walked into the House of Commons. Why? Exactly as Mirabeau said in the tennis court on the eve of the French Revolution, when the King's soldiers tried to drive out the representatives of the people. He said: "We are here by the power of the people, and we will not be driven hence except by the power of the bayonet."

John Wilkes had the people back of him. They knew he was a profligate and a libertine. They knew that he was as unworthy of popular respect or confidence as any man could be, but the people of Middlesex said, "By God, we are going to determine who will be our representative in the House of Commons, and we do not propose that the House of Commons, acting under the instigation of the King, shall do so for us."

When he was released from prison they were so close to civil war, and the throne of George III so trembled in the balance that when he walked into the House of Commons, not a man dared to gainsay his right to take his seat, although the records showed that he was not a member. He took his seat and he served as a member of the House, and after three years, on May 3, 1782, John Wilkes moved the House that the resolution of condemnation, the resolution of expulsion, the resolution making him ineligible to sit in the House of Commons be canceled, and thereupon the record of the House was brought out, and his former enemies had the humiliation of seeing the clerk do just as was done in our time for Andrew Jackson. A great black line was run across the record which had condemned John Wilkes.

Back of this contest was the belief of the English people that if representative government were worth anything, the people of a district or community had a right to their own selection, whether they exercised that right wisely or unwisely. It was a matter of no concern to the House of Commons.

Now, in the course of that debate, it may interest the Members—perhaps I ought not to take so long—to know that Mr. Justice Blackstone was a member of the House of Commons, and that he was very much in the King's favor. The first edition of the Commentaries had appeared a short time before this great debate, and in Blackstone's first edition of the Commentaries he said [reading]:

> "Next, as to the qualifications of persons to be elected members of the House of Commons. Some of these depend upon the law and custom of Parliament, declared by the House of Commons: (b) others upon certain statutes. And from these it appears—"

Then he goes on and gives a list of disqualifications which were prescribed by law and says [continuing reading]:

> "But subject to these standing restrictions and disqualifications, every subject of the realm is eligible of common right."

There the first edition of the Commentaries ended, and when Mr. Justice Blackstone arose in the great debate on Wilkes and stated that in his judgment the fact that he was in prison disqualified him to sit as a member of the House, Grenville read to Mr. Justice Blackstone what he had said in the Commentaries, and no such restriction was there. Blackstone, in the second edition of the Commentaries, and all subsequent editions, has the following—

> "though there are instances wherein persons in particular circumstances have forfeited that common right, and have been declared ineligible for that Parliament by a vote of the House of Commons or forever by an act of the legislature."

That, of course, was put in to square his vote in the Wilkes case with his views as a commentator.

You might say, if that was the law of Mr. Justice Blackstone, it would indicate that a similar power was intended to be vested by the Constitution in the Congress. But the analogy wholly fails, as between an omnipotent

Parliament, which is responsible to no one except to the people, and the Congress of the United States, which has to act *vis-a-vis* the reserved rights of the states, because there were no constituent states or reserved rights against which Parliament had occasion to act. They could say tomorrow, if they wanted to, that nobody except a man 50 years of age should sit in Parliament, and no court could gainsay it.

If you will now again recall what took place in the Constitutional Convention, if you will now recall what Madison said as to the dangers of which every man was conscious—the use of power by a majority of the House—you will see why they named the qualifications in the Constitution and simply followed the principle that, so far as the determination of the election, returns and the legally prescribed qualifications are concerned, each House should be the judge thereof, as against the judiciary, which, as I have said, had claimed the right to determine these questions.

Now, gentlemen, my argument is drawing to a close, but there is another phase of this question to which I want to make passing reference.

The Supreme Court of the United States has held that while these special provisions with respect to each House of Congress confer a broad discretion, yet, nevertheless, they must not be construed as inconsistent with other rights conferred by the Constitution, or, especially, with the general scheme and structure of our dual form of government; that they must be limited so as to promote and not to destroy the great object.

In that connection I want to call your attention to this fact, which while it may not be applicable to the extent that I could invoke it in a court of justice, yet I do think should animate the spirit with which you interpret and exercise this power to pass upon the qualifications of members.

What would be the nature of the Senate's action if it refused the seat to Mr. Smith? Obviously it has not passed upon the returns or the election of a member, because it is not disputed that the sovereign people of Illinois, by a majority of over 70,000 in an election that was absolutely free of any scandal or suggestion of the purchase of votes, elected Mr. Smith as its choice, and elected him with full knowledge that Mr. Insull had contributed to his campaign fund. Upon that issue the people of Illinois had passed, and it was a question for their conscience and not for the conscience of the Senate.

Therefore, if the Senate of the United States should bolt the door on Colonel Smith, and simply say, "Whatever be the opinion of the people of Illinois, or of the governor of your state, acting under his power to fill a vacancy, nevertheless, we do not think him fit, and our judgment in the matter is final. We do not say he was not elected. We do not say he was not appointed, but what we do say is that we declare him ineligible to a seat in the Senate"— if the Senate of the United States should say that—it is essentially punitive. You cannot disguise it. It is essentially punitive. It is not judging the election and returns. It is punishment, and it is a very grievous punishment. Theoretically it is a punishment for life, because if Colonel Smith, by reason of moral unfitness, is thereby disqualified from sitting under these credentials, unless another Senate should reach a different conclusion, the same reason is just as applicable, on that theory, if 50 years from now, if his life were spared that long, the people of Illinois should send him back by 1,000,000 majority. In other words, what you are seeking to do is to pass what is well known in English law as a bill of attainder. You are declaring him perpetually disqualified to fill an office. It is true that such a declaration is not like that of a court, where you could call it *res adjudicata*. Another Senate may have an entirely different opinion about it, but, nevertheless, barring the continuing power of the Senate to decide the question as it sees fit, the thought remains that the disqualification does not go merely to these credentials. It does not merely treat his credentials as a scrap of paper, but denies his eligibility while he lives, ever to sit in the Senate on the ground of moral unfitness.

Why is he thus sought to be subjected to a life sentence, so far as a great civic right is concerned, because, as I said at the beginning, a sum of money was contributed by a man who was the owner of public utilities to a campaign fund which was used in Mr. Smith's election?

You will remember that we started the discussion with the clear recognition in the report of the Reed committee that no statute, either of the United States or of the state of Illinois, had forbidden Mr. Insull to contribute to that campaign fund, and no statute had limited the amount.

Furthermore, the Constitution of the United States forbids both the nation and the states from passing any bill of attainder or *ex post facto* law. A bill of attainder is a legislative act which inflicts punishment without judicial trial. If the punishment be less than death, the act is termed a bill of pains and penalties, and the Supreme Court has held that within the meaning of the Constitution, bills of attainder include bills of pains and penalties. An *ex post facto* law, as defined by Chief Justice Marshall, is a law which renders an act punishable in a manner in which it was not punishable when it was committed.

Gentlemen, the Supreme Court of the United States passed upon those provisions both of the state and of the Federal Constitution, in two of the great cases of the courts. I refer to Cummings against the State of Missouri in 4 Wallace, and the other, a contemporaneous decision, in re Garland, reported in the same volume.

In the Cummings case the plaintiff was a Catholic priest who lived in Mississippi. The carpet-bag government of Mississippi had imposed a new constitution, which provided that no one could be a priest, or pursue any gainful occupation or profession unless he could take an oath that he had taken no part in the War of the Rebellion against the Federal Government.

Cummings could not take the oath. He had been a Catholic priest who had fought with his section and people, and thus an attempt was made to indict him for continuing to serve as a Catholic priest.

The Supreme Court said that constitutional provision was clearly a violation, because, in effect, this provision attainted him; that it had not only attainted him, but it was *ex post facto* in making something punishable that was not punishable at the time it was done.

In the Garland case, Garland was a distinguished Democrat who subsequently became Attorney General under Grover Cleveland. An act had been passed in those harsh reconstruction days, which provided that no man could ever appear in the Supreme Court of the United States, unless he could take an oath that he had taken no part in the War of the Rebellion. Garland sought as a lawyer, and previous member of that bar, to appear in a case. The Supreme Court held that this attempt to impose a disqualification upon a man by a retroactive measure was entirely wrong.

I appreciate that if this were a juridical question, these provisions, except as they vindicate great constitutional ideals, would not be applicable. A law or an act can be politically anticonstitutional, and yet it may be juridically constitutional; or, in other words, putting it this way, there are many acts which are in violation of the Constitution but which the judiciary of the nation cannot pass upon because the questions are essentially political in their nature, and beyond the fair power of the judiciary to intervene.

But that does not alter the solemn obligation of men who sit as judges, as you do, and as your companions of the Senate will do, in this matter. You are not sitting as party men. You are not sitting as legislators. You are sitting as judges to respect the great ideals of the Constitution.

Certainly it is not consistent with those great ideals, even if you think that Mr. Smith, having heard that Insull contributed to his campaign, ought to have insisted upon the money being returned, even if you think there was impropriety in it, even if you think it was not in good form—put any interpretation you please upon it—yet, unless he had been disqualified by reason of a statute existing at the time, and if he did it in the innocent way which the Reed committee describes, you are, in fact, visiting upon him *ex post facto* punitive vengeance of the most ruthless kind.

I say of the most ruthless kind. I think Colonel Smith would rather die than have the stigma of being called forever a man ineligible to sit in the United States Senate. It was his great ambition. Six years ago he sought the same great position. He was defeated. He bore his defeat like a man, and supported his successful adversary. He came up again, against overwhelming odds, as I said at the beginning, apparently accomplishing the impossible, and now to say that he shall be disqualified, that this stigma shall be put upon him because of an act which was not illegal when done, and which is not illegal today, is vengeance of the most ruthless kind. I say to you, Senators, solemnly, that if it be illegal for a rich man who is connected with corporations to give to a campaign fund where the candidate is a public official, I would like to know, in the last 50 years, how many could honestly plead innocence of the charge.

Take yourselves. You are sitting Senators. You come up for reelection. Suppose Judge Gary, of the United States Steel corporation, out of his vast fortune, should contribute to your campaign fund. It is just as easy to say that he contributed because of past favors or prospective favors as to say that Mr. Insull contributed to Mr. Smith's campaign fund because of past services on the public utilities commission, or prospective services in the short time that he would serve if he were elected a United States Senator. There is no distinction. It would leave nearly every President of our time in an invidious position if the gift to a campaign committee can be construed as an improper gift to the candidate of a party by reason of the fact that the man who gives the money either has or may have a sympathetic interest with the policies which the candidate is advocating.

I am not unappreciative of the dangers of money in politics. I know the danger is great. There is danger that our country, which is getting stupendously rich, may become corrupt. I was glad that Senator Goff brought up the question in this morning's session as to whether this most useful inquiry of the Reed committee, with which we have no quarrel, cannot lead to some constructive legislation. Let us hope that there is, under the seventeenth amendment, power to pass an effective corrupt practices act applicable to primaries. I do not think there is, but let us hope there is.

I do not think I differ wiith Senator Goff at all, but I

say, with great respect, that there could be no greater disqualification against the powers of the State than to apply a uniform rule, because if you give to the comparatively few people of Idaho, for example, the right to spend $25,000 in a campaign for Senator, and say that in the State of New York with 10,000,000 people, in Pennsylvania with 9,000,000, and in Illinois with 8,000,000, they can not spend any more than the 60,000 people of Idaho, you simply have put the three populous States at a manifest disadvantage as compared with States of lesser population. An amount sufficient to conduct a campaign of education in the larger states might have the most corrupting influence in a state of small population.

Out of the Reed committee and out of this great controversy, let us hope there will grow a sentiment that will establish the rules of the game in political warfare, whether by State or Federal action.   But, surely, the folly of the man who burned down his barn to smoke out the rats would be slight indeed compared with that of a nation which, entering upon an irrational and indiscriminate system of legislation, would tear down the constitutional edifice of the country and destroy the rights of the States in a matter so vital to them as the right to choose their own Senators.

The State of Illinois has a motto: "National union; State sovereignty."

That is a good paraphrase of that famous saying of Mr. Justice Miller, I think it was, in the case of *Texas v. White*, when he spoke of the "indissoluble union of indestructible States." We will have an indissoluble Union. We need not worry about that. The economic causes, that are more potential than man-made laws, or even constitutions, are welding this country together in unity, from which, whether desirable or undesirable, there can be no escape. But when it comes to political centralization to accomplish some reform of the hour—sometimes a misguided reform—when it comes to tearing down the basic right of the States, the greatest of all rights of the States, if that can be successfully done, your indissoluble union of indestructible States becomes merely one of those phrases that does not represent realities. The States then have been proved to be destructible and not indestructible.

I do not know what Colonel Smith's fate will be, but what I do know is that his fate will not end this controversy. The battle is on. If anybody supposes that all the feeling in this matter is against Colonel Smith, then I think he is mistaken, because, so far as I can see, there is a ground swell of feeling, which is about the healthiest symptom I have seen in 50 years, to the effect that the political centralization of this Government has gone entirely too far; that it is about time that the States should reassert their ancient liberties.

Colonel Smith, if he has the door of the Senate shut in his face, may not live to see his triumph, as John Wilkes did, but, if you will allow me this concluding thought, last October I spent the most interesting two hours, I suppose, that I ever spent in the Supreme Court in 30 years. From the very beginning of the Republic, Madison had asserted that the President had the power to remove, and that that power could not be restricted by Congress. Congress had never acceded to that. In one of the stormiest crises of our national life, when the great triumvirate of Webster, Clay, and Calhoun trained their batteries upon Andrew Jackson, Jackson had only the intellectual power of Thomas H. Benton to defend him. In that hour they passed a resolution designed to dishonor and disgrace Andrew Jackson. They wrote it in the Journal of the Senate, that he had violated his oath of office as President of the United States in removing Duane.

A generation later another President of the United States, misjudged Andrew Johnson, trying to do the best he could with an impossible situation, was haled before the bar of the Senate, impeached by the House, and was about to be dismissed and disgraced from the greatest position in the gift of any people, for removing Mr. Stanton. But finally, by reason of the salutary two-thirds rule, Mr. Johnson was technically acquitted, although morally convicted. On this late October day in the Supreme Court, Chief Justice Taft unrolled his manuscript in the case of *Myers* v. *The United States*, very nearly a century after Andrew Jackson's condemnation and about half a century or more after Andrew Johnson's condemnation. The Supreme Court said that both of them were justified. It seemed to me that the shades of Andrew Jackson and Andrew Johnson must have been lingering behind those Ionic pillars listening to their vindication. It took a long while to come, but it came.

So, in this matter, to which I have given the best I can of brain and physical energy, the fight may be temporarily lost, but it will never be abandoned. Colonel Smith may fall in the struggle, but the State of Illinois will not surrender its sovereign rights; and there are other States that feel very keenly about this crisis, some of the States represented by the distinguished Senators who are here, who have voiced what seems to me to be true constitutional doctrine.

What, then, do we seek of the committee? The Senate asks you to consider two questions. The first is, What, on the face of the evidence before the committee, should be done except to follow the unbroken precedents of the Senate by administering to Col. Smith the oath and giving him his seat, subject to that ever continuing right to expel him for any cause of expulsion to which the Constitution is applicable.

Second. What should be the decision, even though he were given his oath, as to whether he should retain his seat in the Senate?

Gentlemen, there are essential reasons, based upon constitutional rights, why this committee should pass upon that first question first. If it be true, as I have argued, that the acceptance by Col. Frank L. Smith's treasurer—call it an acceptance by Frank Smith if you will—of a campaign contribution from Mr. Insull and from Mr. Studebaker, and from Mr. Copley, is not any reason for refusing him the right to take his oath upon the undisputed credentials, then every day that you keep Colonel Smith out of the Senate you have done him a wrong, and a continuing wrong to the great State of Illinois, because Illinois has a right to have present at this hour in the Senate two Senators, to cast two votes upon any measure that requires a vote. Mr. Smith, as an individual, has a right, if I am correct in that theory, to take the oath of office, and then to submit himself to any proceedings to expel.

Therefore, we earnestly ask the committee, without in any way concluding its labors, to make a partial report if they are convinced that my contention is sound, stating that the only testimony that was adduced against Colonel Smith is the testimony in the report of the Reed committee, which you will summarize in your own way as you read the testimony; and that upon that testimony there is no constitutional disqualification or any reason why he and the great State that sent him should not have a present seat in the Senate.

I cannot conclude without thanking you for the great patience you have shown me, both those who agree with me and those who may disagree with me, in listening to me with kindliness and forbearance. I have tried to fight the good fight and to keep the faith of the Fathers, as I understand the faith of the Fathers, and I only hope that each Senator, not only on this committee but each Member of the United States Senate, when he votes upon this great question may enjoy the same consolation.

XIII

THE NORTHERN SECURITIES CASE

Few cases in the judicial history of this country excited wider attention a generation ago than the Northern Securities case. It remains a notable landmark in American jurisprudence.

It was the result of a titanic struggle between two great groups of bankers, the Morgan-Hill interests and the Standard Oil-Harriman interests, to control the Northern Pacific Railroad. The result was one of the greatest panics that ever took place in the history of Wall Street, when Northern Pacific stock reached a bid of $1,000 a share and the stock exchanges of America and Europe were convulsed by the resultant crash in securities. To end the panic the two groups of bankers made a treaty of peace and formed the Northern Securities Company to own their joint holdings in the Northern Pacific stock.

When President Roosevelt ordered his Attorney General, Philander C. Knox, to institute a suit to dissolve this combination as a violation of the Sherman Anti-trust Law, the suit became the political sensation of the hour. Mr. Beck was at that time an Assistant Attorney General and took part in the taking of the testimony in this great equity cause. When it was ready for argument, he was selected by the Attorney General to present the case for the Government before the statutory court of four judges.

While Mr. Beck had at that time gained some national reputation for his successful argument in the Lottery Case, yet he was not well known west of the Mississippi and as he entered the St. Louis Court on the occasion of this notable argument his youthful appearance and modest, almost self-effacing, manner created something of a sensation. A St. Louis paper at the time made the following comment:

"When Mr. Beck walked into the Federal courtroom to open the argument in the Northern Securities case Wednesday a murmur of surprise went around the room. He slipped quietly into a chair and, sliding down to a comfortable position, threw his head back to the angle usually affected by men who wear nose glasses with thick lenses.

"There was a change, however, when he rose to address the court. He held a crowded court room for three hours and a half while he discussed dry figures. Some said it was his voice, others that it was his persuasive manner that constituted the charm of his talk. During the long speech, the voice did not once quaver, or grow husky and the persuasive manner which kept him leaning far over the table toward the judges did not abate."

The result of the case is now a part of the judicial and economic history of the country. Both the court of first instance and later the Supreme Court sustained all the contentions of the Government. Mr. Beck did not take part in the argument before the Supreme Court for when he appeared in St. Louis on March 18, 1903, he had already decided to resign as Assistant Attorney General to enter a New York law firm and had only deferred his resumption of private practice in order to argue this notable case.—EDITOR.

May It Please the Court:

There will be little tendency either on the part of court or counsel to minimize the importance of this controversy. Few have ever been presented to any court which affected corporate interests of greater magnitude, and still fewer, which more vitally concern the welfare of the American people. As the three conditions of modern commercial life are production, transportation, and credit, and as in a country of such vast area as that of the United States the problem of transportation is only secondary in importance to production itself, this case in a measure involves the industrial liberty of the citizen. I am not unaware that there are able apologists for railroad monopoly who contend that it is inevitable and beneficent, and that freedoom of competition is an "iridescent dream." I shall not discuss this economic phase of the question, for State and Nation have declared with unmistakable emphasis by positive law that the safety of the people lies in the free play of competition. *Sic ita lex*, and in this forum any other contention is wholly out of place. If the Government shall prevail, an important and salutary principle will be reaffirmed, by which great aggregations of capital will be prevented from stifling competition, no matter how ingenious or indirect their methods may be. The majesty of the law will in that event triumph over paper devices and collusive agreements. If, on the contrary, the law shall be so impotent as to sacrifice substance to shadow, and the present method of creating a monopoly in transportation shall be judicially recognized, then a "coach and four" has been driven through the Federal statutes enacted for the prevention of such monopoly. If competing carriers can form a stable, permanent, and controlling combination with indefinite and perpetual powers through the simple device of a so-called "holding corporation" organized under a State charter—a form which, as will be hereafter argued, is far more inimical to the public interests than the traffic arrangements or technical trusts which the law has hitherto condemned—then both the interstate commerce act of 1887, with its inhibition of pooling, and the act of July 2, 1890, with its sweeping condemnation of all combinations in restraint of trade or attempted monopolies, will be—not repealed by the Government in accordance with law—but made a dead letter by the power of individuals, who will thus show the impotence of the declared will of the American people.

This legal controversy is, in one sense, recent, for the particular act complained of is the virtual merger, in November, 1901, of two theretofore competing transcontinental lines into a single corporation; but in a broader sense the controversy is much older, and the formation of the Northern Securities Company was but another, and— let us hope—final attempt to accomplish a purpose which the Supreme Court of the United States had five years before declared unlawful. Indeed, this persistent and obstinate struggle between these great transcontinental lines on the one hand to stifle competition, and the United States Government on the other, to promote it, is one of the most interesting and significant struggles between the power of capital and the power of the law that the history of civilization presents. I do not mean to impute to the great masters of transportation a persistent, deliberate, and conscious attempt to violate the laws of the land, for I prefer to think that with them consolidation is an impulse —born of self-interest—and that they have struggled on from method to method, and from purpose to purpose in the blind and unconscious hope that the ultimate object of crushing competition would be accomplished in some manner which would receive the sanction of the law. But it is none the less significant that this present attempt to obtain judicial approval for the present colossal merger is consciously or unconsciously an attempt to secure a result which the American people, acting through their legislature, have as constantly and persistently prohibited, and which the Supreme Court in opinions hereafter referred to has repeatedly condemned.

It was a very serious question with the Government's law officers whether, assuming all the properly pleaded facts, it would not be content to submit the case to this tribunal upon bill and answer, but as the defendants had denied any intent whatever to form a combination, notwithstanding the decision of the Supreme Court that the intent would follow as a conclusive presumption from the very nature of the acts, yet we thought it would be more satisfactory to your honors to put before you all the facts that would explain these ingenious averments of the answers, and thus give the court the fullest information as to the subject of this controversy.

In doing this the Government went into the camp of the enemy, and called upon every defendant who had sworn to an answer to testify in words of ordinary speech as to his participation in this merger, rather than in the guarded and subtle phraseology of a legal answer. We were content to submit this case upon the pleadings, and upon the defendant's own admissions as to what they did.

The defendants, however, were not content to rest their case upon the answers of their own clients, but filled three printed volumes of testimony with a mass of irrelevant evidence, which was designed either to prove that the act of Congress, under which the Government's petition was framed, should not have been passed, or that, in any event, others had violated its provisions with impunity.

To fittingly characterize such testimony it is necessary to employ the familiar analogy of the cuttlefish, which, however, has especial application to the case at bar, for the dictionary informs us that a cuttlefish is "a cephalopod of the genus Sepia, having an internal shell (a holding company), large eyes, and ten arms furnished with denticulated suckers (the constituent companies), by means of which it secures its prey. It has an ink bag, opening into the siphon, from which, when pursued, it throws out a dark liquid that clouds the water, enabling it to escape observation." The inky fluid used by the Northern Securities Company to escape a decree will be found in these bulky volumes of irrelevant testimony.

I venture to say that when your honors come to read this mass of testimony you will justify the use of the analogy, and you will be of the opinion that this case can be fairly and fully adjudicated upon the defendant's own admissions, with the aid of such presumptions of law and fact as have been sanctioned by judicial experience.

With this preliminary explanation of the pleadings, I pass to a narrative history of this transaction as developed from the testimony itself. I shall endeavor not to weary your honors with long citations from the testimony, yet I trust the court will indulge me if at some critical point of the case I read the testimony of the actors themselves, and I again remind the court that as to every finding of fact the Government will invoke the sworn admissions of the defendants themselves.

West of the Mississippi, and between that river and the Pacific Ocean, lies a commercial empire, 1,100 miles wide and 2,000 miles long, in which dwell twenty millions of people, who, by productive labor, are creating unbounded wealth, to which, however, the problem of transportation at reasonable rates is a vital necessity. Congress recognized this, and as early as 1853 authorized surveys of a route for a railroad from the Mississippi to the Pacific, and lines were surveyed near the thirty-second, thirty-fifth, thirty-ninth, forty-second and forty-seventh parallels. At that time communication with the Pacific Ocean was either overland, attended by unnumbered hardships and dangers, or around Cape Horn. The conclusion was then reached that each of these projected routes was practicable except that along the thirty-fifth parallel. In fact, four great transcontinental lines in the process of time have been constructed in the United States to serve the great public purposes which were then in mind. These systems are the Atchison, Topeka and Santa Fe, the Union Pacific, the Northern Pacific, and the Great Northern.

Appreciating the vast public purposes which the facilities of transportation would serve, Congress aided the construction of these lines from time to time with prodigal generosity. In the single decade between 1860 and 1870 it gave 200,000,000 acres of land, and advanced nearly $65,000,000 to some of the trans-Mississippi railroad companies; and this prodigality was supplemented by the various States through which the lines passed, which with equal liberality gave immense areas of their unsettled domain to the pioneers in railroad construction.

Confining our attention to the two northwestern transcontinental lines, a brief statement of their corporate history may not be uninteresting and inapplicable.

The original Northern Pacific was chartered in 1864 by Congress, and received a land grant of 47,000,000 acres. After the failure of its great projector, Jay Cooke, in 1873, it was reorganized in 1875, and the work of construction was vigorously pushed. It again went into the hands of a receiver in 1893, and was reorganized in 1896, by the amalgamation of fifty-four different companies, which gave it a mileage of 4,706 miles, and a total issue of stock and bonds of $380,000,000. It was reorganized under a special charter granted by the State of Wisconsin. Its present mileage is 5,019 miles, and its outstanding stocks and bonds are $495,000,000.

The history of the Great Northern Railway dates back to 1857, when the Territory of Minnesota granted a charter to the Minnesota and Pacific Railroad to build a road to the Pacific Ocean. It was again incorporated in 1864, but in the panic of 1873 shared the fate of its great rival, and went into the hands of a receiver. It was then that its master spirit, James J. Hill, became influential, and he organized a syndicate of Canadian capitalists to purchase the road. Desiring in 1889 to bring the road, with the various extensions which had been subsequently acquired, under a common organization, he discovered an old charter granted by the Territory of Minnesota in 1856 to the Minneapolis and St. Cloud Railroad, and this company, with the other constituent companies, were merged, and the corporate name changed to the Great Northern Railway. Its total mileage is 5,249 miles, and its outstanding stock and bonds are $469,000,000. An inspection of the map will clearly show that the two lines were in the fullest sense parallel and competing, for with common eastern and western termini they serve the transcontinental and trans-Pacific traffic of the same territory from the lakes and the Mississippi to Puget Sound.

Both the States through which these lines passed and the Federal Government early felt that public policy required that all railway systems should remain competitive. It would serve no useful purpose to recite the various constitutional and statutory provisions of the several States which declare the public policy to which I have alluded. It manifested itself in the organic and statutory laws of all the States of the Union. It is questionable whether the statute books of any State are free from some provision, and in many States, such as in Pennsylvania, the matter was regarded as of such permanent importance that the people, disregarding the ordinary methods of legislation, reconvened in constitutional convention in order to write into their organic law the inhibition of such restraints of trade as the consolidation of parallel and competing railroad lines would necessarily occasion.

Indeed, neither constitutional nor statute law was necessary to make such inhibition the declared public policy of the American people, for such consolidations are but one form of restraining trade, as was repeatedly pointed out in the discussions which preceded the passage of the interstate-commerce act of 1887, and the Sherman anti-trust law of 1890. The declared policy of our people, as heirs to the common law, had been to oppose any combinations which tended to the creation of a monopoly or which unreasonably restrained commerce.

It is not, however, with the policy of the States that we are now concerned. It is enough that the assumed evils of railway consolidation, whether effected by technical consolidation or by pooling and traffic agreements, or otherwise—had so powerfully impressed the public mind as to awaken the long dormant power of the Federal Government to regulate interstate commerce. To give this power over interstate commerce the Federal Government had been created, and yet so conservative had it been that from 1787 to 1887 the Federal statutes, with very few and unimportant exceptions, made no attempt to interfere with interstate commerce. So far as legislation was concerned, interstate commerce was left absolutely free, and it was only its growing subjection to the despotic and oppressive methods of great corporate interests that finally led Congress to exercise its long latent but none the less great power in the interests of freedom of trade.

The Federal Government did not act hastily or unadvisedly in the matter. The Forty-ninth Congress, on March 7, 1885, appointed a special committee, known as the "Cullom Committee," to investigate the grievances against the railroads. This committee took a large amount of testimony, and made an elaborate report to Congress, which is published in two volumes as Senate Report, first session, Forty-ninth Congress, volumes 2 and 3. As the result, Congress passed the act of February 4, 1887 (24 Stats. L., 379), entitled "An act to regulate commerce." The provisions of this familiar act need not be recited, except to quote section 5, which showed the declared intention of Congress as to the methods which at that time were adopted by the carrying companies in their efforts to eliminate competition. Section 5 provides:

> Sec. 5. That it shall be unlawful for any common carrier subject to the provisions of this act to enter into any contract, agreement, or combination with any other common carrier or carriers for the pooling of freights of different and competing railroads, or to divide between them the aggregate or net proceeds of the earnings of such railroads, or any portion thereof; and in any case of an agreement for the pooling of freights as aforesaid, each day of its continuance shall be deemed a separate offense.

It will be argued hereafter that the method adopted

in the case at bar of incorporating the joint ownership
of two competing carriers into a holding corporation violates the spirit if not the letter of this section, and is in
substance and effect an incorporated pool.

It was soon evident that the mere inhibition of the specific method of pooling would not answer the public demands, which became more importunate as the various
industries of the country, between which there had theretofore been the fiercest competition, were at that time
forming with incredible rapidity into great amalgamations
of capital known as "trusts." Congress, therefore, in
1890, after prolonged debate, and with little dissent upon
the final vote, passed the sweeping act of July 2, 1890,
called the "Sherman Anti-Trust Law," whereby not only
all combinations in restraint of trade were forbidden,
but every attempt to monopolize foreign or interstate
commerce of this country or any part thereof was made
illegal and a misdemeanor. As will be hereafter shown,
and as is now accepted law, this important act was more
than a mere declaration of the common law as to restraints
of trade, for while the common law permitted reasonable
restraints of trade and only forbade those which were unreasonable, yet Congress reached the deliberate conclusion
that the interests of the American people demanded a
sweeping and absolute prohibition of *every* agreement in
restraint of trade, and of *every* attempt to monopolize
any part of trade or commerce.

Pools and traffic arrangements thus being forbidden,
and railway and industrial combinations being likewise
forbidden by both State and Federal law, this conflict between the law and the railroads entered into a new phase
when the same result was sought to be accomplished by
a method of pooling shares of stock in the hands of a trustee, by the method known as the "community of interest"
plan, whose perfect development in the form of an incorporated "unity of ownership" is to be found in the
merger which is now under consideration in this suit.

It is instructive to review the first attempt of the defendants to defeat the policy of the law by the method
of individual stock holdings, and the fate it met at the

hands of the highest court of our land; and this illustration is more pertinent because both the parties and the railways then concerned are the same parties and the same railways which formed the Northern Securities Company. I refer to the leading case of *Pearsall* v. *Great Northern Railway Company* (161 U. S., 646).

As already stated, in 1893 the Northern Pacific Railway Company passed into the hands of a receiver. Mr. J. P. Morgan, a financier of astounding genius—and to whom, with no abuse of the term, the much-abused expression "Napoleon of finance" may well be applied—undertook the colossal work of reorganizing this company. The details of the reorganization are not now important except as they affect the plan which was obviously then under consideration by both Mr. J. P. Morgan and Mr. James J. Hill to secure the practical merger of the Great Northern and the Northern Pacific, and the elimination of competition between them, and which plan bore its final fruit in the Northern Securities Company. Mr. Hill and his immediate associates, whose moral control of the Great Northern is conceded by the testimony in this record, and Mr. J. P. Morgan and his associates, who had assumed the task of guiding the Northern Pacific through the difficult process of reorganization, clearly reached the conclusion to combine forces and merge interests, so that the motive for competition would cease. Accordingly, the Great Northern Railway Company and the holders of the majority of the outstanding bonds of the Northern Pacific Railway Company entered into an agreement with the firm of J. P. Morgan & Co., by which the property on the foreclosure proceedings was to be sold to a committee of bondholders, who were to organize the new corporation which should issue bonds to the aggregate amount of $100,000,000 or more. These payments the Great Northern Railroad was to guarantee, and in return for its guaranty the capital stock of the new company should be $100,000,000, of which one-half was to be transferred to the shareholders of the Great Northern. *This stock was not to be issued directly to the Great Northern Railroad Company as a corporate entity, but was to be as-*

signed either to its stockholders individually or to a trustee for their use.

The State of Minnesota, by an Act of March 9, 1874, thus affirming the declared policy to which I referred, provided that—

> no railroad corporation or the lessees, purchasers, or managers of any railroad corporation shall consolidate the stock, property, or franchises of such corporation with, or lease or purchase the works or franchises of, or in any way control any other railroad corporations owning or having under its control a parallel or competing line; nor shall any officer of such railroad corporation act as the officer of any other railroad corporation owning or having the control of a parallel or competing line; and the question whether railroads are parallel or competing lines shall, when demanded by the party complainant, be decided by a jury as in other civil issues.

It was further provided by the Act of March 3, 1881, of the laws of Minnesota that—

> No railroad corporation shall consolidate with, lease, or purchase, or in any way become owner of, or control any other railroad corporation, or any stock, franchise, or rights of property thereof, which owns or controls a parallel or competing line.

Upon a bill filed by a stockholder to prevent the consummation of this indirect merger, the question arose primarily as to whether the acts of 1874 and 1881 could, under the Constitution of the United States, impair the unexecuted contract rights of the Great Northern Railway Company to consolidate with other lines running in the same direction; and secondly if such were a constitutional exercise of power, whether the mere purchase by a trustee of the stockholders or the stockholders themselves individually, of the Great Northern Railway Company of one-half of the capital stock of the Northern

Pacific Railway Company (about to be formed) and a guaranty by the Great Northern Railway Company of the proposed bond indebtedness of the Northern Pacific Railway Company was a violation of the provisions of the acts of 1874 and 1881, which in effect forbade the consolidation of parallel and competing lines. The case was argued very ably before the Supreme Court by counsel, at least one of whom appears now as counsel in the present case. The Supreme Court held that the State had the power to pass the prohibitory statutes and that the proposed indirect method to eliminate competition through the medium of individual stock ownership was a virtual consolidation of the roads and void as against the public policy of the State.

The view which the Supreme Court took, in an opinion by Mr. Justice Brown, is most instructive. It tears the ingenious corporate device into tatters, and with unmistakable emphasis says that in the opinion of the court, as in the opinion of Congress, there was a just and reasonable public policy which forbade the elimination of competition and the tyranny of monopoly. The court looked at the substance and not the shadow of the transaction. It permitted no fine-spun theories of corporate entities and the separate acts of stockholders to affect the question. It held in substance that corporations as personal entities only existed in the fiction of law, and that all that is done is done by men who, when a statute founded upon public policy, and *a fortiori* a penal statute, is under consideration, cannot shield themselves behind charters. Detailed reference will be made to this notable opinion hereafter in the argument on the law.

In considering the transaction, the legality of which is involved in the case at bar, it is important to remember this first and unsuccessful attempt to merge the control of these two transcontinental systems into a common ownership. It is most significant, for it throws a searchlight upon all that subsequently took place.

The policy of such a combination, as is now under consideration, is not the impulse of a day or the matter of a year. As fully testified to both by Mr. Hill and Colonel

Clough, the Great Northern Railway Company has had for many years a fixed and continuous policy, from which it never deviated and toward which it moved as slowly, and apparently as irresistibly, as a glacier. It is true that there were many stockholders of the Great Northern, as well as of the Northern Pacific, and it is not contended that all of the stockholders in any sense consciously combined to effect the common object. It is enough to say that Mr. James J. Hill and a group of associates controlled capital stock of the Great Northern to the extent of $35,-000,000 and through their holdings, and through the executive offices which they held, controlled the policy of the Great Northern with a harmony on the part of the stockholders that amounted to the unanimity of an "opera chorus." As Sheridan says in *The Critic*, "when they do agree upon the stage, their unanimity is wonderful."

On the other hand, after the Northern Pacific had gone into the hands of a receiver, and its reorganization had been undertaken by the banking firm of J. P. Morgan & Co. (the fiscal agents of the company), the stock was vested in a voting trust which he controlled. The testimony discloses that in all which subsequently took place the real parties to every transaction were comparatively few and absolutely potential. Mr. James J. Hill represented the Great Northern and spoke as absolutely for its policy as though he had owned every share of its capital stock. Mr. J. P. Morgan, acting either personally or through one of his partners, spoke with the same *ex cathedra* authority for the Northern Pacific, and in the momentous struggle which subsequently developed between the Union Pacific interests (the third of the four great transcontinental lines in the United States), Mr. E. H. Harriman, either personally or with his banker, Mr. Jacob H. Schiff, of Kuhn, Loeb & Co., spoke with equal authority and potency for the great corporate interests which they represented. Indeed, as will subsequently appear, the vast holdings of the Northern Pacific, which were subsequently acquired by the Union Pacific interests, were never taken in the name of those corporations, but were held in the name of Harriman and Pearce.

The actors in the drama, therefore, were few, and to discover that which was done it is only necessary to read the testimony of James J. Hill, J. P. Morgan, and E. H. Harriman (the "great triumvirate" of this colossal transcontinental combine), and the history of the transaction will then be secured from the lips of those who by their deeds made its history.

It is clear from Mr. Morgan's testimony that prior to the decision in *Pearsall v. Great Northern Railway Company*, in March, 1896, he and his associates, who, through the pooling trust, controlled the insolvent Northern Pacific Railroad, and Hill and his associates, who had absolute control of the Great Northern, were working in harmony for the purpose of eliminating competition, and that the legality of their attempts was under serious consideration.

Defeated in this attempt to amalgamate the Great Northern and the Northern Pacific systems in the manner described, these masters of finance and transportation next determined to eliminate competition by adopting the community of interest plan, and this plan had its final development, as will be hereinafter stated, into an incorporated unity of ownership plan, which absolutely destroyed competition by removing all motive for it.

It may be well at this stage to define what the "community of interest" plan is, and fortunately we have a definition in the testimony in this case, which the great financier, Mr. J. P. Morgan, has given us. He was asked the question:

Q. *What is community of interest?*

A. *The community of interests is that principle that a certain number of men who own property can do what they like with it.*

Q. *But they sha'n't fight one another?*

A. *There is no fighting about it. If they choose to fight their own property—but people don't generally do that.*

Q. *Is not this community of interest idea one of working harmony?*

A. *Working in harmony—yes.*

Q. *Even though they own competing and parallel lines?*
A. *No; they own them all.*

In this lucid and practical exposition of "community of interest" the great financier has undone much of the work of our learned adversaries, for they will argue to your honors at great length that these two railroads are still competing lines, notwithstanding their common ownership. The client evidently does not agree with his counsel, and with clearer insight Mr. Morgan tells us, in substance, that the lines cease to be competing and parallel when controlled by a common ownership.

Accordingly, the ink was hardly dry upon the opinion of the Supreme Court in *Pearsall v. Great Northern Railway Company* before Hill and his associates, representing the Great Northern Railway, had acquired from Mr. Morgan $26,000,000 of the stock of the reorganized Northern Pacific, and Mr. Morgan and his associates, on the other hand, acquired stock in the Great Northern Railway to an unascertained amount.

This state of harmony was disturbed by the Union Pacific interests in the following sensational manner:

As will be seen by the map, which is printed in volume 2, page 504, of the Record, there lies to the south of both systems the great central railway system, whose eastern termini are Chicago and St. Louis, and whose western terminus is Billings, in the State of Montana, where it joins the Northern Pacific. It also connects with both of the Northwestern railway systems at St. Paul. This system, known as the "Burlington," has nearly 8,000 miles of trackage and a total capital stock and bonds of $360,-000,000. While only incidentally, and to a minor extent a competitor with either the Great Northern or the Northern Pacific, it was in the fullest sense a competitor of the Union Pacific, and this competition threatened to become more serious, inasmuch as the Burlington, during or before the year 1900, commenced to make surveys to carry its lines to the Pacific coast.

Learning of this attempt, and in order to get the traffic which the Burlington system could give either to the Union Pacific lines or the Northwestern transcontinental lines, the Union Pacific interests, acting through Mr. E. H. Harriman and Kuhn, Loeb & Co., quietly commenced in the fall of 1900 to purchase the Burlington system. They succeeded in acquiring about $9,000,000 of the stock—when it was apparent that control could not be secured in the open market, and the parties resold their stock.

It is clear that this attempt of the Union Pacific interests alarmed both the Great Northern and the Northern Pacific companies, and, accordingly, early in 1901, Mr. Hill, acting for the Great Northern, and Mr. Morgan, for the Northern Pacific, opened negotiations with the directors of the Burlington system for the purchase of the Burlington stock, and succeeded in March, 1901, in purchasing 1,066,600 out of 1,112,000 shares at $200 a share, for which each of the purchasers joined severally in bonds to the amount of $222,400,000.

In this manner the entire Burlington system with its 8,000 miles of trackage, its vast assets represented by $360,-000,000 of capital stock and bonds (par value), passed jointly into the hands of the Great Northern and Northern Pacific, and while, unquestionably, the purposes of the acquisition may in part have been for the sagacious purposes of developing traffic, to which Mr. Hill, in many pages of testimony, has given eloquent testimony, yet it is difficult to escape the conclusion that the acquisition was also made, partly to prevent the construction of a rival transcontinental line to the Pacific coast, and partly to secure, as against the Union Pacific system, the vast traffic which originates on the Burlington system, and which is destined for points west of its western terminus.

When the news of this *coup d'etat* became public, the Union Pacific interests naturally took alarm. Their representatives, Mr. Schiff and Mr. Harriman, at first determined to make peace, provided that their interests were recognized in the transcontinental combine; and thereupon, in the month of March, 1901, they formally demanded of Mr. Hill that the Union Pacific interests should be admitted to participation in the Burlington deal.

To the refusal of Hill and Morgan to divide a considerable portion of the transportation world with Harriman the sensational events which followed are directly attributable. Indeed, should a dramatic poet essay to describe in rolling hexameters this modern Iliad of the financial world, he would liken the Burlington system to the fair Briseis, and, substituting Harriman for Achilles, invoke the muse with:

> "Achilles' wrath, to Greece the direful spring
> Of woes unnumbered, heavenly goddess sing."

Indeed, the counterpart of the disastrous speculative war which followed is to be found in a modern romance of exceptional power, wherein the great novelist, Zola, describes a warfare of the Bourse, and pictures a mighty contest between Sacchard, a financier of Napoleonic audacity, on the one hand, and the silent Gunderman, who probably typified a Rothschild. But truth is always stranger than fiction, and in dramatic details and disastrous results the fiction of Zola is tame in comparison with the events which resulted from this refusal to permit Harriman to participate in the Burlington deal, and which shook to its very center the equilibrium of the financial world, for, upon this refusal, Mr. Harriman and his associates determined upon a counter *coup d'etat*, which was as audacious and difficult of its class as Napoleon's passage of the Alps and his sudden appearance on the plains of Italy. The capital stock of the Northern Pacific was $155,000,000, and Mr. Harriman and his associates determined to "delve one yard beneath the mines" and blow their adversaries skyward by purchasing in the market the control of the Northern Pacific Railway, thus menacing the Hill-Morgan monopoly in the Northwest, appropriating the Burlington system, and diverting its traffic over the Union Pacific. With extraordinary rapidity and success they acquired in the month of April, 1901, thirty-seven millions of the common stock and forty millions of the preferred stock of the Northern Pacific, thus giving them a complete majority of the entire capital stock, but unfortunately for them, as the sequel proved, less than a majority of the common stock. Hill and Morgan first became aware of this *coup d'etat* early in May, 1901.

How successful it was they could not at that time determine.

As the result of this extraordinary contest, with the added stimulus of the speculative fever which had caught the public, the extraordinary panic of May 9 took place, which sent Northern Pacific stock to $1,000 a share, and carried with it a shrinkage in other securities to the extent of hundreds of millions of dollars, and consequent ruin to many of the speculative public.

Great as were the financial actors in this remarkable drama, it was obvious that they had unwittingly created a financial condition which might involve even them in irreparable loss. The money markets of the world were convulsed, the equilibrium of the financial world shaken, and many speculative interests in a critical condition. It was perfectly obvious to all the contestants that to continue the struggle would mean destruction to values generally, with a possibility of a repetition of the panic of 1873, and that therefore peace at any price must be secured.

When the smoke cleared away from the field of battle, a meeting was held between the various interests for the purpose of effecting, if not a treaty of peace, at least an armistice that would suspend hostilities.

Mr. Hill had previously testified that on the "show down" of this gigantic speculative poker, the Union Pacific interests had shown a clear majority of the entire capital stock of the Northern Pacific.

This was apparently a "winning hand," but unfortunately the Achilles of this Iliad proved, like his predecessor, vulnerable in the heel, for while Harriman held a majority of all of the stock ($78,000,000 out of $155,-000,000), and at a stockholders' meeting would thus control the corporation, yet the Hill-Morgan interest owned a majority of the common stock, and they claimed that the directors, who had been chosen under the voting trust by Mr. Morgan, could retire the preferred stock. This stock could not be retired before the first of January, 1902, and the date of the annual meeting of the stockholders was the preceding October 1. Thereupon, Hill and Morgan met their adversaries with a threat to post-pone the annual meeting until the Northern Pacific pre-ferred stock could be retired. If retired before an annual meeting, they remained in control, for the Union Pacific interests, notwithstanding their majority of both classes of capital stock, would lose control by reason of holding only a minority of the common stock.

As the result of this conference, an inspired bulletin was given to the public by the participants in the peace conference. When closely read it affords persuasive proof that the idea of a holding company, in which the warring interests shall all be represented, was determined upon in the negotiations which succeeded the panic of May 9. It must be remembered that these masters of the markets were diplomats, and that neither Talleyrand nor Metternich would more gravely weigh their language. Every word in their official announcement would have its purpose and significance. Remembering this, let me read the bulletin which appeared in the Wall Street Summary of Saturday, June 1, 1901:

> It is officially announced that an understand-ing has been reached between the Northern Pa-cific and the Union Pacific interests, under which the composition of the Northern Pacific board will be left in the hands of J. P. Morgan. Cer-tain names have already been suggested, not now to be made public, which will *especially* be rec-ognized as *representative of the common inter-ests*. It is asserted that *complete and permanent* harmony will result under the plan adopted *be-tween all interests involved*.

"Representatives of the common interests!" "Com-plete and permanent harmony." How could permanent harmony be guaranteed except by an incorporated hold-ing company, which for all time would concentrate in the hands of a few the vast transportation interests which had been at war. Permanence could not be predicated upon any mental attitude, but the pooling of stocks into a company of perpetual powers would insure permanent relations so far as any legal device could do so. And what were the "common interests?" Obviously those which had been at war—the Union Pacific, the Great Northern, and the Northern Pacific. As the zoologist can construct the prehistoric monster from a bone, so it is easy to construct the entire agreement from the sententious phrases of the inspired bulletin and of the events which followed.

What was agreed upon in May, 1901, was this:

1. J. P. Morgan to nominate the board of directors for the Northern Pacific road, which should represent the Union Pacific and the Hill-Morgan interests.

2. The preferred stock of the Northern Pacific to be retired.

3. A holding company to be formed, which would purchase the stock of the Great Northern and the Northern Pacific, and which should thereby purchase the Harriman holdings and insure a representative of the Union Pacific interests in the merged properties.

It is obvious from Harriman's testimony that such was the result of this memorable struggle. He had pledged the credit of the Union Pacific Railroad, and its underlying company, the Oregon Short Line, to the extent of $78,000,000 to get control of the Northern Pacific. He was satisfied to surrender these holdings in return for representation in the holding company which he regarded as sufficient to protect the interests that he represented.

As indicating when the idea of the holding company was formed, he testifies explicitly that he agreed to sell his holdings in the Northern Pacific in September or October of 1901, and that the values at which the respective stocks of the Great Northern and the Northern Pacific were to be taken over had been then determined. The compact was carried out to the letter.

Mr. Morgan returned from Europe in July, and at once took control of the situation under the agreement of arbitration.

It appears from Mr. Morgan's testimony that the understanding was more than a truce. It was a definitive treaty of peace. The "community of interest" plan was invoked to settle the conflict between the three great trans-

continental systems, and Mr. Morgan promptly selected
the board of directors for the Northern Pacific Company,
and selected such as would represent all three interests,
and thus insure that "harmony" which the law assumes to
be prejudicial to the public. With the purchase of the
Burlington, and its elimination as a possible transconti-
netal competitor, with the practical division of the Northern Pacific system between its former owners and the
Great Northern and the Union Pacific interests, the time
naturally seemed most opportune to the participants in
this gigantic combine to place their "community of interest" on a stable basis by incorporating it.

It was easily apparent that the method of "community
of interest" could not be wholly effective, inasmuch as
it was psychological or temperamental in character, and
was only of value so long as the mental attitudes of the
participants continued in the direction of harmony. Thus
the process of consolidation took a new phase when the
community of interest was changed by the formation of
the Northern Securities Company into the far more stable
and effective method of *unity of ownership*.

Undoubtedly this plan of a so-called "holding corporation" had long been in the minds of both Hill and Morgan.

It may be true that the settlement of the Burlington
contest had no *necessary* relation to the formation of the
Northern Securities Company, but it is clear from both
Hill and Morgan's testimony (especially that of Mr. Morgan), that the tremendous contest over the Northern Pacific between the Union Pacific and the Hill-Morgan interests did powerfully suggest to the minds of Hill and
Morgan the absolute necessity of accomplishing without
further delay their long-cherished plan of unity of ownership between these two competing transcontinental lines,
the plan which, as Mr. Morgan frankly testifies, they had
tried once before and found to be illegal by the decision
in the *Pearsall* case.

Accordingly, steps were immediately taken to put their
plans into effect, and they were accomplished with almost
incredible rapidity. The day that witnessed the retirement
of the Northern Pacific stock witnessed the application

for a charter for the Northern Securities. At first Mr. Morgan thought (as shown in the testimony previously recited at length) that the purpose could be accomplished by pooling their holdings of stock in a preexisting trust company. But this was open to the previous objection that not only had no trust company sufficient capital to accept so large a financial responsibility, but the acquisition of the trust company by the control of a majority of its stock would, of necessity, mean the domination of the stock thus pooled.

A trust company being impracticable, it was decided to secure a charter, and this was no easy task, as Mr. Morgan testifies.

It is thus apparent from Colonel Clough's testimony that as early as March, and with the Burlington purchase in actual progress, the matter of this holding corporation was under active discussion. Its delay, as he states, was due to the absence in Europe of Mr. Kennedy, who did not return until June. The inference is fair that Mr. J. P. Morgan's absence in Europe was also not without its weight. It will be convenient at this point to group certain dates.

January 1, 1901, J. P. Morgan dissolves the voting trust of the Northern Pacific road.

January, 1901 (Hill testifies about the middle), Hill and Morgan begin negotiations for purchase of the Burlington.

March, 1901, Harriman and Schiff demand a participation in the Burlington deal, which Hill and Morgan refuse.

April, 1901, negotiations for purchase of Burlington concluded.

April, 1901, Harriman interests begin to purchase Northern Pacific stock and acquire by May 9 a majority of all stock.

May, 1901, Hill-Morgan interests commence to purchase Northern Pacific common stock and secure a majority of that stock, it being understood that the Northern Pacific preferred stock is to be retired.

May 9, 1901, panic due to Northern Pacific "corner."

May 11, 1901, representatives of Hill, Morgan and Harriman meet at Harriman's office and make peace by agreeing that Morgan shall name the next board of directors of the Northern Pacific Company. Harriman gives his proxy for $78,000,000 of Northern Pacific stock to Morgan.

July 1, 1901, deed executed to secure bonds issued for the purchase of the Burlington system.

July 4, 1901, J. P. Morgan returns from Europe, and on July 23 names a board for the Northern Pacific which represents all three interests.

July 23, 1901, meeting of directors of Northern Pacific. Five resign and five new ones, nominated by Morgan, succeed them.

September, 1901, Harriman opens negotiations with Morgan & Co. for sale of Union Pacific's Northern Pacific holdings.

October 1, 1901, annual meeting of stockholders of Northern Pacific and selection of directors nominated by J. P. Morgan.

October, 1901, Morgan interests agree to buy Harriman's holdings in Northern Pacific for the "holding corporation" about to be formed.

November 13, 1901, board of directors of Northern Pacific Railway meet and elect directors and officers.

November 13, 1901, meeting of the directors of the Northern Pacific road and passage of a resolution to retire the preferred stock of the Northern Pacific road.

November 13, 1901, application and issue of charter of the Northern Securities Company.

November 18, 1901, Northern Securities Company purchases, as previously agreed, $78,108,000 of the stock of the Northern Pacific Railway Company, from E. H. Harriman and Winslow S. Pierce, trustee for the Union Pacific interests.

November 20, 1901, Chicago, Burlington and Quincy Railroad Company leased to Chicago, Burlington and Quincy Railway Company.

November 22, 1901, Mr. Hill as president of the Securities Company addresses a circular letter to stockholders of

Great Northern strongly advising them to exchange their securities for Northern Securities stock.

November 30, 1901, Mr. Hill addresses individually a similar letter to all inquiring stockholders.

December 27, 1901, Northern Securities Company purchases convertible bonds of the Northern Pacific Railway Company to the amount of $34,000,000.

January 1, 1902, it converts these bonds into the common stock of the Northern Pacific road, which, with the stock previously purchased on November 18, 1901, gave it practically all of the common stock of the Northern Pacific. It had also acquired at that time 986,689 shares of the 1,250,000 shares of the Great Northern.

Comparison of these dates will theretofore show that between January 1, 1901, and January 1, 1902, a group of men, representing and acting for the three great transcontinental railway systems, namely, the Union Pacific system, the Northern Pacific system, and the Great Northern system, had consolidated into a new company formed by them for the specific purpose, the Burlington, Northern Pacific, and Great Northern systems, with their aggregate trackage of approximately 20,000 miles, and had accomplished this extraordinary and unprecedented amalgamation in a manner which preserved harmonious relations between the combined systems and the Union Pacific system. This arrangement, if sustained by the courts, would be effected in a mode that is *permanent in character, absolute in power, and infinite in possible extension.*

If there were no other testimony than the naked facts, no court would assume that this extraordinary combination of circumstances could happen, as the world was once supposed to be created, by a fortuitous concourse of atoms. But with the positive testimony of Hill, Harriman, and Morgan, it cannot be questioned that all of these occurrences were interdependent and the designed result of a combination of men of powerful resources, who thus sought to place the control of these systems and the regulation of the vast interstate traffic which they carry in the hands of a few men.

It has already been shown that there was considerable

discussion as to what charter could be secured to protect such extraordinary powers. After careful consideration by eminent counsel, it was finally decided that the State, which had won a bad pre-eminence for its reckless sale of corporate privileges to secure petty fees, was the state whose protective power should be invoked. Accordingly the charter was applied for in New Jersey on December 13, 1901, and the transaction required no expenditure save $30,000, the bonus due to the state. With this exception, the whole transaction was nothing more than the exchange of pieces of paper, both being certificates of ownership; the buyers were the sellers and the sellers were the buyers, with this important difference, that the part owner of the property of the Northern Pacific Railway, or the Great Northern, found himself a part owner of the property of both. Had the two constituent companies formally consolidated, no different results would have been accomplished. Had the Great Northern and Northern Pacific formally merged their corporate identity and issued new capital stock in retirement and exchange for the pre-existing holdings, the result would have been precisely the same as in the exchange for the certificate of the Northern Securities, with the single exception of the name. Between a technical merger and a transfer to the so-called holding company is the difference between tweedle-dum and tweedle-dee. Throughout this argument I have referred to the Northern Securities as the so-called "holding company." It is far more than a holding company. Its powers are broad enough to operate its properties and, indeed, its powers are broad enough to do anything that serves the interests of its incorporators.

No more extraordinary charter was probably ever granted than this one. A few of its salient features are:

(1) To purchase the shares of stock or bonds of any corporation of any State, Territory, or country, or to purchase any real or personal property whatever.

(2) To dispose of them in any way, to anyone, on any terms, at any time, and at will.

(3) As owner of such stock and bonds or property "to exercise all the rights, powers, and privileges of owner-

ship;" in other words, to do all that the original owners of such stock or property could do.

(4) "To do any acts or things designed to protect, preserve, improve, or enhance the value of any such bonds or other securities or evidence of indebtedness or stock."

(5) To exercise these powers, infinite in character, forever.

(6) Under the laws of New Jersey, to increase its capital stock to any sum whatever for such purposes.

(7) The control of these powers is vested in a board of directors, who can meet and transact business either in or out of New Jersey at pleasure, and who may appoint of their number "an executive committee, of which a majority shall constitute a quorum," which committee "shall have and may exercise all or any of the powers of the board of directors, including power to cause the seal of the corporation to be affixed to all papers that may require it."

(8) The board of directors, besides managing the business generally, shall have power from time to time to fix and vary the amount of working capital of the corporation.

(9) The board of directors have the final right to determine when the books shall be opened to the inspection of the stockholders.

(10) The board of directors can make by-laws and amend or repeal them at pleasure.

Such extraordinary powers were never yet granted to a corporation unless it be one of New Jersey origin. In a few words, its powers may be classified as follows:

(1) Infinite in scope.
(2) Perpetual in character.
(3) Vested in the hands of a few.
(4) By methods secret even to stockholders.

It will be interesting to follow out the possibilities of such a corporation. The original idea of a holding corporation, as explained by noted financiers, is to enable the minority to rule the majority. Thus, if two constituent companies have a joint capital of $100,000,000, it will take $51,000,000 to control them; but if a ho' '.1g corporation can be formed and can acquire $51,000,000 of stock, then $26,000,000 will dominate the holding corporation, which will in turn dominate the $100,000,-000 corporation. Thus the quarter will dominate the three-quarters. This idea, however, is modest as compared with the Northern Securities Company, for, not only does a majority of the Northern Securities Company, namely, $201,000,000 control the Burlington, Northern Pacific, and Great Northern systems and all subsidiary companies, whose aggregate capitalization, including funded debt exceeds $1,000,000,000, but the board of directors, whose holdings of Northern Securities may be comparatively insignificant, can, during the tenure of their office, appoint a committee with power to act and to use the seal of the corporation at pleasure. This committee may be only three in number, and a majority is determinative. Thus, in the last analysis, two men may control the unlimited powers of the holding company, which, in turn, controls the vast powers of the Burlington, Northern Pacific, and Great Northern companies, and all subsidiary companies. When, in the history of corporate organization, was there ever a charter which concentrated such vast and immeasurable power in the hands of so few?

The extent of the "harmony" under the treaty of peace may be measured by a classification of the present boards of directors of the Northern Pacific, the Chicago, Burlington and Quincy, and the Northern Securities Company.

It will thus be seen that in the two systems that were the subject of the quarrel, namely, the Northern Pacific and the Burlington, that all three interests are represented on the boards of directors, and that the board of directors of the Northern Securities Company is about equally divided between the three parties to the compact, namely, the Great Northern, the Northern Pacific, and the Union Pacific interests. A summary of these systems under the present arrangement is as follows:

	Miles	Stocks and bonds outstanding
Union Pacific (1901)	5,543	$988,000,000
Controls Southern and Central Pacific	9,441	901,000,000
Owns large interest in Northern Securities	----	400,000,000
Controls—		
Great Northern	5,249	469,000,000
Northern Pacific	5,019	495,000,000
Control—		
C. B. and Q. Ry. Co.	----	100,000,000
Which leases C., B. and Q. R. R.	8,171	360,000,000
Total	33,423	$3,713,000,000
Per mile		111,000

The effect upon the public may be measured by the unprecedented capitalization of $111,000 per mile. It is said that in early days the prejudice in New York against banks was such that some of the oldest banks of that State were obliged to do business under the cover of furnishing water. The above capitalization suggests the wondering question why the Northern Securities did not take out a charter as a "water" company!

The formation of this railway combine of unprecedented size, and clothed with powers so unlimited and extraordinary in scope naturally alarmed, not merely the people of the great Northwest, who were dependent for their very lives upon the facilities for transportation which these companies furnished, but also the whole American people, who see in this combination the prelude to a still greater one which would control all the railways in America.

An attempt has been made in defendant's testimony, to which detailed reference will be made hereafter, to suggest that these two companies are only competitive to a limited and trivial extent. But such evidently was not the opinion of the governors of Minnesota, Montana, South Dakota, Idaho, and Washington, whose executive officers sprang to arms as though facing the sudden peril of an invading army. Each of these states had either constitutional or legislative provisions which forbade within their borders the consolidation of these parallel and competing lines. It was a novel proposition to them that the laws of these states could be nullified by the simple device of a New Jersey charter. The governor of Minnesota not merely called attention to the illegality of the combination in his annual message to the legislature of the state of the years 1902 and 1903, but he called the governors and attorney generals of the states, through which these lines passed, into conference, and this conference (held at Helena, Montana) was attended by the governors and attorney generals of Minnesota, Montana, South Dakota, Idaho, and Washington. These officials, representing the people of these states, unanimously adopted the following resolution:

> In our opinion, the consolidation or threatened consolidation of the Great Northern, Northern Pacific, and Burlington Railway systems in the several states through which they run as parallel and competing lines is contrary to sound public policy, and also, with the exception of Idaho, is in violation of the Constitution or laws of said states, and mindful of the obligation which the law imposes in such cases upon the officials of the several states here represented, we hereby give our unqualified approval and endorsement to any proper and suitable proceeding which may be instituted in any court having jurisdiction by the sovereign state of Minnesota, or any other state affected thereby, designated, designed, and intended to speedily and finally test and determine the validity of such consolidation or threatened consolidation. And further, we unanimously protest against any combination or consolidation which restricts

or stifles free competition in the trade or commerce of the country.

Not contented with a mere protest, the state of Minnesota, on January 7, 1902, applied to the Supreme Court
of the United States for leave to file a bill to enjoin the
combination, and the Supreme Court for reasons given in
184 U. S., 199, decided that they were without *original*
jurisdiction to decide the controversy.

A greater power was about to intervene, for the President of the United States, mindful of the welfare of the
entire people, requested the opinion of his Attorney General as to the legality of the procedure, and on February
19, 1902, Attorney General Knox authorized this statement:

> Some time ago the President requested an
> opinion as to the legality of this merger, and I
> have recently given him one to the effect that,
> in my judgment, it violates the provisions of the
> Sherman Act of 1890, whereupon he directed
> that suitable action should be taken to have the
> question judicially determined.

By the authority of the President, therefore, the Government filed the present bill to enjoin this combination
as a violation of the act of July 2, 1890. On April 7 the
State of Washington filed an application in the Supreme
Court for leave to file a bill, and this was granted by the
Supreme Court on April 21, and during the same month
the attorney general of the state of Minnesota commenced a new suit against the Northern Securities Company, which suit was removed to the United States circuit court, where it is now pending. It thus appears that
not only the Federal Government, but the officials of five
states, have voiced the public policy of state and nation
against the proposed merger, and the suggestion, therefore, that the merger does not affect competitive traffic,
and therefore the public interests to any appreciable extent, may profitably be dismissed.

Having thus stated the essential facts of the controversy, as to which there can be little substantial dispute, I pass to the law applicable to the transaction.

To exclude the suggestion that individuals could, when formed into a corporation, violate the act under the pretense that they did not act as individuals, and that a corporation formed by a state was beyond the purposes of the act, Congress further provided:

> Sec. 8. That the word "person" or "persons," wherever used in this act, shall be deemed to include corporations and associations existing under or authorized by the laws of either the United States, or the laws of any of the Territories, the laws of any state, or the laws of any foreign country.

It will thus be seen that five distinct acts have been made offenses by this act:

(a) No person or corporation shall make any contract in restraint of trade.

(b) No person or corporation shall engage in any combination, whether in the form of a trust or otherwise, in restraint of trade or commerce.

(c) No person or corporation shall monopolize any part of trade or commerce.

(d) No person or corporation shall attempt to monopolize any part of the trade or commerce among the several states.

(e) No person or corporation shall combine with any other person or corporation to monopolize any part of the trade or commerce among the states.

If either of the defendants to this bill shall be proved to have committted any one of the offenses above stated, the United States is, as to him, or it, entitled to relief. In other words, the question involved in the present case is—

Did either the Northern Securities, *or* the Great Northern Railway Company, *or* the Northern Pacific Railway Company, *or* James J. Hill, *or* William P. Clough, *or* D. Willis James, *or* John S. Kennedy, *or* J. Pierpont Morgan, *or* Robert Bacon, *or* George F. Baker, *or* Daniel

Lamont, make a contract in restraint of trade, or engage in a combination in restraint of trade, or monopolize any part of trade or commerce, or attempt to monopolize any part of trade or commerce, or combine or conspire with others to monopolize any part of the trade or commerce?

These questions must necessarily involve a definition of a contract in restraint of trade under the Federal statute and the definition of a monopoly under the Federal statute, and as to that, fortunately, the decisions of the Supreme Court leave us in no doubt. These decisions are comparatively few, and therefore I shall review them and subsequently summarize the propositions which they seem, to me, to clearly establish.

Obviously, the first and leading case is *Pearsall v. Great Northern Railway Company* (161 U. S., 646), to which reference has already been made, and which, while it construed the statutes of the State of Minnesota which forbid the consolidation of parallel and competing lines, yet lays down principles of law as to what is a monopoly or contract in restraint of trade equally applicable to the Federal law of July 2, 1890.

As to the question of public policy the court says (Mr. Justice Brown) (p. 675):

> We do not deem it necessary to express an opinion in this case whether the legislature could wholly revoke the power it had given to this company to extend its system by the construction or purchase of branch lines or feeders, since the possibility of an extension of the road, even to the Pacific Coast, may have had an influence upon persons contemplating the purchase of its stock or securities, so that a right to do this might be said to have become vested. *But we think it was competent for the legislature, out of due regard for the public welfare, to declare that its charter should not be used for the purpose of stifling competition and building up monopolies. In short, we can not recognize a vested right to do a manifest wrong.*

This opinion, however, is of controlling force in the question as to whether intent is a necessary ingredient. Much testimony has been offered in the case at bar to prove, on the one hand, that the gentlemen who formed the Northern Securities Company did not intend to restrict interstate trade or form a monopoly, and on the other hand that they did. But the Supreme Court, in the case above cited, clearly disposes of the question by ruling that intent was wholly unimportant; and this ruling has been followed in all subsequent cases, to which allusion will be presently made.

On the same day that the Pearsall case was decided the Supreme Court handed down another decision to the same general effect in *Louisville and Nashville Railroad Company v. Kentucky* (161 U. S., 677); and again emphasized the disposition of the courts to give full force and effect to all legislation forbidding restriction of competition in transportation by the consolidation of parallel and competing lines. The Constitution of the State of Kentucky, of 1891, provided that—

> No railroad * * * shall consolidate its capital stock, franchises, or property, or pool its earnings, in whole or in part, with any other railroad * * * or common carrier company owning a parallel or competing line of structure, or operate the same, etc.

By the act of March 7, 1854, the Louisville and Nashville Company, which had been incorporated in 1850, was given power "to unite their road with any other connecting therewith." It sought to acquire the control of the Chesapeake, Ohio and Southwestern Railroad Company, a competing line; and it sought to do this through the medium of a judicial sale. The Supreme Court sustained the action of the Court of Appeals of Kentucky, in an opinion by Mr. Justice Brown, and held that the consolidation was illegal.

Anticipating the argument which will probably be made in the case at bar, that a decision adverse to the right of consolidation would effect the stockholders who had invested large sums of money in the proposed consolidation, the Supreme Court, in the opinion referred to, well says (p. 691):

> In reply to the argument that millions of dollars have been invested in the securities of the company upon the faith of what was supposed to be its admitted powers, and that its capital stock of $1,500,000 in 1856 has expanded to $51,000,000, it is sufficient to say that in making such investments capitalists were bound to know the authority of the company under its charter, and to put the proper interpretation upon it; and that we are not at liberty to presume that investments were made upon the faith of powers that do not exist; and, if they were, the Commonwealth is not bound to respect investments made under a misapprehension of the law. Indeed the argument proves too much, and would justify the inference that capitalists put their money into the road upon the assumption that it had been given irrevocable right to absorb to itself every road which might thereafter be constructed within the limits of the Commonwealth.

The argument now addressed to the court that a decree favorable to the Government would impair vested rights of property, and that under the bill of rights Congress may not forbid men to dispose of their property as they please, is thus met by Mr. Justice Brown in the case referred to.

Thus the Supreme Court, at the first opportunity, took occasion, in the most emphatic and ample manner, to support and vindicate the declared public policy of state and nation with respect to railway monopolies.

In neither of these cases was the United States a party litigant. In the *Pearsall case* it was a stockholder's bill, and in the *Louisville and Nashville case* it was the State of Kentucky which sought to vindicate its own laws.

The contest between the people and the railways assumed

a new phase when the Federal Government, acting under and in pursuance of the legislation above referred to, in the great case of *United States v. Trans-Missouri Freight Association,* 166 U. S., 290 (1897), summoned eighteen railroads, which formed the Trans-Missouri Freight Association, on the ground that the association violated the act of July 2, 1890.

In this case, as well as in the subsequent case of *United States v. Joint Traffic Association* (171 U. S., 505), the whole question was argued, and reargued, and thrice argued by eminent counsel in behalf of the railways, and in each case the Supreme Court reached conclusions which were adverse to a far less direct and offensive combination of competing railways, and in so doing laid down definitive principles which clearly rule the case at bar. Indeed, it may be here stated that every contention now urged by counsel for the defendants in the case at bar was also urged in the cases above stated, and negatived by the court of last resort.

In the *Trans-Missouri case* some fifteen competing interstate railways had formed a freight association, by the rules of which they agreed to be governed within a prescribed territory. These provided for the appointment of a committee "to establish rates, rules, and regulations," and to consider changes therein. Their conclusions, when unanimous, were to rule, but in case of difference, the question was to be referred to the managers of the various lines, and if they disagreed, it was to be arbitrated. Any party to the agreement could change the rates upon five days' previous written notice, and the right to change the rates was reserved, even though the association disapproved of the change, provided that ten days' previous notice was given. Compliance with the rules was provided for by penalties to be assessed against the offending line, and any one of the parties could withdraw from the association on thirty days' notice.

The agreement is inoffensive in comparison with the present merger case. It had only reference to the maintenance of rates; there was no distinct pooling of earnings; the active management of the properties did not pass to a common source of control, except as to the maintenance of rates, and as to these there was the right of any party, upon the prescribed notice, to make his own rates or to withdraw entirely from the association. There was neither permanence, unity of control, or any real power of government vested in the central organization. The Supreme Court in an opinion by Mr. Justice Peckham held that the act of July 2, 1890, had not only declared the common law, but had materially extended it by prohibiting every contract or combination in any form in restraint of trade or commerce.

In the later case of *United States v. Joint Traffic Association* (171 U. S., 505) decided in 1898, these conclusions were elaborately reargued and reviewed by the court. In that case thirty-one railroad companies formed themselves into an association known as the "Joint Traffic Association," which was, in substance, the same as that passed upon in the *Trans-Missouri case.* There was, however, the further disclaimer of any intention to violate the interstate commerce act, and the duty was enjoined on the managers to cooperate with the Interstate Commerce Commission to secure stability and uniformity in rates, fares, and charges.

The agreement was for five years only, and the method of the enforcement of the regulations was left to the managers, with power to act. As stated, the grounds of the *Trans-Missouri* decision were reargued as though not settled, with the additional argument that the act of July 2, 1890, as previously construed by the Supreme Court, would necessarily be unconstitutional as an invasion of the liberty which is guaranteed by the fifth amendment.

The two cases which were decided on the same day as the Joint Traffic cases, namely, *Hopkins v. United States,* 171 U. S., 578, and *Anderson v. United States,* idem, 604, need not be referred to at length, for, in the first place, they did not present a case of combinations between railroads in restraint of trade, and, for the better reason, as the court properly held, they did not refer to legitimate interstate commerce at all, as they constituted intra-state combinations whose purpose was to afford local facilities to interstate trade. They were therefore not within either the legislation referred to, or, indeed, within the constitutional power of Congress.

The Sherman anti-trust law was next under review in the case of *Addyston Pipe Company v. United States,* 175 U. S., 211, which, while not a case of competing railroads, yet rediscussed and reaffirmed certain legal principles which are applicable to the present case. The Addyston Pipe case presented a combination between manufacturing companies of different states to allot territory between themselves, and in this manner divide and control interstate trade in the commodity which they manufactured. It was there argued that the power to regulate commerce had reference only to protection from state legislation and not to private contracts, and that therefore legislation which sought to impair the freedom of contract between individuals was unconstitutional and void under the fifth amendment. The court held otherwise.

One case of a Federal appellate court remains to be considered. I refer to *Chesapeake and Ohio Fuel Company v. United States* (115 Federal Reporter, 610), in which the Circuit Court of Appeals for the sixth circuit passed upon the legality of a combination which, like the present, sought the protection and assumed legality of a corporate charter. In that case, various coal companies formed a corporation under the laws of the State of West Virginia, called the Chesapeake and Ohio Fuel Company, to allot between the constituent companies the respective portions of certain interstate trade in their commodity and fix the prices of the same. The opinion was delivered by Circuit Judge (now an associate justice of the Supreme Court) Day. The opinion follows the doctrine of the preceding cases.

As to the question of intent, the court says (p. 623):

> "It is to be remembered in this connection that it is the *effect of the contract upon interstate commerce, not the intention of the parties in entering into it, which determines whether it falls within the prohibition of the statute.*"

As to the suggestion that the coal transported by the combination was a very small percentage of the entire competitive interstate traffic in the commodity (an argument advanced in the case at bar), the court says (p. 623):

> "It is further contended that the competition is such in the market for which this coal is intended, and the coal produced by the operators, parties to this agreement, is such a small fraction of the quantity sold that it can not affect prices materially. It is not required, in order to violate this statute, that a monopoly be created. It is sufficient if that be the necessary tendency of the agreement. In *U. S. v. E. C. Knight Co.*, 156 U. S. 1. 15 Sup. Ct., 249, 39 L. Ed., 325, Chief Justice Fuller said:
>
> 'Again, all the authorities agree that, in order to vitiate a contract or combination, it is not essential that its result be a complete monopoly. It is sufficient if it really tends to that end, and to deprive the public of the advantages which flow from free competition.' "

This comprises the applicable decisions of Federal appellate courts. It is apparent that they cover every phase of the question, and, by an inspection of the answer, every contention urged at the case at bar. Before returning, therefore, to the facts of the present case, it may be desirable to summarize the doctrine of these decisions and then apply them to the facts of the present merger. With this end in view I submit the following propositions:

1. Public policy requires free competition between competing transportation lines and forbids all attempts to restrict such competition or create a monopoly.

2. The police power extends to corporations which are engaged in a public service, and which are, therefore, subject to legislative control so far as become necessary for the protection of the public interests, and it is competent for the legislature of a state with respect to domestic trade, and Congress with respect to interstate trade, to

prohibit either corporations or individuals from combining, either directly or indirectly, to eliminate competition.

3. The purchase of a stock by a railroad corporation in a competing line is contrary to public policy and void, and this even though accomplished by individual stockholders, acting in behalf and for the interests of the purchasing company.

4. Where the direct and necessary result of a given combination is to eliminate competition, and thereby restrain trade, the intent to accomplish that result will be presumed and need not be formally proved.

5. It is not important that the proposed combination does not secure a complete monopoly of a given subject of commerce; a partial monopoly is equally offensive to public policy.

6. The fact that the power of the combination has not been exercised to increase prices or rates is not important. The law is concerned not with what is done, but with the power to do it.

7. The law will look to the substance and not to the form, and will not permit a monopolistic combination, no matter by what corporate or legal device it may be attempted.

8. Corporations as personalities only exist as a fiction of the law and for practical and beneficial purposes which subserve public interests. Where such fiction is invoked to violate criminal statutes or to defeat sound public policy, such fiction will be disregarded and the law will look to the acts of the individuals who control the corporation as the acts of the corporation itself.

9. Therefore, the mere fact that such a consolidation takes the form of a purchase by the stockholders of one company individually of a portion of the capital stock of a competing line will not legalize the transaction, and this notwithstanding the fact that the capital stock so purchased is less than a majority, provided it be purchased with a view to the control of the competing line.

10. The liberty guaranteed by the fifth amendment to purchase and sell property is clearly subject to the police power of the state and nation, and does not sanction pur-

chases and sales of capital stock with a view to a practical consolidation of parallel and competing lines.

It would, therefore, seem clear, under the indisputable facts of this case and the decisions thus reviewed, that all of the defendants did engage in a combination in restraint of interstate trade and that they did seek to monopolize a part of it, and that they intended to do so is conclusively presumed from the admitted facts. Even if the court had the slightest hesitation in reaching this conclusion as to the individual defendants, it could have none as to the Northern Securities Company. It is a "person" under section 8, and, taking over under its broad charter powers nine-twelfths of the Great Northern stock and practically all of the Northern Pacific stock, it absorbed both systems, created a unity of ownership, and thereby restricted trade by the elimination of competition. Courts are too practical to ignore the known and natural results of human action. In dealing with the question, they regard as an axiom the proposition that to remove the motive for competition is to destroy competition itself. It is obvious that the officers of the Great Northern, chosen by the Northern Securities, can have no motive to compete with the officers of the Northern Pacific in the operation of their respective systems, for the prosperity of the Great Northern is the prosperity of the Northern Pacific and vice versa. They have a common owner and a common master, and it is of no practical consequence whether the people use one or the other as a carrier, as the entire proceeds of their joint traffic necessarily go into the common treasury of the Northern Securities Company. To suggest that competition is possible where competition is useless is an absurdity. As previously stated, in the case of *Pearsall v. The Great Northern Railway,* the Supreme Court answered the question by holding that the ownership by the stockholders of the Great Northern Railway of even half of the Northern Pacific Company's capital stock was a virtual amalgamation of their systems, and it follows that where a third company owns all of the Great Northern and owns practically all the Northern Pacific Company, that, *a fortiori,* such restriction of competition,

which is but a convertible term for restraint of trade, has
taken place. Without affirmatively discussing so clear a
proposition, I shall simply review in conclusion the legal
answers which the defendants attempt to make to the
Government's propositions.

The defendants do not seriously dispute the fact of the
practical amalgamation. Both in the answers filed in the
case and in the testimony of their witnesses their case
amounts to little more than one of confession and avoid-
ance. They seek to be relieved from the consequences of
their concerted action upon subtle legal quibbles which,
if sustained by the court, would, as stated in the beginning of this argument, make a dead letter of the Sherman anti-trust law.

1. They contend, in the first place, that it is the right
of each stockholder of the Great Northern and the Northern Pacific to freely dispose of his property at pleasure,
and that such right is guaranteed by the fifth amendment
of the Constitution.

The answer to this is obvious:

(a) Assuming the right to dispose of property, it does
not follow that the stockholders may combine to exercise
that right in a manner that will violate the Federal law
against monopolies. The very essence of the common-law
offense of conspiracy is either to do an unlawful thing, or
to do a perfectly lawful thing in an unlawful manner, and
there are many unlawful conspiracies in which the act of
each individual, taken by itself, would be perfectly lawful, but in which the combination, by reason of its opportunities for oppression, becomes unlawful. The entire
theory of the law as to trusts is built upon this principle,
for in every form of trust or combination in restraint of
trade the gist of the offense is the concerted and therefore
injurious action of individuals, and the individual acts, innocent in themselves, are stamped with illegality because
their joint effect is offensive to public policy.

In *Pennsylvania Railroad Company v. Commonwealth
of Pennsylvania* (7 Atlantic Reporter, 368) the president
of the Pennsylvania Railroad Company and the president
of a projected railroad company, which would compete,

signed a contract, by which the latter agreed to put the control of its company into the hands of persons to be named by the president of the Pennsylvania Railroad Company. This was to be effected by the stockholders of the projected company transferring their shares to the trustee named. It was there argued that the right of stockholders to sell their shares could not be enjoined, but Judge Simonton, in an opinion, which was affirmed by the Supreme Court of Pennsylvania, decided to the contrary.

(b) The case at bar involves more than the mere right of stockholders to sell. Conceding for purposes of argument that some of the defendants who are stockholders can not be held responsible for the sale of their individual holdings, yet, as pointed out by Mr. Justice Brown in *Louisville and Nashville Railroad Co. v. Kentucky* (161 U. S., 677), the legality of such a transaction depends not merely upon the power to sell, but also the power to buy. He says (p. 691):

> Besides this, however, in order to support the proposed consolidation of these two systems, the parties are bound to show not only that the Louisville and Nashville Company was competent to buy, but that the Chesapeake Company was also vested with power to sell. To make a valid contract it is necessary to show that both parties are competent to enter into the proposed stipulations. It is a fundamental principle in the law of contracts that to make a valid agreement there must be a meeting of minds, and, obviously if there be a disability on the part of either party to enter into the proposed contract there can be no valid agreement.

As the act of Congress makes it unlawful for any "person" or "corporation" to monopolize, or attempt to monopolize, interstate traffic, it is obvious that the present pleadings and proof will support a decree against the Northern Securities Company for the act of acquiring practically all of the Great Northern and Northern Pa-

cific stock, even though the court should reach the conclusion that as a matter of abstract theory each stockholder of these two systems had the right to sell his stock.

(c) Stockholders can not, however, veil unlawful acts
under a corporate charter. It is true that as between the
corporation and the stockholders, and for purposes of
corporate government, the law treats the corporation as
a separate entity from the stockholders, but it is unquestioned law that the fiction of a corporation's separate existence can not avail the individuals who compose it as
between them and the state, and especially where the provisions of a remedial or penal statute are concerned. Violations of the law can not be excused under the plea of
charter privileges. This was clearly ruled in the case of
State v. Standard Oil Company (49 Ohio State, 137.), in
which the majority of the stockholders of a corporation
transferred their stocks to certain trustees, under an agreement which was in effect a violation of the anti-trust laws
of that state. Thereupon, the state instituted a proceeding in *quo warranto* to forfeit the charter of the corporation. The defense was made that in point of fact the
creation of the trust was not the act of the corporation
but of individual shareholders. The Supreme Court of
that State overruled this contention, and forcibly stated
the law.

2. The defendants next contend that they are acting
under charter rights, conferred by a sovereign state, with
which the nation is powerless to interfere.

It is well to analyze this contention. A large number
of individuals, scattered throughout the world, but many
of them living in the States of Minnesota, Montana, Idaho,
North Dakota and Washington, were the stockholders of
the two great railway systems which passed through these
states. They are, moreover, citizens of the United States.
The laws of all five states and the laws of the United
States forbid any combination between these competitive
systems which would insure a monopoly of traffic. Forthwith, certain of these stockholders go a thousand miles to
the State of New Jersey, obtain a piece of paper, which
purports to give them the power to obtain the ownership

of these railway systems, and under this pretended power acquire the ownership and ultimate control of both systems. When confronted with the violation of the laws of the states through which the systems pass, and of which many of them are citizens, and with the laws of the United States, of which most of them are citizens, they reply: "We are not individuals, or a combination of individuals; we are simply a single person, namely, a New Jersey corporation. It has given us the power, and we propose to exercise it."

If there were no Federal law in existence, the answer to such contention is obvious. A corporation as a separate entity is purely a fiction, and those who act under it are human and responsible beings, whose obligation to obey existing laws cannot be in any wise affected by the pretended merger of their identity in a paper charter. No state can authorize a combination of men to violate the laws of another state. As Mr. Justice Brown said in the *Pearsall* case, the law cannot recognize a "vested right to do a manifest wrong."

But whatever the powers of the State of New Jersey may be as against the laws of Minnesota, Montana, Idaho, North Dakota and Washington—and fortunately this difficulty of conflicting state powers need not be decided in this case—it is obvious that they are powerless when invoked against the Constitution of the United States. It provides for its own supremacy, and the laws made thereunder, and among these powers, as to which it is supreme, is the power to regulate interstate commerce; and under this power, as was decided in the *Joint Traffic and Trans-Missouri* cases, the Federal anti-trust law has been duly enacted. *It is the supreme law of the land*, the laws of New Jersey to the contrary notwithstanding. Any other view would make the state, through its power to create corporations with indefinite powers, superior to the Federal Government and supreme in matters of legislation. The proposition is indefensible.

Much will doubtless be said by our learned adversaries as to the sacred rights of sovereign states to charter corporations with extensive powers to do business in other states. Doubtless the ingenuity of counsel will endeavor to characterize this suit of the Federal Government as an unjustifiable invasion of the right of the State of New Jersey to form individuals into a corporation in such way and upon such terms as she may think proper. The more charitable view would be that the State of New Jersey has not sought to give a legislative "indulgence" to a corporation to violate the laws of other states and of the Federal Government, and that the sweeping language of the present charter must be read in connection with the general statute laws of New Jersey so that the powers granted are only such as are "for lawful purposes."

Unfortunately for this indulgent view of New Jersey's purposes, the highest court of that state, in the case of *Trenton Potteries Company v. Oliphant* (58 N. J. Eq., 524), has held in effect that the courts may not read into the sweeping provisions of its corporation laws such qualifying sentences as will bring these laws in harmony with the general provisions of law with respect to monopolies. And, unfortunately, too, the executive officers of New Jersey have openly proclaimed the policy of the State to peddle charters to do anything, in any manner, anywhere, and in any way, provided the thirty pieces of silver, for which the interests of the public are to be betrayed, are duly paid to the State.

Unquestionably, this laxity does not concern other states as long as the exercise of these charter privileges is confined to the State which creates them, but it is common knowledge that New Jersey, whose sense of justice was once proverbial, has been the "city of refuge" for those who seek there the privileges denied them by the wholesome laws of other states. I deny *in toto* that New Jersey has any right to send beyond its borders corporations armed with letters of marque and reprisal. Far from seeking to invade state's rights by this proceeding, the Federal Government, as the common guardian of all the states, is seeking to vindicate the integrity of their internal laws, as well as its own, and against the lawless laxity of New Jersey's corporation laws.

Whatever may be the rights of other states with respect to their internal commerce there can be no question as to

the power of the Federal Government to protect interstate commerce from invasion.   In this matter the United
States is dealing with "national highways," and with a
character of commerce as to which its powers are plenary.

Upon the rock of Federal supremacy as to interstate
commerce the Government firmly rests, and, like a house
builded upon a rock, it cannot fall.

3. Defendants contend, however, that the mere ownership of shares by the New Jersey corporation has no direct
or immediate relation to interstate commerce, and, is,
therefore, not within the scope of the Federal power.
Even if this corporation were only a holding corporation,
I could not concede the contention.   As was said in *Gibbons v. Ogden* (9 Wheat., 1):

> "But it is almost laboring to prove a self-evi-
> dent proposition, since the sense of mankind, the
> practice of the world, the contemporaneous as-
> sumption and continued exercise of the power,
> and universal acquiescence have so clearly estab-
> lished the right of Congress over navigation and
> transportation of both men and their goods as
> not only incidental to but actually of the essence
> of the power to regulate commerce."

Transportation is, therefore, commerce, and its vehicles
are instrumentalities of commerce, and as such, when engaged in interstate trade, are so fully within the scope of
the Federal power that Congress may even regulate the
form of brakes used in railway transportation, and the
States may not forbid their entrance into their borders.
*These interstate railway systems, therefore, are Federal in-
strumentalities, their roadbeds are "national highways,"
and their business is essentially interstate commerce.* The
corporations created for their management and operation
are but the method of evidencing ownership and regulating power of control. Prior to the merger, all of the stockholders of the Northern Pacific owned the Northern Pacific. The Northern Pacific property is not pieces of
paper, called shares of stock, but property of intrinsic
value. The capital stock of a corporation is but the

method of measuring the value of these assets, and each certificate is but the evidence of the stockholders' proportionate participation in the assets of the business and its profits. It is true that in the interim between stockholders' meetings the stockholders designate directors as their agents, who operate the property in the stockholders' behalf, but the directors are none the less the servants of the stockholders, and have, and can have, no powers except such as are given to them by the stockholders in accordance with the law of their being. The directors operate the road under directions given by the stockholders at annual meetings, and represent their policy. The stockholders clearly operate the road. Theirs is the "ultimate control." *Qui facit per alium facit per se* is an old axiom of the law, and approved common sense.

The fact that the largest stockholder of the Northern Pacific and the Great Northern is itself a corporation cannot make this less a truth. The stockholders of the Securities Company are the individuals who previously owned the constituent systems. The merger changed the character of their ownership, but not the fact of ownership. To acquire the ownership of Federal instrumentalities of commerce is, therefore, to act directly upon such instrumentalities when such acquisition operates to eliminate competition and create monopoly. As was clearly decided in the Supreme Court cases hereinbefore recited, the law concerns itself not alone with that which is done but with the power to do, and the acquisition by a single person or combination of the full title to competitive inter-state railway systems carries with it the unquestioned power to exercise to the fullest the rights of such ownership and such ownership has an immediate and direct relation to commerce.

I do not admit, however, that this New Jersey corporation is simply a "holding" company. As previously explained, it is an "owning" company with the fullest rights of ownership. It may not merely acquire but it may dispose of the things acquired, and it is further given authority to "do anything" which may be necessary to enhance the value of the securities thus acquired. These remarkable powers must be read in connection with Colonel Clough's testimony as to the difficulty which the defendants had in securing a charter with ample powers; the defendants desired the power not merely to hold the stock of these two competitive systems, but to vote it and thus determine its policy, to collect its dividends and thus enjoy the usufruct, and to do any act which might increase the value of the properties thus jointly acquired. The right to vote the stock operates directly upon interstate commerce, for it necessarily regulates such commerce. At annual meetings of the constituent systems, the Northern Securities Company, through its proxies, can by resolution direct its servants, whom it selects, to increase rates or to lower them, to refuse traffic or to accept it, to give preferences or to decline them, to borrow money or to spend it, to build extensions or abandon existing lines. This power to command constitutes that monopoly of commerce which is not merely directly related to commerce, but is the conduct of commerce itself.

We are not dealing in this case with an abstract power. If the court will look at the exhibits printed in a separate column, it will perceive upon the record an actual exercise of such power, for the Northern Securities Company, at the annual meetings of its constituent companies, voted sufficient of its holdings of stock to direct its policy and select its servants. Whatever, therefore, may be said of the mere abstract acquisition of property, yet, when the right to control the property at annual meetings is actually exercised, the contention is remarkable that the interference with commerce is not direct but only remote and collateral. It may be argued that such exercise of power only takes place at the annual meetings of shareholders, and that in the interim the directors operate the company, and for this proposition the *Pullman Palace Car Company v. Missouri Pacific Company* (115 U. S., 597) case may be cited. But it is obvious that that case had reference to a construction of particular contracts between a railroad company and the Pullman Palace Car Company, and that the question of the actual control of a railroad under the interstate-commerce law and under the Constitution of the United States did not arise.

Some reliance also may be placed upon the case of *United States v. E. C. Knight,* but the distinction between that case and this is obvious. In that case the Sugar Trust purchased the plants and other assets of manufacturing companies, and it was held that manufacturing was not, *per se,* commerce, even though manufactured products might enter into interstate commerce; but we are here dealing with transportation, which, as Justice Johnson said in *Gibbons v. Ogden,* is as indistinguishable from commerce "as vital motion is from vital existence." Transportation being commerce, its instruments are federal instrumentalities when engaged in interstate traffic, and the federal power assuredly extends to the master as well as to the servant engaged in such commerce.

The full extent of this power is well set forth in the Lottery Case (*Champion v. Ames,* 188 U. S. 321) recently decided by the Supreme Court, and as to which I may be presumed to have some knowledge, as I had the honor of representing the Government. In that case Mr. Justice Harlan quotes with approval the opinion of Chief Justice Waite in *Pensacola Telegraph Company v. Western Union Telegraph Company* (96 U. S., p. 1), as follows:

> "The powers thus granted are not confined to the instrumentalities of commerce, or the postal service known or in use when the Constitution was adopted, but they keep pace with the progress of the country, and adapt themselves to the new developments of time and circumstances. They extend from the horse with its rider to the stage coach, from the sailing vessel to the steamboat, from the coach and the steamboat to the railroad, and from the railroad to the telegraph, as these new agencies are successively brought into use to meet the demands of increasing population and wealth. They were intended for the government of the business to which they relate at all times and under all circumstances. As they

were intrusted to the General Government for
the good of the nation, it is not only the right,
but the duty, of Congress to see to it that intercourse among the States and the transmission
of intelligence are not obstructed or unnecessarily encumbered by State legislation."

It is obvious, therefore, that the driver of the stage
coach, who, in colonial days, carried freight and passengers from state to state, was engaged in interstate commerce, and while thus engaged was subject to the regu-
lative power of Congress. A firm or corporation owning
such stage coach thus employed as an interstate common
carrier could not be less subject to Federal power than an
individual owner.

If one owner subjects himself to Federal power by engaging in interstate commerce, then a hundred owners
who act collectively equally do. Legislation has heretofore been directed toward the governing board of the carrier as the most direct method to enforce the provisions
of law, but it does not follow that mandatory provisions
of law could not be directed with equal validity to the
owners themselves.

For the courts to assume to discriminate between owner
and employee would be, I think, most mischievous. In
another court room of this building, a learned and able
Federal judge is hearing an injunction proceeding in which
the right of organized labor to affect the movements of
interstate trains is directly under discussion. I know nothing about the merits of that case, and would of course
express no opinion concerning them. It is enough to say
that under Federal decisions, notably *In re Debs,* that those
who control organized labor, even though they be neither
employees nor stockholders of an interstate carrier, and
have, therefore, no direct relation to it, can yet be enjoined, if they seek by combination to induce the employees
of such carrier to prevent its operation by organized
violence. Shall it be said that the law is impotent to reach
the owners, when they combine to restrict competition?
I know of no decision that would cause greater social discontent than a decision which would uphold the absolute

and drastic power of the Federal Government by injunction when invoked against the employees, and, on the other hand, abdicate power as to the masters of these employees. The law knows no such distinction, and it has no respect of persons. It sweeps away the obstructions to interstate commerce without respect to those who place them there.

It is too late a day to deny the plenary power of the Federal Government over interstate and foreign commerce. This power is "vested in Congress as absolutely as it would be in a single government having as its constitution the same restrictions on the exercise of the power as are found in the Constitution of the United States." (Mr. Justice Johnson in *Gibbons v. Ogden,* cited with approval by Mr. Justice Harlan in the *Lottery Case*).

All interstate railroads are treated as national highways, and while a State may create a corporation to engage in interstate commerce, or to occupy these national highways, yet when such corporations do so, they are subject to the plenary power of Congress, any condition of their charter or any regulation of the State of their incorporation to the contrary notwithstanding. Thus, the Supreme Court affirmed the power of a State to form a corporation to construct an interstate bridge, but it denied the power of the State to regulate the tolls for passage over the bridge which the corporation exacted. (*Covington Bridge Co. v. Kentucky,* 154 U. S., 204).

Under this power it has not only chartered interstate railways, but, in point of fact, chartered by the act of July 2, 1864, (13 Stats., 365), the Northern Pacific Railroad Company, to which one of the defendants has succeeded. Having chartered it, it exercised absolute rights over its regulation. It imposed upon the corporation the duty to "construct, furnish, maintain, and enjoy a continuous railroad and telegraph line" (sec. 1). It provided that "a uniform gauge shall be established throughout the entire length of the road" (sec. 5); and it required the operation of a telegraph line along the entire line provided, with the proviso that the rates charged to the Government shall not be higher than for individuals (sec. 5). It required the Northern Pacific "to permit any other railroad which shall be authorized to be built by the United States or by the legislature of any Territory or State in which the same may be situated, to form running connection with it, on fair and reasonable terms" (sec. 5). It prohibited the corporation from making a mortgage or lien (sec. 10). By the later act of June 25, 1868 (15 Stats., 79), it required the company to make annual reports to the Secretary of the Interior.

Congress has, however, rarely exercised this plenary power over interstate railways however incorporated. This policy of inaction, however, was practically abandoned on the passage of the commerce act of 1887, which constituted the Interstate Commerce Commission, with its advisory powers over every detail of interstate transportation. It requires rates to be reasonable; prohibits unjust and unreasonable charges; prohibits preferences to persons or to localities and discriminations; requires equal facilities for the interchange of traffic; prohibits a greater charge for a short haul than for a long haul; prohibits pooling contracts; requires the publication of rates; forbids the change of rates except upon public notice; requires publicity as to rates; prohibits the collection of charges other than the established rates, and requires full reports.

If, therefore, Congress can charter corporations to engage in interstate commerce, and if it has plenary power to regulate the manner in which citizens shall engage in interstate commerce, and if it can provide that corporations created by states which engage in interstate traffic shall only do so in the manner and under conditions which Congress prescribes, then assuredly it must have power to prevent an attempt, either on the part of individuals or of state-made corporations, to monopolize interstate commerce. The Federal power will not "strain at a gnat and swallow a camel."

3. Defendants may contend that the testimony fails to establish a specific intent to violate the statute.

Where the nature of the act itself is a violation of the statute, no formal proof of intent is necessary; it will be conclusively presumed. In this, as in any legal matter, no one can escape responsibility for his conscious acts by the plea that he did not intend to do them. The formation of the Northern Securities Company, with its capital stock equivalent to the combined value of the Great Northern and the Northern Pacific, as fixed by the defendants, and the subsequent acquisition of practically all of said stock, and the direct acquisition of both systems by one corporation and the unity of control thereby resulting, are acts of unmistakable meaning, and the intent to do them follows irresistibly.

Even if formal proof of intent were necessary, it is respectfully contended, without reciting the testimony, that the testimony of Hill, Morgan, and Clough clearly show the purpose to unite the control of both roads in a common corporation, and thus create a monopoly of theretofore competitive traffic.

4. Defendants further contend that in fact they have only done that which others have done both before and subsequent to the passage of the Sherman Act. In other words, they make the extraordinary plea that their unlawful act should suffer no interference at the hands of the law because others have been guilty of the same violations of the law. It may be admitted that long prior to the Federal legislation in question there had been a steady process of consolidation between the great railway interests of the country. Many of these consolidations were in no sense restrictive of commerce but were legitimate and healthy extensions of existing lines. Others were specifically authorized by States within whose borders the railways run. Others took place before the passage of the Federal antitrust law, and could not be governed by its provisions. Apart from this, and conceding *arguendo* the existence of other violations, the absurdity of the argument that a man can claim immunity because others had been guilty of a similar violation, is so transparent that defendant's counsel seek to hide it under the suggestion that this testimony is offered to prove a contemporaneous construction of the statute.

As to this it is enough to say:

Contemporaneous construction as a method of interpreting statutes is only available when uniform and of long continuance.

It is only of value where the language of the statute is ambiguous.

In the case of *United States* v. *Graham* (110 U. S., 219), a statute provided certain mileage, and made no distinction in traveling in and traveling out of the country. It was found as a fact that from the time the act was passed, in 1835, until the decision there had been a uniform departmental practice to distinguish between traveling outside of the country and traveling inside of the country. Chief Justice Waite held that the language of the act was entirely clear, and that the uniform interpretation put upon it to the contrary by the executive officers of the Government for a period of fifty years could not affect the act. He said:

> "Such being the case, it matters not what the practice of the Departments may have been or how long continued, for it can only be resorted to in aid of interpretation, and it is not allowable to interpret what has no need of interpretation. If there were ambiguity or doubt, then such a practice, begun so early and continued so long, would be in the highest degree persuasive, if not absolutely controlling in its effect. But with language clear and precise and with its meaning evident there is no room for construction, and consequently no need of anything to give it aid."

In *Fairbank v. United States* (181 U. S., 283), the limitations of the doctrine of contemporaneous construction are fully suggested and discussed. In that case, the court set aside a uniform construction of nearly a century, on the ground that the language of Congress was free from doubt.

The antitrust law of 1890 is of recent passage and has been the subject of considerable litigation. Many suits have been instituted under it, but it cannot be fairly said that the Government has acquiesced in any construction of its provisions. Certainly no instance is cited in the list of supposed violations of the law where two corporations have transferred nearly all of their capital stock to a third corporation created expressly for the purpose of insuring a perpetual unity of ownership. Such is the present case. Until it can be shown that a similar case exists upon which no executive action was taken, the argument from contemporaneous construction becomes wholly untenable. Even if such a case could be cited, the action or non-action of the officers of the Government cannot nullify the will of Congress.

5. It is next suggested that although the merger does restrict to some extent competition in interstate traffic, yet that such traffic is but a small percentage of all the traffic of these two roads, and therefore should be disregarded on the principle of *de minimis*.

It is to be observed that the act expressly makes it an offense to monopolize or attempt to monopolize "any part" of commerce. Even assuming that the competitive interstate traffic was only two or three per cent of the total of the defendants, yet that in itself means a considerable volume of traffic, and, as to those who are unjustly deprived of the benefits of competition, it is as harmful as though it were a hundred per cent of the entire traffic. However, the elaborate tables offered by the defendant, which purport to establish the percentage, are misleading, for they refer exclusively to stations within the lines of the companies, and wholly ignore the vast volume of transcontinental traffic which originates on other roads to the east of the eastern termini or to the west of the western termini. The entire traffic which the Burlington sends over the lines of the Northern Pacific and the Great Northern, and which was sufficient in volume to justify them in paying over $200,000,000 to acquire the Burlington, is wholly ignored in determining to what extent competitive traffic is affected by this merger.

The court need, however, do no more than inspect the map, which is found on page 504, vol. 2, of the Record. In *Louisville and Nashville R. R. v. Kentucky* (161 U. S., 677), Mr. Justice Brown determined the competitive nature of the traffic by such inspection, and the map in the present shape clearly shows that these two systems are competitors for nearly 2,000 miles, and stretching from the Great Lakes to Puget Sound. They have common eastern and western termini, and, as to all transcontinental traffic, were competitors prior to the merger. If positive testimony is needed, the testimony of Mr. Mellon, president of the Northern Pacific, would be sufficient.

6. The defendants further contend that though the merger does restrict interstate commerce, it accomplishes beneficial purposes in the development of traffic. This is the familiar argument of the beneficence of monopoly. It should be addressed to Congress and not to the courts. The benefit to the people of this merger may be all that its master spirit, Mr. James J. Hill (for whose far-reaching and empire-building plans I, personally, have both respect and admiration), claims it to be, but I apprehend that the people will continue to entertain their old-fashioned prejudice against monopoly, and the arguments addressed to the courts will fall upon as deaf ears in this respect as when addressed to the legislatures and peoples of the States immediately affected. If the merger be so beneficial, the emphatic protests of the executive officers of five States would seem to be unnecessary. However, these questions are all for the legislative and not the judicial branch of the Government. The courts already have enough *quasi*-legislative powers, whose burden is heavy, not to willingly assume a supervisory power over the wisdom or folly of legislation. It is possible that the concentration of property interests, including railroad transportation, is an economic tendency as irresistible as gravitation. It is possible that the law itself will be as impotent to stop it as to affect by legislative enactment the procession of the stars. This, however, neither the officers of the law, nor the courts charged with the duty of interpreting and enforcing it, can recognize. The American people are both conservative and practical, and when they recognize that monopoly is beneficent and competition is an evil, they will repeal existing laws and by positive legislation facilitate and legalize railway monopoly. Until that time, the law should be fairly, fully, and impartially enforced,

for it is everlastingly true that the imperative need of this country, both at the hands of capital and of labor, is not more law, but more obedience to law.

The noble founder of Pennsylvania, in speaking of the great Commonwealth that he had founded on the banks of the Delaware, said:

> "That government is free to the people under it where the laws rule and the people are a party to those laws, and all the rest is tyranny, oligarchy, and confusion."

This simple statement expresses the "whole law and the prophets" of free government. A generation ago countless thousands died that government by the people should not perish from the earth. It should never be forgotten that it may be threatened from within as from without, and that its mighty purposes can be defeated as readily by judicial decision or executive inaction as by open foe. In the case at bar the United States stands for the enforcement of the laws. The wisdom of these laws must not be questioned, or their purposes defeated by judicial decision. However public spirited the purposes of the defendants in forming this merger may have been, and whatever its resultant good or evil, it clearly violates existing laws, whose provisions must be enforced, unless government by the people is to be justly deemed a self-confessed failure. It has never been a failure and will not be, I confidently predict in the case at bar, which I now submit to the Court with my deep appreciation of the patience with which your Honors have heard me.

XIV

THE GREAT LAKES CONTROVERSY

One of the greatest functions of the Federal Government is to compose quarrels between the States in matters which are not, as such, within the province of the Federal Government, but which are reserved to the States. The Constitution contains a clause which permits the States to make treaties with each other, but always subject to the consent of Congress, and it further created a Supreme Court, before which, as before an international tribunal of arbitration, the sovereign States could litigate their differences. As the Supreme Court has largely answered its primary purpose of interpreting the Constitution, it is not strange that its great function as an international tribunal is assuming an ever-larger importance in its work.

Since the beginning of the government, a large number of suits have been brought by States against other States, as original actions in the Supreme Court. Possibly the most important of these is the case, which is still pending, in which the States of Wisconsin, Minnesota, Ohio, Pennsylvania and New York are litigating against the States of Illinois, Missouri, Kentucky, Tennessee, Mississippi and Louisiana. The question relates to the right of the State of Illinois to make a diversion of the waters of Lake Michigan into the Mississippi watershed, not only for sanitary purposes, but also to create a great waterway from the Lakes to the Gulf.

This case has taken several forms and has already been the subject of three opinions by the Supreme Court. In order to ascertain the facts of the case, the Court referred the matter to a former associate and since appointed Chief Justice of the Court, Charles Evans Hughes, and the following argument was made on June 2, 1927, by Mr. Beck before the Special Master to sustain his contention that the regulation of commerce was a political and not a justiciable question.—EDITOR.

My colleagues have graciously assigned to me the privilege of arguing the fundamental question of law, which underlies this great controversy between sovereign States. That question involves no less than the authority, power and dignity of the United States. Its Government is more deeply interested in the proper solution of this controversy than the complainant and respondent States collectively can possibly be.

We have been reminded that the complainant States contain thirty millions of people, but in the adequate solution of this problem more than one hundred million people are deeply concerned, and for these, only the United States can speak.

It is, therefore, amazing that this case should proceed to judgment in the absence of the United States, for the attempt of the complainants to litigate their rights without paying the United States the scant respect of making it a defendant, is to produce the play of Hamlet without the character of Hamlet.

For this unprecedented and unjustified omission the respondents are not responsible. They did not choose the parties to the controversy, the form of proceedings or the forum. The complainants in deciding these questions refused to implead the only Government which has exclusive and plenary authority in the matter. Upon their heads, then, be the consequences of this fatal omission.

To prevent an irresponsible suit of this character by individual States, the Congress has expressly provided that any action to remove an obstruction to navigable waters must be instituted by the Attorney General of the United States. (Act of March 3, 1899, Section 12, 30 Stat. at L. 1151). On this ground, alone, respondents could confidently ask the dismissal of this action. Even if this informality were waived, the inescapable fact would still confront the Master that the rights of the United States cannot be litigated in its absence.

I shall not, however, discuss these questions of procedure, important and controlling as they are, but shall address myself to the "height of the great argument" by contending that under both principle and authority the respondents need no other or better shield of defense than the express authorization, which Congress, through its administrative officer, gave to the Sanitary District to divert the waters of Lake Michigan.

Any other conclusion, as I will presently show, cannot be reconciled with the long line of Supreme Court decisions, which, without shadow of turning, have sustained the plenary and exclusive power of the United States to determine and control the uses of its navigable waters.

Beginning with the case of *Gibbons vs. Ogden,* decided more than a century ago, and culminating in a suit between the *United States vs. The Sanitary District* in respect to this very matter, in which the complainants, then participating as *amici curiae,* urged the paramount authority of the United States, the current of authority is unbroken. To reverse it now is a more difficult feat than to reverse the current of the Chicago River.

In the complexity of its issues of fact, few, if any, more important cases than the instant case have ever arisen in the courts of this country. The testimony has taken a wide range of human speculation, and some of it, in its scientific hypotheses and mathematical estimates, has almost reached the limits of human thought. Time and again complainants' counsel, with the frenzied license of the poet, have attempted to give "airy nothings a local habitation and a name." And yet, despite all the formidable tomes of testimony, the inescapable fact remains that the case could be disposed of on the averments of the bill, or upon the single undisputed fact as given in evidence, that the Sanitary District is doing nothing that has not the express authorization of the Federal Government. In this respect, the testimony may be likened to the subject matter of the controversy, the Great Lakes, for its superficial area is out of all proportion to its depth.

The great patience, with which the Master has heard the testimony for a period of nearly six months, and the industry and skill, with which complainants' counsel have attempted to prove a vast volume of irrelevant facts, should not, however, blind the Master to the conclusion that the complainant States have wholly mistaken their forum. Their testimony should have been addressed in the first instance to the Secretary of War, as the administrative representative of Congress, or to Congress itself. Indeed, much of this testimony has been considered many times by Congress and its appropriate Committees, and never in the last quarter of a century has either Congress or the Secretary of War denied to the Sanitary District the right to make some diversion of the waters of Lake Michigan for the purposes of the Sanitary Canal.

We base, therefore, the defense, not merely upon the legal power of the Federal Government, but upon a compelling equity, which would induce this court, if it had judicial duty in this controversy, to refuse, as a court of equity, its sanction to any such gross breach of faith as would necessarily follow the issuance of the injunction herein prayed for.

Only one governmental power is competent to revoke this permit, and that is the political department of the Government, which gave it. To complainants' counsel we therefore say:

> "Til thou cans't rail the seal from off the bond,
> Thou but offends't thy lungs to speak so loud."

Our opponents may reply that this was the language of Shylock, but certainly there is nothing in this case that likens Chicago to Shylock. It is not Chicago that is asking a pound of flesh. At the instance of the complainants, the Federal Government has exacted from Chicago conditions which, I venture to say, are without any precedent in the history of American municipalities. We are not complaining of the terms, which the Secretary of War imposed as the conditions of the diversion. He was obliged to take into consideration the welfare of the complainants as well as of the respondents and, indeed, of the whole American people. In the exercise of a political discretion, vested in him by Congress, he provided a temporary solution of a difficult problem, and did so in the common interest of all.

But we confidently submit that if the Federal Government, either through its political department or in this proceeding through its judicial department, should break faith with Chicago and, having taken the benefits of the agreement, refuse Chicago the benefits of the diversion, the analogy of Shylock might not be wholly inappropriate.

In the relations of the States as between themselves and in the greater relation of the Federal Govrnment to the

States, there is the solemn obligation and the highest duty
of good faith, and there would be a gross breach of faith,
if the understanding between the United States and Chicago for the temporary solution of this difficult problem
were treated as a "scrap of paper." Such a result is to me
unthinkable.

This case, however, involves considerations even greater
and deeper than this question of good faith. In this, as
in any case, it is supremely important that the division
of powers between the three departments of the Government should be strictly observed. The vice of complainants' case is that it asks this court to regulate commerce,
although the Constitution vests that power exclusively
in Congress, and Congress, through the power delegated
to the Secretary of War, has settled the problem.

Our learned opponents are not unconscious of this answer to their suit, and on this account have urged in different forms that this is not a case in law or equity, but
an arbitration between sovereign nations and as such to be
determined by some undefined and nebulous principles of
policy, which influence independent nations in such arbi-
trations to compose their differences.

There are fugitive expressions in some opinions of the
Supreme Court—largely *obiter dicta*—which, read super-
ficially and in the absence of the context, suggest that any
cause of controversy between sovereign nations, however
non-justiciable it may be, may be made the subject of a
suit in the Supreme Court between the States of the Union,
and that the court is empowered to direct any solution
that may be necessary to compose such differences.

This is a serious constitutional heresy. It is in the first
place founded upon a false predicate, to which little or no
attention has been paid. The States of the Union are not
and never have been strictly and fully sovereign states.
To call them such has always been a misnomer.

Before the Revolution they were the common colonial
dependencies of the British Empire. When the first Continental Congress formed a provisional government, however inchoate it was, the Colonies to some extent had
yielded their sovereignty. They surrendered more by the

Articles of Confederation. Under the Constitution of the United States they yielded all of their sovereignty in the sphere of power vested in the United States.

It is misleading, therefore, to compare a controversy between States, which are linked together in a common Union, and which, since the Constitution, have had their powers distinctly delimited, with a controversy between wholly independent sovereign nations, which have no common allegiance and which must, therefore, adjust their quarrels as best they can. It is an even greater heresy to suggest that the States in creating the Constitution and thereby surrendering their powers to make war against each other, had thereby authorized the Supreme Court to make any adjustment of their differences, which might be necessary to compose their quarrels.

In the case of *Pacific Telephone Co. vs. Oregon*, 223 U. S. 118, Chief Justice White, after reviewing "the settled distinction * * * between judicial authority over justiciable controversies and legislative power as to purely political questions," as first stated in *Luther vs. Borden*, 7 Howard 1, and after referring to the argument in that case that the judiciary could differ with the judgment of the President as to the manner of discharging his great responsibility, quoted the following vigorous answer of the Supreme Court in that case to such a contention:

> *"If the judicial power extends so far, the guarantee contained in the Constitution of the United States is a guarantee of anarchy, and not of order."*

The Supreme Court has held that it can only consider a case, if it be of a *justiciable* character and admits of a *judicial* remedy.

If it be political in its nature, the only remedy is for the States, in a matter within their reserved powers, to compose their own differences and then to submit them to Congress for ratification.

The leading case of *Louisiana vs. Texas*, 176 U. S., 1, presented a "controversy" between States, which threatened good relations between the two States and, to that extent, the harmony of the Union. Louisiana filed a bill against the State of Texas and her health officer, and contended that, under the pretense of executing the quarantine laws of Texas, that State and its health officer were virtually discriminating against the port of New Orleans by refusing entry to its vessels on the pretended ground of yellow fever in New Orleans, although it admitted vessels from other ports where the plague was far more prevalent. Louisiana, therefore, averred a deliberate discrimination against its chief port of entry by an abuse of a reserved power of the State over quarantine regulations.

This court held that one State could not sue another State on the alleged ground of an abuse of law by a public official of the defendant State. Here was a case where a real controversy existed between the States of a character which, as between independent nations, might well result in war, and if the judicial power is as broad as the complainants in the instant case now contend, a controversy was presented involving a breach of comity, which, as between truly sovereign nations, might lead either to arbitration or war.

After discussing the authorities Chief Justice Fuller concluded:

> "*Jurisdiction over controversies of that sort does not embrace the determination of political questions,* and, where no controversy exists between States, it is not for this court to restrain the Governor of a State in the discharge of his executive function in a matter lawfully confided to his discretion and judgment."

Moreover, there can be no controversy between constituent States in respect to a subject matter, which is not within their governmental competence.

They cannot litigate with each other as to the manner in which the Federal Government shall regulate interstate commerce.

In *South Carolina vs. Georgia*, 93 U. S. 4, it appeared, that prior to the Constitution, a compact was made by

South Carolina and Georgia, under which a branch of the Savannah River was made the boundary line between the two States, and the navigation of the river over a specified channel was provided for. The Federal Government by Act of June 23, 1874, had appropriated $50,000 "for the improvement of the Savannah River." This court dismissed the suit on the ground that neither South Carolina nor Georgia had any further power in the matter, since the power over this navigable waterway had been vested in the Federal Government.

Once again the subject came before this court in the first case involving the present defendant, the Sanitary District. I refer to *Missouri vs. Sanitary District*, 180 U. S., 208.

In that case Missouri sought to enjoin Illinois from polluting its river by the use of the sanitary district canal. In an elaborate opinion by Mr. Justice Shiras, this Court again reviewed all the decisions. It sustained its own jurisdiction because of the averment of the bill of a direct injury to the health of the people of Missouri by the pollution of the river. This was regarded as presenting a controversy of a justiciable character, but it gave no countenance to the suggestion that *any* differençe between States gives jurisdiction to this court and that the court is authorized by the Constitution to make any decree that seems necessary in the interest of harmony. The decision was obviously based upon the fact that no question of navigation or commerce presented itself in that case, and the Federal Government had no direct duty in respect to a question of pollution.

This court cannot take jurisdiction of an alleged controversy between the States in respect to a matter, as to which no State has any power under the Constitution, and that even if the subject matter of the controversy be one which is within the reserved rights of the States, it is nevertheless not a "controversy" within the meaning of the Constitution, unless it be susceptible of a judicial determination under known principles of law and by judicial remedies.

Notwithstanding the broad language of the Constitution, this court remains a court. It is not an academic forum or a council of conciliation, or even an international tribunal of arbitration. It is not the judicial branch of a League of Nations, whose judgments are measured only by its own caprices and benevolent disposition.

Even though there be a "controversy," it must present a "case in law or equity." The fugitive *obiter dicta* in some opinions, to which I have referred, and which were largely used, *arguendo,* by the learned Justices in sustaining the power of the court to entertain original jurisdiction in a proper case, mean little more than that such litigation cannot in respect to procedure be determined solely by the narrow rules that govern litigations between individuals. The great philosopher of the court, Mr. Justice Holmes, has said that the susceptibilities of a State are something more than those of an individual, but due regard for such susceptibilities cannot destroy the Constitution.

Therefore, the Supreme Court, as in this case, is slow to dismiss a suit, even though the bill of complaint be plainly inadequate, and it refuses to apply as between quasi-sovereign states narrow and technical rules of evidence. It is nevertheless true that all that has been delegated to this court is "judicial power," and not legislative or executive power, and that judicial power means the power to judge between the States under recognized principles of law and in cases where the remedy is one which the court can give without usurping powers which have been delegated to other branches of the government.

I therefore address myself to the great question, which underlies the whole argument, and that is that such a regulation is essentially a *political* and not a *judicial* function, and therefore that this court, under the grant of "judicial power," is wholly incompetent to make such a regulation of commerce as would result if the court granted the relief prayed for.

The regulation of waterways for purposes of navigation has always been peculiarly a political question, and the Constitution in more than one paragraph manifests the unmistakable purpose to leave an essentially political question to a political body, which, being responsible to the people, can be best trusted to act in the common interest of all. The only relation, which the judiciary ever bears to it, is the purely auxiliary one of interpreting and enforcing regulations of trade, which either exist at common law or by positive statutes.

Commercial intercourse is the very basis of civilization. From the dawn of history and even in prehistoric times the construction of roads, whether by land or water, has been one of the primary and principal political functions of the State.

The facilities of transportation concern the life of the state, and involve the relations of nations. Today the thoughtful student gives less attention to the personal history of dynasties and far more to what is now called the economic interpretation of history. Rome became the greatest empire of ancient times, as much through her genius for the construction of roads as for her martial power, and England, the greatest world empire of modern times, has maintained its proud position in the councils of the nations almost wholly through its domination of the waterways of the world.

Of all methods of intercommunication, one of the oldest and most practicable was the water route. It is this circumstance that has given such political significance to the sea power, as Admiral Mahan has shown in his classic book on that subject. Individual nations have grouped themselves about inland seas and cities have grown upon river banks.

From the earliest times, in recorded history, the genius of man has supplemented the natural waterways by canals. Few mechanical achievements of man are older.

Egypt, the cradle of civilization, had canals ten thousand years ago. Babylon's greatness was due to her canals, the greatest of which is said to have been over seven hundred miles long. China has had its canals since the dawn of history, and the Grand Canal, which connects the Yangtze-Kiang to the Pei-Ho, was nearly one thousand miles long. If Marco Polo is to be believed, it was the

Chinese who first constructed the lock which enabled a vessel to be raised from one level to another.

Long before the Suez Canal and nearly fourteen centuries before Christ, the Mediterranean and the Red Seas were connected by canal. Rome connected the Rhone with the Mediterranean by a canal, and one of the earliest of the Caesars made the Eternal City a seaport by means of a canal from the Tiber to the sea.

The union of distant waterways by a canal has in all periods of history been the dream of sagacious empire builders. Long before the Rhine was connected with the Danube, Charlemagne had conceived the idea. The greatest contribution of France is the canal which connects the Bay of Biscay with the Mediterranean. To France also must be given the credit of the first attempt to connect the Atlantic and Pacific Oceans by a canal, and it remained for Theodore Roosevelt to realize the majestic dream of De Lesseps. England holds its vast empire today partly through the Suez Canal, and all her political policies are constantly shaped by the necessity of preserving this link between her island empire—that "precious jewel set in a silver sea"—and the mighty empire of India. These artificial waterways have appealed to the imagination of the myriad-minded men of history, for one of the great canal builders was Leonardo Da Vinci, and Michelangelo could forget his sculptor's chisel and his painter's brush to solve similar mechanical problems.

If this controlling influence of commerce and the purely political nature of its problems be true of other countries, it is peculiarly true of America, and has been so from the very beginning. Its discovery was due to an attempt to secure a waterway to India. The very character of its colonization has always been influenced by trade routes. Its political problems from the beginning have been influenced and at times controlled by regulations of commerce. No trade route has had either an older or a more continuing influence upon the development of America than the connection of the Great Lakes with the Gulf of Mexico through the mighty channel of the Mississippi River. Joliet as early as 1673 perceived the immense possibilities of the Lakes-to-the-Gulf route, and both La Salle and Father Dablon suggested even in those primitive days the feasibility of avoiding the short portage from the Chicago River to the Des Plaines by the construction of a canal. Thus, long before there was a State of Illinois or a City of Chicago, the water route from the Lakes-to-the-Gulf had not only been conceived as a possibility, but in favorable seasons of the year was used as a natural water-way by Indians, trappers and fur-traders.

The philosophic student of history realizes the immense influence which the valleys of the Ohio and Mississippi had in shaping the destiny of our country and, indeed, in determining the fate of Europe. Modern history might have been differently written if a young Virginian soldier, George Washington, had not been directed to go to the Ohio Valley and order the French to vacate. This fateful circumstance induced England to make war against France, and, in the war of the Spanish succession to espouse the cause of Frederick the Great instead of aligning herself with France and Austria in defeating the pretensions of the Hohenzollern. Had Frederick the Great then been defeated, as he nearly was and would have been, but for the aid of England, there might have been no Hohenzollern dynasty, and possibly no World War.

It was to insure the free navigation of the Mississippi that Jefferson swallowed his constitutional scruples and purchased from Napoleon a trans-Mississippi territory of over a million square miles for a song.

The Mississippi has always exercised an immense influence upon the destiny of America. Its control and regulation have been matters of solicitude to our statesmen. Often our foreign policies have been determined and our domestic political issues shaped by questions, to which the Father of Waters has given rise. Generations come and go, political policies appear and disappear, but "Ole Man River" flows on to the discomfiture of statesmen and nations.

Our foreign and domestic political issues have always been shaped and defined by economic questions, which grow out of regulations of commerce, whether by internal improvement, protective tariffs, or commercial treaties. Even when our country was a feeble congeries of states on the Atlantic seaboard, and its statesmen regarded the Appalachian Range as our inevitable western boundary, yet there were sagacious men, who looked beyond the Alleghanies and saw that in the undeveloped wilderness to the west lay the future greatness of America, if convenient trade routes could be provided.

Of these none exceeded, either in practical interest or far-seeing sagacity, George Washington. The construction of canals had an especial fascination for him. He was the first colonial statesman to advocate the linking of the Atlantic coast with the Mississippi Valley. His correspondence shows that the possibilities of water routes to develop and cement the union of the colonies were constantly in his mind. As early as 1774 he introduced a bill in the Virginia House of Burgesses for the improvement of the navigation of the Potomac for 150 miles beyond tidewater. On his victorious return from the war he again plunged into the subject, which had fascinated him from the time, when on horseback he had penetrated into the unknown wilderness beyond the Alleghanies.

In a letter to Edmund Randolph, in 1785, he said:

> "The great objective for which I wish is for the navigation of the Rivers James and Potomac extended to connect the western territory with the Atlantic States. *All others to me are secondary.*"

He was the founder and president of the Potomac Company, which sought to connect the headwaters of the Potomac with Lake Erie. His vision predicted the possibility of a waterway route from the Potomac to Detroit, when the latter was only a military outpost. Always a broadminded American, his interest was not confined to the transportation route for his native state, for he advocated, long before Clinton, the practicability of a water connection between Lake Erie and the Hudson River.

Writing on October 10, 1784, to the Governor of Virginia, Washington, having traced out for him the different routes and distances from the Potomac to Detroit and having emphasized the economic value to Virginia of some connection with the "fur and peltry trade of the Lakes, and for the produce of the country which lies within," then added:

> "But in my opinion there is a political consideration for so doing, which is of still greater importance. I need not remark to you, Sir, that the flanks and rear of the United States are possessed by other powers, and formidables ones too; nor how necessary it is to apply the cement of interest to bind all parts of the Union together by indissoluble bonds, especially that part of it, which lies immediately west of us, with the middle states. For what ties, let me ask, should we have upon those people? How entirely unconnected with them shall we be, and what troubles may we not apprehend, if the Spaniards on their right, and Great Britain on their left, instead of throwing stumbling-blocks in their way, as they now do, should hold out lures for their trade and alliance? What, when they get strength, which will be sooner than most people conceive (from the emigration of foreigners, who will have no particular predilection towards us, as well as from the removal of our own citizens), will be the consequence of their having formed close connexions with both or either of those powers, in a commercial way? It needs not, in my opinion, the gift of prophecy to foretell."

In another letter to David Humphreys, dated July 25, 1785, Washington wrote:

> "My attention is more immediately engaged in a project, which I think big with great political, as well as commercial consequences to these states, especially the middle ones; it is by removing the obstructions and extending the inland

navigation of our rivers, to bring the states on the Atlantic in close connexion with those forming to the westward, by a short and easy transportation. Without this, I can easily conceive they will have different views, separate interests, and other connexions. I may be singular in my ideas, but they are these; that, to open a door to, and make easy the way for, those settlers to the westward (which ought to progress regularly and compactly) before we make any stir about the navigation of the Mississippi, and before our settlements are far advanced towards that river, would be our true line of policy."

His political sagacity was further indicated by the fact that, when nearly all his contemporaries were worried about Spain's control of the free navigation of the Mississippi, he perceived that the immediate problem was to develop and populate the hinterland east of the Mississippi and then the navigation of that river would take care of itself. Thus he writes to Richard Henry Lee, on August 22, 1785:

"However singular the opinion may be, I cannot divest myself of it, that the navigation of the Mississippi, at this time, ought to be no object with us. On the contrary, until we have a little time allowed to open and make easy the ways between the Atlantic States and the western territory, the obstruction had better remain. There is nothing that binds one county or one State to another, but interest. Without this cement the western inhabitants, who more than probably will be composed in a great degree of foreigners, can have no predilection for us, and a commercial connexion is the only tie we can have upon them. It is clear to me, that the trade of the Lakes, and of the River Ohio, as low as the Great Kanawa if not to the Falls, may be brought to the Atlantic ports easier and cheaper, taking the whole voyage together, than it can be carried to New Orleans; but, once open the door to the latter before the obstructions are removed from the former, let commercial connexions, which lead to others, be formed, and the habit of that trade well established, and it will be found no easy matter to divert it; and vice versa. When the settlements are stronger and more extended to the westward, the navigation of the Mississippi will be an object of importance, and we shall then be able, (reserving our claims,) to speak a more efficacious language, than policy, I think, dictates at present."

Our nation came into being by reason of a dispute with the Mother Country over restricted trade relations. The exact nature of that controversy is not always correctly understood. Prior to the Revolution the general principle, which regulated the Mother Country toward its colonial offspring, was that each colony should have complete freedom in its local affairs, but that matters of general concern and especially the regulation of foreign trade and industry should be within the exclusive control of parliament. Few, if any, of the colonial leaders, at least at the beginning of the controversy, ever questioned the right of Parliament to establish a uniform commercial system for the empire.

The real grievance of the Colonists was the attempt to impose taxes upon them *for purely revenue purposes,* and not as a regulation of trade. To this kind of a tax the objection was made that "taxation without representation was tyranny." The same view was expressed in Parliament by some of its greatest statesmen, like Pitt and Burke. When the elder Pitt arose from his sick bed and justified the resistance of the Colonies in his immortal speech, he said:

> "There is a plain distinction between taxes levied for the purpose of raising a revenue and duties imposed for the *regulation of trade* for the accommodation of the subject."

These facts are not recited in a spirit of pedantry, but to emphasize the clear conception of the founders of the American Republic that the regulation of trade was not only *essentially* a political problem, but that it was one of the most important, if not the most important, function of the legislative branch of the government.

When, therefore, these wise statesmen came to formulate the Articles of Confederation, and later the Constitution of the United States, they used words and made provisions in the light of a fundamental conception of government, which was to them indisputable, and that was that a regulation of trade, which could make or unmake the prosperity of states, cities, and even individuals, was a matter of such supreme importance that it could only be committed to the representatives of the people in their legislative assemblies.

When our nation came into being and when the Constitution of the United States was formed chiefly to create a central power that could regulate commerce, such regulation was regarded as a political function of the government. To the Fathers it would have been inconceivable that any power less than the supreme legislative power of the nation should control this vital matter of regulating commerce.

The genesis of the Constitutional Convention was in the meeting at Mount Vernon of the Commissioners of Maryland and Virginia to regulate commerce along the Potomac, and through the later assembling of five States at Annapolis and their invitation to all the States to unite in a convention to amend the Articles of Confederation in the interest of commerce.

This great convention met and, however acute the differences were upon nearly every other subject, its members agreed with substantial unanimity that the States should no longer have the power to regulate commerce between them or with foreign nations, but that a Congress of the American people should be created under a new government, which would have plenary and exclusive power in this vital matter.

It is a common error to suppose that the commercial

power of the Union rests simply upon the commerce clause of the Constitution. Such is not the fact. It is also based upon many other grants of power, and it is significant that all these powers are granted to Congress and none of them to the Executive or the Judiciary.

The commercial power of the nation partly rests upon the power of taxation, for I have already shown that to the men who framed this Constitution, the idea of a tax as a regulation of commerce was very familiar.

Following this power of taxation comes the express power—

> "to regulate commerce with foreign nations and among the several States and with the Indian tribes."

Then follows the power to establish

> "uniform laws on the subject of bankruptcy throughout the United States, to coin money, and to fix the standard of weights and measures; to provide for the punishment of counterfeiting the securities and current coin of the United States; to establish post offices and post roads; to promote the progress of science and the useful arts."

In the closing hours of the Convention, Franklin moved to add to the Post Road clause an express power to construct canals, but the motion was rejected as superfluous, as the power already existed under the Commerce clause.

Consider the simple language of the grant to regulate commerce. It does not say that the Federal Government or the United States shall regulate commerce. If it did, there might be room for argument that the power could be exercised by the Executive or the Judiciary or the Congress. On the contrary, the power is granted to Congress *and to Congress alone.* Evidently, the framers had in mind the system of government under which they had lived, which gave this power to Parliament as the supreme council of the realm. Let us consider the reasons which probably influenced them.

The Constitution could have said: "The judicial department of the government shall have power to regulate commerce." If so, an impossible political burden would have been put upon the Federal judiciary, and its prestige would have been fatally impaired. The judges, serving for life, are not responsible to the people. Those of the Supreme Court were originally only five in number and there could not, therefore, be a representative of each State on the bench. Moreover, the very nature of judicial duties would make it impracticable for a court to consider regulations of commerce in that spirit of accommodation and compromise which is always the characteristic of a legislative body. Obviously, to the judiciary the power could not have been granted without destruction.

The Constitution might have granted it to the Executive, but here again the President of the whole people is a citizen of only one State, and his policy might represent a purely local and sectional view. Moreover, if granted to him, his power would be that of a dictator.

The power was therefore granted to the "Congress," not only because the regulation of commerce is essentially a law and its enactment belongs to the law-making body, but because no such law could come into being unless the House of Representatives, directly responsible to the people every two years, and the Senate, as the representative of the States as States, concurred in the wisdom of the regulation.

There are two other and even more significant clauses of the Constitution, to which I invite the very special consideration of the Master. They are to be found in Art. 1, Section 10.

The first provides:

> "No state shall, without the consent of the Congress, lay any impost or duties on imports or exports, except what may be absolutely necessary for executing its inspection laws."

The framers feared that otherwise the States by imposts and tariff duties might regulate trade. Hence, the prohibition.

The second is:

> "No state shall, *without the consent of Congress*, lay any duty on tonnage, * * * *enter into agreement or compact with another State*, or with a foreign power."

The second clause, in its reference to possible agreements or compacts between the States, is the most significant. It clearly contemplates that there are many questions arising between two or more States or groups of States, which they could best settle themselves. The Constitution did not intend to terminate all diplomatic relations between the States. It realized that they would frequently have grievances growing out of their close and intimate relations. Obviously, the subject matter of these grievances could not be a matter over which the Federal Government has exclusive control, for one State cannot have a controversy with another State as to the manner, in which Congress shall exercise its powers. Therefore, the agreements or compacts between the States, which are contemplated by this clause, refer to the collision of interests and sentiments between them in the exercise of powers reserved to the States.

It is very significant that even in respect to those matters, which otherwise would not be within the cognizance of the Federal Government, it is especially provided that there could be no compact or agreement between the States "without the consent of Congress." Note again that it is not the consent of the Executive, nor of the Judiciary, which is made necessary. The Constitution might have said that the States could make compacts between themselves provided they were submitted to the Supreme Court. It did not.

The Convention declined to give the Judiciary any such revisory powers. Indeed, they had thrice voted down a proposition that the Supreme Court should be associated with the President as a "council of revision" over all laws, whether of the States or the Nation.

Nor does the clause say that such compacts are valid, if submitted to the President and ratified by him.

The framers evidently had in mind the fact that most compacts or agreements would have relation to matters of boundaries and intrastate commerce. If in respect to such *intrastate* matters, two or more States made an agreement, it was without validity unless ratified by Congress.

To me this is most significant as demonstrating that the framers could never have intended that the Judiciary should, in a suit between the States, make any regulation of commerce.

Let us suppose that these two groups of States had never come into this court, but had met and divided the waters of Lake Michigan between the Great Lakes states and the Mississippi Valley states. Would their amicable agreement as to such allocation have had any validity unless ratified by Congress?

Is it not equally true that if the two groups of States, now litigating at the bar of this court, should agree upon a consent decree, which would provide for the nature and character of the diversion, the seal of this court could give it no efficacy, unless and until Congress had ratified it?

If the two groups of States could not by a compact or agreement divide the waters of Lake Michigan without the consent of Congress, and if they could not agree to a consent decree of like import without such consent, can it be that this court can itself make such a regulation of commerce without the consent of Congress?

Undoubtedly, it was the intention of the Fathers to encourage the States to settle their controversies between themselves, in respect to matters which were within their competence respectively, by compacts and agreements. The policy was a wise one, and it has been followed consistently and to a great advantage in the history of the nation. From the beginning of the government up to the year 1924, there have been 39 original actions between the States and 32 compacts between States, and it is interesting to note that since 1880 the compacts have relatively increased as against the prior period.

Congress has rarely failed to ratify these agreements between the States.

Nevertheless, the consent of Congress was necessary, because of the possible effect of such compacts upon the "general welfare."

The thought comes unbidden to my mind that the great controversy in the instant case should have been similarly adjusted, or, at least, an attempt should have been made thus to adjust it. There is no reason why the two groups of States, who are complainants and respondents at this bar, should not have negotiated an agreement for the proper allocation of the waters in question, and such an agreement, if submitted to Congress, would probably have been ratified by Congress.

Neglecting that reasonable course, the complainants have attempted to force this court to make a compulsory agreement, although the court not only lacks the power to regulate commerce, but could not enforce even a voluntary agreement in the matter, unless it had first been ratified by Congress.

The commercial power of the union, in respect to its navigable waters, rests upon an even more solid foundation than the clauses to which I have referred. Especially as to boundary waters, the maritime power in respect to foreign nations is the plenary power of a sovereign nation. It was early recognized by the Supreme Court that this power was greater in respect to transportation by water that it was by land. As to the latter, the difficulty still remained to divide the indivisible by separating land commerce into interstate and intrastate commerce, but the "admiralty and maritime jurisdiction" of the Federal Government gave a power over navigable waters that took less account of this distinction. Nevertheless, the leading decisions on the commerce power, commencing with *Gibbons vs. Ogden*, preferred the commerce clause as the principal basis of the power over navigation.

At first, the maritime power was regarded as restricted to waters which had an ebb and flow, but in *Genesee Chief vs. Fitzhugh*, 12 Howard 443, the Supreme Court included all navigable lakes and rivers, and regarded the Great Lakes as in the nature of inland seas and, therefore, more similar to the ocean than to a river.

The fact is, as previously stated, that all the power, which the States, if they had been, in fact, independent sovereign nations, enjoy in respect to navigable waterways, was vested in the Federal Government and the control of the States over purely local facilities, like quarantine, port regulations and wharfage, is only by the sufferance of the Federal government. In a word, the navigable waters of the United States are the public property of the Federal government, held by it as the trustee of the American people and to be used and regulated in such manner as it thinks proper.

If we now turn to the third Article of the Constitution, which creates the Judiciary, we will find a total absence of any authority to regulate commerce or to legislate in any capacity. The original draft of Article 3 stated that the "jurisdiction" of the Supreme Court should be as therein stated, but that was evidently regarded as too vague, and the clause was amended to read:

> "The judicial power of the United States shall be vested in one Supreme Court and in such inferior courts as the Congress may from time to time ordain and establish."

In its earlier form, Article III, Section 2, read:

> "That the jurisdiction of the national judiciary shall extend to cases which represent the collection of national revenue, impeachments of any national officers and questions which involve national peace and harmony."

Had the judiciary article thus remained, there would be much force in complainants' contention that this court could settle any controversy between the States "which involves the national peace and harmony."

When, however, this clause came to be considered, this indefinite grant of jurisdiction was stricken out on August 27th, by the Committee on Detail, and the grant was greatly narrowed by the present provision that "the judicial power shall extend to cases in law and equity."

This expression, "judicial power," has added significance

when we recall one of the great but little known contests in the Convention.

The framers of the Constitution were students of government and history and they undoubtedly followed with intense interest the long struggle in France between the Executive and the Judiciary, which had culminated a short time before the Philadelphia Constitutional Convention met. The Judiciary of France, called the *Parlement*, had acquired the power to nullify a law when they deemed it unjust or unwise. No law had any validity until it was "registered" by the Judiciary. If the Judiciary refused to register a law favored by the King and his Council, or by the legislative assembly of France, which rarely met, the only recourse that the Executive had was to bring pressure upon the judges to register it. From the earliest times until the French Revolution, the history of France was marked by a continuous battle with varying fortunes between the legislative power of the King and the judicial power of the *Parlement*.

Some of the ablest men in our Constitutional Convention, in the extreme of their distrust of democratic institutions, favored a similar council of revision, to consist of the President and the Supreme Court, which would have the power to nullify any statutes, either of Congress or of a State legislature, which the council deemed unauthorized or even inexpedient.

It is surprising that among those who favored this plan, which would have thrown the judiciary into political strife and destroyed its prestige, were James Madison and James Wilson. Voted down on June 6th, 1787, it was again brought up on July 21st and was defeated by a bare majority of one vote. Again the attempt was renewed, and this third time the project was decisively defeated.

Thus the framers attempted to follow the doctrine of Montesquieu by separating the three great departments of the government, but as a substitute for the so-called "Council of Revision" it conferred upon the President a qualified veto.

Having thus rejected the attempt to confer legislative powers upon the judiciary, the framers of the Constitution, in creating the Supreme Court and authorizing the creation of inferior courts, conferred upon them only "judicial power," and such power to a convention largely composed of American lawyers could only mean the power to interpret and enforce the laws of the land, but never to make the laws.

It is true that in a qualified sense the Supreme Court, in determining that the laws of a State transgress the powers delegated to the Federal Government, or in interpreting the statutes of Congress, which often contain words of enumeration rather than of definition, lays down many rules of law, which become in effect regulations of commerce, but every such judicial declaration is in the last analysis an interpretation either of the Constitution or the statutes of Congress or the common law.

The Supreme Court has always recognized that its power was only judicial, and not legislative or executive, and has always disclaimed the power to decide political questions. It has always accepted the political decisions of the legislative and executive branches of the Government. The decisions of the political department of the Government, if not inconsistent with the Constitution, are conclusive upon the courts. Even the questions that are quasi-judicial are similarly conclusive, for the decision of Congress that a claim is an equitable obligation of the Government and appropriating money for its payment, cannot be questioned by the judiciary. (U. S. vs. Realty Company, 163 U. S. 427).

I have already indicated, but it should again be emphasized, that no question is so essentially political in its nature as a regulation of commerce.

The formative period of our history is largely one of the political regulation of commerce.

This generation often complacently regards itself as the most constructive in our history, but I sometimes wonder whether the two decades from 1820 to 1840 were not as amazing in their achievement as the extraordinary period in which we are now living. A new direction was given to the movement of the nations when Jefferson acquired

Louisiana and the "Father of Waters" thus flowed un-
vexed to the sea.

It was an era of great constructive decisions. *Marbury
vs. Madison* established the power of this court on a firm
foundation; *McCulloch vs. Maryland* enormously expanded Federal power by implication; the *Dartmouth
College* case gave stability to property rights, and in *Gibbons vs. Ogden,* the United States assumed responsibility
for the navigable waters of the United States.

The steamboat was developed and the water-ways became of controlling importance. Federal internal improvements began when Calhoun, in 1816, introduced a
bill to appropriate a bonus, which the government had
obtained from the United States Bank, as a perpetual fund
for constructing roads and canals. To him the political
aspects of these commercial agencies far transcended the
economic, for he argued, as Washington had argued before
him, that roads and canals were imperatively needed, if
the East and West were to remain under a common flag.
Then followed the long struggle over the constitutionality
of internal improvements, when an appropriation was
sought for the Cumberland Road, that great link between
the East and West which we owe to the genius of Gallatin.

In the meantime, New York, by one brilliant stroke,
had made its chief city the metropolis of America by constructing the Erie Canal and, at the same time, laid the
foundations for the future greatness of Chicago. Pennsylvania, the supremacy of whose chief city was threatened by the Erie Canal, constructed a canal from Philadelphia to Pittsburgh, with a portage over the Alleghany
Mountains. Virginia and Maryland, not behind, constructed the Chesapeake and Ohio Canal, which became
the future route of the Baltimore and Ohio Railroad.

The American people then first became conscious of
the vastness of the natural resources of the continent and
were impressed even more with the fact that these resources would be as valueless as though they were in Mars,
unless transportation facilities could be provided.

At the end of the Napoleonic war, the war-ridden
masses of Europe commenced a steady migration towards

America and, in turn, the older States of the Atlantic seaboard commenced to push across the Alleghanies by various routes. One mighty tide proceeded by the Mohawk Valley to Lake Erie and thence westward. Another crossed the Alleghany Mountains and poured into Ohio and Kentucky. A third moved northwesterly from Virginia into the Ohio Valley. A powerful impetus was given to this movement by the cession of the so-called Northwest Territory to the United States and the sale by it of the public lands to settlers.

The proportions of the movement can be measured by the fact that in 1790, only, 100,000 white people lived west of the Alleghanies, while in 1815 they numbered 1,600,000.

It is not too much to say that the canal and the railroad have played as great a part in welding the States into an efficient union as the Constitution itself, and the present immeasurable power of the United States began with the movement of nations into the Mississippi Valley. Of all these far-sighted dreams of power, none was older in time, or more continuous in its appeal to the imagination, than the project of uniting Lake Michigan to the Mississippi. If realization of that dream was halted by the development of the railroad, yet its full realization is for a future day, for, unless we are less progressive than the Fathers, the time will come when the barges of commerce will pass freely from Lake Michigan to the Gulf.

All these facts, and many others which could be cited, unmistakably show that the whole problem of regulating commerce from the great focal point of Chicago, eastward through the Great Lakes and southward through the Illinois and Mississippi Rivers, is a problem which can be viewed by the Secretary of State from an international standpoint, by the Secretary of War from a military standpoint, by the Secretary of Commerce from an economic standpoint, and by the Congress of the United States, to whom the ultimate decision is given, from all the standpoints combined.

This question of policy involves many factors. No principle can be laid down in a given case that one use of water is to be preferred to another, and the relative advantages of different waterways involve considerations of a political character.

Only two principles of action can be suggested that are rigid and infallible.

The first is that considerations of local expediency must yield to the larger considerations of national interests.

The second is that the only organ of the Government, which is competent to decide these trying questions of expediency and to balance the even more delicate question of relative equities, is the Congress of the United States, in whom the exclusive power was vested.

Upon these two considerations hang "all the law and the prophets" of this case, and they effectually dispose of every contention therein.

Congress has occupied the field from the very beginning of the Government. It has done so continuously, and is now doing so. The executive branch of the Government has always and is now carrying out the wishes of Congress in this matter.

The Secretary of State is endeavoring as best he can to adjust the very delicate international questions which arise in the matter as between this country and Canada.

The Secretary of War in providing for the common defense, in making his recommendations to Congress, is influenced by the great objective to which his department is dedicated.

The Secretary of Commerce, in developing the industries of this country, has urged and is urging in official reports and public addresses the immense advantages to the millions, who inhabit the Mississippi Valley, of a Great-Lakes-to-the-Gulf Waterway, which would diminish the cost of railroad transportation, and to that extent afford much needed relief to the overburdened agricultural interests of the country.

I do not mean that the courts may not have a proper, even though an auxiliary duty, in this problem. Undoubtedly, they have. The suit that the United States Government, brought to restrain the Sanitary District from diverting more water than the permit of the Secretary of

War permitted, was a matter within the judicial cognizance of the Federal courts, for it was an attempt by the peaceful processes of those courts to enforce compliance with the statutes of the United States. Because we are a law-abiding people, the executive branch of the Government did not, without resort to the courts, enforce the permit, as was clearly within its power. But it is to be noticed that the case of the *United States vs. Sanitary District,* which the Supreme Court decided in 1925, did not make or pretend to make any judicial adjudication of the amount of water which the Sanitary District could divert. It never suggested at any time during the long progress of that case that the Federal courts could themselves make a regulation of commerce by allocating the waters of the lake. All that the Government asked and all that the Supreme Court decided was that an order of the Secretary of War was equivalent to an act of Congress, and that as Congress had decided the question by making a regulation of commerce it was imperative that the Sanitary District should comply with it. Upon no other theory could the suit have been sustained. The difference between judicial power to *enforce* a regulation of commerce and an attempt to make such a regulation by judicial power, is admirably illustrated by this case. The first is within the competence of the court; the second is not.

I have hitherto argued this great question upon principle, and it only remains to show that the decisions of the Supreme Court fully confirm the conclusions, which would follow inevitably, even if it were a case of first impression.

The Supreme Court has consistently and continuously emphasized the doctrine that the regulation of commerce is purely legislative and as such vested exclusively in the Congress. Its decisions, as set forth in 271 volumes of its reports, can be searched in vain for any justification of the contention that the Judiciary can regulate interstate or foreign commerce.

Take, for example, the first great case upon the subject, that of *Gibbons vs. Ogden,* the great masterpiece of Marshall's genius as a jurist and sagacity as a statesman. (9 Wheaton, 1.) There is no suggestion that the Supreme Court could decide whether the steamboat company should or should not have a monopoly of the right of navigation in the Hudson River. The decision went no further than to hold that the State of New York could not grant a monopoly of such right over a navigable river even though wholly within its borders. The great Chief Justice said:

> "This power, like all others vested in Congress, is complete in itself, may be exercised to its utmost extent, and acknowledges no limitations, other than are prescribed in the Constitution * * * If, as has always been understood, the sovereignty of Congress, though limited to specified objects, is plenary as to those objects, the power over commerce with foreign nations, and among the several states, *is vested in Congress as absolutely as it would be in a single government*, having in its Constitution the same restrictions on the exercise of the power as are found in the Constitution of the United States."

In other words, as to interstate commerce, from the standpoint of constitutional jurisprudence, applying the principle thus laid down by the great Chief Justice, it follows that if the United States were not a Union of States, but a single nation for all purposes, it could authorize the diversion now in controversy, and it would only have to reckon with the possible rights of Canada; and under the present development of international law the right of Canada to enjoy an uninterrupted flow of the waters is not a perfect right, but is what international jurists call an "imperfect right," for it is controlled more by the comity of nations than by any fixed obligation recognized by international law.

No case more aptly demonstrates my contention than the second *Wheeling Bridge Company case* (18 How. 421), in which a conflict arose between an opinion of the Supreme Court and an opinion of the Congress as to what was an obstruction to navigation.

Pennsylvania had filed an original bill to secure the removal of an alleged obstruction to the navigation of the Ohio River. Congress had not then acted. The Supreme Court in a previous decision (13 How. 518) had entered a final decree which declared the bridge in question to be such obstruction and directed its removal. Before the defendants complied with the decree of the court, Congress passed the Act of August 31st, 1852, in which it said that the bridge in question was a lawful structure.

Pennsylvania argued that such an act of Congress, which in effect nullified a former adjudication by the Supreme Court on the merits of the question, was unconstitutional as an invasion of the judicial power of the court. But the court said:

> "Now, whether it (the bridge) is a future, existing or continuing obstruction depends upon the question whether or not it interferes with the right of navigation. If in the meantime, since the decree, this right has been modified *by the competent authority*, so that the bridge is no longer an unlawful obstruction, it is quite plain the decree of the court cannot be enforced. There is no longer any interference with the enjoyment of the public right inconsistent with law, no more than there would be where the plaintiff itself had consented to it after the rendition of the decree."

I have already quoted for another purpose, from the very pertinent decision of the Supreme Court rendered about fifty years ago in the original action between *South Carolina vs. Georgia* (93 U. S. 4). This decision is most illuminating in the present controversy, because of the marked resemblance of the facts in the two cases. South Carolina complained that Georgia was improving "the southern channel of the Savannah River at the expense of the northern by increasing the flow of water through the former, thus increasing its depth and water-way." The Supreme Court decided that, whatever the rights of the two States were under their original compact, they had lost such rights when they delegated to the Federal Government the power to regulate interstate commerce.

The argument has been advanced, and will doubtless be pressed, that the Secretary of War, in granting the permit of March, 1925, granted it for a purpose and with a motive which was not within the Federal power.

Unfortunately for this contention, it was decided as early as the case of *Marbury vs. Madison* that this Court would never interfere with the action of the Executive when the act was discretionary. Chief Justice Marshall, in that most famous of cases, said:

> "It is scarcely necessary for the court to disclaim all pretensions to such a jurisdiction (mandamus to the President). * * * The province of the court is, solely, to decide on the rights of individuals, *not to inquire how the executive, or executive officers, perform duties in which they have a discretion.*"

The Supreme Court has never swerved from that doctrine and the only instances in which it has controlled the action of an executive, have been to compel the doing of an act, as to which the executive officer had no discretion.

Peculiarly is this true of the action of the Secretary of War and the Chief of Engineers under the River and Harbor Act of 1890 and 1899. This court has recognized that it is wholly impracticable for Congress to provide specifically the manner in which river and harbor improvements shall be made and has, therefore, sustained the power of Congress to delegate to its officials a broad discretion in the matter.

Thus, in *Monongahela Bridge Co. vs. United States*, 216 U. S. 177, the Supreme Court, in construing the Act of March 3, 1899, said:

> "*Congress intended by its legislation to give the same force and effect to the decision of the Secretary of War that would have been accorded to direct action by it on the subject.*"

Indeed, in *Sanitary District of Chicago vs. United States*, 266 U. S. 405, in which the United States filed its bill upon the validity of a similar permit by the Secretary of War and the Sanitary District at that time defended its course on the ground that the Secretary of War had no authority to limit the amount of the diversion, the Supreme Court said:

> "This withdrawal is prohibited by Congress, *except so far as it may be authorized by the Secretary of War.*"

Similarly, I contend in the instant case that, as the action of the Secretary of War in granting the permit of March 3, 1925, is equivalent to a direct statute enacted by Congress to the same end, complainants are as little entitled to question the reasons and motives of the Secretary of War as to question the reasons and motives of Congress, if the Congress had acted directly, instead of indirectly.

Who can say what were the motives of the Secretary of War in the matter? Who can definitely say that the only motive which impelled his action was a spirit of humanity for the unfortunate condition, in which Chicago would be placed, if it were forbidden to divert the waters further?

If it were of any importance, it could be shown that many motives might well have prompted the action of the Secretary of War and, as he was merely the delegated representative of Congress, he was fully justified in taking into consideration any motive which might have actuated Congress to grant such a permit by direct legislation. He may have argued, as Congress might have argued, that, as the Federal Government had for more than a century encouraged Illinois to connect Lake Michigan with the Illinois River by a canal, and as the Federal Government had permitted, more than a quarter of a century ago, the diversion of waters for this purpose into the canal, a moral obligation rested upon the United States—and a sovereign nation can be moral—not to destroy a useful public work, under conditions that would be most harsh and oppressive. To regulate commerce it is not necessary to create an epidemic in the third city of the world.

Again, the Secretary might have thought, as the War Minister of the nation, that the long-dreamed-of inner route from the Lakes to the Gulf, to prevent obstruction to our commerce, if the St. Lawrence River were ever closed to American ships, would well justify a permit to the City of Chicago, if it was at the enormous expense of constructing the canal, to use it, incidentally, for sanitary purposes.

Again, the Secretary might well have reasoned that, if he immediately stopped the diversion, and the sewage of the third city of the world was at once diverted into Lake Michigan, Chicago, as a great port of entry for commerce, might become so unhealthy that that commerce would be largely, if not wholly, destroyed.

Again, he might have reasoned that, pending negotiations between the United States and Canada for the control of these boundary lakes and rivers, it was desirable that the Secretary of State, in the conduct of these negotiations, should have as an argument the existing diversion of waters.

And, again, he might have reasoned that the internal development of America, and especially the economic welfare of the Mississippi Valley, required the continuous development of the Lakes-to-the-Gulf water-way and that, as the Federal Government was quite unwilling to provide enormous sums to secure that development, it was good policy, from a financial standpoint, to allow Chicago to divert the waters, if it would continue to maintain the Sanitary District canal.

It is conceivable that even the legitimate considerations of a purely political nature, in the narrower sense of that word, might have influenced the Secretary of War. He might have argued that, as Congress has never affirmatively forbidden the diversion and has never nullified the permits, which from time to time the Secretary of War has given to Chicago, the fair inference must be that the Congress has approved of some diversion of the waters, for any of the reasons above mentioned, and that, as such action by

Congress presumably represented the preponderate will of the American people, it was wise statesmanship to permit the diversion.

Or, the Secretary might have reasoned that the irrepressible warfare between the farmer and the manufacturer, which at the moment seems in danger of degenerating into a new conflict of the sections, was so menacing that it was the course of enlightened politics to encourage, and not obstruct, the slow development of the Lakes-to-the-Gulf water-way, in order to satisfy the inhabitants of the Mississippi Valley that their government was not indifferent to their welfare.

However, it is not necessary to determine which of these motives may have influenced the administrative agents of Congress, for, as stated, the judiciary is without any power whatever to question the motives of a public official in the exercise of a discretion. Undoubtedly, a discretion may be abused, but, if so, the remedy is not in the discipline of the courts, but in that of the people.

Chief Justice Marshall recognized this in *Gibbons* vs. *Ogden,* when he said:

> "The wisdom and the discretion of Congress, their identity with the people, and the influence which their constituents possess at election, are, in this, as in many other instances, as that, for example, of declaring war, the sole restraints on which they have relied to secure them from its abuse. They are the restraints on which the people must often rely solely in all representative governments."

Our form of government would finally dissolve if the legislative branch of the government sat in judgment upon the motives of the judiciary, or the judicial branch of the government sat in judgment on the motives of either the legislative or the executive branches of the government. Necessary coordination requires the willing acceptance by one department of the actions and decisions of another department when such actions or decisions are matters of discretion. No one would seriously contend that, if this diversion had been sanctioned by a direct Act of Congress, the Supreme Court could nullify the law, by attributing to Congress, as the sole motive for the legislation, the purely humanitarian purpose of saving Chicago from an epidemic and, as stated, it has no greater right to question the motive of the Secretary of War, whose act, in legal effect, is the act of the Congress itself.

If further authority were necessary, it would be sufficient to cite the very analogous case and conclusive decision in *Wisconsin vs. Duluth,* 96 U. S. 383.

Between Wisconsin and Minnesota and near the City of Duluth was a boundary stream. On one shore was the city of Duluth and on the other, Superior City. Duluth, once humorously called "The Zenith City of the Unsalted Seas," needed a harbor. The city cut a channel close to the Minnesota shore by means of a canal and the diversion of the waters into this canal so changed the boundary river that the natural entrance at Superior City began to fill up. As a result incoming ships used the Duluth channel and made that city their port of entry. The Federal government, in connection with its river and harbor work in the Great Lakes, and under appropriations for "the harbor of Duluth," spent various sums of money in dredging both channels. Wisconsin brought suit to prevent Duluth from further diverting the waters of the old river and its natural flow into the canal above referred to. This Court held that the suit could not be entertained, as the whole matter was in charge of the Federal government and only Congress, or its administrative agents, could act. The Court, after referring to the Government's policy for many years of appropriations through the River and Harbor Bill for the benefit of the Great Lakes and expended by the Government's engineers, said:

> "If then Congress, in the exercise of a lawful authority, has adopted and is carrying out a system of harbor improvements at Duluth, this court can have no lawful authority to forbid the work. If that body sees fit to provide a way by which the great commerce of the lakes and the

countries west of them, even to Asia, shall be
securely accommodated in the harbor of Duluth
by the short canal of three or four hundred feet,
can this court decree that it must forever pursue the old channel, by the natural outlet, over
water too shallow for large vessels, unsafe for
small ones and by a longer and much more tedious route? While the engineering officers of
the government are, under authority of Congress, doing all they can to make this canal useful
to commerce and to keep it in good condition,
this court can *owe no duty to a State* which requires it to order the City of Duluth to destroy
it."

The facts in that case and the instant case are so similar
that it would only require the elision of the word "Duluth" wherever it occurs and the substitution of the word
"Chicago," to make the opinion of the Supreme Court in
Wisconsin vs. Duluth applicable, with little revision, to
the instant case.

It seems an idle superfluity to cite these and many other
cases to the same effect when, in a recent case between the
parties to the instant case and in respect to the same controversy, the Supreme Court conclusively decided the
question.

In that case the Secretary of War had granted a permit
to the Sanitary District to divert 4,167 cubic feet of water
per second from Lake Michigan. The Sanitary District
refused to acknowledge the validity of this limitation and
the United States Government brought an action to enjoin the Sanitary District from any greater diversion. The
present complainants all appeared as *amici curiae* in support of the government's contention that the permit of the
Secretary of War was conclusive.

This court, on January 5, 1925, unanimously decided
the case in favor of the United States. After again sustaining the constitutionality of the delegation of power to
the Secretary of War, it said:

> "This withdrawal is prohibited by Congress, *except so far as it may be authorized by the Secretary of War.*"

It is further noteworthy that, in affirming the decree for an injunction, the court pointedly called attention to the fact that a "large part of the evidence is irrelevant and immaterial to the issue that we have to decide," and this for the reason, as the court added, that "we are not at liberty to consider them (the dangers to the City of Chicago) *as against the edict of a paramount power.*"

It is a poor rule that does not work both ways and now that Chicago has complied with the new permit of the Secretary of War, may it not say, in turn, that neither the Special Master nor the Supreme Court is "at liberty to consider" prejudicial results to the Lake States "as against the edict of a paramount power?"

This is especially true, for at the instance of the United States Government, this court, in affirming the order for the injunction, said that it was "without prejudice to any permit that may be issued by the Secretary of War according to law."

Responsive to this intimation that the decision did not deprive the Secretary of War of further power in the matter and that, therefore, the court's decree was not *its* decision as to the amount of the diversion, but only an affirmance of the continuing power of the Secretary of War to prescribe the diversion, the Secretary of War issued the permit, under which Chicago is now diverting the waters.

Few cases could be cited where a Secretary of War had a more delicate question of judgment to determine than had Secretary Weeks in 1925. The fate of a great city and the commercial welfare of great States were alike involved, but, above all, there were grave considerations of national policy, of international relations, of military considerations and of economic welfare, and, last but not least, humanitarian considerations, which made his brave and sagacious act a task difficult of determination, but one which I venture, as his friend, to say,

was one of the most useful and beneficent of a conspicu-
ously successful and noble career.

So just and human a man could not ignore the humanitarian aspect of the problem. The preservation of life is
a primal law, which is written into our hearts by God,
and Secretary Weeks might have recalled the words, which
were put into John Milton's mouth in an imaginary "Conversation between Abraham Cowley and John Milton,"
wherein Milton is made to say:

> "But, you will say, there is no such law. Such
> a law there is. There is the law of self-preserva-
> tion written by God, Himself, on our hearts.
> There is the primal compact and bond of society,
> not graven on stone, nor sealed with wax, nor put
> down on parchment, nor set forth in any express
> form of words by men when of old they came
> together; but implied in the very act that they
> so came together, pre-supposed in all subsequent
> law, not to be repealed by any authority, not in-
> validated by being omitted in any code; inas-
> much as from thence are all codes and all au-
> thority."

If the permit had been displeasing to Congress, it could
have nullified it by a new act of Congress, and concededly
its decision would have been final. Congress, by its tacit
acquiescence in the action of Secretary Weeks, has ratified
his action and who can dispute that such action is final?

Our opponents, while conceding the power of the Federal Government to divert navigable waters to a different
channel for purposes of navigation, will probably argue
that that is the limit of its authority and that, in such diversion, it may not exceed the amount which may be necessary for such purpose.

A regulation of commerce is not so simple as that argument would indicate. It necessarily involves many complex and related questions, of the wisdom of which Congress can alone judge. As Madison pointed out in the
Constitutional Convention, commerce is often "indivisible" in the practical administration of government.

An illuminating case in this connection is *United States vs. Rio Grande Irrigation Co.* 174 U. S. page 690. In that case the Supreme Court considered the validity of acts of Congress, which permitted the use of waters for mining, agricultural, manufacturing and other purposes. In one of these statutes, the Federal Government permitted the use of water for irrigation and reclamation. When, however, such uses interfered with navigability, the United States brought a suit against the Rio Grande Irrigation Company to enjoin it from appropriating waters for these purposes, and the respondents pleaded these acts of Congress in defense.

Mr. Justice Brewer said:

> "Obviously by these acts, so far as they extended, Congress recognized and assented to the appropriation of water in contravention of the common-law rule as to continuous flow. To infer therefrom that Congress intended to release its control over the navigable streams of the country and to grant in aid of mining industries and the reclamation of arid lands the right to appropriate the waters on the sources of navigable streams to such an extent as to destroy their navigability, is to carry those statutes beyond what their fair import permits."

Unquestionably, the United States could forbid altogether the diversion of the waters of Lake Michigan by the Sanitary District, if it believed that it was unfairly prejudicial to the interests of navigation. Undoubtedly, it could, if it so desired, give an unlimited power to the Sanitary District to divert such waters, and it is an inevitable corollary that it can prescribe the amount of any permitted diversion, even though the diversion were wholly for a purpose other than navigation. *A fortiori,* it can permit the diversion of these waters, where its purpose, in whole or part, is to create a new navigable waterway, as in the case of the Sanitary District canal. It is of no consequence whether the chief, or even exclusive, purpose of the Sanitary District is to use the waters for drainage purposes. It is enough that the United States, in the exercise of its political discretion, is satisfied to permit the use of the waters for purposes other than navigation, when it has reached the conclusion, of which it is the sole judge, that such use of the waters, whether for mining, irrigation, or sanitary needs, is not unreasonably prejudicial to the general interests of navigation.

Our complex civilization frequently requires the Federal Government, in exercising its express powers, incidentally to control subject matters otherwise beyond the Federal field of power.

Finally, let me test the soundness of my argument by the following supposition.

Assume that Chicago had never diverted the waters of Lake Michigan and had turned its sewage into the Lake. In that event, its docks would have "smelled to heaven." The United States has spent many millions of dollars upon the improvement of the harbor of Chicago. Let us then suppose that Congress, acting upon the complaints of all who used the port, had directed the Sanitary District to divert the waters of Lake Michigan in order to force the waste products of this great industrial city into the Mississippi watershed, as the least of two evils. Would complainants seriously argue that Congress was without power to make this adjustment of a difficult problem? Could the complaining States, as against the paramount authority of the Federal Government over the navigable waters of the United States, have reasonably asked this court to frustrate the action of Congress?

How does the case differ in principle, if Chicago with the knowledge and approval of the Federal Government, adopts this solution of the problem? When the Federal Government occupied the field of power and affirmatively asserted its authority over the navigable waters, the responsibility became that of the United States and the complainant States have no standing to question the manner in which the United States has exercised a power expressly delegated to it by the Constitution. Whatever may be the title to the soil under navigable waters, the waters themselves are the public property of the United States, to be administered by the federal government as the common trustee for the welfare of the American people. In discharging its duty as such trustee, it need have had no greater motive than to maintain the welfare and prosperity of the City of Chicago. If this be conceded, then what authority can sit in judgment upon its motives? Certainly not this court.

If the Master should conclude that the rightful decision of the case involves the balancing of the equities between the complainants and the respondents, here again he should not find such balance against the respondents, unless it has been clearly and fully proved that it rests with the complainants.

In such balancing of equities the welfare of the people of Chicago cannot be neglected. Whether the large lake cargo steamers can load as heavily with a lessened lake level, or whether the bathers at the Wisconsin ports have been affected, or the apple trees of Michigan robbed of their fruit, are all insignificant as compared with the health and the lives of three millions of people.

The welfare of Chicago concerns the welfare of the entire nation. Its swift rise to greatness is a ninth wonder of the modern world. It is the city, "whom the merchants that pass over the sea have replenished; by great waters the harvest of the river is her revenue and she is a mart of the nations."

If her commercial greatness has been that of Venice in her golden days, her achievements in art are not unworthy of the Queen of the Adriatic, for, since Venice arose, like Aphrodite from the sea, man has had no greater pageant of beauty, even though it were evanescent, than the Dream City, which Chicago, nearly twenty-five years ago, erected upon the shores of Lake Michigan to commemorate the daring and genius of a man, who sought to make the unknown Atlantic itself a waterway to India.

Complainants have argued and will argue that the Secretary of War in granting this permit could not take into consideration humanitarian considerations. I deny this. It is in effect to say that the Congress, for whom the Sec-

retary acted, could not be influenced by such considerations.

Cannot a sovereign nation be humane? Is it compelled
in exercising its political duties to ignore considerations
of humanity? To give the lake carriers a larger cargo and
thereby greater profits, is it obliged to condemn a great
commercial city to the dangers of an epidemic?

The welfare and prosperity of three millions of people
are in the Master's hands. It is idle to minimize the danger, which will result, if this diversion of water were immediately enjoined and the sewage of one of the greatest
commercial cities of the world was discharged into the
lake, where are now intakes of drinking water.

Chicago may well say to this court: "Who shall save
me from the body of this death?"

Fortunately, no such responsibility rests upon either the
Master or the Court. It is upon Congress.

The present great flood in the Mississippi valley gives a
striking proof of the fact that only the United States can
solve this difficult problem. Mark Twain once said of the
Mississippi:

> "One who knows the river will promptly aver
> —not aloud, but to himself—that ten thousand
> river commissions, with the mines of the world at
> their backs, cannot curb it or confine it; cannot
> say to it, go here or go there and make it obey;
> cannot save a shore it has sentenced; cannot bar
> its path with an obstruction which it will not tear
> down, dance over and laugh at."

Our Government has expended in the last fifty years
nearly 200,000,000 dollars upon the Mississippi, and the
problem of its regulation seems more vital and imperative
than it did when the majestic river flowed through an
unbroken wilderness. What the Nile is to Egypt, the Mississippi has been to the United States, and few internal
improvements have been the subject of greater study and
more acute concern than the utilization of this mighty
river to connect the greatest lake system in the world with
our Mediterranean, the Gulf of Mexico. The present situa-

tion in the Mississippi Valley, as the swollen river spreads death and destruction over the area of an empire, clearly shows that the solution of this problem is essentially political, *and that only one power is competent to solve it, and that is the Congress of the United States.*

For this court to frustrate the will of Congress, to tie the hands of the Secretary of War and the Chief of Engineers, and itself to make a regulation of commerce as to the amount of water that can be fairly diverted from Lake Michigan to improve the water route to the Gulf, *would be an act of judicial usurpation.*

Even the pendency of this suit in the courts, for which, as previously argued, there is no justification under the Constitution, serves to obstruct the other departments of the Government and especially Congress, for the appropriate committees of both the Senate and the House have for years had this matter under very careful consideration, and Congress would probably have long since disposed of it, but for the pendency of this group of suits in the court. A fine respect for the judicial branch of the Government has induced Congress to refrain from final action until the Supreme Court decides that the solution of the problem is not within its competence, and a fine respect for the Congress of the United States should induce the judicial branch of the Government to dispose of this suit as a palpable abuse of the processes of the court.

"If it were done, when 'tis done, then 't-were well, if it were done quickly."

I must apologize to the Master for the length of this argument, which can only be justified by the magnitude of the interests involved. I am especially conscious of this trespass upon his inexhaustible patience, for my argument supports a thesis, which under principle and authority, seems to me indisputable. However, I have been encouraged by the patience and consideration which the Master has shown to all counsel in this case. The case has been a great one and aptly recalls the following saying of Chief Justice Coke:

"I find, a mere stranger in this case, such a one as the eye of the law (our books and book-cases) never saw, as the ears of the law (our reporters) never heard of, nor the mouth of the law, (for *judex est lex loquens*) the Judges, our fore-fathers of the law, never tasted: I say, such a one, as the stomach of the law, our exquisite and perfect record of pleadings, entries, and judg-ments, (that make equal and true distribution of all cases in question) never digested."

XV

THE CONSTITUTION AND THE FLEXIBLE TARIFF

Mr. Beck has devoted much of his private and official life to the study of the Constitution. He believes that none of the three great departments of the Government should either attempt to transfer or yield any of its authority to the other because of danger in disturbing the nice equipoise in the distribution of governmental power which has made a great nation with liberty under law.

When the Ways and Means Committee of the House of Representatives, following the Presidential election of 1929 and the inauguration of the successful candidate, brought to the floor of the House a bill to revise the tariff rates, he noted that the bill continued and extended authority to the President to raise or lower tariff rates in his discretion upon recommendations of a tariff commission as to any inequality of competition between domestic and foreign manufacture. This authority in a more restricted form first appeared in the tariff act of 1922.

Notwithstanding the fact that the provision was sponsored by his party associates, Mr. Beck's reverence for the Constitution and his belief in the unwisdom of this enlarged transfer of the taxing authority of Congress to the President, led him, on May 22, 1929, to make in the House of Representatives the following argument in opposition to the proposed transfer. While the argument changed few votes in the House, it was not without its effect in the Senate, where in a subsequent debate it was freely and frequently quoted. The Republican members of the Senate Finance Committee refused to accept the new proposal and the Senate, after a very able debate, denied any such power to the President in passing upon the administrative features of the Tariff Bill. As this book goes to press, the matter is still an issue betwen the two Houses.—EDITOR.

Mr. Chairman and Ladies and Gentlemen of the House:

I do not rise to discuss any tariff duty in the proposed bill. I am frank to say—and it may be a naive statement—that with the possible exception of one schedule—the sugar schedule—I have no such independent knowledge as to justify me in differing from the conclusions reached by the majority of the members of the Committee on Ways and Means, in whose exceptional knowledge and integrity of purpose I have complete confidence. I do not propose to discuss the sugar schedule, although I have some opinions with respect to the merits of that proposed change in the tariff bill to which I may give expression later.

I am rather seeking to challenge the attention of the House to what seems to me to be a question of fundamental importance and one very gravely affecting the dignity of Congress and the peculiar prerogatives of the House of Representatives. I refer to that provision in the administrative features of this law which provides in substance that the President may determine whether or not, as between foreign producers who export to this country and domestic producers, there is any inequality in conditions of competition; and if he finds such inequality, to determine in his final discretion, although with the aid of the Tariff Commission, the duties by way of increase or such duties by way of decrease as will compensate for this purely theoretical equilibrium between the conditions of competition in the markets of this country. To enable the President thus to exercise the most ancient prerogative of Congress, or of any legislative body in any free country in the world, namely, the prerogative of imposing taxes, the President is authorized to change classifications and duties, and he is further authorized to change, if necessary, the method of valuation by adopting the American market price as against the price in the market of export. Thus the President has an absolute discretion, between the maximum and minimum of the statute, to impose whatever duties he pleases upon his determination of a condition which is far more of a theory than a matter of precise ascertainment. If there is, by reason of some human, spiritual, economic, or financial cause, some inequality that puts a producer in Europe who exports to America at a disadvantage with the American producer, or puts the American producer at a like disadvantage with the foreign exporter, then the President may by a change in duties restore the theoretical equality. It cannot be denied that that is the most far-reaching transfer of the power of Congress to the President that has ever been proposed in Congress.

It would give me less concern if it had not received the support and confirmation in the speech that our esteemed

424 MAY IT PLEASE THE COURT

colleague, the gentleman from New Jersey, [Mr. Fort] made yesterday afternoon, to which I shall presently refer.

But before doing so I want to suggest to the House a curiosity I felt, when my attention was first drawn to this remarkable provision of the proposed law by the very able speech of the gentleman from Georgia [Mr. Crisp], in which speech, so far as it referred to the constitutionality of this proposed flexible tariff provision, I heartily concur.

I want to consider first what was the genesis of such a provision which, at the very time we were disputing with the Senate the question as to whether or not the Senate can initiate a bounty for farmers, without usurping the constitutional prerogative of this House, proposes to transfer an almost absolute power of taxation on every article of merchandise within a given minimum and maximum to the President of the United States.

Having had some experience with the Executive branch of Government, I suspected that this proposal did not originate in the Committee on Ways and Means. I suppose it arose in the mind of one of these theoretical economists, who had recently been a professor in some college —and they are as full of ideas as a dog is of fleas—who first persuaded the Tariff Commission to do what every other Government bureau does, namely, having acquired power, to reach out for more power. Having persuaded the Tariff Commission, and the Tariff Commission having persuaded the Treasury Department, the Treasury Department then sends the recommendation to the Committee on Ways and Means, and, as an administrative measure, the committee concludes that the greater wisdom of the Executive branch of the Government should prevail; and if Congress accepts the recommendation of the Committee on Ways and Means an ancient power of Congress is transferred to the Executive, because a governmental bureau seeks more power.

The provision, if adopted by Congress, will ultimately be submitted to the Supreme Court of the United States, and I am not prepared to say that the proposed law may not receive the pontifical absolution of that great court, for the very obvious reason that that court from the beginning, as it must be in a democracy, assumes any state of facts, however far reaching, however far from reality, or any method of reasoning that does not do plain violence to common sense, in order to sustain what it regards as the will of Congress. That is the vicious circle in this and many other respects in which we are moving in this country. One individual in an executive bureau conceives an idea that greater powers ought to be given to the Executive, and then the appropriate department approves it, and then your committees approve it because the department did, and then the Congress enacts it because the committee approves it and then the judiciary adds its final sanction out of respect for the legislative will. Ever thus a new innovation in our laws is made a part of our system of government, which gravely affects the future development of American institutions.

I shall now refer briefly to the remarks of our colleague from New Jersey [Mr. Fort], who not only gave his blessing to the proposed change but desired that it should be expanded; and in order that I may not do injustice to his thought I ask your attention while I read it.

Speaking yesterday he said, answering the objection that the flexible tariff clause was an unauthorized delegation of legislative power to the Executive:

> "The second reason is that Congress, it seems to me, has lost nothing but trouble in its delegation of other like powers, as, for example, over railroad rates."

Let me interpolate that there is no just analogy between railroad rates and a tax, and if I had the time I could readily demonstrate it.

Mr. Fort continues:

> "I believe we will be a stronger body, both in fact and in the public mind, if we rid ourselves of as many details and administrative matters as possible, for we will then have—what sometimes we now lack—time for the thoughtful consideration of matters of vital public policy. Let us

make the rules and declare the policies and let
somebody else attend to the details."

That, as an abstract truth and as applied to details,
which are essentially or predominantly executive in character, might well receive the concurrence of any thoughtful man, but the details of which he was speaking were
details of taxation, and taxation is the first and greatest
function of a legislative body, and it is the one function
that has hitherto distinguished a free nation from one that
is not free. All the great battles of English liberty were
fought about this question whether any power, even that
of an absolute monarch, could impose a duty without the
consent of the great council of the realm. As we know,
one English king lost his head in trying to impose taxes
without the consent of Parliament; another lost his crown
for the same reason; and the most glorious chapters of
English history are those when Pym, Eliot and Hampdon,
distinguished members of the House of Commons, were
willing to risk their heads upon the block rather than surrender the power of the Common to decide the methods
of taxation, which my brother from New Jersey calls
"details."

Mr. Morton D. Hull: Will the gentleman yield?

Mr. Beck: Yes.

Mr. Morton D. Hull: Is not consent given by the delegation of the power?

Mr. Beck: To say that the transfer of a power is the
exercise of that power is to say that the abdication of an
essential and vital parliamentary function is a proper
discharge of that function, and that would make mean-
ingless all parliamentary institutions. In other words,
suppose that Parliament—and it never would—should vest
in King George the power to impose any tax he pleases—
even considering that Parliament were subservient enough
to do it—would that be consistent with the historic ideals
of the English-speaking race? I venture to say it would
not.

I wish to say, in respect to the statement of Mr. Fort,
which I have just quoted, for whose judgment I have profound respect—and his argument in other respects was

able and generally had my concurrence—I doubt whether he reflected the views of the President. I know perfectly well, and we all rejoice in the fact, we who are his friends, that the gentleman from New Jersey enjoys a relation to the President which is peculiarly close. We are glad that the President has the advantage of so wise, so disinterested, and so loyal an adviser, and we are equally proud and glad that a member of this House enjoys, to such an especial degree, the confidence of the President. But the President could not have sanctioned this statement that we were simply to proclaim a policy, like protection, and then allow the President to impose the duties that would carry it into effect, and that is the substantive meaning of this novel idea: We are to become an academic debating society to discuss certain broad principles but we are to permit the Treasury Department and the President to work out the details. Of course, the details might often be so different from the spirit of the general policy that the will of Congress would be destroyed. The President could not have sanctioned the suggestion that we were to proclaim a policy and then, as the gentleman from New Jersey said, have the Congress impose a nominal duty, and then authorize the President to impose a maximum duty, which might be a thousand per cent, and then say to the President: "We want the products of American manufacture and of the American farm to be protected. And now it is for you, Mr. President, to raise or lower the duties as you think best, in your discretion, in order to carry out this policy."

If that were to be done, what becomes of the provisions of the Constitution, which state that all legislative power is vested in the Congress? What becomes of the special provision that the Congress shall impose taxes for the common defense and general welfare? What becomes of the yet more restricted provision that any bill to raise revenue shall originate in the House of Representatives? What becomes of all three, if you can set up a mere academic proposition and then leave to the President the power to raise or lower taxes at will?

I have said that can not be the President's view, and to

sustain that contention let me read to you what he said on the 15th of October, 1928, in a speech he made in the city of Boston. And they are golden words, the doctrine of a true constitutionalist. The most ardent lover of the Constitution in respect to this question could not ask more than these words I now read:

> "The Tariff Commission is a most valuable arm of the Government. It can be strengthened and made more useful in several ways.— But

A portentous "but"—

> the American people will never consent to delegating authority over the tariff to any commission, whether nonpartisan or bipartisan."

[Applause.]

> "Our people have the right to express themselves at the ballot upon so vital a question as this.
> "There is only one commission to which delegation of that authority can be made. That is the great commission of their own choosing, the Congress of the United States and the President. It is the only commission which can be held responsible to the electorate. Those who believe in the protective tariff will, I am sure, wish to leave its revision at the hands of that party which has been devoted to the establishment and maintenance of that principle for 70 years."

It may be said—and I am sure the question has arisen in the minds of a great many on this side of the aisle who are doing me the kindness to follow me—but after all, has not this question been decided by the Supreme Court; did not the flexible tariff provision of the act of 1922 receive the sanction of the Supreme Court; and if so, is there any question of constitutionality in a judicial sense that remains to be discussed.

I venture to say there is a marked difference between the provisions of the flexible tariff of 1922 and those contained in the present bill. Let us consider them. I fear I will not have the time, and yet this question is of such tremendous import and I am so anxious that the members of this House, particularly those not of the legal profession, shall see exactly how far the Supreme Court has gone in sanctioning these delegations of authority—

[Mr. Garner: Will the gentleman from Pennsylvania permit an interruption.

Mr. Beck: Certainly.

Mr. Garner: The gentleman from Pennsylvania is making a wonderful argument and a splendid contribution to this subject, and, if the gentleman will permit, I am going to yield him such time as he may need to conclude his remarks. [Applause.]

Mr. Beck: I thank my friend, the distinguished leader of the minority, heartily for his very great courtesy. I will try to justify it to the best of my ability.]

I was about to say that I want this House to understand the extent to which the Supreme Court has given any judicial sanction to the delegation of the taxing power, and when I do this I shall not rest my argument, even though I assume that the Supreme Court may hereafter, in its policy of resolving all doubts in favor of an act of Congress, find it possible even to go as far as to validate the provisions of this act.

The first and the greatest case in this matter was the case of *Field v. Clark* (143 U. S., 649), and I want to read the provisions of that statute. It was the McKinley reciprocity statute, and I want to read the language in order that you may see exactly what was there passed upon. That act said:

> "That with a view to secure reciprocal trade
> with countries producing the following articles,
> and for this purpose, whenever and so often as
> the President shall be satisfied that the govern-
> ment of any country producing and exporting
> sugars, molasses, coffee, tea, and hides imposes
> duties or other exactions upon the agriculture or
> other products of the United States which, in

view of the free introduction of such sugar,
molasses, coffee, tea, and hides into the United
States, he may deem to be reciprocally unequal
and unreasonable—"

That in that event, to summarize, he shall have power
to impose certain duties which Congress specifically prescribed.

This case was argued very ably and, as I remember, the
only serious doubt any constitutional lawyer had was that
the President was to be the judge of whether the legislation of other countries in the matter of imports was reciprocally unjust as compared with the benefits that they
received from our free list. It certainly gave him the
power to do something more than ascertain a tangible
fact, which was capable of precise statement and about
which there could not be any reasonable difference. Some
argued that it was a question of policy whether or not
there was this lack of reciprocity. However, the Supreme
Court—Chief Justice Fuller and Justice Lamar dissenting
—sustained that power on the ground—and it must have
been upon this basic premise—that it was a practicable
thing to ascertain with precision whether the laws of another country were lacking in reciprocity as compared
with the advantages that our free list gave to them, and
that was sanctioned and has become a part of the fundamental law.

The countervailing duties case is thoroughly defensible
and involves no delegation of power whatever. Of course,
the Congress can pass a law imposing a duty and then provide that upon the happening of a certain contingency,
like a bounty granted by a foreign government to their
exports, that in that event an additional duty equivalent
to the bounty can be imposed.

No one questions this at all, because you will see that in
both classes of cases the fact to be ascertained, upon which
the will of Congress changes, is an ascertainable fact susceptible of precise statement, admitting of no reasonable
discretion as to its existence as a fact, and what is to happen has been prescribed by Congress, so that the President

merely discharges the ministerial duty of proclaiming the existence of a fact and notifying the world that by reason of that fact a different duty is prescribed. Here is no delegation of the taxing power.

Now we come to the flexible tariff act of 1922 and there approach ground that I think many old-fashioned constitutionalists, of whom I claim to be one, wonder how the Supreme Court could have reached its decision in the case of *Hampton v. United States* (276 U. S., 394), but when we remember the undoubted policy of that court to accept, if at all possible, any legislation that Congress makes as within the Constitution—a policy so conservative and so tenaciously adhered to that less than 50 Federal statutes from the beginning of the government have ever failed to receive the pontifical absolution, to which I referred—we can understand their desire to accept what was theoretically and presumably the will of Congress. Let me compare the provisions of the act of 1922 with the provisions in the bill now under consideration. The act of 1922, which is the existing law, provided that the President, whenever he finds that the cost of production of an article made abroad and exported to our shores and the cost of production of a like article made in this country are unequal, that thereupon the President can make a change in duty of not more than 50 per cent from the established rate in order to adjust the inequality in the cost of production.

The Supreme Court, when they rendered this decision, necessarily accepted two basic facts, and if they did not it is incredible, in my opinion, that they would have sanctioned this power to transfer the taxing power to the President.

The first basic fact was that the costs of production of a foreign article were susceptible of exact computation and ascertainment and could be put into the form of a precise statement and that their actuality could be for all practical purposes established.

The second basic premise was that it was practicable by a mathematical computation so to adjust the rates that there would be a compensation for the difference in the costs of production.

Unfortunately, both premises we now know to be quite inaccurate. The court accepted them because Congress did, but experience has shown that costs can not always be estimated.

The Supreme Court is not to be criticized for assuming these premises because Congress assumed them. Indeed, the court can not do otherwise than assume any state of facts which the Congress assumes for the purpose of its legislation; but we know now, and the committee's report establishes that you can not in all cases, or in many cases, ascertain with any degree of accuracy the costs of production abroad, and we also know without much outside information the surpassing difficulty, if not impossibility, of making a mathematical computation of the difference between the cost of production, if and when ascertained, and the existing duty.

It is because these two premises are now recognized by the Committee on Ways and Means to be unsound that the Tariff Commission proposes to extend the whole basis of the statute to a new basis that is not only insusceptible of ascertainment, but in the final analysis is only an economic theory. Because this act says, not that there shall be the power of the President to increase a rate of duty to adjust an inequality in the cost of production, which is question of fact, however difficult to be ascertained, but this statute says that there shall be ascertained by the President "inequalities in the conditions of competition." What are these inequalities? Are they inequalities that relate to the human spirit, or inherent in the good will, or in the political advantages that a government may give its own people, or are they inequalities purely of a financial character? To what extent is there any definite restriction on what the President is to find except that he is to reverse the immortal epigram of President Cleveland—he is to say it is not a condition but an economic theory that confronts us. The President is to determine a theory—moral, political, economic, financial, or what you please—determine it in his discretion, and then within a limit of 50 per cent increase or 50 per cent decrease make such adjustments as will meet the theoretical inequality, which will inevitably be very largely a matter of conjecture.

I have stated frankly to this House—and I hope I shall never make a speech which will be lacking in frankness—that I am not prepared to predict that the Supreme Court may not sanction this delegation of power, as they accepted the provision of the 1922 act. It is certainly a portentous and dangerous step to take—to substitute for a certain standard an inexact and speculative standard like the one proposed.

I say that is a long step beyond anything Congress has done.

[Mr. Moore of Virginia: Will the gentleman yield?

Mr. Beck: I yield to the gentleman from Virginia.

Mr. Moore of Virginia: Will the gentleman state how the court divided in the last case he mentioned?

Mr. Beck: They were unanimous. The Supreme Court is very much like Hamlet following the ghost of his father in the first act of that great tragedy. The court follows that ghostly thing we call the will of Congress. It follows it as the Prince of Denmark followed the ghost, with timidity and trembling, because it never knows how far the Congress is going or into what abyss of unconstitutionalism the ghost may lead it. [Laughter and applause.] But finally there comes a time when the court sees it is approaching some perilous cliff, and it says, "Whither wilt thou lead me, speak, I will go no further." [Laughter.] For example, the court in *Veazie vs. Fenno* gave its judicial sanction to the power of Congress to destroy by a perversion of the taxing power the undoubted right of State banks to issue currency.

Then came the case of *McCray vs. the United States*, where they held that a statute, which said that if oleomargarine was colored pink, or any other color than the color of butter, it could have a very moderate tax, but if it resembled butter, there was a prohibitive tax. Then Congress, following that doctrine of the court, passed the child labor law, which I argued in the Supreme Court, and which sought by another perversion of the taxing power to prohibit the manufacturers in the States from employing child labor, and it was at that point— and I, as a lover of constitutional institutions, thank God for their decision—that the Supreme Court said, "Whither wilt thou lead me? Speak, I will go no further," and they invalidated that law. I shall not be surprised when this particular provision comes before the court, if it does come, to hear the court say, "We have carried this doctrine of delegating essential legislative powers to the extreme limit, and we will go no further."]

But suppose, gentlemen of the House, that this is sustained by the Supreme Court? Does that answer our constitutional scruples? Some of you may recall a speech I had the great honor of making in this House on February 22, which was received with so much indulgence by the members of the House, and you will remember that I spoke of the large sphere of political power in which constitutional provisions can be invoked, but which are beyond judicial view because they are essentially political in character; and it is that fact that makes it obligatory upon us, if we are the worthy heirs of the great traditions of the English-speaking race, to bear in mind in the exercise of these powers the great historic principles of English liberty, the greatest of which is that a free people should never be willing to be taxed except by the consent of their representatives in Congress assembled. [Applause.]

Ah, you will say, but there are two obvious distinctions between the great quarrels between the English lovers of liberty and arbitrary English kings in the times of the Tudors and the Stuarts, which culminated disastrously for one Stuart, Charles I. You will say the essential distinction is this, first, that the tax to be imposed, unquestionably in substance by the President, is, after all, imposed by a President who is also elected by the American people, and who is responsible at periods of four years to the American people. But the answer to that is that the Constitution of the United States did not intend to leave this kind of taxation to any one man, even though he be the President of the United States. [Applause.] The Constitution took great care to say that the legislative powers were to be vested in a Congress which, in the Senate, would represent the States as States, and in the House should every two years be the fresh expression of the majestic will of the people. The Constitution also provided specifically, in order that there should be no question as to whether the imposition of a tax is a legislative act, that the Congress shall impose taxes, and that bills to raise revenue must originate in the House of Representatives. That is what the Constitution says, and however pleasant it may be for us to divest ourselves of further responsibility and visit all the burdens as well as the powers of taxation on the President, the fact remains that the Constitution forbids it; and it is no answer, in connection with these ideals of the English-speaking race, to say that the President is elected.

The second distinction is that Congress authorized the President to impose these increased duties. That is the question raised by the interruption of my friend upon the left. As I said to him then, and I venture to say now, can it make it a less indefensible betrayal of the great principles of the English-speaking world to vest in one man, however august his power, however great his dignity, however noble his personality—for this House to say to him as a subservient body, "We turn it over to you; you find out whether there is an inequality in competition; you determine what you think is necessary to equalize the difference in competition. We do not care to discharge the duty vested in us by the Constitution; we want to resolve ourselves into a debating society to discuss abstract problems and general policies, and we will leave to you, Mr. President, the nice function of determining what duties shall be imposed to adjust our country to a purely conjectural condition of economic equality." [Applause.]

Some will say that the President does not impose any taxes under this provision. You know the difference between the adjudication of a State statute by the judiciary and a Federal statute is that with a State statute the judiciary looks through the form at the substance, and with a Federal statute the form is more liberally accepted as a fair statement of the substance, and in that way statutes that are often wanting in constitutional power are accepted. Look through the form at the substance of this idea. The President appoints the Tariff Commission. Under this law it may be wholly composed of one party. I am not quarreling with that provision; that may be wise. The President can remove them at will. Under the case that I argued in the Supreme Court—*Myers v. United States* (272 U. S.), one of the very greatest I ever had the privilege of arguing in that great and noble court —the power of the President to remove every member of the Tariff Commission is established beyond peradventure.

So that, with his power of appointment, stimulating gratitude, and his power of removal, stimulating fear, the President controls the Tariff Commission. I do not mean that this President or, please God, any President that may be elected hereafter in our lifetime, would use that influence with the Tariff Commission; but the power of the President over the Tariff Commission is very strikingly shown by the fact that when a Tariff Commission recommended a reduction of the duty on sugar a former President of the United States ignored their recommendation and refused to make the reduction. So that a Tariff Commission is a good deal like a board of directors. It may have some potential usefulness, but, generally, it is a debating body and its executive head controls. The President is to determine what is called an "inequality in the conditions of competition," and then the President is authorized to raise or lower any item in the whole tariff structure in his sole discretion in order to adjust the country to what he calls an equality of competition.

Do not think for one moment if this law is passed and validated by the Supreme Court, which is very doubtful —do not suppose that there will be any judicial review by anybody, because there can not be any judicial review as to the exercise of this discretionary power. If there be one principle that is established in this country beyond any other by the Supreme Court in a number of decisions, it is that they will never interfere with an act of political discretion by an Executive, least of all by the President of the United States. They declined to even entertain a suit against Andrew Johnson for enforcing a bill which Andrew Johnson had declared unconstitutional.

Therefore, it will be in the discretion of the President, and as the compensatory duty is likewise vested in the discretion of the President, the President can in his discretion destroy an industry by reducing the tariff or destroy one competing industry in favor of another by imposing an increase of duty, and there is no officer or court who can call his act into question. He would be as arbitrary as a Tudor monarch. I should be amazed if such a principle should become a law.

I only want to address myself to one other thought, particularly to my colleagues and esteemed friends of the Committee on Ways and Means, and especially to the leader on this side of the House.

[Mr. Crisp. Mr. Chairman, will the gentleman yield for a question before he goes further?

Mr. Beck. Certainly.

Mr. Crisp. Is it not just as constitutional and just as logical to transfer to the President upon a finding of facts by the Secretary of the Treasury, as to the financial needs of the Government, the power to raise or lower income-tax rates 50 per cent as this proposal?

Mr. Beck. Yes. If this law be valid, you could pass a law to the effect that the President, by the advice of some auxiliary body, could raise or lower income taxes, or change any form of taxation at his pleasure, if some economic or moral abstraction is used as the basis of his action.

Mr. Linthicum. Mr. Chairman, will the gentleman yield there?

Mr. Beck. Certainly.

Mr. Linthicum. The gentleman was speaking a moment ago about the Tariff Commission. During a former presidential term Mr. David J. Lewis, of Maryland, a member of the Tariff Commission, as his term was about out, was given to understand by the President that if he would submit his resignation, to be held by the President, he would be reappointed. Mr. Lewis absolutely refused to do it and somebody else was appointed in his place.]

Mr. Beck. I wanted to say a final word on the question
of policy, irrespective of the question of constitutionality.
I am a Republican and a protectionist. If this provision is
in the bill, with the possible exception of sugar, all the
other items in the bill have my hearty concurrence; and
even as to sugar I may hereafter be convinced that the
proposed increase is justified. But as to the question of
protection, are you not playing with fate when you, as
the friends of protection, put this provision in the law?
It is a beautiful law so long as you have a high-tariff President. You do not have to wait for Congress to propose
anything. As the exigences seem to justify, the President
sends for the Tariff Commission and tells them to make a
report upon this or that duty, and up goes the duty.

But are you so certain that three years or seven years
from now we will have a high-tariff President. Politics
are precarious and now in a very fluid state. There might
be an upheaval in Europe that will cause a disruption of
our economic system in this country, and the higher the
wave is the more destructive its violence will be when the
wave breaks. Let us imagine a low-tariff Democrat President, like my friend from Tennessee [Mr. HULL], one of
the old guard for tariff for revenue only. Suppose the
gentleman from Tennessee should become the next President of the United States. [Applause.] Well, that wish
may be on the Democratic side the father to the thought.
[Laughter.] You cannot repeal the flexible tariff provision then, because the same election that would put
the new President in power would also carry at least
more than a third and probably more than a half in
the House and Senate, and the cause of protection
in this country may then be confronted with a far greater
peril than a possible revision of the tariff by Congress.
Then you will be face to face with the fact that a single
man, the President of the United States, under a power
that you gave him and under a power that you encouraged
him to exercise, will summarily reduce tariff rates at a
rate so rapid and bewildering that a great many manufacturers in this country will rue the day when they ever
vested such power in a single functionary, who may be a

low-tariff man or a high-tariff man as the exigencies of politics may determine.

[Mr. Gifford: Will the gentleman yield?

Mr. Beck: Yes.

Mr. Gifford: I was thinking of the same question asked by the gentleman from Georgia [Mr. CRISP], who made a parallel between income-tax rates and tariff rates. I would like to ask the gentleman if the delegation of power is not given to the Secretary of the Treasury to even a greater degree in respect to the bargaining clause in the income tax law?

Mr. Beck: If I correctly understand what the bargaining clause is, it is an adjustment of claims for taxation and therefore an executive function.]

Now, gentlemen, I am drawing to a close. I certainly am appreciative of the attention the House has given me. I appreciate the fact that I may not have met the views of my party associates, but I want again to recall, if I may, one single thing I said from this place on Washington's Birthday. I said, quoting a portion of the Farewell Address, that the greatest menace to the perpetuity of our institutions and the greatest possibility of the destruction of the nice equipoise between the Executive and the congressional power was the aggrandizement of the Executive and the diminution, the persistent self-destruction, of Congress by its own surrender of its vital powers of legislation. I believe that peculiarly applies to this matter. You give the President of the United States this power of taxation. He already has great power over banks; he has power with respect to railroads; but as my friend from Georgia so well said in his speech on May 15, which I may say was the incentive—I will not say the inspiration, because my speech is much too poor to use the word "inspiration"—but the incentive of my speech was the argument of the gentleman from Georgia [MR. CRISP] that this flexible tariff law was an unconstitutional delegation of legislative power. If you give to the President this enormous power over every manufactured commodity, the power to ascertain the fact, which if he finds it no one can dispute and which, having found, he is the judge of the appropriate remedy—you have given him power which admits of infinite abuse. Now, I honor, admire, and esteem too much the present President of the United States to think for one moment that he would abuse it. I am equally confident that if the gentleman from Tennessee, whom I unintentionally nominated for President a few moments ago [laughter], were to be President he would not abuse it; but as I said on February 22, let an unscrupulous and ambitious man become President of this country, with all the powers he has under the Constitution and all that have been given him since the Constitution by the development, I might almost say the perversion, of that instrument, and you have a man so powerful that if he cares to exercise that power nothing but his own death would ever unseat him, unless it were a political revolution. [Applause.] He would have the power to make terms with the greatest industries of this country and give them increased duties or he could terrorize them by the threat of reduced duties, if he saw proper.

If I were the majority member of the Committee on Ways and Means or the floor leader, I would stop and think whether there may not be some truth in what I have said. I would stop and think whether it would not be advisable to permit a debate on this great subject by allowing an amendment on the flexible tariff, or preferably I would take out of this bill this flexible tariff provision, which I understand was inspired by the Tariff Commission in search of greater power. Take it out and make it the subject of a separate bill. Let us debate it with all the care and attention and with all the time that is demanded by a question of surpassing importance, because it goes to the very fundamentals of a free Government. [Applause.]

Then if the House reaches the conclusion that it is safe to vest any such power in the President let them do it, but let us not sacrifice a great principle, an imponderable to a ponderable, a sacred right of Congress to a temporary expediency by so interweaving it with a tariff bill, otherwise admirable, that there can be no fair or reasonable debate upon what I believe in truth to be a momentous and utterly indefensible change in the character of our Government. [Applause.]

XVI

THE VALIDITY OF RESALE PRICE CONTRACTS

The American Gramophone Company, the selling agent of the Columbia Gramophone Company, entered into a contract with the Boston Store of Chicago for the sale of gramophones and records at a stipulated price on condition that the Boston Store should not sell the articles below a named resale price. The Boston Store violated the contract as to the maintenance of the resale price and the American Gramophone Company brought suit to enjoin such violation.

Mr. Beck delivered the following oral argument on January 16, 1918, in support of the validity of the contract and, while the argument is a masterful statement of the sound economic and legal reasons supporting the contract, the Court refused to reverse its prior decisions to the contrary. Two Justices (Holmes and Van Devanter), dissented. It is interesting, in this connection, to note that economic progress again refused to halt at the mandate of the Court, for such resale contracts are daily used in business and are now enforced by business through refusal to sell to any retailer not maintaining the stipulated resale price, a procedure which the Court has itself subsequently approved. *United States* v. *Colgate and Co.*, 250 U. S. 300.—EDITOR.

May It Please the Court:

The ultimate facts of this case are these:

The appellant, a Chicago department store, requested the appellee, the Columbia Gramophone Company, to sell to it certain merchandise. The Gramophone Company, possibly having in mind the propensity for price cutting of some department stores, stated that it would sell these products to the department store if the latter would agree not to sell at less than listed prices.

The department store made a contract to purchase the goods on these terms and conditions, and, as soon as the goods were delivered, it at once proceeded to violate the condition as to the resale price.

Whatever the opinion of the Court may be with respect to the enforcibility of the contract, there cannot

be any division of opinion with respect to the moral turpi-
tude of the department store's act. It may not be a
violation of Federal law to cheat at cards, but the knavery
of the act is not thereby lessened.

The question before the Court, which I propose to discuss, is whether the Gramophone Company is without
redress for its damages sustained through an admitted violation of contract. If it be without remedy, then such a
contract is the only contract in so-called restraint of trade
upon which the "light of reason" does not shine. It will
thus constitute the only exception to the wise and comprehensive doctrine of this Court in the Standard Oil cases,
that the validity of business contracts, which involve some
literal or technical constraint of trade, depends upon the
reasonableness or unreasonableness of such contracts from
the standpoint of the public welfare.

*In other words, I ask the Court to consider whether
such a contract is so tainted with original sin that it is
fatally predestined to judicial damnation!*

The Court will thus see that I do not contend, as has
generally been contended in previous cases of a similar
character, that *all* such contracts are necessarily valid. I
do challenge the doctrine that all such contracts are necessarily invalid. I seek to apply to this class of contracts
principles of a constructive jurisprudence which will consider the varying circumstances under which such contracts can be made, and will adjudge them valid or invalid
as the public interests may require. Such was the unbroken policy of the courts of England and the United States
prior to the enactment of the Sherman Anti-Trust Law,
and such is still the accepted doctrine of the English Courts
to this hour. Indeed it may be added that so far as my investigation goes it is the accepted doctrine of the jurisprudence of every leading commercial nation, unless this
Court shall now say that the United States is an exception.

No business contracts are more usual and normal in
all commercial nations than those which impose a resale
price, and in no nation, so far as my investigation goes,
has the validity of such a contract been questioned except
in the United States, nor would such validity be ques-

tioned in this country had it not been for the sweeping language of the Sherman Anti-Trust Law, which, as first interpreted, seemed to forbid all restraints of trade, whether reasonable or unreasonable.

As this Court has since disavowed this rigid and inelastic construction of the statute, the question is, I respectfully submit, still open to forensic discussion.

This question is of great importance. It not only vitally affects vast property interests, but equally concerns the opportunity and ability of thousands of small retail dealers to exist.

It involves a controversy between would-be monopolists and anti-monopolists, for, as will hereafter appear, a limited resale price system makes for the widest distribution of products and the most extensive opportunity to participate in a branch of commerce, while the system of unlimited price cutting, as practiced by department stores, chain stores and mail order companies, inevitably tends to the destruction of competitors, and to the monopolization of traffic in the hands of a few great business enterprises in each city. This case may, moreover, be the last phase of a great legal-economic controversy, an irrepressible conflict between legitimate and illegitimate commercial methods.

It will be contended that the question is foreclosed to controversy by the decision of this Court in the case of *Dr. Miles Co. vs Park & Sons Co.*, 220 U. S., 373. It is true that certain reasoning in that case, largely *obiter dicta*, seems to indicate a conclusion that under any and all circumstances a vendor is legally powerless to impose upon his vendee a resale price; but as will hereafter appear, the decision itself is not inconsistent with the contention that such a contract is not necessarily unlawful, and will not be adjudged void unless under all the circumstances it is clear that the contract is prejudicial to the public welfare.

This Court has repeatedly stated that its opinions are to be interpreted, according to the facts upon which they were based, and that no generality of expression definitely fixes the law unless such expressions are necessary to the decision of the case.

As was said by this Court in *Woodruff vs. Parham,* 8 Wallace, 123, such *obiter dicta* "can only be received as an intimation of what they (the Court) might decide, if the case ever came before them, for no such case was then to be decided," and was therefore not "a judicial decision of the question."

All that was necessarily decided in the case of *Dr. Miles Co. vs Park & Sons,* 220 U. S., 373, was, that *where an article of commerce was absolutely monopolized* by a given producer, and where therefore no competitive conditions existed in that line of commerce to protect the consumer, and where the producer, being thus an absolute monopolist, imposed upon all distributors and retailers an interlocking system of contracts, *which made competition in prices an impossibility,* that such producer could not, as against one, *who sustained no contractual relation whatever to the producer,* compel him to submit to such price maintenance system.

To decide otherwise would have been to negative altogether the possibility of freedom in trade, and I am not suggesting that this case requires either reversal or modification.

I contend, however, that this decision should not be extended beyond its essential facts or so interpreted as to put the business interests of this country into a rigid and inelastic straight-jacket.

CHIEF JUSTICE WHITE—Mr. Beck, did this Court in its decision in the *Dr. Miles case,* reserve the question you are now discussing?

It did not reserve it, because no question, such as is presented by this record, was before the Court. The system there condemned wholly destroyed competitive conditions. The present case is one of simple purchase and sale, and deals solely with the respective rights of vendor and vendee.

In considering the question above suggested, the Court, I respectfully submit, should commence with the presumption in favor of liberty of contract. Such liberty is one of the most sacred rights guaranteed by the Constitution, and upon it the amazing edifice of American industry has been largely built. Presumptively, a vendor and a vendee are entitled to determine the conditions upon which the vendor will sell and the vendee will buy. Such liberty, however, is not absolute, and obviously the vendor and vendee cannot make a contract that is either criminal, immoral or against public policy in being prejudicial to the common welfare.

That an agreement between a vendor and vendee as to the resale price of an article is not inherently criminal or immoral is clear beyond question. Each is dealing with his own property. The vendor has generally the right to say upon what conditions he will part with his commodity, for he is under no legal obligation to sell it, and the vendee has an equal right to say upon what conditions he will part with his money, for he is under no obligation to buy.

If such a contract is plainly prejudicial to the public welfare, then it is "a restraint of trade," and, when related to interstate or foreign commerce, is as such within the Sherman Anti-Trust Law. If, however, such a contract in a given case is not clearly prejudicial to the public welfare, then the presumptive right of the contracting parties to "do as they will with their own" should be respected.

In determining this question, it should be borne in mind that the public policy which interferes with the right of contract is something more than an opinion that a given contract is unwise. The judiciary, to whom in cases of this character the duty has been immemorially assigned of determining the public policy of the nation, will not condemn a contract simply because it may question its wisdom. It may be economically unwise for a producer to market his products through a middleman, but that ground would not justify a court in pronouncing contracts with middlemen invalid. In other words, the judiciary in declaring the public policy of a nation in the matter of enforcing contracts does not sit as a legislature to determine the wisdom or folly of business transactions. It is only when the judicial enforcement of a contract would amount to a public evil that a court refuses to extend the process of law to such enforcement. Obviously such denial should be interposed with the greatest hesitation and only in clear cases, for in the matter of business contracts business men are ordinarily better judges of business methods than legislators or courts. Their practical experience is better than theory, and the wise nations know that the public interests are advanced by the least possible interference with the delicate mechanism of business.

Ordinarily public policy requires that men should respect their contracts, for that involves the element of good faith, without which neither citizens can deal with each other nor even nations sustain relations of comity.

The second concern of public policy should be the right of business men to determine by contract their own interests. It is only when such liberty of contract and such enforcement of good faith in making contracts would result in a greater evil to the public interests that the interference of law is in any manner justified.

It is often erroneously assumed that at common law all restraints upon the alienation of personal property were invalid. In support of this, Coke's illustration, that the vendor may not sell a horse upon condition that the vendee shall not resell him is generally instanced. Coke never said that his horse could not be sold under a condition that it should not be resold at less than a stipulated price. In any event, that horse has been ridden to death, and is as old and spavined as Don Quixote's famous charger. The age of the aeroplane need not go back to that of the wheelbarrow for its economics. As a matter of fact the genius of the common law did not lay down any such narrow restriction upon the right of contract. It is not and never was the law that all restraints on alienation, whether complete or partial, were invalid at common law.

The erroneous assumption to the contrary arose out of a misconception of the following passage from *Coke on Littleton,* Section 360:

> "And so it is, if a man possessed of a lease for years, or of a horse, or of any other chattell reall or personall, and give or sell his whole interest or propertie therein upon condition that the donee or vendee shall not alien the same, the same is void

because his whole interest and propertie is out of him, so as he hath no possibilitie of a reverter, and it is against trade and traffique, and bargaining and contracting between man and man."

Coke, in the context of this very passage, however, and Littleton, in the section of his *Tenures*, on which it is based, both stated that the rule referred only to *total* restraints upon *every* mode of alienation, and did not include restraints that were not *total*, or that left free *some* right of alienation.   As this widely current misconception, which has found wide expression in the text books and has had some reflection even in judicial decisions, requires correction, the exact language of these venerable and learned authorities deserves quotation.

Chapter 5 of the Third Book of *Coke's Institutes*, written about the time that Shakespeare was writing Hamlet, treats "Of Estates upon Condition."   After discussing conditions in general, conditions precedent, impossible conditions and illegal conditions (all relating to land), and after noting some differences between conditions in contracts and conditions in real property, the commentator returns to conditions in real property, and quotes *Littleton's Tenures*, Section 360, as follows:

> "Also, if a feoffment be made upon this condition, that the feoffee shall not alien the land to *any*, this condition is void, because when a man is infeoffed of lands or tenements (*pur ceo que quant home est enfeoffe de terres ou tenements*), he hath power to alien them to any person by the law. For if such a condition should be good, then condition should oust him of *all* the power which the law gives him, which should be against reason, and, therefore, such a condition is void."

In the first paragraph of his notes on this passage, Coke unequivocally supports this distinction:

> "And the like law is of a devise in fee upon condition that the devisee shall not alien, the condition is void, and so it is of a grant, release,

confirmation, or any other conveyance whereby a fee simple doth pass. For it is absurd and repugnant to reason that he, that hath no possibility to have the land revert to him, should restrain his feoffee in fee simple of *all his powers to alien.* And so it is if a man be possessed of a lease for years, *or of a horse, or of any other chattell reall or personall, and give or sell his whole interest or propertie therein upon condition that the donee or vendee shall not alien the same, the same is void, because his whole interest and propertie is out of him, so as he hath no possibilitie of a reverter, and it is against trade and traffique, and bargaining and contracting between man and man*: and it is within the reason of our author that it should ouster him of *all* power given to him."

Here text book writers on restraints of alienation have generally stopped. Lord Coke's horse, like the wooden horse of the Greeks, is supposed to have fighting forces within its belly sufficient to capture the fortress of modern industry.

Let us, however, read on. Coke then proceeds to quote:

"But if the condition be such, that the feoffee shall not alien to *such a one,* naming his name, or to any of his heirs, or of the issues of such a one (Mes si le condition soit tiel, que le feoffee ne alienera a un tiel, nosmant son nosme, ou a ascun de ses heires, ou de issues d'un tiel), &c., or the like, *which conditions do not take away all power of alienation from the feoffee,* &c., *then such condition is good."*

Here is Littleton's express statement that restraints, that fall in any degree short of complete denial of the right of alienation, that "do not take away all power of alienation"—are good.

That Littleton would have held valid a restraint like that of the agreement certified in the present case, which leaves the vendee free at any time, anywhere, and upon any conditions, to sell the article to anyone, provided only he sell at the particular resale price to which he expressly assented when he bought the article, can hardly be doubted. That Coke shared this view is plain from his notes:

> "If a feoffment in fee be made upon condition that the feoffee shall not enfeoffe I. S. or any of his heirs or issues, &c., this is good for he doth not restrain the feoffee of *all* his power."

Page after page then follows of sections from Littleton and notes thereon by Coke, all discussing examples of partial restraints upon alienation that are valid, because they are not unlimited and do not prohibit *all* power of alienation.

It seems amazing that a legal and economic problem of the twentieth century should be considered in the light of law as expounded centuries ago. Littleton wrote his famous Institutes a full quarter of a century before Columbus discovered America, and Coke his famous commentaries upon Littleton in the reigns of "Eliza and our James."

It is necessary to go back to these fountains of the law, for nearly all discussions of restraints of trade in recent years have started with the assumption that at common law all were invalid, and that it was necessary to look to modern decisions for a more liberal doctrine.

As I have shown, the common law favored liberty of contract. One could search the year books and the earlier common law reports in vain for a single case that held a resale price contract illegal. If any such decision exists, it is yet to be cited.

The decision of *Mitchell vs. Reynolds,* 1 P. Wms., 181 (decided in 1711), and all subsequent cases thereafter, simply recognized the common law, and the only change of doctrine was the growing recognition by the courts that all restraints upon alienation, growing out of contract, should be recognized as within the fair rights of the contracting parties, unless such restraints were clearly prejudicial to the public welfare. As society emerged from the primitive conditions of Littleton's and Coke's times, and the great industrial era of the steamship, the railroad and the telegraph came, the courts and legislatures of the leading nations recognized that the true welfare of society required the greatest possible liberty of contract not clearly inconsistent with the public welfare.

Probably no decision made a more thorough analysis of restraints of trade than the case of *Mitchell vs. Reynolds,* and no modern decision adds anything in substance to the concluding paragraph of Chief Justice PARKER'S opinion in that case, when he said:

> "In all restraints of trade, where nothing more appears, the law presumes them bad, but if the circumstances are set forth, that presumption is excluded, and the court is to judge of those circumstances and determine accordingly, and *if upon them it appears to be a just and honest contract, it ought to be maintained.*"

In this spirit there has been an ever broadening recognition of liberty of contract. In the earlier decisions, it was held that if the restraint were for an unlimited time, it was invalid. Now an indefinite period is sustained. It was originally held that if the restraint was general, i. e., extending over the entire nation, it was bad, although if restricted to a locality, it was good.

Now as shown in the case of *Roussilon vs. Roussilon,* 14 Ch. D., 351, a restraint, which was as wide and round as the globe, was held good when applied to a business which was equally world-wide. The test remains whether the contract is reasonable or unreasonable, and whether the restraint is due or undue. Possibly the rule cannot be more definitely stated.

This pronounced tendency, observable not only in England and America, but in all leading commercial countries, was in America temporarily checked by the interpretation placed upon the decisions of this Court in the *Traffic Association Cases* (166 U. S., 290 and 171 U. S. 505). Those cases temporarily postponed a rational solution of a legal-economic question by placing a too literal interpretation upon the statutory condemnation in the Sherman Anti-Trust Law of "restraints of trade." The Sherman law, originally intended as a mere method of policing the channels of interstate and foreign trade to free them from such obstructions *as were unlawful at common law*, had become an economic theory, and had attempted to reconstruct society by defending the primitive individualism of the age of the wheelbarrow from the greater individualism, which in this age of steam and electricity finds its highest expression in association and co-operative contracts. Had the drastic and unyielding interpretation of the law, as laid down in the *Joint Traffic cases*, been adhered to, it would, to use the language of Justice Holmes in his dissenting opinion in the Northern Securities case, have made "eternal the *bellum omnium contra omnes* and disintegrated society, so far as it could, into individual atoms."

A law thus interpreted was an anachronism in the age of the railroad and telegraph. It was in recognition of this fact, and responsive to the clear interests of modern commerce, that this Court in the leading cases of *Standard Oil Co. vs. United States* (221 U. S., page 1 and decided in 1911) again reviewed the whole subject and definitely established the principle that the Sherman Law simply affirmed with respect to interstate and foreign commerce the principle of the common law as to restraints of trade, as modified and developed by progressive decisions of English and American Courts.

Chief Justice White in this notable opinion referred to the fact that England had repealed the earlier statutes forbidding "engrossing, forestalling, etc., upon the expressed ground that the prohibited acts had come to be considered as favorable to the development of and not in restraint of trade," and he added that the common law gave "an instinctive recognition of the truisms that the course of trade could not be made free by obstructing it, and that an individual's right to trade could not be protected by destroying such right."

This Court further stated that the Sherman Law also indicated "a consciousness that the freedom of the individual right to contract, when not unduly or improperly exercised, was the most efficient means for the prevention of monopoly, since the operation of the centrifugal and centripetal forces, resulting from the right to freely contract, was the means by which monopoly would be inevitably prevented."

This Court significantly added that "freedom to contract was the essence of freedom from undue restraint on the right to contract."

To prevent confusion and to make clear this emancipation of commerce from undue restraints on the liberty to contract, this Court expressly said that any expressions in its decisions in the *Traffic Association Cases,* above referred to, "are necessarily now limited and qualified."

Since this notable decision, the law is unquestioned that unlawful restraints of trade, either at common law or under the Sherman Anti-Trust Law, "only embraced acts or contracts or agreements or combinations which operated to the prejudice of the public interests by *unduly* restricting competition or *unduly* obstructing the due course of trade, or which, either because of their inherent nature or effect, or because of the evident purpose of the act, etc., injuriously restrained trade."

In a later case this Court added that "the statute did not forbid or restrain the power to make *normal* and *usual* contracts to further trade by resorting to all *normal* methods, whether by agreement or otherwise, to accomplish such purpose" *(U. S. vs. American Tobacco Co.,* 221 U. S., 106, 179).

Under modern commercial methods, when the relations of producer, middlemen, retailer and consumer are intimately interwoven, I know of no contract more "usual" and "normal" in the sale of standardized goods, than contracts for resale prices. If our jurisprudence condemns such contracts, then it is not responsive to the genius of this industrial age.

As the legal test of a contract is the public welfare, it inevitably follows that the judicial declaration of public policy must conform to changing economic conditions. In this respect, as in all others, "new occasions teach new duties," and the rapid changes of a progressive and complex age must at times "make ancient good uncouth." This Court has never failed to recognize this fact and to adapt its declarations of public policy to the ever changing needs of an ever changing age. Even before the *Standard Oil* and *American Tobacco* decisions, this Court, in 1910, emphasized the duty of the judiciary to determine the reasonableness or unreasonableness of particular contracts in the light of such changing conditions, when it said in the case of *Dr. Miles Medical Company vs. Park & Sons,* 220 U. S., 406:

> "With respect to contracts in restraint of trade, the earlier doctrine of the common law has been substantially modified in adaptation to modern conditions. *But the public interest is still the first consideration.* To sustain the restraint it must be found to be reasonable both with respect to the public and to the parties, and that it is limited to what is fairly necessary in the circumstances of the particular case for the protection of the covenantee. Otherwise, restraints of trade are void and against public policy. As was said by this Court in *Gibbs vs. Baltimore Gas Company,* 130 U. S., page 409: The decision in *Mitchell vs. Reynolds,* 1 P. Wms., 181, is the foundation of the rule in relation to the invalidity of contracts in restraint of trade; *but as it was made under a condition of things and a state of society, different from those which now prevail, the rule laid down is not regarded as inflexible,* and has been considerably modified. Public welfare is first considered, and if it be not involved, and the restraint upon one party is not further than protection to the other party requires, the contract may be sustained. *The question is whether under the particular circumstances of the case, and the nature of the particular contract involved in it, the contract is or is not unreasonable.'* "

The profound changes, which modern inventions have made in commercial methods, have been freely recognized by the courts in determining the reasonableness of contracts in restraint of trade. As was well said by the New York Court of Appeals, in *Diamond Match Company vs. Roeber,* 106 New York, 473:

> "Steam and electricity have for the purpose of trade and commerce, almost annihilated distance, and the whole world is now a mart for the distribution of the products of industry. The great diffusion of wealth, and the restless activity of mankind, striving to better their condition, has greatly enlarged the field of human enterprise, and created a vast number of new industries, which give scope to ingenuity and employment for capital and labor * * *. The tendency of recent adjudications is marked in the direction of relaxing the rigor of the doctrine that all contracts in general restraint of trade, are void, irrespective of special circumstances. Indeed, it has of late been denied that a hard and fast rule of that kind has ever been the law of England (*Roussilon vs. Roussilon,* 14 L. R. Chancery Division, 351). The law has for centuries permitted contracts in partial restraint of trade, when reasonable. * * *. *It is clear that public policy in the interests of society favor the utmost freedom of contract within the law, and require that business transactions should not be trammelled by unnecessary restrictions.*"

Applying these considerations to the precise question now under consideration, it is obvious that when a vendor sells a commodity to a vendee, upon condition that he shall not resell the article at less than a minimum price, that no *general or absolute* restraint of alienation exists.

The vendee is free to sell to whom, and upon what conditions he pleases, with the one exception noted. Unless it is plain that such a contract is prejudicial to the public welfare, it must be sustained as within the constitutional rights of both vendor and vendee.

In determining this question, this Court must recognize that there is a wide variety of circumstances under which such restrictions are imposed.

For example, the article may be a necessity of life, or, as in the case at bar, a mere luxury. It may be a restriction upon the wholesaler or one upon the retailer. If the former, the possible effect upon the consumer is contingent and remote, for the retailers may compete between themselves as to prices.

The commodity may be sold under competitive conditions or, as in the *Dr. Miles case*, under non-competitive conditions. In that case an absolute monopoly existed. As Justice Brandeis, when still a member of the bar, well said:

> "The position of the independent producer, who establishes the price at which his own trademarked article shall be sold to the consumer, must not be confused with that of a combination or trust, which, controlling the market, fixes the price of a staple article. The independent producer is engaged in a business open to competition. He establishes his price at his peril, the peril that if he sets it too high, either the consumer will not buy or, if the article is, nevertheless, popular, the high profits will invite even more competition. The consumer who pays the price established by an independent producer in a competitive line of business does so voluntarily; he pays the price asked, because he deems the article worth that price as compared with the cost of other competing articles. But when a trust fixes, through its monopoly power, the price of a staple article in common use, the consumer does not pay the price voluntarily. He pays under compulsion. There being no competitor he must pay the price fixed by the trust, or be deprived of the use of the article." ("Cut-throat Prices," Harpers' Weekly, Nov. 15, 1913.)

I have already discussed in our main brief, pages 111-138, the immense and vital difference between the existence of competitive and non-competitive conditions as bearing upon the reasonableness of a contract for a resale price, and without repeating what is there better stated, I need only refer briefly to the controlling importance of this question of fact.

[Mr. Justice Day: Will you in the course of your interesting argument give the court your views as to the effect of such restrictive contracts upon the consumer?

Replying to your Honor's question, it is not possible to dogmatize with respect to such effect. The effect upon the consumer differs in different cases. It may be appreciable or inappreciable; direct or indirect; beneficial or at times prejudicial. Such a restriction upon resale is only one of a number of factors in the equation.]

It may, however, be safely asserted as a general rule, that any commercial method which makes for economical production and distribution does not prejudicially affect the consumer, but on the contrary generally benefits him. If the producer is not at liberty to distribute his goods through wholesalers and retailers with price restriction, then, if he have capital enough, he will be driven to market direct to the consumer, and as this is generally regarded as the more expensive method, presumptively the increased cost of this method of distribution will fall upon the consumer. This is especially true in commodities that are specialties and not necessaries of life. Take for example the phonograph. Generally it is sold either in a shop devoted exclusively to phonographic goods, or in a shop which sells similar commodities, as other musical instruments. The producer does not sell anything but the phonograph and its accessories. If he sells these through his own system of branch stores, the entire overhead charge presumptively falls upon the consumer of his merchandise; but if he utilizes retailers who deal in other musical instruments, as pianos, organs, violins, etc., then the overhead charge of such a retail store is divided between the purchasers of the phonographs and other kinds of merchandise, and the wider the variety and volume of goods sold the smaller the burden of the overcharge. It is, therefore, an economical method of distribution for the producer of phonographs to share with the producers of other commodities the expenses of distribution, and presumptively the consumer gets the benefit of this method of co-operation.

If the resale contract is forbidden, then the producer, if he have sufficient capital, will be unwilling to resort to this method of distribution, and will take the more expensive one of marketing his goods direct to the consumer, especially as he is confronted with the danger that if he markets through department stores, the sale price of his goods may be destroyed by the temptation of the department store to utilize goods of standard value as so-called "leaders," not to make a fair profit but to attract customers to the store.

For these reasons it may well be doubted whether the prohibition of resale contracts will not in the long run burden the consumer, although it may be conceded that temporarily he may profit in a given purchase by getting a commodity more cheaply. Undoubtedly the consumer who buys at a bargain-counter sale of a department store is temporarily benefited by paying less money, but as this process too often destroys the power of the producer to distribute economically, the continuing benefit to the consumer may well be doubted.

I do not concede that public policy should *solely* regard the interests of the consumer, for society is like an orchestra in which each instrument is essential to an harmonious result. Nevertheless the consumer, especially when necessaries of life are involved, must be a matter of first and chief consideration. Public policy, however, must necessarily take into account the retailer, the distributor and especially the producer, for if the producer cannot economically produce, the consumer must suffer a partial or total deprivation of the product and enhanced prices.

It is obvious that that which chiefly concerns the consumer and generally results in a possible enhancement of prices is the absence of competitive conditions, and, when

these do not exist, a contract, which restricts a vendee
from reselling at less than a fixed price, may at least temporarily affect the consumer.

This was the fact in the *Dr. Miles case,* for there a complete absence of competitive conditions existed, and the
fixed resale price necessarily affected the consumer. Where,
however, competitive conditions exist, the inevitable
working of economic laws protects the consumer not only
in giving him the opportunity, if he thinks the resale price
unfair, to purchase a competing product, but also because the existence of competitive conditions normally
affects the reasonableness of the resale price.

Take for example the business with which the present
case is concerned. If the complainants were the sole producers of phonographs and phonographic records, their
power to impose upon their immediate vendees a resale
price would affect the consumer, whose only protection
would be that if the price were excessive, the consumer
would refuse to buy what is a mere luxury. My clients,
however, are obliged to compete in the sale of sound-pro-
ducing instruments with many other producing companies—some producing cheap phonographs, and others,
as the Victor Talking Machine Company, high grade
products. Under these circumstances, if the Columbia
Company by its contract with a retailer imposes an excessive resale price, the consumer will buy the products of
other producing companies, and this power and opportunity on his part will necessarily influence the judgment
of the producer in determining his vendee's resale price.
He will not fix one calculated to drive his customers to
other producers.

In this connection it should be emphasized that to condemn the power of the producer to impose resale prices
will accomplish nothing, except to impose upon the producer additional expenses, which are generally shifted to
the consumer, who thus pays a higher price for a product.

Economic laws are as the tides. They move irresistibly
and beyond the power of statute or judicial decision to
control. No one questions, for example, the right of the
producer, if he has sufficient capital, to establish his own

depots for the marketing of his products, and in that event to charge the consumer all that the traffic will bear. If he have not sufficient capital to establish his own marketing depots, he can at least consign his goods to his own agents with a similar result. It is well known that the consignment plan is far more expensive than the distribution of a product through independent distributors and retailers.

It inevitably follows that if the public policy of the nation, as declared by statute or judicial decision, should unreasonably interfere with the right of contract in the matter of resale prices, that the strongest producers will, as in the case of the Standard Oil and other great concerns, be driven to market their own products. The result will be that the consumer will not only pay as much but, other things being equal, he will pay more for his product, because upon him the burden of increased expenses generally falls.

Thus the small producers may be driven out of business, and only the large producers remain; and this inevitably will tend toward monopolization with all its evils.

Here again is illustrated the futility of interfering with the normal contracts of business, and emphasizes that which we have already quoted from Chief Justice White's philosophical opinion in the *Standard Oil case* that the undue attempt of law to interfere with economic processes to prevent so-called restraints of trade, generally ends in restraints of trade and is in the long run of little, if any, benefit to the consumer. Viewing the controversies of the last generation philosophically, it may be the fact that the greatest restraint of trade has been that of the drastic letter of the Sherman Anti-Trust law.

The present theory of the law is that its processes should be used to conserve competitive conditions. It should not further interfere with the liberty of contract; and where competitive conditions exist, there is no longer a justifiable reason for forbidding a contract between a vendor and vendee, which prescribes a resale price.

I cannot leave this branch of the subject without also referring to the fallacy that competition consists exclusively in prices. A resale price may or may not affect competition in prices, but it cannot affect competition in quality and service, and the modern tendency to standardize prices in standardized goods not only leaves open, but actually stimulates, the competition in the quality of products and the many commercial methods, which may be summarized under the word "service."

For example, there is the keenest competition between the Columbia in marketing its phonographic records and the Victor Talking Machine Company. Each endeavors to secure the most advantageous distributing facilities, the services of the greatest artists for the purpose of making records, with resulting greater popularity and reputation for its products. Each endeavors in its laboratories to improve its products and make them more perfect.

The truest competition consists in these elements, and it is a narrow conception of the public welfare which ignores these elements in exclusive consideration of the question of prices.

Here again in determining the public welfare, the varying conditions of different branches of commerce should be borne in mind. Between one pound of sugar and another there may be little or no competition in quality, but between the phonographic record of one company and that of another acute competition does exist, irrespective of prices.

In concluding this branch of the discussion, I again emphasize the thought that even if competition in prices is the only element to be considered, that the reasonableness *even from the standpoint of the consumer* of resale prices must depend upon the existence or non-existence of competitive conditions, *and this in itself shows the danger* of holding too broadly and rigidly that all resale price contracts are void.

The resale price may be a reasonable or an unreasonable one. Here, the workings of economic law generally result in the fact that if the resale price be unreasonable, the consumer, unless it be a necessary of life, will not take it, and sooner or later it must be abandoned. If the resale price be reasonable, the consumer gets an equivalent for his money. Here the reasonableness of a resale price is best determined by vendor and vendee, *for the vendee will not buy for resale, if the resale price is, in fact and not as a juridical theory only, an effective restraint on alienation.*

Many other considerations, upon which the question of reasonableness may depend, could be instanced, but there is one of such overshadowing importance, and which in itself so fully illustrates the danger of invalidating all resale prices that I content myself with reference to it, especially as it is intimately related to the facts in the present case. In determining whether resale price contracts are prejudicial to the public welfare, the court should, I submit, take into consideration *whether the vendor has any economic justification for imposing upon his vendee a resale price.*

Ordinarily a vendor who sells a commodity to a vendee and parts with his title is not concerned with his vendee's disposition of the article. It does not matter to him whether the vendee uses the article, or gives it away or sells it.

The subject matter of the article or the commercial methods, which apply to its sale, may well give the vendor a substantial interest and right in his vendee's disposition of the article.

Thus the common law which forbade altogether total restraints on alienation yet recognized the peculiar consideration which arose out of a slave or an heirloom. The seller of either could for sentimental reasons sell under promise that his vendee should not resell under any circumstances.

A like distinction exists between the case where the vendor, having sold his article for a price, no longer concerns himself with it *and the case of a vendor, who, on selling his article, proceeds to co-operate with his vendee in finding for his vendee a market for the article.*

In the time of Coke, a vendor sold his commodity, and had no further practical interest in its resale. If human society were still in a primitive stage, this might be an ideal condition; but under modern commercial methods, where the manufacturer of a commodity, not a necessary of life, must often create the market for his wares, not only for himself, but for his distributors and retailers, it is obviously impossible for the manufacturer to sell his goods, and after taking his price give no further attention to them.   That considerable part of all modern commerce, which are luxuries or specialties, and which are subject to the competition of their rival articles in the same line of commerce, and which are marketed under special brands and trade-marks and which thereby acquire an especial and stable value, cannot be developed or even maintained by the manufacturer simply selling his goods to those who apply for them.   His business does not consist in selling over a counter or in a restricted locality, where a shop would be known.   He offers to sell his commodity to one hundred millions of people over a territory three thousand miles wide, and as few of his customers ever see his producing plant, or business office, it is obvious that he must create the necessary demand in the public mind to sell his goods.   For such nation-wide sales no market overt, or public exchange exists.   The public knowledge of the existence of his goods, and the need for them, must be a matter of a long and very expensive educational campaign, and he must convince millions of people that they require the purchase of his goods.

Take for example, the case at bar.   Twenty-five years ago the phonograph was unknown.   If invented at all, it was a mere scientific toy, and its utilization as a musical instrument in millions of homes was an undreamed possibility.   My clients and other producers proceeded to spend many millions of dollars in educating the public to the desirability of the instrument.   One of these companies has spent over twenty million dollars in newspaper advertising and in printing, catalogues, posters, and trade emblems.

The manufacturer has thus at enormous expense created not merely the demand for his goods on the part of his vendee, but also that which enables his vendee, generally a wholesale distributor, to sell to the retailer, and the secondary demand, which enables the retailer to open an attractive shop, and interest the consumer.

The demand having been thus created, the efforts of the manufacturer cannot cease.   They must continue ceaselessly, for the article is not a necessary of life, and sooner or later its hold upon the public mind as a novelty ceases. Thus, each month, the manufacturer widely advertises new records, and again brings to the public mind the desirability of purchasing a phonograph, not from the complainant as the manufacturer, for the producer rarely deals directly with the consumer, but from the retailer, who in turn buys from the distributor.

This immense and continuing service in developing and maintaining the value of the product is no part of any contract of sale between the manufacturer and his immediate vendee. It is a gratuitous service, so far as any contractual obligation is concerned. The manufacturer could withhold it, and if he did, his business, and that of his distributors and retailers would sooner or later dwindle.

It does not follow that the public necessarily pays a larger price. The more phonographs and records sold, the less the proportionate overhead and the greater the ability of the manufacturer to develop the business. The maintenance of a reasonable price leaves a larger amount for the development of the trade as a whole, and the larger the amount of such trade, the less the cost of production, and the less the cost of production, the greater the ability of the manufacturer to lessen his price from time to time. Of this, the Ford motor, a veritable miracle in economical production, is the ubiquitous proof.

That greed may in some instances and for a time defeat this chain of causation, does not destroy the economic fact that a manufacturer, who has developed a business, which enables him to employ ten thousand employees and market products amounting to many millions of dollars in value, does enable the manufacturer to market his product at a less cost, and ordinarily it is to his business interests to do so. A single phonograph of the type sold could not be made for the price at which it is sold, but the manufacture of a million phonographs makes possible, and generally results in, a cheapening of price. This is the secret of the prodigious commercial success of the Ford motor. It is the secret of all similar economic successes. *It has led, not to a restraint of trade, but to a prodigious expansion.*

We are not arguing for any power on the part of the

manufacturer to impose prices upon distributors and retailers *with whom he has no contractual relation.* The
manufacturer should have no power to project his control
over the thing he sells beyond the person to whom he sells
it.   His right to do so should only exist under his own
contracting power.   Having sold his article, whether to
distributor or to retailer, upon such terms as he and his
vendee think fair and reasonable, and the title thus having
passed, the article, so far as the manufacturer is concerned,
becomes a free article of commerce, and the power of the
manufacturer is ended, when the price and other conditions of his contract with the vendee are fulfilled.   Certainly he cannot *by mere notice* affixed to his commodity,
as in the *Sanatogen case,* impose his will as to resale price
upon every one into whose hands the commodity may
come.   Such a power would be inconsistent with the freedom of commerce.*

I simply maintain that when a manufacturer has created the demand for an article, and at great expense is
aiding his vendee in finding a market, that it is not unreasonable, but is consonant with the soundest business
methods for him, as the owner of the article, to provide
that his immediate vendee, who might otherwise be unable to sell the article, shall not, by cutting prices, make
it impossible for the manufacturer to extend him aid.

This Court has recognized this economic truth and its
legal justification in *McLean vs. Fleming* 96 U. S., 245,
when it said:

> "Suppose the latter has obtained celebrity in
> his manufacture, he is entitled to all the advan-
> tages of that celebrity, whether resulting from
> the greater demand for his goods *or from the
> higher price the public are willing to give for the
> article,* rather than for the goods of the other
> manufacturer, whose reputation is not so high
> as a manufacturer. * * * Everywhere courts
> of justice proceed upon the ground that a party
> has a valuable interest in the good will of his
> trade, and in the labels or trade-mark which he
> adopted to enlarge and perpetuate it."

This principle was thus based upon the law of good will, which for many years has led English and American courts to sustain contracts in partial restraint of trade. The distributor or retailer who sells a phonograph, sells something more than a piece of wood and metal. He sells something that has acquired a unique value in the market, by reason of the good-will inherent in a valuable brand. The retailer, who sells a Columbia phonograph, could not sell it to the same advantage if it were not known as a Columbia phonograph, for the manufacturer, by the expenditure of many millions of dollars, has created a stable value for his products. That his good-will and its value are materially impaired by indiscriminate price cutting is clear beyond contradiction.

In more primitive times, good-will was only the habit of the public to return to a particular store; but in this more complex age, good will in a business, which deals in a branded product having a nation-wide market, is the same habit to buy an article, whose value and character are guaranteed by a given brand. Such good-will is an asset, and the right to protect it by reasonable agreements, even though such agreements do partially, but not unreasonably, restrain trade has long been recognized by courts of equity.

The rule is firmly established and is familiar, that in the case of the sale of a business having a good-will, restrictive agreements for the protection of the good-will thus sold may be validly made within reasonable limits. The reasoning which supports the rule is that the transfer of the good will thus sold, can only be adequately protected to the purchaser by compelling the seller to observe such restrictive covenants not to compete, as are reasonable to protect the good will against injury by the seller. The seller is not permitted to destroy or impair the value of the good-will, which he has sold, by competing against it.

Does not the above reasoning apply with equal force to the case of a manufacturer, who, instead of selling his good will as an entirety, makes a contract by which the vendee (through being given an opportunity to sell large quantities of the branded product in which the good will inheres) is *entrusted with the protection of the manufacturer's good-will.*

While there is no technical agency or trusteeship in such a case, may it not be reasonably contended that when a dealer bargains with the manufacturer of a branded article for permission to purchase for resale considerable quantities of an article, and can procure the goods only by agreeing to protect the good will, that the manufacturer entrusts the dealer with the actual handling of a portion of the manufacturer's good-will? He permits him to become a distributor of the product which embodies the good-will, to the extent that the observance of reasonable resale restrictions will protect the good-will, and violation will seriously injure it.

Bearing in mind the fact that the subject-matter in this class of cases is limited to the branded product of the manufacturer as affected by his direct agreement with his dealer, and to such articles only as the dealer has obtained from the manufacturer pursuant to such agreement, it seems clear that the very limited restraint upon trade is less broad in subject-matter than that in case of a sale of the good will,—and that it is as reasonable a restraint.

The ultimate question is whether it is reasonable for a vendor to say to his immediate vendee:

"I will sell you a machine, which has a greater value because of the good will attached thereto, provided that you will not injure that good will by selling at a price less than that which measures the good will."

The business sense of the community, whether regard is had to the class of manufacturers, or distributors, or retailers, believes that this is reasonable, and if the courts shall deny the rights of the manufacturer to make such a contract, then they will fail to take into account the changed commercial methods, which we have discussed, upon which the industries of this country, amounting to billions of dollars, have in great part been built. An overwhelming preponderance of opinion in the business world favors this efficient method of expanding trade. The chief dissenters form the small minority, who seek to monopolize trade by destroying their competitors through unfair competition.

There is another and very important consideration, which requires a recognition of this freedom of contract. Commerce in the time of Coke was a very primitive affair. It was even more primitive in Littleton's time, for he wrote about the time Columbus discovered America. There have been other discoveries since then. Commerce then consisted of articles which were largely necessaries of life. They were sold in a restricted community, for travel was difficult. They were sold over the counter, or in a local market by a physical comparison of the things to be sold. The purchaser tried to buy at a fair price, and to resell at a fair price, and in most cases a fair price was a result of the conflicting views and necessities of the vendor and vendee. The present times present a new condition, which largely disturbs the just equilibrium of competition, and which a wise and progressive judiciary must take into account.

In the great centers of population, department stores, chain stores and mail order houses have come into existence, unknown to Coke's time, when the cobbler was a cobbler, and the horse dealer a horse dealer. The department store sells ten thousand articles, and the customers that throng the aisles of these vast establishments number in the course of a year many millions. To attract these millions to his store, its owner advertises his wares by full page advertisements to millions of people and no method of gaining public patronage is more common than to sell a standardized product at less than cost in order to gain a profit by the probable purchase by such customer of other articles at a large profit. The advertisements of the department store make this fact notorious. Each day they advertise their so-called "bargain sales," often without profit, and, since nearly all of them retire from business as multimillionaires, the conclusion is reasonable that what they lose on one article, a so-called "leader" (often a discreditable trap for the unwary) whose value they have thus sacrificed, or pretended to sacrifice, they make up by large profits on other articles. No trade method is more reprehensible or more restrictive of honest business.

It is generally recognized that the incessant struggle of legitimate business interests for some limited form of price maintenance largely has its origin in these unreasonable and piratical practices.

A department store, as shown in the facts certified to this Court, having purchased a line of phonographs and records from my clients under an express contract not to resell at less than the listed price, promptly advertises to sell them at a price less than the generally advertised and agreed price. Sometimes this price is less than the cost of production. What is the inevitable result? Sooner or later the department store, to a very substantial degree, restrains trade by destroying its competitors, and, with the elimination of many competitors, the demand for the manufacturer's product quickly dwindles, and with a lessened demand, his power to expand commerce by increasing the demand for his products is necessarily destroyed.

Let me give the Court an actual instance, to which testimony was given at a recent hearing before the Federal Trade Commission.

A New York department store, which shall be nameless, purchased on more than one occasion goods having a standard value from the producers and then proceeded to cut the prices below that of any other retail house. As one of these producers testified, the very morning that the public announcement was made by display advertisements of this ruthless cutting of prices, the producer was beset with demands from other retailers to remedy the evil or take back their goods; and finally the producer, who was facing the destruction of his retail trade, went to the department store and was compelled to buy back the goods, which he had sold the department store at a large preferential discount, at the retail price which the department store was offering them to the public.

Can it be that this kind of commercial blackmail is for the public welfare? Can it be that a contract to desist from this form of piracy is a restraint of trade? Can it be that public policy requires the Court to give its sanction to such unfair dealing because of an assumed temporary advantage to the consumer?

One recalls the vigorous and amply justified comment of Mr. Justice Holmes, in his dissenting opinion in the *Dr. Miles case,* where he said:

"I cannot believe that in the long run the public will profit by this Court permitting knaves to cut reasonable prices for some ulterior purpose of their own, and thus impair, if not to destroy, the production and sale of articles, which it is assumed to be desirable that the public should be able to get."

The learned Justice proceeded to say that such conduct was "fraudulent and has no merits of its own to recommend it to the favor of the Court."

In this connection the Court should apply the doctrine of the so-called "unfair trade" cases, *i. e.,* cases involving fraudulent or unfair efforts to violate common-law trade-names as distinguished from technical trade-marks. The trend of the decisions in such cases is constantly toward a more extensive protection against all unfair practices. While the question has usually arisen in suits between the manufacturers or dealers in competing products, the rule should also protect a manufacturer of a branded article, the trade name of which involves his entire goodwill, from the unfair competition of a dealer, who seeks to violate his agreement with the manufacturer. The Federal Trade Commission Act declares the legislative policy of the nation to be opposed to "unfair methods of competition in commerce" (§5). How could the public policy of the nation be more comprehensively expressed?

Take the facts certified to this Court in the case at bar. The manufacturer sells his product under the name "Columbia" and its goodwill inheres largely in the value and use of that trade name. The dealer, a department store, seeks to obtain a stock of Columbia records for sale to its customers. It enters into a dealer's contract, by which it agrees not to resell except at list prices. When it has thus obtained the records, it proceeds to cut prices. The breach of contract is so glaring that the inference of fraudulent intent may reasonably arise from the fact that the dealer, having persuaded the manufacturer to supply it with a stock of records upon the dealer's agreement not to cut prices, thereafter proceeds to cut prices.

If it be actionable "unfair trade" for one manufacturer or dealer, to steal a part of the good will, which inheres in the goods of another manufacturer, by unfairly simulating the latter's trade-marks or labels (through which the public recognizes the origin of the article),—why is it not actionable "unfair trade" for a dealer,—who can get Columbia goods from the manufacturer only by agreeing not to injure the trade name,—to proceed, when he thus gets the goods, to partially destroy the good will by deliberately breaking the agreement, on the faith of which the manufacturer let him have the goods?

The only difference seems to be that in the former case, the price cutter not only takes away from the manufacturer a part of the latter's property, but he also appropriates to himself what he has stolen; in the latter case, he merely destroys that much of the property of his victim.

In each case, however, the actionable wrong is that the value of the trade name to its owner has been lessened and in some cases destroyed by the fraudulent or unfair dealing of the other party.

Can a rule of law be for the public welfare that is a shield of fraud? Does the public gain any real or permanent advantage, when business contracts, entered into in good faith, are treated as "scraps of paper?"

It is, however, contended that my clients are within the prohibition of the law because the certified facts submitted to the Court show that the contract now under consideration was made not with one retailer but with five thousand retailers, and constituted, to use the language of the certificate, "a system." The "system" which was condemned in the *Dr. Miles case* was an inter-locking system of contracts imposed upon the wholesalers, to whom the Dr. Miles Medical Co. sold, and the retailers to whom he did not sell, and this system was justly condemned by this Court.

It does not follow that because a producer makes five thousand resale price contracts instead of one that he is

therefore condemned by the law.   If the producer of
goods, for which there is a nation-wide demand, is entitled to make one resale contract, he must be equally entitled to make fifty thousand, for apart from the fact that
uniformity of contract is a modern method of business,
is the fact that the Clayton Law in spirit, if not in words,
requires such equality of treatment.   To deny to the producer the right to make 5,000 contracts with 5,000 retailers, while conceding his right to make such a contract
with one retailer, would virtually deny the right altogether. *A right cannot depend upon the number of times that
it is exercised.*   Either the right exists or it does not exist.
In the former event, if my clients were entitled to make
this contract with the Boston Store, they were entitled to
make it with every retailer under similar circumstances.
Any other view would be a travesty on the regulation of
business by law in an age when the business man deals
with thousands where the producer in a former age dealt
with scores.

Between the policy of *unlimited* price restriction
through mere notice and the policy of a *partial* price restriction through the right of contract, there is, we submit, a twilight zone, in which the forces of commercial
freedom should have full play, at least until the legislative
department of the Government declares otherwise, and
we earnestly press upon this Court, in justice to the vast
interests that are concerned in this controversy, that this
Court should recognize the existence of such a twilight
zone, not by creating a new law but by recognizing the
fundamental liberty to make a reasonable contract and the
rule of common law, which only forbade a complete restraint on alienation.

In so doing, it will not, as we have previously shown,
declare any new law.   It will simply recognize the doctrine of English and American courts for the last two centuries, which sustains the right of contract, unless the exercise of such right is plainly prejudicial to the public welfare.

This Court is not required to put business enterprise in
a straight jacket. We are confident that it has no disposition to interfere unduly with the liberty of contract.

Much less in maintaining the freedom of trade does it desire to give judicial sanction to unfair and fraudulent trade methods.

I submit that this Court can without violence to its previous decisions say, and the economic welfare of the American people imperatively requires it to say, that a manufacturer has the right to determine, within reasonable limits *and under competitive conditions,* the price for which he will sell his goods, including the imposition upon his immediate vendee as a *part of such price,* of a reasonable resale price.

When he requires, as a consideration for such sale, that his vendee shall not resell at less than a minimum price, he is not projecting his power beyond the fair limit of his contractual rights, and upon the other hand, the vendee is not obliged to buy, and if the conditions be unreasonable, can refuse to buy, and such vendee whether he buys or refuses to buy, is equally within his constitutional rights.

CHIEF JUSTICE WHITE: Assuming, Mr. Beck, that this Court's decision in the *Dr. Miles case* is against your contention, and that the evil consequences, to which you referred, are taking place or have taken place, is not your true remedy to appeal to Congress rather than to this Court? I am not suggesting that this Court has decided the question in the *Dr. Miles case,* but if it has, is not your true appeal to Congress?

Assuming the fact to be as suggested by your Honor I cannot concede that our appeal should necessarily be to Congress. It is part of the genius of our institutions that questions of public policy are to some extent committed to the judiciary, especially where judicial process is invoked to enforce contracts.]

Undoubtedly the courts of England and the United States, in determining whether a contract is or is not against public policy, do to some extent exercise a function, which is quasi-legislative; but the practical genius of Anglo-Saxon jurisprudence has permitted this because a court can more readily adapt its declarations of public policy to the changing needs of successive generations than can the letter of a statute. It has generally and for many centuries been a judicial function to determine when a given contract is or is not in restraint of trade. Congress recognized this, and in employing in the Sherman Anti-Trust Law an apt legal term it still left to the Judiciary the right and duty to determine what was a restraint of trade.

Napoleon said, on the eve of the 18th Brumaire, that his nation had not yet "defined what we meant by the executive, legislative and judicial powers," and he characterized Montesquieu's definition as misleading. In this country, we also now recognize that there is some overlapping in the functions of the three departments of the Government.

This Court recognized this fact when, in the *Standard Oil cases*, it reconsidered the interpretation which it had placed in the *Joint Traffic decisions* on the Sherman Anti-Trust Law by broadening and liberalizing its interpretation of the expression "in restraint of trade." If, therefore, it be assumed that this Court too broadly condemned all contracts for a resale price in the *Dr. Miles case*, which I have not conceded, it would simply follow its own precedent, if in this case it shall qualify and limit the alleged doctrine of the *Dr. Miles case* by making it inapplicable to such a contract as is set forth in the case now certified to this Court.

Edmund Burke once said "that the greatest struggles for constitutional liberty in England turned upon the questions of taxation." In the last 25 years, and possibly in the next quarter of a century, the great struggles in this country have turned and are turning upon the true liberty of contract. Upon that foundation, built by the Constitution itself, we stand in this case, for as was said by a very distinguished English Judge (SIR GEORGE JESSELL), in *Printing Company vs. Sampson*, 19 Equity Cases, L. R., 462:

> "If there is one thing more than any other which public policy requires, it is that men of full age and competent understanding shall have the utmost liberty of contracting, and that contracts when entered into freely and voluntarily, shall be held good, and shall be enforced by courts of justice."

XVII

THE CONSTITUTIONAL POWER OF CONGRESS TO EXCLUDE ALIENS IN THE ENUMERATION OF THE CENSUS

> The House of Representatives had under consideration a bill for the taking of the census and the establishment of a ratio for the apportionment of members of the House among the several states, as provided in Article 1, Section 2, of the Constitution. During the discussion of the bill, Henry St. George Tucker, a distinguished member from the State of Virginia and a recognized authority on Constitutional law, made an argument in support of the proposition that, in arriving at the ratio to be used for the apportionment of representatives among the several states, the Constitution required that aliens should be excluded. The following address, delivered by Mr. Beck on June 10, 1929, demonstrated, in my opinion, with almost mathematical exactitude that Mr. Tucker's argument had no justification in the Constitution.—EDITOR.

Mr. Speaker, Ladies and Gentlemen of the House:

I listened to the address of the distinguished gentleman from Virginia with pleasure, as I always do when he addresses the House, and if he failed to convince me of the soundness of his contention, it was not due to any lack of respect on my part for his ability as a student of the Constitution or because he failed to say anything that could be said in support of his contention. The gentleman from Virginia holds a high and very deserved place in this House as an interpreter of the Constitution. He has brought to the great subject the researches of a lifetime and his auditors have the added satisfaction that any view he expresses is not actuated by any ulterior or partisan motive but is dictated by his lifelong loyalty to the Constitution.

If I understand his argument correctly, he was, as he says, "driven to the conclusion" that the framers of the Constitution did not intend, when they used the word "persons," in Article 1, section 2, of the Constitution, to include aliens. The title of his address, as given in the CONGRESSIONAL RECORD, might suggest a narrower contention that the framers of the Constitution did not intend either to include or exclude aliens but left it to the discretion of the Congress in making the enumeration.

While this latter contention could, in my judgment, be more plausibly supported, yet I doubt whether the gentleman from Virginia intended to suggest it, for he has been a zealous student of *Madison's Debates,* and they have doubtless satisfied him, as they must any careful reader, that, whatever else they intended, the framers of the Constitution did not intend to leave the time and the method of enumeration to the discretion of Congress. It was first suggested in the convention of 1787 that it should be left to Congress, but the wise men of the convention speedily saw that this would admit of the same legislative jugglery as the States practice when they so gerrymander districts as to give to one party a wholly disproportionate representation. They rejected the idea of leaving the precise method of the enumeration to the discretion of Congress and required that it be made in a specific way every ten years.

Notwithstanding the title of his address, I think the gentleman from Virginia will agree with me that the framers of the Constitution intended to either include or exclude aliens from the enumeration, and the only question that seems to admit of discussion is the nature of their decision.

The gentleman from Virginia tells us that he is "driven to the conclusion" that they did not intend to include aliens. I am driven to the conclusion that they did, and I should not regard the question at this late day in the history of the Republic as even debatable, were it not that the gentleman from Virginia has given to his contention, which he confesses is "novel," the great authority of his name. Indeed, the fact that it is a novel contention, 140 years after the Constitution became operative, in itself refutes his contention. Undoubtedly, questions may arise in the interpretation of the Constitution, even at this late day, which are novel, although the occasions must necessarily be few. I remember, as Solicitor General, arguing in the Supreme Court one question as to whether the clause of the Constitution, which prohibits any preference to any port, included the ports of a Territory. This question had never been raised and, in the nature of the case, it could not well be raised until there were Territories having ports of entry and until Congress sought to discriminate against them.

When, however, a "novel" question has reference to a matter which has arisen every decade in the practical workings of the Government and it is clear that, during a period of over 140 years, a uniform construction has been adopted, then it can be fairly said that that construction of the Constitution has been definitely determined by usage and can not at this late day be reasonably questioned. Our Constitution was in its creation an evolution and it has remained an evolution ever since. Its development is due to formal amendment; to usage, which we call practical construction, and to formal judicial interpretation. Of amendments there are few; of judicial decisions there are many, but, far exceeding in importance either amendments or judicial decisions, the practical interpretation of the Constitution by those who conduct the machinery of the Government has always been accorded most persuasive force.

May I again refer to a case which I had the privilege of arguing in the Supreme Court. It was unquestionably one of the greatest cases of this generation in determining the form of our Government. It was the so-called *Removal from-Office Case,* in which the question was again raised whether the President had the power to remove any official whom he had appointed by and with the advice and consent of the Senate. It was true that the Constitution nowhere vested in express language any power to remove in the President, and it was equally true that very eminent men, at different periods of our country's history, had from time to time suggested a doubt as to whether the power of the President was drawn from his appointing power, which he shared with the Senate, or from his general executive power to see that the laws were faithfully executed. The case was finally decided in the great decision of Chief Justice Taft in *Myers v. United States* (272 U. S.), and it is significant that the Chief Justice rested his decision in large part upon the fact that, in the First Congress of the United States, in which were many men who had sat in the Constitutional Convention, a decision was then reached after prolonged debate that the President's power to remove was a part of the Executive power vested in him by the Constitution and that Congress could not either impair or destroy it.

Similarly, in this case it cannot be questioned that, in every previous enumeration, in apportioning Members of the House of Representatives aliens have been included in the basis of representation, and if the gentleman from Virginia is correct, then this Nation from the beginning has never been properly organized and there has been no true basis of representation. All of us will shrink from such a conclusion.

It is significant in this connection that another distinguished Member of this House—I refer to the gentleman from the fourth district of Kansas—while himself desiring to exclude aliens from the enumeration, has been unable to concur in the conclusion of Mr. Tucker that the Constitution already works such exclusion. On February 13 last, the gentleman from Kansas [Mr. Hoch] made a very able argument in support of a proposed constitutional amendment which would work such exclusion, and his argument clearly accepted as an unassailable fact that the Constitution in its present form requires the inclusion of aliens. His views are the more important because he had reached the conclusion that the time had come to exclude aliens from the enumeration, and it is fair to assume that if he could have construed the Constitution differently he would have done so.

Before passing to a closer discussion of the question, I want to notice two false premises upon which, it seems to me, the argument to which I am replying was based.

The first is that there were no aliens in the United States when the Constitution was adopted and that the question, therefore, had no serious consideration. Three or four times in the course of his address our colleague from Virginia reiterated this statement. Indeed, in his peroration, referring to the first period of the Republic, he said, "Why put in aliens when they were not here? There were not any aliens here; I mean practically none, of course."

The second premise of his argument was the statement

that to include aliens was to give them an undue influence in the Government and that it was essential that they should be excluded to prevent such undue influence. Our friend from Virginia linked the presence of aliens in this country to "a splinter in the hand, a cinder in the eye; indeed, any foreign substance in the human body is liable to create irritation, friction, distress, and swelling, and so forth." He argued that any other interpretation would "admit aliens to a large influence in the Government of the United States," and as an illustration of his theory he stated that if two districts had each 500,000 people and one of them consisted wholly of American citizens and the other was equally divided between citizens and aliens, that the latter "would have double power over the other district."

I challenge the soundness of both premises. They seem to me without justification in fact.

Taking his first premise, long before the Constitution was adopted, there had already set in a great tide of immigration to this country. Especially in the Middle States there were many aliens. When the Constitution was adopted aliens were very welcome in this country. It was then recognized that its future greatness would depend to some extent upon migration to this country. The American people were then not as sensitive about aliens as they are now, for they all recognized that many were the descendants of men who were once aliens. One of the counts against George III in the Declaration of Independence was this:

> "He has endeavored to prevent the population of these States; for that purpose obstructing the laws for naturalization of foreigners and refusing to pass others to encourage their migration hither."

In many of the Colonies there were the most liberal provisions with respect to aliens. Thus in Massachusetts no length of residence was required and in others only an oath of allegiance, while in others any permanent residence qualified a man to vote if he was a freeholder.

Pennsylvania especially had a heterogeneous population.

Its chief city was then the true cosmopolitan city of the country. Recognizing the existence of many aliens in America, the naturalization laws of Pennsylvania were so liberal that any alien who had resided in Pennsylvania for one year and owned real estate was made *ipso facto* a citizen and accorded all the rights of such. The Constitution itself recognizes the necessity of naturalization in more than one passage.

Thus the framers of the Constitution could not have been ignorant of the fact that there were then many aliens in the United States and that many more were to come, and it is a plausible conjecture that, because they were truly a part of the population, subject to the laws of the country, they used the word "persons" in describing whom should be enumerated.

Equally without foundation is the second premise that to include aliens in the population is to give them an undue influence in the councils of the Nation, for that ignores the basic theory of representative government. Aliens are human beings, and as such have rights in any country in which they are domiciled, not only under the principles of natural justice but also by the provisions of the Constitution itself. Aliens help to create the wealth of our Nation; they are subject to its laws and must comply with all its demands of taxation.

The gentleman from Virginia suggested that if all the people of the United States could be called in a town meeting to determine upon questions of common interest aliens would naturally be denied a right to vote. That may be true, but, nevertheless, citizens who voted would necessarily act for the common benefit of all the inhabitants, who would be obliged to respect the laws thus enacted. As such a town meeting is impossible, we have adopted the principle of representative government, and while only citizens can vote for such representatives such fact is not inconsistent with both the moral and political obligation of the representatives to act in the common interests of all, as all, whether citizens or not, are affected by such laws and are obliged to obey them. Aliens, therefore, who have become part of our household and who have cast their lots permanently with ours, and who presumably have a wish to become citizens when permitted to do so, have a just right to be represented, although they cannot select the representatives, and the framers of the Constitution recognized this when they included them in the enumeration.

The only exception to this fundamental rule of public justice was the nontaxed Indians and the slaves. The former were regarded as *sui generis* and the right of the latter to be represented, even though they were regarded as property, was recognized by the Constitution by enumerating them to the extent of three-fifths of their number. Why include slaves and exclude alien freemen?

Not only was the argument of my friend from Virginia defective in its fundamental premises, but his method of construing the Constitution was, it seems to me, too narrow. His is the textual method of taking the words of the instrument and trying to determine the true meaning from the words themselves. The Constitution can never be adequately construed by this method and my friend's argument demonstrates the fact, for he himself shows that the word "persons" has been used in the Constitution in twenty-seven different places and that it does not always have the same meaning in any one place. This is probably true. It certainly illustrates the fact that to determine what the framers meant by the word "persons" in Article I, section 2, you must consider not only the text of the Constitution, but also the debates in the Federal Convention and the historic background of that great document. It is therefore a singular fact that my friend from Virginia makes no reference to the debates in the Constitutional Convention and none whatever to the historic controversy between the great and the little States as to the basis of representation, and yet it cannot be denied that Article I, section 2, was the final outcome of a controversy which began in the First Continental Congress and which became the greatest source of controversy in the Federal Convention itself.

When that controversy is recalled it seems clear and would be indisputable but for Mr. Tucker's argument that the word "persons" did include all human beings except those who were specifically excluded from Article I, section 2, and it will not be disputed that there is no express exclusion of aliens from the "persons" to be enumerated.

Words are always an imperfect medium of thought. As Justice Holmes once said, they are but the "skin of a thought." Nearly all the great controversies of history have turned upon the meaning of words, because no words can ever be used that fully express the meaning of those who employ them. Indeed, the meaning of words may often depend upon the inflection of the voice. The sardonic Disraeli was wont to reply to those who sent him the gift of a book, "I shall lose no time in reading your book," and to others he would reply, "I am lying under a sense of obligation to you for the gift of your book." Here the same words are susceptible of two precisely opposite meanings.

For this reason, the textual method of weighing the meaning of a general expression, like "persons," while it must be the first step in any discussion of meaning, is only the first step. To ascertain the true meaning, it is obligatory that we put ourselves in the mental attitude of those who used the words, and to do so we must understand the subject matter of their discussion and the purpose of the debate.

I therefore shall invite your attention in a brief reference to the genesis of Article I, section 2, and I think you will then see that, with the exception of negro slaves and of nontaxed Indians, it was the clear intention to enumerate the entire population, without respect to whether a given person was a full-fledged citizen or only, as an alien, a potential citizen.

Article I, section 2, was the culmination of a long-standing controversy between the Colonies, each of which had become by the act of revolution an independent and fully sovereign nation. The First Continental Congress constituted a provisional government of the most informal character. It was little more than a conference of newly created independent States for the purposes of common defense. It was the "United States" in embryo. It exercised many of the rights of a sovereign power and, among others, issued currency to pay the expenses of the new

Government. The obligation to redeem such currency was distributed among the thirteen Colonies by apportioning to each a quota, for which each was individually responsible. Thereafter the expenses of the Government were largely met by requisitions, addressed to each State, but each State reserved the right to honor or dishonor the requisition as it seemed proper.

As to the method of estimating the quota, the Continental Congress had first suggested that it be based upon real-estate holdings, and for this purpose the Congress of 1783 had required the States to make returns of their lands, buildings, and inhabitants. Anticipating that this would not result satisfactorily, they recommended to the constituent States that the quota be based upon the number of inhabitants. (Journals of Congress, VIII, p. 129.) The difficulty of either method was due to the fact that, in the first place, there was no satisfactory method of estimating the value of taxable real estate, and, on the other hand, there was no authoritative census of the inhabitants.

The result might easily be anticipated. At first some States honored the requisition, and others disregarded it or were tardy in their payment; and as the financial affairs of the inchoate Government went from bad to worse, none of the States fully met the requisitions of the Government. This led to very great dissatisfaction, for each State had an equal voice in the new Government, and the injustice of allowing a State which contributed little or nothing to the national expenses or to the recruiting of the armies the same voice as a State which measurably met its share of the common burden soon became the source of great discontent.

Shortly after the Declaration of Independence attempts were made to put the form of the Government into more definite shape, and as a result the so-called Articles of Confederation were proposed in 1777 and tardily adopted in 1781. Under these articles each State was represented in Congress by not less than two nor more than seven Members, but each State was entitled to only one vote. Article VIII provided:

"All charges of war and all other expenses that shall be incurred for the common defense or general welfare, and allowed by the United States in Congress assembled, shall be defrayed out of a common Treasury, which shall be supplied by the several States in proportion to the value of all land within each State, granted to or surveyed for any person, as such land and the buildings and improvements thereon shall be estimated according to such mode as the United States in Congress assembled shall from time to time direct and appoint."

This was the first attempt to have an equitable apportionment of expenses, although the relative power of each State in the new Government remained the same, and the cause of the grievance was thereby in no respect removed.

I need not detail the terrible breakdown of the new Government under the Articles of Confederation. Congress attempted to apportion the expenses of government upon the value of the lands in each State, but, as to the costs of the Army and Navy, it was agreed by Article IX that Congress had power—

to make requisitions from each State for its quota in proportion to the number of white inhabitants in each State.

In this lay the germ of Article I, section 2, of the Constitution. The "white inhabitants," which excluded the Indians and the negroes, were taken as the basis of the quotas, because it was found impracticable to value the taxable real estate and it was believed that the number of white inhabitants would be a fair measure of the relative wealth of the various States.

This method of apportionment proved a complete failure, not because it was not sound in theory but because the conditions of poverty and the general demoralization that followed the treaty of peace made it impossible to carry out any such plan. For example, the Government made a requisition upon the States to raise $8,000,000, and only $400,000 was actually contributed. The receipts of the Confederation in the last 14 months of its existence were less than $400,000. It was the so-called "critical period" of our history, and the new Nation nearly died at its birth.

The result of this financial chaos and the conflicting commercial regulations was the calling of the great Federal convention of 1787. The great problem that confronted that convention was due to the facts that I have recited. It confronted far more than the raising of revenue. It involved a question of political justice. Long before the convention met there were two opposite schools of thought in conflict. The one prevailed in the smaller States and the other in the larger. The small States were morbidly conscious of their new dignity as a nation and insisted upon absolute equality between the States that formed the Union. The larger States had a deep sense of the injustice of allowing each of the thirteen Colonies an equal voice when they differed so greatly in wealth and population and contributed so disproportionately to the common fund.

The sense of this injustice was manifested in the First Continental Congress and, as the war progressed and contributions of money and men by the different States varied not merely proportionately but in varying degrees of loyalty to the common cause, the unfairness of allowing a State which contributed few men and less money the same vote as a State which taxed its resources of treasure and men to the utmost became more glaring. Therefore the great problem of the Federal Convention of 1787 was to reach an adjustment that would satisfy the pride of the little States, as sovereign nations, and the just demands of the larger States that political power should be proportioned to political burdens. Virginia and Pennsylvania were the two largest States, and before the convention met their delegates had met in caucus and formulated what was subsequently called the "Virginia plan." The second section of that plan provided:

> "*Resolved, therefore,* That the rights of suffrage in the National Legislature ought to be apportioned to the quotas of contributions or to the number of free inhabitants, as the one or the other rule may seem best in different cases."

This plan, which was our Constitution in embryo, was bitterly assailed in an angry debate of many weeks by the delegates from the little States, which, in turn, submitted the so-called "New Jersey plan," but even that plan made the following provision in section 3:

> "*Resolved*, That whenever requisitions shall be necessary, instead of the rule for making requisitions mentioned in the Articles of Confederation, the United States in Congress be authorized to make such requisitions in proportion to the whole number of white and other free inhabitants of every age, sex, and condition, including those bound to servitude for a term of years, and three-fifths of all other persons not comprehended in the foregoing description, except Indians not paying taxes."

It will thus be noted that in the Articles of Confederation and in both the Virginia plan and the New Jersey plan the apportionment was to be based upon the population in language so general as not to exclude aliens. It was a numbering of the people without respect to whether they were citizens or aliens and only the New Jersey plan made the exception of Indians not paying taxes and of three-fifths of the slaves. The Indians were excluded because they were regarded as nomadic, wild tribes, and in no true sense a part of the population, and the real dispute was as to the slaves, which the Northern States claimed could not be regarded as inhabitants, because they were regarded by their owners as property, while the slaveholding States insisted upon their being included in the enumeration. The three-fifths rule, as proposed in the New Jersey plan, which was put forth by the smaller States, was in the nature of a compromise.

I need hardly remind the House of the great discussion, lasting many weeks, with which the convention began and which related wholly to the question whether the States should be represented in both Houses of Congress on an equality or in proportion to their wealth or numbers. It resulted in a grave crisis, which nearly disrupted the convention, but the first and great compromise of the convention was finally reached through the influence of Doctor Franklin, whereby the principle of equality of right was recognized in the Senate and the equity of proportional representation was to be recognized in the constitution of the lower branch of Congress.

After this compromise had been adopted the debate then began as to the basis of representation in this House, and the only question was as to the method of allotment.

When the debate had been concluded the convention, sitting as a Committee of the Whole, on the 13th day of June made their report, and section 7 provided:

> "The rights of suffrage in the first branch of the National Legislature (the House of Representatives) ought not to be according to the rule established in the Articles of Confederation but according to some equitable ratio of representation, namely, in proportion to the whole number of white and other free citizens and inhabitants of every age, sex, and condition, including those bound to servitude for a term of years and three-fifths of all other persons not comprehended in the foregoing description, except Indians not paying taxes in each State.

It will hardly be questioned that aliens were included in the comprehensive expression, "white and other free citizens and inhabitants of every age, sex, and condition."

Unable to agree upon equality in the Senate, the report of the Committee of the Whole was referred to a compromise committee, and that committee reported in favor of equality in the Senate and proportionate representation in the House and recommended that property, as well as persons, ought to be taken into account in order to obtain a just index of the relative rank of the States. This was on the insistence of the larger States, which apprehended a shifting of the population to the West and South, which would ultimately subject the larger States, which would have the greater wealth, to the oppressive demands of the smaller States, and time has verified this prediction. Therefore, the method of apportionment was again recommitted to five members, who proposed a scheme whereby the first

House of Representatives should consist of 56 Members, who were to be distributed among the States upon an estimate of their population, but authorized the Legislature, as future circumstances might require, to increase the number of Representatives and distribute them among the States upon a compound ratio of their wealth and the number of their inhabitants, and this was adopted.

It was then proposed that the first Congress should consist of 36 Members from States which held few or no slaves and 29 from the slave-holding States, and this was objectionable to the latter. Accordingly, a counterproposition was made to return to the principle of numbers alone and to provide a periodical census to adjust the shifting of their population or wealth, and to gain this provision for the future it was agreed to count the slaves on the basis of three-fifths of their numbers.

The subject was long and earnestly debated, and while I have no time to quote from the debates, which would be very illuminating, the fact remains that at no time during the debates was it suggested for a moment that aliens were not to be included among the inhabitants. The culmination of the debate came when the northern States, speaking through Gouverneur Morris, agreed to accept the principle of the three-fifths rule, provided that direct taxation should be in proportion to representation. It was thought that this would result in an equitable balance, for if the slave-holding States had an undue advantage by the inclusion of three-fifths of the slaves, who were regarded as property, yet they would bear a correspondingly greater burden in the apportionment of direct taxes.

Accordingly a new resolution was referred to the Committee of Detail, which provided that the first Congress should consist of 65 Members, but that—

> * * * the Legislature of the United States shall possess authority to regulate the number of Representatives in any of the foregoing cases upon the principle of their number of inhabitants, according to the provisions hereafter mentioned, namely, provided always, that representation

ought to be proportioned according to direct taxation.

It then provided for a census to be taken within 6 years from the first Congress and thereafter every 10 years "of all of the inhabitants of the United States."

The Committee of Detail, after considering this proposition, reported that there should be one Representative for every 40,000 inhabitants, but another effort was made to exclude the slaves from the enumeration and the debate broke out afresh. The principle of a three-fifths allotment to the slave inhabitants was, however, retained and suffered no change when the draft of the Constitution was again referred to the Committee of Style and that committee reported the Constitution in its present form, which provides:

> "Representatives and direct taxes shall be apportioned among the several States which may be included within this Union according to their respective numbers, which shall be determined by adding to the whole number of free persons, including those bound to servitude for a term of years, and excluding Indians not taxed, three-fifths of all other persons."

I apologize to the House for this very lengthy statement of the genesis of Article I, section 2, but if there be any who are inclined to support the thesis of the gentleman from Virginia, that the framers did not intend to include aliens in the enumeration, then this lengthy explanation will not be in vain, for it seems to me conclusive that when they deliberately used the expression "persons" in their method of enumeration, they used it in the comprehensive sense of all human beings who were inhabitants of the several States, except in so far as they expressly excluded persons who were Indians not taxed and slaves, the latter being enumerated on a purely artificial basis of three-fifths of their numbers.

It is clear that the framers never intended to leave the matter to the discretion of Congress. They compromised their differences by establishing a hard and fast rule, and they reaffirmed this when they adopted the Fourteenth Amendment, whereby it was provided that—

> "Representatives shall be apportioned among the several States according to their respective numbers, counting the whole number of persons in each State, excluding Indians not taxed."

To argue that the Congress could at this late day arbitrarily exclude aliens from the enumeration would be a very dangerous step, and happily the Congress has refused to take it. If the Congress can exclude any class of inhabitants, it is difficult to understand where the destruction of the constitutional provision would stop. We have seen in the last nine years that even the positive mandate of the Constitution that there should be a reapportionment every decennial census has been violated. In my judgment, the two most fatal blows which have been struck against our form of government in recent years are the refusal for so many years to reapportion on the basis of the Constitution and the asserted right of the Senate to exclude a duly elected Senator because, in its judgment, the State which accredited him had made an unwise choice. That either proposition could be seriously entertained makes one despair of the permanence of a written form of government.

I hope I owe the House no apology for this discussion of a question which for the time being may seem academic. Can the discussion of any constitutional principle be academic? Certainly the subject assumes a gravely practical character when we reflect upon the wreckage of those portions of the Constitution, which were the basis of the great compact. Macaulay imagined a New Zealander of a later age who, standing upon a broken arch of London Bridge, would survey the ruins of the historic edifices of London, but an observer, who would study our Constitution as the Fathers designed it and as it now exists, would see in the subject matter of this discussion a greater wreckage.

Little is now left of the great compromises of the Fathers. The sovereign States were to be represented in the Senate by representatives of their own choice. Today the accepted doctrine is that the States only nominate Senators and that their final choice must be "with the advice and consent of the Senate."

Such Senators were to be selected by the State legislatures. They are now elected in a popular election.

Taxation was to go hand in hand with apportionment, but under the Sixteenth Amendment the larger part of the taxes have been levied for nine years past without apportionment among the several States and without regard to a decennial census or enumeration.

As a result the theory of equitable representation in proportion to the burdens of government, which was the great objective of the Fathers, has been destroyed.

"Can such things be and overcome us as a summer cloud without our special wonder?"

INDEX

(The figures refer to pages)

A

B

PAGE

496   INDEX

PAGE

PAGE

PAGE

S

INDEX 509